GOD'S AMEN
IS REVEALED IN THE MATRIX OF WISDOM

MW01487226

PATTERNS FOUND INHERENT IN THE
MATRIX OF WISDOM

MATRIX OF WISDOM

Universal Mathematical Matrix
Prima Materia (Perennial Matrix)

(a) Big Bang: Explosion: Dot
(Time and Timelessness)

(b) Implosion: Line
(Ambiance of God)

(c) Kamea of Saturn: Angle
(Worldwide Religious Diversity)

(d) 12 Sign of the Zodiac: Circle
(Tetrahedral Forces of Creation)

(e) Kabbalistic Tree of Life
(Cosmology - Consolidation)

(f) Star of David in Genesis
(Tetrahedral Forces of Creation)

MATRIX OF WISDOM

Ego-consciousness   Unconscious Mind

(g) Time & Timelessness
(God revealing His Presence)

(h) Pythagoras' Multiplication Matrix
(MATRIX OF WISDOM Origins)

KAMEA OF THE SUN

6	32	3	34	35	1
7	11	27	28	8	30
19	14	16	15	23	24
18	20	22	21	17	13
25	29	10	9	26	12
36	5	33	4	2	31

KAMEA OF THE MOON

37	78	29	70	21	62	13	54	5
6	38	79	30	71	22	63	14	46
47	7	39	80	31	72	23	55	15
16	48	8	40	81	32	64	24	56
57	17	49	9	41	73	33	65	25
26	58	18	50	1	42	74	34	66
67	27	59	10	51	2	43	75	35
36	68	19	60	11	52	3	44	76
7	28	69	20	61	12	53	4	45

Pythagoras' Multiplication Matrix

1	2	3	4	5	6	7	8	9	10
2	4	6	8	10	12	14	16	18	20
3	6	9	12	15	18	21	24	27	30
4	8	12	16	20	24	28	32	36	40
5	10	15	20	25	30	35	40	45	50
6	12	18	24	30	36	42	48	54	60
7	14	21	28	35	42	49	56	63	70
8	16	24	32	40	48	56	64	72	80
9	18	27	36	45	54	63	72	81	90
10	20	30	40	50	60	70	80	90	100

William John Meegan

The opinions expressed in this manuscript are solely the opinions of the author and do not represent the opinions or thoughts of the publisher. The author has represented and warranted full ownership and/or legal right to publish all the materials in this book.

God's Ambiance
Is Revealed in the Matrix of Wisdom
All Rights Reserved.
Copyright © 2016 William John Meegan
v4.0

Cover Image © 2016 William John Meegan. All rights reserved - used with permission.

This book may not be reproduced, transmitted, or stored in whole or in part by any means, including graphic, electronic, or mechanical without the express written consent of the publisher except in the case of brief quotations embodied in critical articles and reviews.

Outskirts Press, Inc.
http://www.outskirtspress.com

Paperback ISBN: 978-1-4787-8047-2
Hardback ISBN: 978-1-4787-7939-1

Outskirts Press and the "OP" logo are trademarks belonging to Outskirts Press, Inc.

PRINTED IN THE UNITED STATES OF AMERICA

DEDICATED TO

The spiritual sages that scribed the indigenous Hebrew and Greek languages symbolically and alphanumerically to the sacred scriptures preserving for all time the Esoteric Science and to the inner esoteric hierarchy of the Roman Catholic Church for their due diligence over the past two milleniums in creating Catholicism's beautiful spiritual literature, artworks, monuments and architecture dedicated to the WORD OF GOD and to the inner esoteric hierarchy of Freemasonry for their incredible architectural and spiritual rendition of the generic religious paradigm (MATRIX OF WISDOM) of the soul embossed upon the city of Washington DC and to Egypt, Taoism, Buddhism, Hinduism, the Native American Indians and to all esoteric religious cultures around the world.

TABLE OF CONTENT

TABLE OF CONTENT

LIST OF ILLUSTRATIONS

INTRODUCTION

MATRIX OF WISDOM is the single most important spiritual symbolic image associated to the indigenous religious paradigm that existed in all cultures around the world in all times and climes from the Dawn of Time. I say the DAWN OF TIME; because, TIME begins at conception not before and the MATRIX OF WISDOM literally recreate creation ex nihilo after the Initiatic Visionary Experience no matter how inane that sounds. The only way that this image that exudes the WORD OF GOD can be intuited is via the psyche of a true spiritual initiate. Every religious culture around the world in all times and climes intuited this MATRIX OF WISDOM on their own volition. The hypothetical Diffusion Process had nothing whatsoever to do with the spiritual development of any religious cultures on earth. I know this to be a fact; for the reason that, I personally intuited this MATRIX OF WISDOM in 1994 long before I learned that it was also known worldwide by all religious cultures and secret societies. Only through a very deep spiritual meditational contemplative analysis of this MATRIX OF WISDOM can the initiate look forward to understanding how the sacred scriptures, artworks, monuments and architecture around the world were intuited and creatively developed out of the WORD OF GOD.

The Esoteric Science is an amalgamation of the knowledge that is inherent in the MATRIX OF WISDOM and the scribes' commentaries on that knowledge. The scribes that wrote the Judaeo Christian Scripture had to create a mythology (historical fictional storyline) to codify that knowledge into a sanctified vessel similar to the Eucharistic chalice on the altar: i.e. the sacred scriptures. The sacred scripture is the Eucharist: i.e. body and blood of Christ. These commentaries (sacred scriptures) are not the WORD OF GOD per se; but, rather the sacred vessels that contain the mystical WORD OF GOD. The MATRIX OF WISDOM is a perfect matrix; because, it unifies the Seven Liberal Arts: Quadrivium and Trivium into a systemic system of thought. The numerics of the MATRIX OF WISDOM are both the Quadrivium and the Trivium; though, most people will not see the numerical digits in the MATRIX OF WISDOM as part of the Trivium nonetheless it is. The scribes of the Old Testament solve that observational and contemplative problem by numbering the Hebraic Coder; thus, numbers per se as humans understand numerical digits were nonexistent in the sacred scriptures other then the alphabet representing the numerical digits. Neither the Quadrivium nor the Trivium that writes the sacred scriptures is the WORD OF GOD per se; though, the mystical nature of the Quadrivium as it is codified into the sacred scriptures via Sacred Geometry does symbolize the WORD OF GOD it is merely the Quadrivium when it is interpret through commentary in human parlance: thus, the WORD OF GOD can only be conveyed to the initiate via God's personal guidance.

The MATRIX OF WISDOM is basically an image of the two part psyche: ego-consciousness and the unconscious mind of every human being that has ever lived. For all intent and purpose the MATRIX OF WISDOM is Aladdin's Carpet. No one can get off this carpet; for the reason that, it is the initiate's psyche. Notice I said Aladdin's Carpet indicating Aladdin's egocentric personality. The MATRIX OF WISDOM is nonexistent; for the reason that, it is merely a commentary on the MONAD: i.e. God. The soul exist: the psyche per se does not exist.

The Esoteric Science is, for the most part, an unknown mystical science that the scribes of antiquity and modernity's secret societies such as the inner hierarchies of major religions and esoteric brotherhoods, such as Freemasonry and the Rosicrucians, developed and codified into the religious and/or other esoteric artworks around the world. The inner hierarchies of these organizations are in the *know*; because, most members in these societies have no idea what esotericism is, nor that such an Esoteric Science even exists. Most members of these organizations merely join them to be part of a social or networking group.

Those that are in the *know* will not say anything about esotericism; for the reason that, they know that the mystical ambiance that is the WORD OF GOD is impossible to convey in the vernacular. Those that know nothing about esotericism will have a tsunami of knowledge on every subject matter in existence to inform the world about.

As for myself, I am a member of the Roman Catholic laity and I am neither a member of a secret society nor am I a member of an inner hierarchy in the Roman Catholic Church. The research outlined in this volume is my own, which was accumulated over forty-two years in pursuit of trying to understand the Judaeo Christian Scriptures and the teachings of the Roman Catholic Church. All of the research in this volume was intuited piecemeal via the guidance of my only confidant: God.

It is of course not easy to obtain knowledge of esotericism especially when you enter into the forest (unknown inexplicable invisible realm) not knowing that it even exists. Everything about beginning to study, on your own, the Judaeo Christian Scriptures is through the lenses of a translation of the original indigenous Hebrew and/or Greek language(s). The lone member of the laity, like me, entering into the texts of the Judaeo Christian Scriptures would not at all comprehend intellectually at the commencement of such studies that the mysticism of the indigenous Hebrew and/or Greek language(s) cannot be translated into another language unless esotericism was known by the translators. If the translators did know esotericism they most likely would have advised their employers to keep the texts in its original format.

Not being a member of an inner religious hierarchy or a member of a mystical brotherhood I have made no vows of secrecy to anyone. I know that esotericism cannot be conveyed per se; however, the secrets that all religions and other secret societies vow not to divulge is what this book is all about. The **HIDDEN** mystical inexplicable WORD OF GOD cannot be divulged to another even if those in the *know* wanted to convey it to the world; however, the secret pledges that members of the hierarchies in religions and secret societies vow never to reveal is what is called the **COVERED**: i.e. the symbolic and the alphanumeric structure of the sacred scriptures, literature, artworks, monuments and architecture, which is never-ever divulge to the masses (general public) explicitly.

The only thing that is left for the average member of the religious laity and members of the secret societies that are not in the *know* to deal with is the **REVEALED**, which is the bland mythological (historical fictional storyline) texts of the sacred scriptures, literature, artworks, monuments and architecture; for the reason that, 99.99…% of the sacred scriptures and literature of the world are published in translation, which rips the mystical vitality from them by excluding the symbolic and numeric structure (Quadrivium) that is inherent in the indigenous languages that writes the sacred scriptures and the mystical literature and artwork of the world.

No matter what I write I cannot express in any way by means of the vernacular or other means the existence of God; however, I can like John the Baptist point to God's Ambiance, which is known all over the world as Christ (offspring of God), Tao, Buddha, Krishna, Horus, etc., etc.; however, being born and raised in the milieu of the Christian mythoi I can only truly express myself from those environs; nonetheless, initiates of other religions should be able to intuit in their belief systems what I am conveying from out of the Christian mythoi.

It is essential that the initiate understand that all religions are one no matter what the crazed fundamentalists in his or her religious institutional hierarchy or what the oceanic laity have to say on the subject. Ridding ego-consciousness of biases, prejudices and preconceived notions such as this are essential to envisaging the higher spiritual nuances that have been placed covertly in plain sight; yet, they are summarily dismissed by the masses without thought; for the reason that, such trivial gobbledygook such as biases, prejudices and preconceived notions that lingers in one psyche dominates and have absolute sovereignty over the psyche. Does it really matter what color a person skin is? Or what nationality he or she is? Or what his or her religion is? Or what language he or she speaks? Or what gender he or she is? These questions are limitless. When it comes to searching for knowledge of God personal biases, prejudices and preconceived notions stirs one's thinking down the wrong pathway of thought into a wealth of knowledge that makes no sense to anyone but oneself. Proof of this is blatantly witness in the twenty-seven thousands (27,000) sects of Protestantism (iconoclasm: i.e. egocentrism) and still there is only one sect of Catholicism (iconography) and that is only in the Christian religion.

Reading the sacred scriptures in any religion, in translation, is the wrong way of reading the WORD OF GOD; though, those that don't know how to read the Hebrew and/or Greek in the Judaeo Christian Scriptures translations, in modernity, it is the only way of getting at the basic surface storyline relating to the mythoi of Judaism and Christianity; however, from that point forward the Hebrew and/or Greek alphabet(s) should be studied relating to their symbolism, numerics, Gematria values and alphabet meanings.

In addition to these basics a great deal of meditational contemplative thought has to be put into the biblical texts to determine what it is saying and what the patterns of sacred geometry in the bible is exuding in those texts; furthermore, one has to study a number of different and diverse systems of thought like Astrology, symbolism, the cerebral lobes of the brain, the Tarot Cards, the bones of the body and religious literature, artworks, monuments and architecture in one's own religious culture. All of the diverse and disparate materials and systems of thought that an initiate chooses to study in search for understanding of the WORD OF GOD have to be unified contemplatively and harmonious into a single Hermetic esoteric systemic system of thought.

I say that a number of diverse disparate system of thought have to be studied to understand the generic spiritual paradigm; because, one system per se is not enough and cannot elucidate the WORD OF GOD. This may be because familiarity breeds contempt. Seeing how a number of diverse and disparate systems amalgamate the ethereal patterns that mystics, shamans and sages of all times harmoniously integrated into different genres of thought will aid the initiate in conceptually understanding the generic spiritual paradigm and this is only if God is the initiate's only confidant. It is an inexplicable concept for the iconoclastic individual to grasp that this MATRIX OF WISDOM is inherent in the psyche and that this matrix per se educates the soul as to how to live in the phantasmagoria of his or her psyche.

This sounds inane and seems to be impossible for a human being to accomplish. I agree that it is impossible and such a task cannot be accomplished via the initiate's own volition without the aid of God. Every profession and/or discipline on the face of the earth can be used to codify the universal generic religious paradigm into its fold. In other words everything in the outer world can be utilized to obtain ethereal spiritual nuances relating to the generic religious paradigm.

In this volume I am going to use a number of genres of thought to outline the generic religious paradigm that is inherent in all religions around the world.

There is a generic mystical paradigm to in all religious and secret societies' literature, artworks, monuments and architect around the world. All the world's religions partake of the same mystical source material: i.e. MATRIX OF WISDOM, to articulate esoterically what is covertly hidden in plain sight: the WORD OF GOD.

I will give a brief outline of the twenty chapters in this book:

CHAPTER ONE: THE FIRST WRITTEN LETTER: BETH ב (KAMEA OF THE SUN) AND THE FIRST HIDDEN LETTER: PEI פ (KAMEA OF THE MOON) OF THE BIBLE

The main focus of this chapter is to illustrate that the first letter of the sacred scriptures called BETH ב is esoterically the entire bible. Inundating and surrounding BETH ב is a hidden letter called PEI פ and the entire Old and New Testaments are commentaries on these materialistic and spiritual letters exuding the WORD OF GOD via the Trivium (BETH ב) and Quadrivium (PEI פ). I illustrate through commentaries and images on these letters that they symbolize two magic squares: i.e. the Kamea of the Sun and the Kamea of the Moon; hence, spirituality permeates every single letter of the bible.

CHAPTER TWO: SERPENT MOUND

Here I discuss how the Serpent Mound Effigy in Peebles, Ohio, USA created by the Native American Indians over twenty-three hundred (2300) years ago, which was esoterically constructed using the very same mystical concepts laid out in the first Hebrew letters of Genesis. I also discuss Dr. William F. Romain's (archeologist) lecture he gave at Serpent Mound on June 18, 2016 that illustrates via the Native American Indians' religious ideology the same mystical paradigm I envisaged and intuited out of other religions' teachings and the symbolism that Freemasonry codified into the streets of Washington DC.

CHAPTER THREE: THREE TORAHS

The Hebrew alphabet is broken down into three separate and distinct categories. In this chapter I will discuss the fact that there are three Torahs is the one bible that mystically corresponds with the categories of the Hebrew alphabet: **REVEALED**: that which is written on the surface texts (historical fictional storyline) of the sacred scriptures, **COVERED**: the symbolism and alphanumeric structure of each and every letter of the sacred scriptures and **HIDDEN**: the WORD OF GOD that cannot be conveyed in any manner in the vernacular. Only God can convey his spiritual ambiance. This chapter is accompanied by a chart of the Hebrew alphabet.

CHAPTER FOUR: SOME MYSTERIES IN THE FIRST CHAPTER OF GENESIS: The Kabbalistic Tree of Life, the Star of David and the Kundalini Serpent

A detail mathematical analysis of the first chapter of Genesis is conducted on the thirty-two (32) times that the word ELOHYM is used in the first chapter of Genesis. In this chapter an interlinear text of the first chapter of Genesis in Hebrew and English is provided that color codes the associate words to the 32-Elohyms, which graphically depicts the Kabbalistic Tree of Life and its four basic categories: Sefirah, Mother letters, Double Letters and Elemental Letters and in addition the Star of David is shown to be mystically associated to the Elemental letters, which the ancient authors obviously wanted the student of the bible to envisage. This mathematical analysis of the Kabbalistic Tree of Life also illustrates the Kundalini Serpent rising upon its central column. In addition this sacred geometry exemplifies what is meant by God dividing the LIGHT from the DARKNESS. In doing this the mystical nature of LIGHT and DARKNESS in found imbued into the Vesica Piscis harmoniously.

CHAPTER FIVE: SOLOMON'S TEMPLE and the SISTINE CHAPEL

The Sistine Chapel is somewhat discussed in relationship to the first chapter of Genesis. A number of patterns found throughout the Sistine Chapel are analyzed. The Sistine Chapel is formatted mystically in a rectangular shape depicting Solomon Temple symbolically representing the east-west corridor of time; however, the symbolism in the chapel is meant to be read and mystically morphed into an octagon shape conceptually showing the mystical nature of Christ crossing the east-west corridor of time into the mystical Garden of Eden.

This chapter goes into a great deal of detail in explaining the mosaics in the floor, the symbolism in the frescoes and the patterns that permeate the chapel. Mainly this chapter focuses on the Cosmic, Archetypal and Existential patterns that dominate the esotericism throughout the chapel. The Kabbalistic Tree of Life and its dynamics are illustrated to be Catholicism primary reason for building and frescoing the Sistine Chapel. Another primary focus of the chapel is to illustrate via symbolism the ethereal Battle Royale that is continuously and everlasting played out between iconography (symbolic though) and iconoclasm (literal mined non-symbolic thinking).

CHAPTER SIX: THE BIRTHS OF ADAM AND EVE

The births of Adam and Eve are discussed along with a study of the first word of Genesis: BERESHITH, which provides an understanding that whatever is written in the bible is precedent and based upon that which has previously been written. The discovery of the Genesis Formula is laid out to illustrate mini-versions of the Kabbalistic Tree of Life, the Star of David and the Crown of Creation: Keter.

CHAPTER SEVEN: ADAM AND EVE IN THE GARDEN OF EDEN

The discussion on Adam and Eve is continued to associate the second chapter of Genesis to the first word of Genesis. The first word of Genesis: BERESHITH is analyzed spherically to illustrate and reveals how many chapters and verses there are in the book of Genesis. This is discussed in relationship to the tetrahedral forces of creation. The Vesica Piscis is introduced from out of the Genesis Formula and the Fibonacci sequence is also discussed in relationship to the Genesis Formula.

CHAPTER EIGHT: THE VESICA PISCIS IN ARTISTIC FORMS

The Vesica Piscis is further discussed and many images are presented from a number of artistic forms.

CHAPTER NINE: SOME MYSTERIES OF CHARTRES CATHEDRAL

A commentary on the mystical nature of Chartres Cathedral mythoi and artwork is outlined discussing the number of fires that took place in its mythological back-story, which is important to understand in order to grasp the mystical message in the building's overall artwork. The mystical message of the West Facade's Rose Window is argued in relationship to the Last Judgment and the Labyrinth on the floor of the cathedral.

CHAPTER TEN: CYGNUS X-3, THE NORTHERN CROSS AND CHILDREN OF THE SWAN

The constellation of Cygnus X-3 is talked about in relation to the basic indigenous spiritual paradigm of creation.

CHAPTER ELEVEN: MATRIX OF WISDOM (PART 1): Development Stages

The development stages of the MATRIX OF WISDOM are outlined step by step from beginning to end to demonstrate to the reader how the matrix is/was created.

CHAPTER TWELVE: MATRIX OF WISDOM (PART 2) Internal Dynamics

A detail numerical analysis of the MATRIX OF WISDOM illustrates that it symbolizes the two part psyche: ego-consciousness and the unconscious mind and the matrix has inherently in its construct a number of graphic images that demonstrate the origins of Pythagorean mathematics and it illustrates the concepts of time and timelessness. This analysis also includes illustrating the graphic images of Kabbalistic Tree of Life and the Star of David. These latter images definitively demonstrate how the Kabbalistic Tree of Life and the Star of David were scribed into the first chapter of Genesis proffering the theory that this MATRIX OF WISDOM is the original source material of the sacred scriptures worldwide.

CHAPTER THIRTEEN: MATRIX OF WISDOM (PART 3): Generating the Genesis Formula

Continuing with the theory of the MATRIX OF WISDOM scribing the sacred scriptures an analysis is conducted on the first word of genesis: BERESHITH linked to the Genesis Formula illustrating how the first word of Genesis and the Genesis Formula was constructed through the dynamics of the MATRIX OF WISDOM transubstantiating into Christ consciousness.

CHAPTER FOURTEEN: MATRIX OF WISDOM (Part 4): Astrology

Through the vibrant symbolism of Astrology the cerebral lobes of the brain can be seen to symbolize the twelve zodiacal signs, which illustrates through Greek and Roman mythology coupled with the mythoi of Genesis clarifies more fully time and timelessness. This analysis mystically generates another analysis of the first four chapters of Genesis extrapolating out to the first eleven chapters of Genesis and then discussing their mathematical structure relating to the spiritual generic pattern radiating outwardly permeating the entire book of Genesis. The Sistine Chapel is discussed again in relationship to Astrology and the east-west corridor-of-time. The MATRIX OF WISDOM is analyzed mathematically symbolizing the planet earth (soul) with stars of the galaxy surrounding it. The mathematics of the MATRIX OF WISDOM demonstrates God's Ambiance outside of the time/space continuum and how God's Ambiance comes into creation via Christ consciousness to create Eve as narrated in the second chapter of Genesis.

CHAPTER FIFTEEN: MATRIX OF WISDOM (Part 5): Religious Architectural Creativity

The basic generic religious paradigm outlined in the first word of Genesis is shown to have been derived directly from the Giza Plateau's Pyramid Complex. It also discusses Christ consciousness in relations to the Pharaoh with Horus consciousness.

CHAPTER SIXTEEN: MATRIX OF WISDOM (Part 6): WASHINGTON DC

Continuing on with the thesis of Religious Architectural Creativity this chapter explores the incredible esoteric resourcefulness that Freemasonry constructed into the streets and monuments in Washington DC that pivots upon the Capitol Building symbolizing it as the axis mundi: Bodhi Tree symbolizing timelessness. The Capitol Building grounds is symbolic of Golgotha (mound of the skull). Freemasonry's presentation illustrates God Ambiance (Christ consciousness) amidst timelessness via the symbolism of the Templar's Cross. The esoteric symbolic techniques outlined in the sacred scriptures are clearly codified into the National Mall and the streets of Washington DC. The symbolism that Freemasonry codified into the city streets of Washington DC were also codified in the past using the mythoi of the War of Independence and the Civil War. In fact Freemasonry, to this date, is continuously working esotericism into the mythoi of the National Mall in Washington DC.

CHAPTER SEVENTEEN: MATRIX OF WISDOM (Part 7): KAMEA OF SATURN

The Kamea of Saturn using the numbers one thru nine (1-9) produces many images and deals with many concepts. The Kamea of Saturn symbolizes the Holy of Holies and is often displayed in an octagon shape, which is the preferred design of all Christian Churches. It developed the Chinese I Ching and the Square, Compass and G of Masonic symbolism and many other religious cultures symbols. Being that it is a Magic Square it can be envisaged along with the rest of the Magic Squares to exude from out of the MATRIX OF WISDOM.

CHAPTER EIGHTEEN: THE MATRIX OF WISDOM (Part 8) THE FIBONACCI SEQUENCE

The Fibonacci sequence is analyzed and discusses with many discoveries that I personally intuited. The Fibonacci sequence is associated to the 46-cromosones of the cell's structure. The Fibonacci sequence has been reduced to a continuous everlasting oscillation process of 24-calculations, which also points to it being the origins of the MATRIX OF WISDOM.

CHAPTER NINETEEN: THE FIRST TWO CHAPTERS OF GENESIS AND THE CYCLES OF DIVINE CREATION

First intuited, out of the first two chapters of Genesis, in December/January 1976/1977 a cycle of nine parts was the kernel of an idea that inspired all the researches in this book. The Cycles of Divine Creation were worked on over the past 40-years; but, has not been fully understood until July 2016 and they are still exuding nuances. These cycles takes the words of the sacred scriptures and astrologically orientates them. The cycles have always been recognized, by me, as the Scales of Libra (Anubis); however, they have much more mystical meaning than that. They symbolize Time and Timelessness. These scales are used nanosecond by nanosecond in the life of the initiate. These scales have nothing to do with physical death; though, symbolically they epitomize the transition from materialism into the Garden of Eden: Ambiance of God.

APPENDIX: DANTE ALIGHIERI'S LA DIVINA COMMEDIA'S MATHEMATICAL SYSTEM

This is a very clear and precise esoteric mathematical analysis of Dante Alighieri's La Divina Commedia Mathematical System researched from April 15, 1983 thru to 1994. This work represents a separate and autonomous literary work outside of the Judaeo Christian Scriptures that lays-out with simple elementary mathematics the same mathematical esoteric science codified to the bible. The Quadrivium (four mathematical sciences: Arithmetic, Music/Harmony, Geometry and Astronomy/Astrology) is codified into the compositional structure of La Divina Commedia's three volumes: Hell, Purgatory and Paradise that contains one hundred chapters and 14,233-verses; thus, with only one hundred (100) three digit numbers (13-base numbers) this very sophisticated esoteric science is covertly hidden. These mathematical patterns graphically depict the Zodiac/Calendar year with the Star of David centrally located and the mathematics also produces an image using the Area Graphics Program via one line illustrating three silhouettes of male heads symbolizing the Trinity: Father, Son and Holy Spirit.

GOD'S AMBIANCE

IS REVEALED IN THE MATRIX OF WISDOM:
THE FIBONACCI SEQUENCE (Golden Ratio)

PREAMBLE

It is not the intension of this work to prove the existence of God, for that is an inexplicable and an unattainable goal for anyone to partake of. God is the only one that can indoctrinate the initiate into His spiritual ambiance; rather, what this work will illustrate prolifically throughout this volume via numerous illustrations and commentaries to augment them, is that there is a generic religious paradigm of spiritual and psychological symbols that are inherent in the psyche that explicitly inspired the mystics of all times to materialistically concretize spiritual contemplative thought via literature, artworks, monuments and architecture. Neither one nor a thousand such illustrations can illuminate nor convince anyone of the presents of God; however, whether the reader is a believer or an atheist there can be no denying the inexhaustible detail scientific nature of the Esoteric Science being introduced in this work that is shown to exist globally in all cultures in all times and climes.

The MATRIX OF WISDOM, from modernity's perspective is an entirely new spiritual way of thinking, was known worldwide by all religious cultures in antiquity. This works can only demonstrate that the basic rudiments of all religions have the same foundational source material. All religions iconographically (symbolically) believe and study the teaching of God in the same manner virtually putting all spiritual cultures on the same contemplative page; however, from an iconoclastic (no symbolism) perspective all religions view God and His teachings from a historical and materialistic perspective essentially isolating their religions from all others secular and religious cultures. Iconographic and Iconoclastic thinking are two diametrically opposite modes of thought and the twain shall never meet.

It would astound both religious and academic scholars to know that the manner that modernity teaches it religions dogma and traditions of its secular mores to the populace would be realistically equivalent to comparing a preschooler's knowledge to that of a mystic saint. The ratio of knowledge would be zero to omniscience. Modernity literally knows nothing about religion. Modernity's religions and academia worldwide are analogous to white sepulchers (Matthew 23:27) similar to being frozen in time eternally maintaining the status quo and essentially that is their true raison d'être: reason for existence. There is nothing wrong with creating a materialistic status quo culture if religions and academia knows that they are confronted by a spiritual impenetrable barrier that cannot be surpassed by egocentrism. I will demonstrate throughout this thesis that a religion is basically suppose to be set us to inform the lone individual (initiate) how to interpret the sacred scriptures on his or her own volition via self-motivation. The sacred scriptures are not just literary texts. The WORD OF GOD is imbued into the universe at large and in all activities of life and in addition it is imbued into how the ancient scribes, artists and architects codified the WORD OF GOD into their individual genres of thought and life's activities.

Religion per se has nothing to do with congregations or fellowships. From Judaism's stance the Jewish male is taught from that perspective. When the Jewish male has his Bar Mitzvah from that point forward he is the sole interpreter of the Torah; whereas, Catholicism teaches that same tradition on a symbolic iconographic level, which is now taught in modernity not from an iconographic (symbolism) perspective; but, from the Protestant's iconoclastic (no symbolism) perspective: meaning the sacred scriptures are taken literally and historically not mystically and symbolically. On an iconographic level the priest, prophet, apostle and all biblical characters are symbolically the lone individual reading the sacred scriptures esoterically. The sacred scriptures are speaking to the individual not to a congregation or to a fellowship. The individual is supposed to be an eternal pioneer not a follower (sniveling lamb) of a charismatic individual rhetorically lecturing, from a pulpit, his biblical opinions, without augmenting them with demonstrable evidence of what he or she is lecturing on.

Religion is supposed to be ORDERLY CHAO; whereas, modernity's secular world has brought religion down to drowning in the deluge (tsunami) of the chaotic psyche. Each individual per se is suppose to be self-motivated to research the sacred scriptures on his or her own volition, which would eventually make every member of the laity, from a materialistic stance, seemingly with a different point of view about his or her religion; though, every member of the laity adheres to the same canonical texts, dogmas and traditions. If every member of the laity truly understood how to read their religious texts using the same original source material: i.e. MATRIX OF WISDOM (Fibonacci sequence[1]) each individual would have a valid interpretation of the sacred scriptures that no other member of the laity has. Each member of the laity would be following his or her own raison d'être (reason for existence[2]).

What Catholicism epitomizes on a totally symbolic level is the psyche of the lone member of the laity envisaging the true WORD OF GOD. Religion has nothing to do with a fellowship; rather, it is God, personally, revealing His ambiance to the lone member of the laity. In the New Testament mythoi, Christ in talking to crowds each person is standing there alone listening to Christ talking to him or her. Christ's message to the lone member of the laity is disparately given to the multitudes, which is analogous to how the Holy Spirit descended upon the twelve apostles on Pentecostal Sunday giving each of them His spiritual ambiance via a different spiritual raison d'être (gift from God: reason for existence).

> "When the day of Pentecost arrived, they were all together in one place. And suddenly there came from heaven a sound like a mighty rushing wind, and it filled the entire house where they were sitting. And divided tongues as of fire appeared to them and rested on each one of them. And they were all filled with the Holy Spirit and began to speak in other tongues as the Spirit gave them utterance. And there were dwelling in Jerusalem Jews, devout men, from every nation under heaven. Now when this was noised abroad the multitude came together, and was confounded, because every man heard them speak in his own language (Acts 2:1-6)."

First notice that the 'rushing wind: i.e. spirit of Elohym (Gen. 1:2) filled the house: i.e. BETH ב: i.e. first written letter of Genesis. Then notice how the wording of Acts 2:1-6; has the Jews, from different nations, being devout men, which is precisely what Freemasonry say, *"making good men better men."* In other words these were people that obeyed the teachings of Judaism and the reason why they were called devout men. They were obeying societal mores, which were both their secular and religious teachings. Language is not necessarily verbal parlance as inferred in the above texts; for the reason that, seeing these devout men were all Jews why give each disciple a different cultural language outside of the Hebrew language? It does not make sense from the perspective of these verses; thus, I see the word LANGUAGE in the sixth (6th) verse to symbolize raison d'être. God allows His message to be broadcast abroad in every possible manner, whether it is through the universe, nature, life's activities, languages and/or the professional skills of the initiate.

The MATRIX OF WISDOM is basically a commentary on the MONAD: i.e. Soul, Christ. When the soul (Christ consciousness) comes into the world of time and space, as a child, it splits into a two part psyche: i.e. ego-consciousness and the unconscious mind. This is essentially the veil of the temple's soul (Holy of Holies) splitting into two parts (Matthew 27:51). The laity from modernity secular perspective neither on an individual nor a collective level ever makes the connection between the child (Christ) coming into the world and the crucifixion of Christ. On a symbolic level these two biblical events are one and the same. Every single child born into the world is CHRIST (Tao, Buddha, Krishna, Horus, etc.); yet, the moment that a child comes into the world the child is named: i.e. crucified to that definition that characterizes and defines him or her. The child is born into the world with an ambiance of a spiritual sheen, which in Christianity would be designated as Christ consciousness; however, the child is quickly educated out of that spiritual ambiance by being baptized into the ways of the world: i.e. family, religious

---

[1] This nuance about the Fibonacci sequence will be clarified as this thesis continues.
[2] Everybody has the same spiritual raison d'être *expressing* it differently in their life's endeavors.

and societal mores: i.e. modernity's secular teachings. Believe it or not the child being educated into the ways of the world, for all intent and purpose, immediately confronts the three temptations of Christ (Matthew 4:1-11) gold, frankincense and myrrh (Science, Theology and Medicine); though, modernity would not think of it that way.

> *I was once told the story about a little four year old girl. Her parents had recently come home with their new born child. The parents watched over their children by listening in on them with a monitor. One day the little four-year old girl goes up to her younger sister's crib and says, "Can you tell me about heaven? I am forgetting all about heaven".*

The average human being tries the rest of his or her life via modernity's secular religious studies to regain that spiritual ambiance lost in the adolescence years. Very few succeed and those that do succeed do it with the guidance of God.

The sacred scriptures are 100% symbolic depicting neither time nor space nor the historicity of any particular culture nor is it discussing any greatness and/or heroics of a particular human being; though, the sleight of hand is in the surface textual exoteric (surface) storyline materialistically suggesting otherwise and that is the psyche's Shadow of Darkness that blankets out the truth of reality for all those that do not truly want to have any conscious knowledge concerning the WORD OF GOD.

The storyline of the sacred scriptures does have some credence as to how to interpret the WORD OF GOD; for the reason that, it canonizes (religiously concretizes) the surface storyline so it will never-ever be changed. Also the nuances of the storyline also have interpretive value on a symbolic level that aid in interpreting its numerical esoteric (abstract symbolism) aspects of the texts properly. As the sacred scriptures are read letter by letter relating to reading the texts word by word the surface storyline essentially goes on the back burner so-to-speak: i.e. out of sight out of mind.

The sacred scriptures have nothing whatsoever to do with morality, ethics, penal or civil codes: i.e. all these are manmade control systems, which of course are necessary to create an orderly cultural materialistic civilization. They are necessary to create devout citizens. The primary purpose of the secular government is to develop the intellect of the citizenry into being good and devout citizens. Symbolically: in point of fact, the sacred scripture begins from the perspective that the initiate (bible student: member of the laity) has already been fully educated and has become accustomed to modernity religious and secular teachings. Judaism, for all intent and purpose, is very much like the Masonic Order, insofar, they try to teach Good (devout) Men to be 'Better Men'. Being an excellent citizen does not determines whether an individual is religious or atheistic. In point of fact most people that believe that they are religious are realistically atheistic; for the reason that, they live their entire lives iconoclastically. An iconoclastic individual is not religious; though, he or she may argue that assessment of iconoclasm.

When the scribes of antiquity spiritually intuited the MATRIX OF WISDOM it was envisaged as a commentary on the MONAD (the number one: Christ, Soul); thus, the MATRIX OF WISDOM pragmatically does not truly exist outside of a means by which the initiate can conceptually cull out the WORD OF GOD with an accurate precision in order to understand what life and reality is all about.

The MATRIX OF WISDOM is a very difficult matrix to divine ex nihilo (out of nothing) especially when it is not even known to exist; though, it is simply, from modernity's standpoint, the first nine multiplication tables brought down to their lowest common denominators (casting-out-nines). Christ said, *"I praise you, Father, Lord of heaven and earth, because you have hidden these things from the wise and learned, and revealed them to little children (Matthew 11:25)"*. It must be pointed out here that the MATRIX OF WISDOM has its source material in the MONAD, which is the commencement point of the Fibonacci sequence[3], which is the true foundation of how the MATRIX OF WISDOM was developed and used to write the sacred scriptures of the world.

---

[3] The Fibonacci sequence was known by the ancient; though, what they called it is unknown; however, as this thesis continues it will become quite obvious that they knew of the Golden Ratio (Golden Means).

MATRIX OF WISDOM
UNIVERSAL MATHEMATICAL MATRIX:
Prima Materia (Perennial Matrix)

9	9	9	9	9	9	9	9	9	9
9	1	2	3	4	5	6	7	8	9
9	2	4	6	8	1	3	5	7	9
9	3	6	9	3	6	9	3	6	9
9	4	8	3	7	2	6	1	5	9
9	5	1	6	2	7	3	8	4	9
9	6	3	9	6	3	9	6	3	9
9	7	5	3	1	8	6	4	2	9
9	8	7	6	5	4	3	2	1	9
9	9	9	9	9	9	9	9	9	9

The mystical ambiance of this MATRIX OF WISDOM defies the known laws of physics; for the reason that, it formulates it own inherent images via sacred geometry that exudes the WORD OF GOD, without any prompting or inventive thought from the initiate. The sum total of all knowledge: i.e. the WORD OF GOD is inherent in these iconographic images and it is the sole responsibility of the initiate not only to divine the MATRIX OF WISDOM; but to cull out from it how it writes the sacred scriptures (build the internal not the external Temple of God) and why it is used to do so. Every moment of life is writing the sacred scriptures; though, that is not consciously envisaged.

The MATRIX OF WISDOM wrote the sacred scriptures through the auspices of the scribes of antiquity through revelation from the Holy Spirit putting mythological themes to the sacred geometry they intuited out of the numerical aspects of the MATRIX OF WISDOM. It is the purpose of this book's thesis to outline how that mystical process takes place.

The reader may eventually obtain an intellectual understanding of the systemic Esoteric Science codified to the sacred scriptures; however, this does not mean that he or she will grasp the significance of the WORD OF GOD. Only God can clarify to the initiate the mystical ambiance of his divine WORD: Christ consciousness. There is no doubt that atheists will find ways of declaring the Esoteric Science as an invention of humanity and that will be; for the reason that, they are after all who they are: atheists: i.e. the egocentric (iconoclastic) elite.

I, personally, don't think that many people will immediately benefit by reading this work's thesis; for the reason that, too often I venture into excruciating details, or not enough explanations, in my attempts to explain the Esoteric Science and I cannot fathom any better way of presenting it. The systemic system of the Esoteric Science housing the ambiance of the WORD OF GOD is far more detailed than I could ever hope to explain. This thesis will be tedious, laborious and psychically excruciating to the uninitiated; for the reason that, such a reader will not know the serenity that the silence contemplative meditational thought offers. The uninitiated is too enamored by the noise and the clamor of modernity's materialistic reality. The initiate learns to silence that which enamors his or her psyche. This is no way or means that one should meditate eternally in a monastic atmosphere; rather, it is learning to slowly back away from those materialistic pleasures that enamor the psyche.

Most Christians and/or Jews and/or Moslems in modernity would not know anything about the MATRIX OF WISDOM and individually and collectively they would think it was a concocted occult and/or hermetic interpretation of the WORD OF GOD. And I would not blame them if they did think that way; for the reason that, iconography (symbolism) is not the manner they were taught to read their sacred scriptures. Modernists are taught to read the sacred scriptures iconoclastically (literally and historically). I agree that iconoclastic thought is the traditional and preliminary way of educating a child into the art of reading via the societal mores. Think of iconoclastic thought as basic generic elementary teachings such as numerics and the alphabet: i.e. symbolic of the Old Testament, which is never-ever forgotten. Iconoclasm is the basic teachings of any elementary school teacher. The teacher can instruct the student into mathematics, the alphabet and how to read; however, sadly the majority of students once they leave the classroom do not read or use mathematics that much more in their lives. You cannot force someone to continue his or her education once they leave the classroom. The whole of life is an educational process.

I, myself, was fully caught up in the fray of modernity systemic system of thought until about August 1974 when I began to work my way out of iconoclastic thought when reading the bible and religious literature and studying religious artworks, monuments and architecture. Religious Bible-Studies should immediately venture into educating the laity concerning the differences between iconoclastic and iconographic thought and how they both are symbiotically and systematically used to write the sacred scriptures of the world. No one can completely rid themselves of iconoclastic thought for it is the way of life live in the phantasmagoria of the psyche (the real world). Iconographic thought is used mainly to be amidst the ambiance of God in the Garden of Eden that should be a 24/7 undertaking, which is symbolized by religious teachings. Going from iconoclastic thought, which the surface text of the bible infers, to iconographic thinking is realistically vanishing (Rapture) psychically to be amidst God's Ambiance in the Garden of Eden: *Two men will be in the field: one will be taken and the other left. Two women will be grinding at the mill: one will be taken and the other left (Matthew 24:40-41)."* Of course this does not mean that the individual vanishes from the face of the earth where iconoclastic thinking people do not see him or her that spiritually vanished; rather, it is like being in a crowded room totally oblivious of everybody around you; for the reason that, the initiate vanishes into God's Ambiance in the Garden of Eden. The ambiance of the world is all around the initiate; but, the initiate is no longer enamored by it.

The amalgamation of iconoclastic and iconographic thinking can be acclimated to one's every thought, word and deed while living life in the material world 24/7; however, because the world is presently in the bowels of Hades it *may* take decades for the individual to works his or her way out of modernistic iconoclastic thought to religious iconographic thinking. As generations go by the religious educational lapses of time will decrease proportional to modernity increases it knowledge of esotericism. What I mean by this is that the basics of the esoteric science can eventually be quickly learned or taught to others; however, the mystical nature of the esoteric science can only be taught to the initiate by God. Since God is infinite there is no way of fully understanding the spiritual forces of creation.

The sacred scriptures of the world are iconographically structured line upon line here a little and there a little (letter by letter via word by word). This systemic system of the esoteric science cannot be understood in a moment of time. It is very much like learning any profession on the face of the earth; however, religiously every soul has to individually learn esotericism, directly from God, in order to understand the WORD OF GOD. This esotericism is not just for an ordained priesthood. Every member of the Roman Catholic laity is a priest after the Order of Melchiezidek. Members of the ordain priesthood are merely curators and preservers of sacred literature and artwork. It is obvious that modernity's present members of the ordained priesthood are not educators of the teachings of Christ (Tao, Buddha, Krishna, Horus, etc.). If the ordain priesthood's raison d'être was to educate the laity to the teaching of Christ they failed miserably in informing the laity of the Esoteric Science, which codifies the WORD OF GOD to the sacred scriptures, literature, artworks, monuments and architecture of their religion.

Personally, I do not believe that the ordain priesthood's mission is to teach religious beliefs. The ordain priesthood's raison d'être is to make available to the laity the untarnished sacred scriptures, literature, artworks, monuments and architecture of its religion around the world so that it is available to the individual member of the laity when he or she wakes up from the stupor of materialism and is willing to give of his or her *whole heart, mind, soul, time, finances and resources* to search for the knowledge of God. God is the only educator of His sacred WORD. No ordained priest has such authority.

This work per se is not solely about Christianity; rather, this work is about the same generic esoteric science that exists running parallel to all other generic religious systems on Earth. Being Christian I will be referencing the Judaeo Christian Scriptures to augment my discussion on the WORD OF GOD. I have neither the intention of proselytizing the iconoclastic teachings of Christianity nor any other orthodox religions on the face of the Earth. My goal is to lay out the generic esoteric science that governs the foundations of iconography found in all religions teachings on Earth that use the original spiritual source materials: i.e. MATRIX OF WISDOM. This will not be an easy task to put into words that will reach the mental acuity of the individual member of the laity that knows absolutely nothing of esotericism. I have to be myself in writing this book and that may be a devastating disadvantage to many readers due to the manner I articulate this thesis.

Neither iconography nor iconoclasm is the WORD OF GOD per se; however, they will on a symbiotic level in scribing the sacred scriptures prepare the initiate to know the WORD OF GOD when he or she envisages it and only God can guide the initiate through that labyrinth.

The sacred scriptures are written from the format of absolute perfection and not too many people know or appreciate that. When a self-motivated initiate such as myself, takes on the task of trying to understand the sacred scriptures via a foreign language (Hebrew) and precision sciences (Seven Liberal Arts and Sacred Geometry) he or she is not going to be immediately educated into it; because, of his or her frail educational limitations. Such an endeavor is like trying to bore through a mountain of granite rock that is miles deep, with a toothpick, not knowing how to read the data or understand the strange ideas that come to mind. Embarking upon such a task the initiate will have absolutely no ideas how deeply mystical the WORD OF GOD is and he or she will neither know the existence of nor what esotericism is.

ANTIQUITY'S SPIRITUAL ACCOMPLISHMENTS
In Literature, Artworks, Monuments and Architecture

Having said all the above I would like to give the reader a heads-up on what the ancient scribes of the sacred scriptures around the world were up against in writing the WORD OF GOD from out of the numerics of the MATRIX OF WISDOM (Fibonacci sequence – Golden Ratio).

First of all the scribes of antiquity had to be able to illustrate comprehensively the concept of diametrically opposing systems that represented both materialism and spirituality. This seems to be a self-evident fact; for the reason that, the world is known to be a realm of opposites; however, materialism versus spirituality appears consciously to be, for the most part, a humanly contrived opposite and not a natural phenomenon that all the other opposites in the material creation seem to inherently exude.

The basic problem that the scribes of antiquity were faced with was to layout the existence of this set of opposites, materialism versus spirituality, which did not appear realistically to have anything to do with the manifested materialistic creation whatsoever. The scribes of antiquity had to do it in such a manner that the iconoclastic world would never know that the WORD OF GOD was codified into the world's literature, artworks, monuments or architecture or that it ever occurred or that it was ever accomplished. It literally is not possible for a person living iconoclastically to ever know of the existence of the WORD OF GOD. The WORD OF GOD is inexplicably silent. The fact that modernity has absolutely no idea that the WORD OF GOD even exist is incontrovertible evidence of that truth. The sacred scriptures per se are not evidence of the existence of the WORD OF GOD. The texts per se are not the WORD OF GOD. It is beyond the ability of any individual to teach the WORD OF GOD; because, of its inexplicable mystical nature. Only God can take on that task and gift it to the worthy initiate.

Of course no scribe or group of scribes could have even so much as conceived of such an ostensibly non-existing problem to be solve unless of course they were gifted with the Initiatic Visionary Experience and it is only God that could have presented the project to the scribes to be accomplished.

The only evidence that the scribes of antiquity had at their disposal that there was the WORD OF GOD to be mystically and stealthily scribed into the sacred scriptures was the existence of the MATRIX OF WISDOM, which guided the scribes of antiquity into how they were to write the sacred scriptures. It is this numinous guidance that writes the WORD OF GOD not the scribes per se. The scribes only conceived of the mythoi that writes the surface texts. This was a very daunting task to accomplish; for the reason that, numerics and symbols had to exist that demonstrably illustrated what materialism per se symbolized and in contrast there had to be numerics and symbols that demonstrably illustrated what spirituality symbolically represented and to accomplish this goal in such a way that ambiguity did not exist in their presentation of these concepts: i.e. materialism versus spirituality: exotericism (Trivium – written text) versus concealed esotericism (Quadrivium – numerical texts).

However, one of the most mystical aspects that the ancient scribes writing the sacred scriptures confronted collectively was not to layout overtly that Christ is the WORD OF GOD; thus, neither God nor the Son of God can actually be seen by the human eye or via the human intellect on its own volition. The whole of the four gospels mystically tell of Christ as he is educating the initiate outside of the time/space continuum; paradoxically, the laity reads the New Testament record of God's Ambiance (Christ consciousness) as if Christ actually existed in the real world of time and space.

The Old Testament talks about Christ via the symbolic and alphanumeric structure of the Hebrew letters; thus, the surface texts of the Old Testament does not speak of Christ overtly; whereas, the New Testament scribes culled out the WORD OF GOD from the esoteric symbolism and alphanumeric structure of the Old Testament Hebraic letters.

The sleight of hand maneuvering in writing the New Testament gospels was to present Christ saying things once or performing an act once in a gospel; though, some of those saying and acts are mentioned in other gospels. Yet, the four gospels as a group symbolize the four mystic elements, which collectively symbolize the LIGHT culled out of the DARKNESS in the first day of creation through diverse methods. These onetime sayings and one time events shield the idea that Christ enters the life of any initiate He talks to. Each initiate literally becomes Christ. These onetime sayings or events are symbolic of multiple events similar to the life of Christ written into four gospels. Every event in the bible is a vignette that is synonymous to the other thousands of other vignettes in the bible. This is why the entire Old and New Testaments are commentaries on the first written letter of the Bible: BETH ב and the mystically hidden letter that inundates and surround BETH ב called PEI פ. This is well worked out on the National Mall in Washington DC where the Capitol Building is the central hub of the city. The entire National Mall going east to west is worked on mystically to illustrate the mysticism of John's gospel that symbolizes the Water Sign of Astrology: i.e. Scorpio; whereas, the other three directions going north, east and south are inferred via the Templar's Cross and/or the gigantic Great Pyramid symbol with the third eye above it that surrounds the Capitol Building's grounds, which is in the shape of a skull: Golgotha, which spherically radiates out God's Ambiance.

John's gospel has been argued in the Christian mythoi as to why it was allowed into the canonized texts of the New Testament. I believe that the Freemasons are expressing the fact that life can be lived beautifully in the Garden of Eden amidst God's Ambiance.

The story of Christ in the New Testament is an amalgamation of many of activities that his followers collectively achieved when they were in the state of Christ consciousness. Christ per se cannot become a materialistic man unless God's Ambiance is imbued into the soul of a lone initiate. When the WORD OF GOD crosses the east-west corridor of time the initiate becomes Christ. The priest of the Roman Catholic Church (Catholicism) literally tells the laity that that every member of the Roman Catholic Church is Christ. Personally, I think that is going too far; because, if a member of the laity is not thinking iconographically he or she is certainly not Christ.

As this thesis is read it will be demonstrated that the MATRIX OF WISDOM will illustrate how the Golden Means (Fibonacci sequence) is the primary symbol that represents the materialistic realm of thought. The Fibonacci sequence per se symbolizes the materialistic activities of the individual initiate, which can do nothing on his or her own volition. In other words; though, the Fibonacci sequence has the potentiality of going beyond the formulation of the MATRIX OF WISDOM it is prevented from doing so; for the reason that, the iconoclastic atheist does not have the mental acuity of going beyond his or her limitations. The Fibonacci sequence's oscillation process is a perfect example of the continuous and never-ending onslaught of redundancy the individual experiences via the world of opposites and this is why the majority of the world is bored stiff with its daily activities via addictions and obsessions: people lives are basically limited by these failings.

Whereas, the MATRIX OF WISDOM can be transubstantiated into what I have come to call the Genesis Formula, which inaugurates the Initiatic Visionary Experience via the first word of Genesis BERESHITH: i.e. *"in the beginning"*. It is the Genesis Formula that literally demonstrates that there is a set of opposites designated as materialism versus spirituality. The MATRIX OF WISDOM illustrate via mathematics very tediously with complicated concepts not only that there is a set of opposites called materialism versus spirituality; but, also why conceptually materialism and spirituality are opposing forces. Note that it is only the organic dynamics of the world that allows opposites to split into two parts: i.e. male and female; whereas, those of natural phenomenon never: i.e. north and south, east and west and up and down never-ever separate for they eternally cling to each other.

The Fibonacci sequence oscillation process symbolizes the fast pace of TIME (Saturn/Cronus), which incorporates the din and clamor of the world; whereas, the Genesis Formula (Jupiter/Zeus) conquers TIME and it is this latter concept of reality that allows the initiate to enter into the Garden of Eden to sit under the Bodhi Tree (axis mundi) and listen to the Still Small Voice: i.e. the silence of God's Ambiance, which the din and clamor of the world has the overwhelming tendency to drowns out.

It should be stated clearly that initially entering into the time/space continuum as a child the MATRIX OF WISDOM: the soul's psyche: ego-consciousness and the unconscious mind is created via the Fibonacci sequence; for the reason that, it symbolically slows down TIME into a repetitive cadence: i.e. infinite redundancy causing addictions and obsessions; whereas, God's Ambiance created via the paradigm exuded out of the Genesis Formula slows down TIME even further causing a sense of TIMELESSNESS as if the world is spinning around the initiate without him or her being enamored by it.

CHAPTER ONE

THE FIRST WRITTEN LETTER: BETH ב (KAMEA OF THE SUN) AND THE FIRST HIDDEN LETTER: PEI פ (KAMEA OF THE MOON) OF THE BIBLE

The first thing to understand about the sacred scriptures is that there is no way that modernity can translate either the Old and/or the New Testament from one language into another for modernity has not the mental acuity to do so. Both of these canonized libraries are systemically and scientifically structured on an esoteric (secret knowledge) level via the Esoteric Science: the SEVEN LIBERAL ARTS: Quadrivium and the Trivium, which are harmoniously integrated and amalgamated throughout the sacred scriptures. These sacred documents are not novels telling historical and/or fictional stories that have no other meaning than what the surface texts are conveying; whereas, religious documents of this spiritual caliber are structured letter by letter esoterically (symbolically - iconographically) and not word by word via exotericism (literally - iconoclastically). In fact the sacred scriptures around the world can only be read: i.e. studied and researched letter by letter esoterically iconographically not word by word exoterically: literally: iconoclastically.

Any translation of the sacred scriptures from around the world into a foreign language wipes out the spirituality of the sacred scriptures by voiding out the entire Quadrivium: Arithmetic, Music/Harmony, Geometry and Astronomy/Astrology: i.e. sacred geometry. Once the sacred scriptures of any religion are translated (via hubris: i.e. ego-centrism) into a foreign language they no longer can be considered the WORD OF GOD.

Each letter in the Hebrew and the Greek alphabets has a symbolic and an alphanumeric structure: i.e. each letter has not only a symbolic meaning it is alphabetized and is given a numerical value and is spelt out, as a word, with several letters with an overall Gematria value; thus, the very first written letter of the Judaeo Christian Scriptures: BETH ב is crammed pack with an abundance of data, which cannot be envisaged via iconoclastic (non-symbolic) thought; on the other hand, the esoteric meaning of the Hebrew and Greek letters can only be grasp via iconography (symbolic thought). The difference between these two diametrically opposing genres of thought is infinite as infinite as the abyss between spirituality and materiality: the twain shall never-ever meet without the auspices of Christ consciousness. Symbolically, spirituality and materiality are analogous to the two hemispheres of the brain working harmoniously in sync with each other.

The Esoteric Science (true Hermeticism) codifies sacred geometry throughout the sacred scriptures of the world via this development of structuring and codifying each letter of the indigenous languages alphanumerically and symbolically and augmenting the texts via the assimilation of the SEVEN LIBERAL ART on a level of iconographic perfection that iconoclastically modernists would consider impractical, implausible and incomprehensible. The rationale that the scribes of antiquity had for developing this Esoteric Science (Hermeticism) to codify into the sacred scriptures of the world is that each religious culture was to be self-motivated and was to independently intuit and record the WORD OF GOD (spiritual forces of creation) on their own. The WORD OF GOD is culled out of the MATRIX OF WISDOM, which is a commentary on the MONAD: Soul (God/Man Christ). The MONAD splits into the two part psyche: i.e. ego-consciousness and the unconscious mind. The MATRIX OF WISDOM via the Fibonacci sequence is the original source material that exudes all manifested creation and writes the sacred scriptures around the world.

Make no mistake about it the MATRIX OF WISDOM: i.e. Fibonacci sequence is the psyche: i.e. ego-consciousness and the unconscious mind brought down into a spiritual/materialistic format so that the initiate can envisage how the psyche and the primeval spiritual forces of creation work in unanimity harmoniously via Christ consciousness. It is inconceivable for modernists to believe that the psyche can be explicitly discussed in such a precise scientific manner; however, this is an inexplicable aspect of the mystical ambiance of the MATRIX OF WISDOM (Fibonacci sequence): the WORD OF GOD.

BETH ב (2) is the first written letter of the TORAH: i.e. sacred scriptures. Its numerical value is two (2); however, when it is spelt out it has the Gematria value of four-hundred and twelve (412). As a mere letter read iconoclastically BETH ב really has no value other than being a letter use to spell out a word; whereas, iconographically BETH ב symbolizes the Birth of Christ consciousness, which Christians call the Pelican; for the reason that, a Pelican folds it head into it breast. Carl G. Jung speaks of this in his work Mysterium Coniunctionis[1]. BETH ב is spelt out: BETH ב (2), YUD י (10) and TAV ת (400). The number 412 is a transposition of the number 1, 2 and 4, which connote the seven directions formatting a sphere: center, up, down and the four directions. I'll discuss the importance of this sphere as this thesis progresses. In the letter/word BETH ב spelt out, YUD י symbolizes the spiritual sun: i.e. Christ

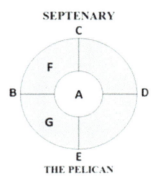

SEPTENARY

THE PELICAN

consciousness; however, the iconoclastic BETH ב symbolizes the materialistic sun: i.e. ego-consciousness and PEI פ symbolizes the moon: i.e. unconscious mind, which will be discussed in a minute. What this means is that ego-consciousness and the unconscious mind are amalgamated, which is why in modernity the world is in total chaos and the individual has absolutely no way out of this chaos on his or her own volition unless he or she can spiritually be Born Again regaining his or her soul's lost spiritual ambiance.

Ego-consciousness has to deflate itself, which per se would be battling against its own archetypal: egotistical survival animal instincts.

In the Old Testament Yahweh (Sun – ego-consciousness) and Elohym (Moon - unconscious mind) are the waters of creation and when they lose the ambiance of Christ consciousness they amalgamate by coming at each other violently like a tsunami creating CHAOS (confusion) in the two part psyche. The psyche's iconoclastic activities can be envisaged as psychically malfunctioning; for the reason that, there is no Christ consciousness separating them from one another. In the real world there are floods periodically worldwide in all times and climes and these floods are used, on a symbolic level, to record esoterically the psychic activity of the individual and/or humanity as a whole losing the *'spiritual ambiance (God) that separates the heavens: TIMELESSNESS and the earth: i.e. TIME Gen. 1:1)'*.

Atlantis is a myth as is the legends of the Garden of Eden and Shangri-La, etc., which speaks of the perfect contented realm: i.e. God's Ambiance, which the MATRIX OF WISDOM provides the soul with that is willing to sacrifice the world of materialism for knowledge of him or herself and to know the **ALL** that can be learned about the spiritual powers of creation: i.e. God. The below image of the city beneath the waters about to receive a fallen angel was found on the Internet, which perfectly illustrates my argument about the psyche. The top, center and bottom commentaries on this image are mine. The fallen angel is obviously an initiate that has lost Christ consciousness and is psychically and summarily tossed back into materialism. This latter about the fallen angel is diametrically opposite of that which is discussed in the fifth day of creation in the first chapter of Genesis when the birds fly out of the waters of the sea to live on the Mastaba: mound of creation: dryland: i.e. earth. The birds are of course angels returning to the Garden of Eden to be with God (sixth day of creation).

---

[1] http://www.amazon.com/Mysterium-Coniunctionis-Collected-Works-Vol-14/dp/0691018162/ref=sr_1_1?s=books&ie=UTF8&qid=1462026710&sr=1-1&keywords=mysterium+coniunctionis

Iconographically the entire Old and New Testaments are commentaries on this one lone letter BETH ב positioned as the first written letter of the Judaeo Christian Scriptures. From modernity iconoclastic (literal and historical) perspective that is impossible, inconceivable and inexplicable; nonetheless, that is one of the main points in this thesis to illustrate demonstrably iconographically (symbolically) that spiritual truth. BETH ב iconographically is the Christian Bodhi Tree otherwise known as the axis mundi (still point in which all creation revolves – center of creation).

BETH ב (2) is mystically inundated and surrounded by the invisible (esotericism) Hebrew letter PEI פ (17). This letter PEI פ esoterically symbolizes the silent MOUTH OF GOD. Here I am going off the discussion, for a second, to point out that Scorpio, which the first verse of Genesis symbolizes, along the ecliptic cycle, is seemingly (?) chasing and trying to grasp the sun that is eternally traveling towards the west. It will be seen how this is an important nuance as this thesis continues.

The letter PEI פ has the numerical value of eighty (80) and the Gematria value of eighty-one (PEI פ is spelt PEI פ (80) and ALEPH א (1) = 81: i.e. 9 x 9 Magic Square – KAMEA OF THE MOON). It is this letter PEI פ codified esoterically to inundate and surround BETH ב that allows BETH ב to be the Bodhi Tree: i.e. axis mundi (center of creation: spiritual Sun) and PEI פ symbolizes all of creation. Later on in this work it will be shown how creation is inaugurated where God's Ambiance surrounds the soul creating the Garden of Eden.

In the iconoclastic world the individual is told he or she is not the center of creation: Everybody's ego-centrism iconoclastically, in modernity, negates that idea. In the esoteric realm of thought every initiate is the Bodhi Tree (center of creation).

PEI פ as the MOUTH OF GOD symbolically has thirty-two (32) teeth: sixteen (16) up and sixteen (16) down and from the mouth come *'God's breathe (spirit of God) that hovers over the face of the waters (Gen. 1:2).* This 'breath of God' is the initial step in the Initiatic Visionary Experience. God comes down upon the good and the evil psyche that is prone and frozen stiff and immobilized, without prejudice, and it is up to the initiate to motivate him or herself into action: i.e. *"And Elohym said (DESIRED), Let there be LIGHT (Gen. 1:3)"*, which perfectly exemplifies the initiate that is sincere in his or her quest to know him or herself and to know God

PEI פ is analogous to a blank sheet of paper and BETH ב sits at the top right hand corner of the page. PEI פ as the KAMEA OF THE MOON is a perfect layout of the unconscious mind. Everybody psyche is generically functioning similar to all other psyche's. Everybody psyche is different; for the reason that, each person has a different raison d'être: i.e. reason for existence – ways of expressing him or herself; thus, the KAMEA OF THE MOON is a perfect Magic Square of eighty-one (81: 9 x 9) numbers; however, PEI פ spelt out, without ALEPH א (1) cannot contain the wisdom of Christ consciousness and its merely the unconscious mind battling ego-consciousness. In this state of mind PEI פ would not be a perfect Magic Square; rather, it's eighty (80) numbers, which is minus one: ALEPH א (1) would be chaotically disarrayed. I will get to that as I continue.

The moment that PEI פ (Gematria value is 81: 9 x 9 Magic Square: also 9^3 cubed), is envisaged all magic squares (squared or cubed) are inferred for future biblical interpretation. Knowing PEI פ is the Kamea of the Moon it is no great leap of logic to see BETH ב as the Kamea of the Sun (cubed 6^3); for the reason that, BETH ב per se symbolizes the conduit of all creation. I will discuss this in a minute and this is the mystical reason that BEREHITH has only six letters. BETH ב can only show half the equation and this will be shown why throughout this work; thus, YUD י, which is the center letter in the word BETH ב (Beth ב – Yud י – Tav ת) symbolizes the sun in the center of the solar system. Since BETH ב is the conduit of all creation and the six letters of BERESHITH infers six cubed (6^3), which is the Kamea of the Sun cubed. This is analogous to the initiate having Christ consciousness seeing psychically peripherally symbolically on a spherical level. What I mean by this is that the spiritually gifted (mystic) apparently has access to omniscience. This will be fully envisaged when I discuss the esoteric symbolism codified to the National Mall in Washington DC (see chapter sixteen). Ego-consciousness can only visualize the limitations forced upon the phantasmagoria of the psyche (tunnel vision = ego-consciousness' agenda): i.e. material creation from the front; though, physical vision has peripheral vision it is only in perspective to tunnel vision.

The Kamea of the Moon: PEI פ is symbolic of the unconscious mind and The Kamea of the Sun: BETH ב is ego-consciousness and both appear to be united; however, without the spiritual ambiance of Christ consciousness they are in eternal warfare; whereas, The MATRIX OF WISDOM is the Initiatic Visionary Experience that destroys PEI פ: the old Kamea of the Moon and destroys BETH ב: the old Kamea of the Sun and gifts the worthy initiate with the Garden of Eden: i.e. a spiritual harmonious relationship with a new BETH ב: Kamea of the Sun (earth) and a new PE פ: Kamea of the Moon (heaven) that represent the ambiance of God in the MATRIX OF WISDOM. Symbolism is not a two dimensional (iconoclastic) tool; rather, it is a three dimensional (iconographic) tool. Iconography sees the whole picture; whereas, iconoclasm is liken to being at a smorgasbord where an individual selects or rejects what he or she pleases; thus, a two dimensional image is iconoclastic and a three dimensional image is iconographic.

Ego-consciousness per se does not exist. It is a by-product of the delusional hubris psyche that is not governed by Christ consciousness. Ego-consciousness not being a self-motivator is created through hubris trying to maintain a self-created status quo.

Psychically, in the normal spiritual course of events Christ consciousness is supposed to be continuously culled out of itself: i.e. MATRIX OF WISDOM (10^3: cubed). The Kamea of the Moon (9^3: cubed) is not added to the Kamea of the Sun (6^3: cubed) in order to totals to 945. It will appear initially to some readers that not presenting the MATRIX OF WISDOM (cubed: 10^3) as the amalgamation of the Kamea of the Sun (cubed: 6^3) and the Kamea of the Moon (cubed: 9^3) as symbols for the Hebrew letters BETH ב and PEI פ would be nonsensical and ridiculous.

The reason why the Kamea of the Sun is not added to the Kamea of the Moon is because it is already inherent in the Kamea of the Moon. Symbolism in the bible multitask continuously and can be used in a number of different symbolic scenarios; thus, BETH ב (2nd Hebrew letter) and PEI פ (17th Hebrew letter) total to QOPH ק (19th Hebrew letter) and that is because from that perspective they represent Christ consciousness, which will be discussed shortly.

The sacred scriptures for the most part economizes symbolism; whereas, the mathematics of the sacred scriptures are not at all times precise as perfection is normally envisaged in modernity; however, as the database of material in the sacred scriptures extrapolates outwardly into a larger mythological storylines explaining the WORD OF GOD, those mythoi are used to denote the same symbolism previously discussed, mathematical precision become extremely accurate.

I can only warn the reader that the spiritual law (God) is far more severe in it judicial verdict and sentencing than any judicial system in modernity. God's way of punishing those that are uninformed of His spiritual laws is to leave them to themselves. Every single soul is so punished with this severest of all punishments for the smallest infractions of God's spiritual laws.

From the very first Hebrew letter of the Judaeo Christian Scriptures, from a totally symbolic perspective, the MATRIX OF WISDOM presents itself, which is Christ consciousness: the ambiance of God or the Eucharistic presence. Christ is not per se the sun; rather, He symbolizes the mystical alchemical marriage of the Sun and the Moon; however, Christ is often symbolized as the Sun; whereas, the symbolism of the Moon is not noted similar to how BETH ב is the first written letter of the Torah and PEI פ is the first hidden letter: if truth be told this is why symbolically women worldwide are second class citizens in modernity Patriarchal societies.

BETH ב (masculine) is iconoclastic two-dimensional thought that dominates false interpretations of the sacred scriptures.

If this MATRIX OF WISDOM did not present itself from the very first letter of the sacred scriptures: BETH ב the TORAH could never have been written. All knowledge of God's creation had to be made available ex nihilo (out of nothing) at the very moment of creation. Throughout this volume I will illustrate prolifically how the sum total of all knowledge flows out from BETH ב continuously creating the Old and New Testaments.

The Hebrew letter BETH ב is said to symbolize the Temple of Elohym. Considering the symbolism of BETH ב I would agree with that; however, I would go further designating BETH ב as the New Testament and PEI פ as the Old Testament and it may well be because of this that BETH ב has been designated as the Temple of God: Holy of Holies.

The initiate has to realize that the bible produces symbols that are not quite accurate mathematically as modernity would like to see meticulously worked out equations; for the reason that, the bible efficiently economizes its resources by crammed packing every single letter of the sacred scriptures with the sum total of all knowledge. BETH ב and PEI פ are both Hebrew letters that symbolize Magic Squares that are fully developed; however, BETH ב as the Kamea of the Sun cubed is 6^3 or 216-cells and PEI פ as the Kamea of the Moon cubed is 9^3 or 729-cells. They do no not combine to total to 945-cells, which is not 1000-cells, which would be the cube 10^3 of the MATRIX OF WISDOM; however, it will be seen below that subtracting 216 from 729 gives the quotient of 513, which is the transposition of 153, which symbolizes the Vesica Piscis and is the aggregate of seventeen (17), which is the numerical position of PEI פ the seventeenth (17th) letter of the Hebrew Coder. Adding 729 + 216 would not be economizing of data in the sacred scriptures, which is a normal process in codifying esotericism to the texts. Totaling these two figures would be a false analysis of the scriptural texts. Normally economizing mathematical equations into the texts will be seen to give seemingly inaccurate mathematics until a larger amount of scriptural textual data illustrates the mathematics in a more precise manner.

I discussed all this and repeat it to illustrate the following equation: $729 / 216 = 3.375$, which is not quite, from modernity standpoint, a meticulous equation representing three and a half (3.5), which symbolizes the three and a half coiled Kundalini Serpent. The Kundalini Serpent symbolizes the spiritual Initiatic Visionary Experience. The Kundalini Serpent will be discussed mathematically more accurately in the discussion on the main body of the texts in the first chapter of Genesis. Right now I will illustrate mathematically that this calculation literally is the seed of thought that illustrates how the entire Old and New Testaments are structured mathematically.

The Old Testament has exactly 929 Chapters and the New Testament has 260 Chapters: $929 / 260 = 3.573...$, which is extremely close to 3.5; however, it gets far more accurate than that. The book of Malachi has four chapters. It says, ***"Behold, I will send you Elijah the prophet before the great and awesome day of the Lord comes. And he will turn the hearts of fathers to their children and the hearts of children to their fathers, lest I come and strike the land with a decree of utter destruction (Malachi 4:5-6)"***

And ***"Truly I tell you, among those born of women there has not risen anyone greater than John the Baptist; yet whoever is least in the kingdom of heaven is greater than he. From the days of John the Baptist until now, the kingdom of heaven has been subjected to violence and violent take it by force. For all the Prophets and the Law prophesied until John. And if you are willing to accept it, he is the Elijah who was to come (Matthew 11:11-14)."***

For all intent and purpose, John the Baptist symbolizes the Old Testament and Jesus Christ symbolizes the New Testament: Kundalini Serpent. Everything about John the Baptist (June 24th) is diametrically opposite to Christ consciousness (December 25th), which are their birth dates 180° apart from each other. This is why the New Testament will be shown to be a direct commentary on the esotericism of the Old Testament texts not its exoteric texts (surface storyline). This is analogous to the Kamea of the Sun being pulled out of the Kamea of the Moon so too does the first day of creation cull the LIGHT out of the DARKNESS.

KAMEA OF THE SUN

6	32	3	34	35	1
7	11	27	28	8	30
19	14	16	15	23	24
18	20	22	21	17	13
25	29	10	9	26	12
36	5	33	4	2	31

KAMEA OF THE MOON

37	78	29	70	21	62	13	54	5
6	38	79	30	71	22	63	14	46
47	7	39	80	31	72	23	55	15
16	48	8	40	81	32	64	24	56
57	17	49	9	41	73	33	65	25
26	58	18	50	1	42	74	34	66
67	27	59	10	51	2	43	75	35
36	68	19	60	11	52	3	44	76
77	28	69	20	61	12	53	4	45

Malachi's four chapters reduces the Old Testament 929 chapters down to 925 and increase the New Testament to 264; however, then there is the last chapter of Zachariah that is the pivotal chapter of the entire Old and New Testaments, which acts like a Bodhi Tree or axis mundi (center of creation). It talks about the Lord coming: ***"On that day his feet will stand on the Mount of Olives, east of Jerusalem, and the Mount of Olives will be split in two from east to west, forming a great valley, with half of the Mount moving north and half moving south"***: thus, 924 / 264 = 3.5 (precise mathematics) the coiled Kundalini. This 924 and 264 ratio is no accident when you realize that 924 / 132 = 7 and 264 / 132 = 2. The numbers 2 and 7 are symbolically the LIGHT culled out of the DARKNESS, which the word LIGHT has a Gematria value of 207.

The number 132 will be seen as the transposition of the number 213, which is arithmetical data obtain when the letters of the Hebrew letter/word RESH ר are reduced to their lowest common denominators. RESH ר symbolizes the spiritual cosmic beginnings of the Initiatic Visionary Experience. It is important NOW that I immediately introduce the reader to an extraordinary analysis of the Gematria value of the letter/word RESH ר. RESH ר is the twentieth (20th) letter of the Hebrew Coder and has the numerical value of two hundred (200) and it is a Cosmic letter. RESH ר spelt out is: Resh ר (200 = 2), Aleph (1) and Shin (300 = 3); hence, the reason that it is the transposition of the number 132. RESH's ר Gematria value if 501: 200 + 1 + 300; however, it gets far more mystical than that. I have mentioned that BETH בּ was the first letter of Genesis and that PEI פ inundate and surrounds it.

The letter RESH ר symbolizes Christ consciousness coming down from the north into the deflated ego-consciousness and this is what mystically creates the first word of Genesis: BE-RESH-ITH בראשית. When the letter/word RESH ר is spelt out and in turn each of its letters is spelt out the following results are obtained:

1. RESH ר: Resh ר (200) + Aleph א (1) + Shin ש (300) = 501
2. ALEPH: Aleph א (1) + Lemmed ל (30) + PEI פ (80) = 111
   a. It is interesting that Resh and Aleph combine to total 612, which is the transposition of 216 = 6³: i.e. Kamea of the Sun, which the Sun is being totally eclipse by the Kamea of the Moon (972 transformed into 729: 9³).
      i. This interpretation is further discussed in the second chapter of Genesis, which epitomizes the total eclipse of the sun.
   b. RESH: Resh (200 = 2) + Aleph (1) + Shin (300 = 3) is obviously a take on Christ's statement in the New Testament: ***"For where there are two or three gathered together in my name, there am I in the midst of them"***, it is ALEPH א that gives RESH ר the ability to become the Kamea of the Sun.
      i. It is obvious that the important nuance in Christ's statement is, *"gathered together in my name"* or else Christ is not present.
3. SHIN: Shin ש (300) + Yud י (10) + Nun נ (50) = 360 (circle)
4. TOTALS: RESH ר 501 + ALEPH א = 111 + SHIN ש = 360 = 972
   a. The number 972 is the transposition of 729 = 9³: Kamea of the Moon symbolizing PEI פ the seventeenth (17th) letter of the Hebrew Coder.
   b. This is LIGHT culled out of the DARKNESS (discussed later).

Throughout this volume this North and South phenomenon separated by the East and West corridor of Time will be discussed ad nauseam.

Another calculation of BETH בּ symbolizing the Kamea of the Sun (6³ cubed) and PEI פ symbolizing the Kamea of the Moon (9³ cubed) is in subtracting that 216 from 729 = 513, which is the transposition of the number 153. The number 153 is the aggregate of the number seventeen (17). The seventeenth letter of the Hebrew coder is PEI פ; however, the 153 also symbolizes the mathematics of the Vesica Piscis.

The above calculations confirms my analysis and interpretation of the first letter of Genesis: BETH בּ surrounded by PEI פ: symbolizing the Kamea of the Moon, which in turn PEI פ and BETH בּ form the nineteenth (19) letter of the Hebrew Coder: QOPH ק, which per se is Christ consciousness and this will also be further discuss in this work. QOPH ק (100) from this perspective symbolizes the MATRIX OF WISDOM, which has 10 x 10 = 100 cells.

Numerous examples of this above material will be discussed and illustrated throughout this volume; thus, it can be envisaged via contemplative thought that by understanding the seemingly innocuous numerical and Gematria data scribed into the sacred scriptures letters and words as symbols a great deal of ostensibly disparate concepts harmoniously interrelate with each other.

Once the reader understands that PEI פ inundates and surrounds BETH בּ the first letter of Genesis it should be easy to understand that though the Kamea of the Sun (6³ cubed) symbolizes Christ consciousness it is still a finite concept in relationship to the infinity that the Kamea of the Moon (9³) symbolizes as PEI פ, which mirror images a blank sheet of paper with BETH בּ at the top right corner symbolically symbolizing the initiate scribing the sacred scriptures since Hebrew is written from right to left. This is because PEI פ is not chasing BETH בּ; rather, PEI פ is continuously releasing BETH בּ to write the sacred scriptures: the book of life.

BETH בּ is a finite phenomenon; for the reason that, it continuously ad nauseam is culled out of the DARKNESS writing creation. The moment that the Kamea of the Sun is culled out of the Kamea of the Moon it become part and partial of the manifested creation: i.e. ink on the canvas so to speak. This is analogous to an individual talking. He or she has to continuously cull out from the unconscious mind that which needs to be discussed. The moment that anybody says or does anything: thought, word or deed it vanishes into the ether; because, TIME continues on eternally vanquishing everything that crosses it path.

It will be extremely difficult for modernity to understand that both ego-consciousness (materialistic mindset: iconoclasm) and Christ consciousness (spiritually minded: iconography) are diametrically opposites ways of thinking and that both of these viable existing concepts are eternally transients nanosecond by nanosecond, which have to be perpetually culled out of the DARKNESS. God lets nobody rest on their laurels.

Christianity continuously has the crucifixion of Christ displayed throughout Christendom. There is no problem with that per se if it is conceptually understood that that the image of Christ on the cross and the symbolism of Christianity is what represents spiritually. There is no problem if the symbolism that symbolizes Christ is continuously being pulled out of the DARKNESS ad infinite every nanosecond of the initiate's life spiritually as the same image as the previous nanosecond; though, it may appear materialistically (iconoclasm) to be conceptually otherwise.

This is why the Old and New Testaments are canonized as a closed hermetically sealed systemic system of thought, which nothing can be added to or taken from. The moment that an indigenous language is translated into another language the entire Quadrivium: four mathematical sciences; Arithmetic, Music/Harmony, Geometry, Astronomy/Astrology are completely erased and eradicated from the sacred scriptures. From that materialistic perspective the bible merely becomes seemingly an iconoclastic fictional historical document, which spews out nothing but nonsense that has no rationale to it, from a spiritual perspective, whatsoever.

Today in the twenty-first century modernity find itself in a permanent state of iconoclasm. Modernity wants everything to remain permanent for all times and climes regardless of what TIME teaches it and erodes into the ethers; because, what modernity has it considers it to be it best concept of a utopia paradise. Modernity is the stubborn Minotaur Bull (Taurus) that does not want change. Modernity is analogous to the bull in the China Shop, it does not want movement. Modernity wants the eternal status quo. That concept relating to the status quo alone epitomizes orthodox religious and academic thought throughout modernity in the twenty-first century. Like the bull on the prairie the religious and academic scholar will charge at anything that moves against its mainstream thought and/or what it sees as threatening its status quo and they will go at it with a scorch earth policy even if it means destroying themselves.

This is what this book is all about going against the status quo by simply interpreting the sacred scriptures iconographically not according to the status quo that interprets the sacred scriptures iconoclastically. Let the Armageddon begin.

CHAPTER TWO

SERPENT MOUND

This concept that PEI פ laid out in the first letter of Genesis: BETH ב was also mystically worked out on the SERPENT MOUND complex created about 2300-years ago by the Hopewell Indians in Peebles, Ohio, USA and the surrounding area. I present here the SERPENT MOUND effigy images; for the reason that, it alone as far as I know, other than the city of Washington DC, of all the spiritual sites around the world, is based upon similar concepts to that of the symbiosis that exist between the two Hebrew letters BETH ב and PEI פ.

The American Hopewell Indians over 2300-years ago created this SERPENT MOUND effigy. A comparative analysis between the two Hebrew letters BETH ב and PEI פ and SERPENT MOUND and the gigantic meteor impact crater that it sits in will reveal a lot of mystical nuances that are not readily available to the Christian or Kabbalistic mindset. When Yahweh (Sun – ego-consciousness) and Elohym (Moon – unconscious mind) are not separated by Christ consciousness: God's Ambiance they are basically representations of animal instincts as is the bear effigy that is carved out of the yardang that SERPENT MOUND sits on.

SERPENT MOUND sits upon a gigantic yardang; however, it is much larger than most people realize. William Romain, an archeologist, did a Vimeo Video of SERPENT MOUND[1], which omits all vegetation and water just showing the dry landscape of the area. Immediately within the first second of this Vimeo video the viewer can see a gigantic sleeping bear artistically worked into the landscape and as the Vimeo video continues the bear's body disappears and SERPENT MOUND is shown coming out of the bear's head. Coming out of the head is symbolic of the Hebrew letter/word RESH ר and I will get into that as I go along; however, I don't want to get ahead of myself; though, I will say here that RESH ר symbolizes the 'head' as in SERPENT MOUND the bear's head contains the serpent effigy. RESH ר is the central most important nuance in the first word of Genesis: BERESHITH בראשית. As it can be seen the English texts goes left (west) to right (east) and the Hebrew goes right (east) to left (west).

SERPENT MOUND'S yardang (symbolically BETH ב) sits inside on the edge of a gigantic meteor impact crater, which I believe symbolizes the Hebrew letter, PEI פ. The sleeping bear (average man or woman living in the world) symbolizes the materialistic ego-consciousness and the unconscious mind about to be spiritually awakened. The SERPENT MOUND effigy is obviously the Kundalini Serpent: BETH ב. The effigy has three and a half coils in its length. I will be discussing the Kundalini Serpent in the first chapter of Genesis illustrating that SERPENT MOUND does exudes the basic concepts of the first chapter of Genesis as was seen with the calculation of dividing the Kamea of the Moon: 9^3 by the Kamea of the Sun: 6^3.

SERMENT MOUND was aligned and constructed with extremely precision mathematics that deals with the Summer and Winter solstices and the Vernal and Autumn equinoxes. Surrounding the SERPENT MOUND yardang are twelve other Hopewell Indian mounds that symbolizes the twelve signs of the Zodiac. The Hopewell Indians of course knew of the 365.25 day calendar year. The Hopewell Indians had to know of the MATRIX OF WISDOM. The Hopewell Indian's precision mathematics codified to the serpent effigy demonstrates that knowledge. The American Indians had thirteen lunar calendar months, which they designed their zodiacal system on. Ross Hamilton wrote a few books on the Hopewell Indian mounds: THE MYSTERY OF THE SERPENT MOUND[2] and STAR MOUNDS[3], which I highly recommend. I

---

[1] https://vimeo.com/926341
[2] http://www.amazon.com/Mystery-Serpent-Mound-Search-Alphabet/dp/1583940030/ref=sr_1_1?ie=UTF8&qid=1462060718&sr=8-1&keywords=THE+MYSTERY+OF+SERPENT+MOUND

mention all this about Astrology at SERPENT MOUND; for the reason that, the first four chapters of Genesis have the twelve zodiacal signs codified to the texts esoterically, which will be discussed at length as this book progresses.

It also should be mention that it is obvious, at least to me, that the gigantic bear effigy image was artistically created out of a large yardang that SERPENT MOUND is a part of and having said that, as a reminder, it should be pointed out that the Sphinx of Egypt on the Giza Plateau: its head was also carved out of a yardang, which is another reference to RESH ר (head). The body of the Sphinx was carved out of the granite rock that was beneath the yardang on the Giza Plateau. This goes to suggest that the SERPENT MOUND's yardang could have been artistically withered down to help form the bear effigy. Carving the bear effigy out of a yardang would have been an enormous project; but, no less difficult than that of creating the serpent effigy.

In addition look at the landscape in the Vimeo film and notice the Brook Creek river bed left of the serpent effigy. It appears to be too uniform to have been created by nature's climatic conditions. Others may say that an ice glacier created that carving in the ground that provided the course for the river; however, nature is never that uniformed in its behavior. If an ice glacier hit the side of that yardang the uniformity of the river bank would have, for at least a fraction of a second, gone chaotic and there is no sign of that kind of upheaval in the river bed. I would think it is quite possible that the American Hopewell Indian created this river as an easy access to that sacred SERPENT MOUND site not only to build it; but, also to conduct their sacred religious ceremonies and to make a permanent memorial to their Shaman's Initiatic Visionary Experience. Ancient Canal System in the Americas[4] definitively shows that the American Indians were quite industrious in developing their cultures and that my hypothesis that Brook Creek is manmade in not out of the realm of possibilities. This all had a great deal to do with the many bear clans throughout the disparate America Indian cultures on the North American continent.

I want to point out that even as I write this meditating on Genesis and Serpent Mound I intuited why the first written letter and the first hidden letter were scribed as the first letters of Genesis: BETH ב and PEI פ and why SERPENT MOUND was structured in Peebles Ohio and why Washington DC sits just on the edge inside of the 48-continental states of the United States.

Look out at the Milky Way Galaxy and reading the reports of astronomers it is learned that the Earth's solar system is acclimated to the Astrological Zodiac via it planetary system. The Earth sits just inside the outer regions of the Milky Way Galaxy just as Serpent Mound sit right on the inner edge of the gigantic meteor impact crater. This is just like BETH ב positioned on the top right hand corner of a single piece of paper symbolized by PEI פ. Later in this work I will discuss Washington DC also mimicking the BETH ב and PEI פ spiritual phenomenon.

I believe that the reason why BETH is visible in the text of the sacred scriptures and the serpent effigy on Serpent Mount is visible and the reason why PEI is invisible in the texts of the sacred scriptures and the gigantic meteor impact crater the serpent effigy sit in is invisible (to most people) is; for the reason that, the Sun is visible and the Milky Way Galaxy for the most part is invisible to most people; because, they sleep at night and rarely see the stars in the night sky.

Knowing about the cerebral lobes and how the Zodiacal Signs are assigned to the right and left hemispheres of the brain different nuance emanating from that knowledge can aid the initiate in understanding the Initiatic Visionary Experience. The whole Milky Way Galaxy symbolizes the brain and the core of the galaxy symbolizes the pineal gland (Kundalini Serpent: i.e. symbolically Serpent Mound). The frontal lobes symbolize ego-consciousness (Leo) and the unconscious mind (Cancer). The frontal lobes symbolize short-term-memory; whereas, the occipital lobes symbolizes Aquarius and Capricorn, which harbors the visual cortex. Aquarius and Capricorn are governed mythologically by Saturn/Cronus known as the Father of Time. What

---

[3] http://www.amazon.com/Star-Mounds-Legacy-American-Mystery/dp/158394446X/ref=sr_1_1?ie=UTF8&qid=1462060768&sr=8-1&keywords=STAR+MOUND
[4] http://www.ancient-wisdom.com/americacanals.htm

TIME does is slow everything down into a nanosecond (one billionth of a second: 1/1,000,000,000), in effect, creating in the phantasmagoria of the psyche the time/space continuum; however, the occipital lobes do not give the initiate the spiritual ambiance: i.e. the intuitive insight that the pineal gland gives by gifting the initiate with the Initiatic Visionary Experience: Christ consciousness: God's Ambiance. There is more to this about the brain and the Initiatic Visionary Experience; but, I will discuss that later when I talk about the brain again.

Dr. William F. Romain's
Lecture on Serpent Mound, June 18, 2016

While writing this book I took a trip to visit Serpent Mound, Peebles, Ohio on June 17-19, 2016 to celebrate the Serpent Mound Summer Solstice Celebration, which was held on a weekend; though, the actual Summer Solstice did not take place until Monday June 20, 2016. While there at the Soaring Eagle Retreat a number of people, including myself, gave talks on Serpent Mound.

Dr. Romain's lecture is titled SERPENT MOUND: Portal to the Otherworld[5]. What was very intriguing to me about Professor William F. Romain's lecture is that in explaining the spiritual belief system of the Native American Indians, via the auspices of their mythoi, I instantly recognized that genre of spiritual thought to be the same that was globally understood by all major religions around that world. I already knew that Serpent Mound coincided with my research on the first chapter of Genesis; but, William F. Romain was providing additional information augmenting his thesis by providing illuminating images that clarified what he was talking about and also his thesis was an academic thesis that validated my own researches. For example I had already known that the first two verses of Genesis represented Scorpio and Sagittarius respectively and between these two zodiacal signs Cygnus X-3 (Northern Cross) was located. Additionally, the first two verses of Genesis are a commentary on the first word of Genesis: BERESHITH בראשית, which per se is a commentary on the first written letter of Genesis: BETH ב and the hidden letter PEI פ that inundates and surrounds BETH ב. What William F. Romain discussed that was astounding to me was his clarification of how Scorpio symbolized by the Hebrew letter PEI פ; though, he was not speaking about the Hebrew letter PEI פ per se. The first hidden letter of the Torah is very large PEI פ with a dot in the center of that Hebrew letter. Notice how the Hebrew letter PEI פ with a dot in the center mirror images Scorpio ostensibly chasing the sun along the ecliptic (see image below). Serpent Mound shows the serpent effigy releasing the Sun. I say 'releasing the sun' rather than chasing it; for the reason that, there is incontrovertible evidence that the Old Testament per se symbolizes the serpent (Scorpio) and the egg coming out of the serpent mouth symbolizes the New Testament. I had already lay out above in the last chapter that calculation coupled with the Old and New Testaments mythoi that discusses esoterically how that calculation was generates.

PEI פ Gematria value is spelt out PEI פ (80 - 8) and ALEPH א (1)[6]. ALEPH א is a silent Hebrew letter and PEI פ symbolizes the mouth of God, which infers that the WORD OF GOD is

---

[5] https://www.academia.edu/26388800/Serpent_Mound_Portal_to_the_Otherworld

[6] I want to put forth here a very dire warning to all motivated initiates that seek to study the Hebrew Alphabet. There are many books (erroneous presentation) on the Hebrew Letters. Many of them desiring to teach the Hebraic language do so from modernity's perspective, which adds thousands of words to modernity's Hebraic languages, which were not created via spiritual consciousness. In addition there are many books on the Hebrew Letter that reinterprets the spelling of the Hebraic Letters chaotically. I recommend that all initiate study the ancient version of the Hebrew Coder. I recommend Rabbi Ginsburgh work: THE HEBREW LETTERS: Channels to Creative Consciousness

silent and it cannot be spoken in the materialistic vernacular; notice, PEI פ has a dot in the center of it as does BETH ב. It will be demonstrated in the analysis on the MATRIX OF WISDOM that the numbers one (1) and eight (8) symbolize TIMELESSNESS and TIME respectively. PEI פ (80 - 8) symbolizes Scorpio; for the reason that, its number is eight (8) as Scorpio is the eight sign of the Zodiac. It has already been demonstrated in the first chapter that the Sun is cubed (6^3) and culled out of the Moon cubed (9^3); thus, not chasing but releasing the Kamea of the Sun into the blank abyss; however, in contrast if the Kamea of the Sun was (6^2) squared and the Kamea of the Moon was squared (9^2) then Scorpio would indeed be chasing the Sun. Subtract Kamea of the Sun (6^2) from the Kamea of the Moon (9^2) the quotient is 45, which is the Gematria value of Adam that symbolized the amalgamation of male and female. Yahweh Elohym had not as yet separated them as narrated in the second chapter of Genesis. In additionally if the Kamea of the Sun squared (6^2 - 36): BETH ב is added to the Kamea of the Moon squared (9^2 - 81): PEI פ the total would one-hundred and seventeen (117), which happens to be the second half of the Genesis Formula, which will be discussed later in this volume.

This alone illustrates how these two Hebrew letters: PEI פ and BETH ב are both symbiotic to each other. The numbers one (1) and eight (8), as a numerical pair, infers the beginning and end (Aleph to Tav or Alpha and Omega) of the LIGHT that comes into the world. Symbolically, in abstract thought numbers come into the world symbolized by the Quadrivium (Mathematical Sciences) and are instantly transubstantiated into the Trivium (Grammatical Arts): i.e. digits; though, numbers symbolize the Quadrivium the digits themselves are grammatical symbolizing the Quadrivium. This latter is what is meant when it is said that the spiritual when it comes into the world is concretized: i.e. into digits, letters or images. This concretization of the spiritual into the material has been illustrated through Albert Einstein's equation $E=MC^2$[7]. The Atomic Bomb is a perfect illustration of that equation just as the numerics of the lettering of the bible are crammed pack with an infinite amount of data, which of course is geared towards a limited thought pattern, which of course does not mean that the overall data couldn't be understood if one was to contemplatively meditate on it properly.

Letters and numbers per se have nothing whatsoever to do with spirituality; however, numbers and letters are the only means that the initiate has to understand the complex spiritual concepts abstractly laid out in the bible. God has one language, which individually and collectively is interpreted as the Quadrivium and the whole world collectively has hundreds of languages via the Trivium to concretize the WORD OF GOD. Therefore, it is easier that each initiate intuit the language of God; rather, than expect God to learn the gibberish of hundreds of languages denoted by the Trivium, which God knows nothing of; for the reason that, the WORD OF GOD has nothing whatsoever to do with the Quadrivium and/or the Trivium per se. The word of God is ethereal beyond word and image. The Quadrivium (mathematics) is used to download the WORD OF GOD via the MATRIX OF WISDOM; for the reason that, it is universally known amongst all cultural languages around the world. Later in this work it will be demonstrated demonstrably how God puts His Word into the world via the MATRIX OF WISDOM and how the WORD OF GOD is translated from that into the vernacular.

The WORD OF GOD codified to the bible via the Quadrivium and the Trivium is very much like how computers record the thoughts and artistic expression of humanity via the binary system of zeros (0s) and ones (1s). The binary system in a universal worldwide mathematic system used by all industrial cultures via their own languages to setup their computer systems and then there is collectively the Internet that makes it a worldwide systemic system.

---

https://www.amazon.com/Hebrew-Letters-Channels-Consciousness-Teachings/dp/9657146070/ref=sr_1_1?s=books&ie=UTF8&qid=1467936070&sr=1-1&keywords=rabbi+ginsburgh%2C+channels+to+creative+consciousness

[7] https://en.wikipedia.org/wiki/Albert_Einstein

It will be seen symbolically in the analysis of the MATRIX OF WISDOM how the numbers one (1) and eight (8) as a pair enters the world unnoticed: TIMELESSNESS and TIME respectively; whereas, every other set in the multiplication tables mirror images the first set in the multiplication tables in the materialistic vernacular disparately. Everything in the material world at one time was the immediate LIGHT culled out from the DARKNESS: numbers two (2) and (7). That spiritual LIGHT (Sun 6^3) has to be continuously culled out of the DARKNESS (Moon 9^3) nanosecond by nanosecond, which in turn allows for religions and secret societies around the world to codify the universal spiritual generic paradigm into their literature, artworks, monuments and architecture via numbers three (3) and (6). Numbers four (4) and five (5) symbolize the tetrahedral forces of the psyche eternally generating all the aspects of the universal spiritual paradigm continuously (cosmologically) throughout the dynamics of the phantasmagoria of the psyche. The moment that the 6^3 (Kamea of the Sun) is not culled out of 9^3 (Kamea of the Moon) then PEI פ simply transforms into the unconscious mind (80 = 8) and Yahweh (26 = 8) transforms into the materialistic Sun God (ego-consciousness) and ALEPH א (number one: i.e. MONAD) vanishes from the equation. ALEPH א symbolizes the consensus of the Trinity.

The second image I am presenting here in my discussion on Serpent Mound from out of William F. Romain's work shows the path to the otherworld crossing a river; however, I would beg to differ on that interpretation and say that the river in this instance comes from north going south crossing the east/west corridor of TIME. Often mythoi of another culture are not only misinterpreted by its indigenous people; but, also by those researching it from outside. I will in this work illustrate several examples of Cygnus X-3 (RESH ר), which resides in the North crossing the east-west corridor of Time, heading southward.

What I see this image actually saying is that the Initiatic Visionary Experience is gifted to the worthy initiate and in the process of receiving this gift the initiate is separated on a spiritually psychic level via Christ consciousness from mainstream thought: i.e. the status quo. This is precisely what William F. Romain's second image illustrates; though, the images have multiple souls on each side of the river the sacred geometry via sacred images and the sacred scriptures is at all times speaking solely to the individual initiate. Images of this spiritual nature neither speak to a fellowship nor to a congregation.

Most people have the impression that Heaven, Hell and Purgatory are spirit realms visited after physical death; however, that is a wrong take on the spiritual archives of the world. The world that modernity is presently living in is Hell: the land of the dead; though, it would be extremely difficult to convince modernity's religious and academic scholars of that truth. Those few people that become mystics and Shamans enter into the Garden of Eden (Heaven). The Garden of Eden is also considered the land of the dead; for the reason that, they have crossed over from Hell into the land of bliss, which those living in modernity would call the land of the dead, a better life; yet, the Mystic or Shaman lives contently on his or her own mastaba (mound of creation) while the rest of humanity lives iconoclastically gorging on their materialistic desires. Purgatory on the other hand would be searching endlessly for the knowledge of God, which becomes fruitless; for the reason that, ego-consciousness is the ruling factor. It is only when ego-consciousness deflates itself that it will be gifted with the Initiatic Visionary Experience and allowed to enter into the garden of bliss: i.e. Garden of Eden.

This exact same phenomenon happened with Adam and Eve's family when Abel converted to Cain's religion going from being a shepherd (archetypal) to being a farmer (existential). What this means is that Abel was being guided by the Animal Envoy (instincts); whereas, Cain was deeply into the Mystery Schools. Cain knew how to farm and to go out and build a city. Where did he learn those skills? Adam and Eve accused Cain of murder when in fact Abel became part of Cain's clan. Abel transcended to be a Good Man and then became a Better Man. How I know this is because this Jewish law has come down through the ages to modern times to where a Jew (religiously not ethnically) converted to a Gentile religion; though, he or she lives, breaths and has children he or she is considered dead in the eyes of his or her Jewish family and in the eyes of

Judaism. This is why most Jews will not marry Gentiles unless the Gentile converts to Judaism. From Judaism perspective they are not murdering the Gentile; however if a Gentile converts a Jew to iconographic thought that is considered cold blooded murder. Bishop John Henry Newman of Oxford University in 1845 lost his tenure at Oxford when he converted to Catholicism from Protestantism. Bishop Newman was literally ostracized in England; for the reason that, he was considered a traitor to his culture. Protestantism is basically the Judaizing of Christianity via iconoclasm.

The reader should ask him or herself, *"What did Abel do to become a better man?"* It is known for a fact that shepherds and farmers are in an eternal conflict; for the reason that, the sheep eat the vegetation leaving a desert in their wake. This is analogous to a priest (shepherd) guiding the laity (sheep - followers) to eat what has already been produced by the farmer. A farmer (self-motivator) plows his own fields and doesn't eat from another's field. The priest is more apt to convert to the inner hierarchy of the church than the laity. In other words the laity is gorging on the accomplishments of the scribes of the bible rather than trying to understand how the bible was written esoterically.

Judaism had a very difficult dilemma to endure in the Exodus period via the biblical mythoi; for the reason that, when they left Goshen in Egypt they were leaving the west going across the Red Sea, which runs South to North, to the East. They were returning to the area that their ancestors originated from. For some reason or other the Israelites could not acclimate themselves to Egypt. I believe that this is because they were too clannish and this is why they did not lose their relationship to the Animal Envoy. I say Animal Envoy because the Egyptian hated the Israelites because of their relationship to the domestication of animals when the Egyptians were farmers. This was very much like the Cain and Abel saga only in this case the Israelites fled Egypt. When the Israelite went from west to east they were returning to where they came from; whereas, the Egyptians crossing the Red Sea is a direct indication that they were violating their raison d'être; though, this biblical story in not a historical fact; rather, it is a religious mythological (historical fictional storyline) fact that expresses spiritual nuances and that psychic doctrine of Judaism still persist to this very day. It appears to be a universal dogmatic principle that exists in the psyche of all humanity until the individual escapes that imprisoned mentality. The Egyptian had to cross the Nile River (running south to north) from east to west to get to the area of the Giza Pyramid Complex, which they called the Land of the Dead.

The Egyptian culture is very much like Catholicism; for the reason that, it is solely based upon symbolism (iconography – comprehensive thought); whereas, Judaism is all about iconoclasm (limited thought), which denotes a one track mind: i.e. tunnel vision.

The Native American Indians, that are not shamanistic, as are all cultures around the world iconoclastic (not thinking symbolically) living in the realm of materialism. All the sacred scriptures or the mythoi of any culture are exclusively for the initiate: i.e. Mystics or Shamans that think iconographically. So those indigenous people around the word that gives commentary on their materialistic cultures' mythoi have little or no idea what they are talking about on a mystical level, similar to how Protestants speak about the Christian religion, for they envisage everything in life fundamentally (literally) from a historical or iconoclastic perspective and they speak about their cultural mythologies via that terminology.

The reader should always realize that from a historical perspective the mythoi of the sacred scriptures can be wrong; however, from a religious iconographic mythological perspective the sacred scriptures are infallible.

SERPENT MOUND, Peebles, Ohio, USA

SERPENT MOUND
LiDAR VIDEO: https://vimeo.com/926341

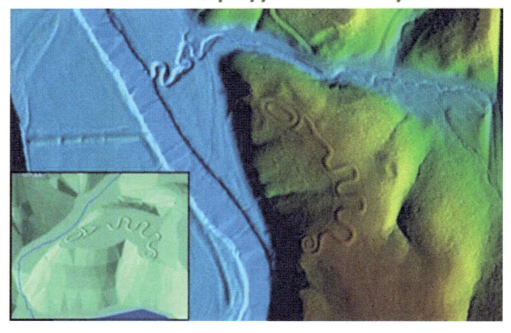

SERPENT MOUND

SOLSTICES, EQUINOXES & LUNAR ALIGNMENTS

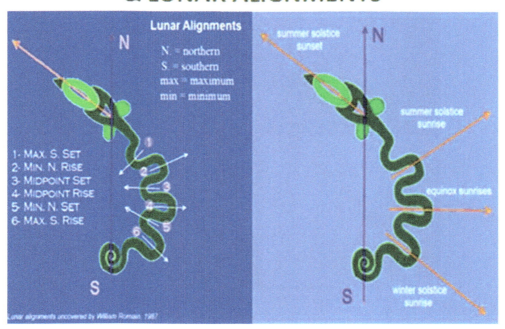

**SERPENT MOUND
RELEASING THE SUN**

**SCORPIO RELEASING THE SUN:
PEI פ RELEASING BETH ב**

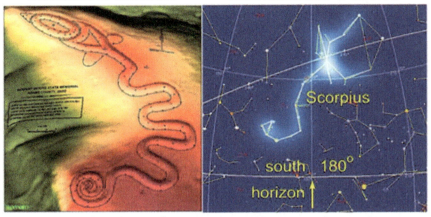

*Romain, William F., 2016 Serpent Mound: Portal to the Otherworld.
Invited presentation. Friends of Serpent Mound, Summer Solstice
Celebration. June 18, 2016, Soaring Eagle Retreat, Peebles, Ohio.*

**RESH ר (river) CROSSING BETH ב (inhabited space)
Spiritually creating BERESHITH ("in the beginning")**

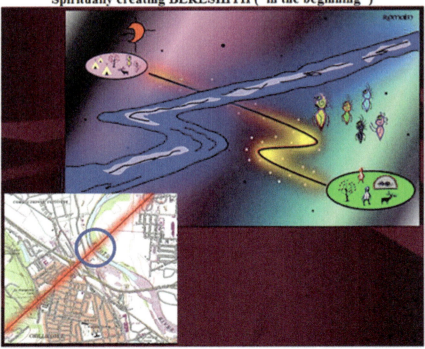

*Romain, William F., 2016 Serpent Mound: Portal to the Otherworld.
Invited presentation. Friends of Serpent Mound, Summer Solstice
Celebration. June 18, 2016, Soaring Eagle Retreat, Peebles, Ohio.*

CHAPTER THREE

THE THREE TORAHS

There are extremely important mystical nuances throughout the Judaeo Christian Scriptures that are not readily apparent to the uninitiated. This is because there are three Torahs in one: i.e. **REVEALED** (sunlight): Archetypal (storyline), **COVERED** (moonlight): Existential (codified numerically beneath the storyline): and the **HIDDEN**: i.e. the inexplicable: Cosmic (the silent word of God). I highly recommend Carlos Suarès works: THE SEPHER YETSIRA[1] and THE CIPHER OF GENESIS[2], which will discuss these concepts relating to the Hebrew Coder in greater detail conceptually.

The **REVEALED** (sunlight) is what is written on the surface textual storyline, the **COVERED** (moonlight) are the symbols, numerics and the alphabetic letters structured into the Hebrew and Greek coders. The SEVEN LIBERAL ARTS: Quadrivium (four mathematical sciences) and Trivium (three grammatical arts) are codified via sacred geometry to that which is **COVERED**. The **HIDDEN** is the WORD OF GOD, which is completely mysteriously silent and can neither be conveyed by the vernacular nor taught to another human being by any materialistic method. The **HIDDEN** can only be envisaged by those that have been Blessed (Christos:"Χρίστος") by God with the gift of the *INITIATIC VISIONARY EXPERIENCE*, which gives the initiate the spiritual and mystical ambiance of the Garden of Eden to read the WORD OF GOD.

The uninitiated would find it extremely difficult to believe that there are THREE TORAHS in one; however, the initiate has to do his or her due diligence in researching and studying the sacred scriptures to earn the right to continuously envisaged and to understand the WORD OF GOD. No one not even those with Christ consciousness are allowed to rest on their laurels.

I highly recommend Rabbi Yitzchak Ginsburgh work: THE HEBREW LETTERS: Channels of Creative Consciousness[3] for those that want to learn more about the Hebrew letters and the WORD OF GOD. There are of course many other scholarly works on the Hebrew alphabet both in books and YOUTUBE videos that can be access for each initiate to learn as much as possible about the Hebrew Coder.

The word of God: the spiritual forces in creation cannot be expressed in the vernacular: i.e. that inexplicable truth cannot be explained either to modernity's laity or to any religious and academic scholar in any reasonable and/or logical discussion. It is nigh unto an impossibility to cross the chasm between iconoclasm and iconography. Modernity's scholars are experts in iconoclasm: i.e. what is known as earthly materialism and/or science couple with its historical background; however, this iconoclasm challenges iconography. In other words a two dimensional thought pattern (iconoclasm) challenges three dimensional thought (iconography).

Every Hebrew letter is alphanumerically structured. In other words each Hebrew letter has a numerical value, Gematria value and an alphabetic letter designate and in addition each letter has a symbolical value. To add to that extremely complex definition of each Hebrew letter each letter is spelt out with several or more alphanumeric and symbolized letters, which exponentially defines the value and meaning of each Hebrew letter.

Most people that do Gematria values of words do not study the alphabetics of the letters in the word, which without would make the Gematria value of words practically meaningless in comparison.

---

[1] https://www.amazon.com/Sepher-Yetsira-Carlo-Suares/dp/0394732731/ref=sr_1_1?ie=UTF8&qid=1467834796&sr=8-1&keywords=the+sepher+yetsira
[2] https://www.amazon.com/Cipher-Genesis-Original-Applied-Scriptu/dp/B002JBMDT4/ref=sr_1_2?s=books&ie=UTF8&qid=1467834930&sr=1-2&keywords=the+cipher+of+genesis
[3] https://www.amazon.com/Hebrew-Letters-Channels-Consciousness-Teachings/dp/9657146070/182-5949294-0810607?ie=UTF8&keywords=the%20hebrew%20letters%20ginsburgh&qid=1462126691&ref_=sr_1_1&s=books&sr=1-1

THE HEBREW CODER

	1	2	3	4	5	6	7	8	9
1 Archetypal	Ox	House	Camel	Door	Window	Nail	Sword	Fence	Serpent
	א	ב	ג	ד	ה	ר	ז	ח	ט
	Aleph	Beth	Ghimmel	Daleth	Heh	Vav	Zayn	Hhayt	Tayt
	1	2	3	4	5	6	7	8	9
10 Existential	Hand	Grasping	Ox Goad	Water	Fish	Support	Eye	Mouth	Fish Hook
	Yud	Kaph	Lammed	Mem	Nun	Samech	Ayn	Pei	Tzadde
	10	20	30	40	50	60	70	80	90
100 COSMIC	Needle	Head	Tooth	Cross					
	Qoph	Resh	Shin	Tav	F-Kaph	F-Men	F-Nun	F-Pei	F-Tzadde
	100	200	300	400	500	600	700	800	900

MATRIX OF WISDOM NUMBERS (Water)

MATRIX OF WISDOM COSMIC (Air)

MATRIX OF WISDOM EXISTENTIAL (Earth)

MATRIX OF WISDOM ARCHETYPAL (Fire)

CHAPTER FOUR

SOME MYSTERIES IN THE FIRST CHAPTER OF GENESIS:
The Kabbalistic Tree of Life, the Star of David and the Kundalini Serpent

Research on the lettering and wording of the sacred scriptures is not only about learning the symbolic and Gematria values of letters and words that aid in defining the words; it is also about envisaging the sacred geometry (Quadrivium) that is codified beneath the surface texts (Trivium). In the next three images the Hebrew and English interlinear version of the first chapter of Genesis is laid out in full and simultaneously I outline the thirty-two (32) times the word 'ELOHYM (God)' is codified to the texts. There is an ancient Egyptian legend that when Antiquity's Hall of Records is discovered there will be thirty-two (32) tablets found.

'Before the final destruction of Atlantis, the Atlanteans are said to have made three sets of 32 tablets, that documented their history, and these were hidden in a "hall of records" in Egypt, Guatemala and Atlantis'.

I repeat this legend about Atlantis: mystically the Garden of Eden; for the reason that, I believe these thirty-two (32) ELOHYMS written into the first chapter of Genesis are symbolically those thirty-two (32) tablets; for the reason that, the sacred scripture globally are Antiquity's Hall of Records. Think about what the word 'HALL' means. It is a straight and narrow passageway: i.e. tunnel vision. That is all the sacred scriptures are iconoclastically one long endless line of texts leading the reader by the proverbial nose down the east-west the corridor of time.

Serendipitously, in December/January 1976/1977 I unintentionally contemplatively cross over into the Garden of Eden under the Bodhi Tree from the east-west corridor of time. What I mean by this is that I began to reread the first chapter of Genesis over and over again trying to understand what it was conveying; thus, I had gone from reading the sacred scriptures chapter by chapter (corridor of time) to just analyzing and studying one lone chapter (Bodhi Tree). This went on for a number of weeks and then I envisaged a nine part cycle, which included the second chapter of Genesis: i.e. seven day week (see chapter nineteen). The discovery of that nine part cycle was the impetus that allowed me to gather all the researches outlined in this volume.

In these three (3) images outlining the first chapter of Genesis I colored coded the **thirty-two (32) ELOHYMS (God) yellow in both Hebrew and English.** I also color code the word that is associated to each and every mention of the word ELOHYM into their separate Kabbalistic Tree of Life categories: **Sefirahs (black), Double letters (Blue), Elemental letters (Green)** and **Mother letters (red)**. An additional fourteen (14) images, that follow this Hebrew and English interlinear version of the first chapter of Genesis, augments this discussion on the Kabbalistic Tree of Life, Star of David and the Kundalini Serpent.

I produce so many images in this thesis; for the reason that, from modernity perspective this Esoteric Science (Hermeticism - Esotericism) is unknown; thus, a brand new science is being introduced; though, this volume cannot possibly provide every though, word and deed that went into accepting and rejecting incalculable concepts and ideas that allowed me to compile this research over forty-two years. I produced these images in this thesis; for the reason that, a self-motivated initiate would see more into them than what I convey in my commentaries on them. I have found, more often than not, to my spiritual advantage that producing images and diagrams relating to my researches tend to exude nuances that were not knowingly intended; however, they are valid mystical nuances that have advanced my researches. That is how mystical the search for the knowledge of God is. God's Ambiance is at all times present; though, initially not envisaged.

Let me also point out that I am not the only person that knows of this esoteric science in excruciating detail. As this work continues it will be obvious that Catholicism and Freemasonry are quite conversant in esotericism in its minute details that I have yet to fathom.

I first obtained the idea about the thirty-two (32) ELOHYMS in the first chapter of Genesis symbolizing the Kabbalistic Tree of Life from Rabbi Aryeh Kaplan's work SEFER YETZIRAH[1] back in 1997 when the book was first published. Upon reading Rabbi Aryeh Kaplan mentioning the thirty-two (32) ELOHYMS in the first chapter of Genesis I wanted to confirm what he was talking about. The Kabbalistic Tree of Life is a tradition in Kabbalistic Judaism that I, at the time, knew nothing about. In my verification process authenticating Rabbi Aryeh Kaplan's work I found he made an error in the classification of one of the Elemental letters and one of the Sefirahs (numbers). Rabbi Aryeh Kaplan followed the traditional interpretation of the Sefirahs rather than what the Torah: sacred scriptures were actually conveying. This was a misinterpretation of the tradition concerning Keter the Crown of Creation, which I will discuss further along in this thesis.

Rabbi Aryeh Kaplan took the first Elemental in the first chapter of Genesis, which is found in the first verse of Genesis: i.e. **"Elohym created"** and named that Elemental as a Sefirah; though, there were three other "Elohym created" in the texts of the first chapter of Genesis that Rabbi Aryeh Kaplan designated as Elementals; thus, it can be envisaged that he was not using reason and logic in his classification process; rather, he used the excuse of tradition, which I will show the foundations of as I continue. The Sefirah in Genesis 1:29: i.e. **"Elohym said (desired)"** Rabbi Aryeh Kaplan designated as an Elemental, which was again illogical seeing there were nine (9) other times that he designated the phrase "Elohym said (desired)" as Sefirahs.

Rabbi Kaplan had no idea that the first two verses of Genesis was, actually, a prelude to the beginning of Creation. The first day of creation, which harbors the first Sefirah, is a reworking mythologically of the first two verses coupled with DESIRE: i.e. "ELOHYM said (desired)". This first Elohym in the first day of creation of Genesis is Keter and all the other Sefirahs descend from it. That in itself is an extremely spiritual nuance; for the reason that, it validates that all creation comes from one lone spiritual nuance. In fact each and every spiritual nuance holds within its precincts the sum-total of all knowledge: i.e. omniscience.

What escapes most Kabbalists is that the words **BETH (412) – SPIRIT (214) – SAID/ desired (241)** all have different Gematria values; however, all three are transposition of each other's Gematria values. These three words **BETH (412) – SPIRIT (214) – SAID/desired (241)** occupy the first three verses of Genesis and each is; essentially, a recapitulation of the other two words. I interpret **BETH (412)** the ego in this context as deflated acquiring Christ consciousness: God's Ambiance DESIRING knowledge of God; whereas, the **SPIRIT (214)** symbolizes the unconscious mind (PEI פ) breathing out that it also DESIRE that knowledge of God and finally "Elohym (Christ consciousness) **"SAID/desired (241)** *let there be LIGHT"*. All three of these words **BETH (412) – SPIRIT (214) – SAID/desired (241)** symbolizes what takes place simultaneously; but, are recorded in this sequence iconoclastically to illustrate ego-consciousness' method of sequencing down the corridor of TIME. **BETH (412)** has to deflate itself first to begin the Initiatic Visionary Experience process. Notice how the Gematria numerical values of **BETH (412)** and **SPIRIT (214** are in reverse of each other as are ego-consciousness and the unconscious mind considered conceptually. It would seem as if the word **SAID/desired (241)** and its Gematria numerical value is a compromise between **BETH (412)** and **SPIRIT (214**; however, I beg to differ and I will illustrate why shortly. Christ consciousness never-ever compromises; for the reason that, it provides a whole new creation and not an amalgamation of the old heaven and old earth and this will be envisaged twice more, outside of the word BERESHITH, in the first chapter of Genesis.

The problem with understanding the sacred geometry culled out of the sacred scriptures is determining the messages that are being conveyed through them. There are thousands of vignettes in the sacred scriptures all saying the same thing using different mythological ways and means of expressing that same idea giving the appearance of linear thought when, pragmatically, linear

---

[1] https://www.amazon.com/Sefer-Yetzirah-Creation-Aryeh-Kaplan/dp/0877288550?ie=UTF8&fpl=fresh&redirect=true&ref_=s9_simh_gw_g14_i1_r

thought has nothing whatsoever to do with esotericism. That is going to be a very difficult dogmatic principle for modernity to accept. The Judaeo Christian Scriptures are extremely large basically to create gigantic mathematical patterns and minor mathematical pattern. The 1189-chapters in the Old and New Testament collectively are analogous to a gigantic jigsaw puzzle and each piece of the puzzle is a holographic image (chapter) of the entire bible mimicking and mirror imaging mythologically all the other chapters.

The reason why Keter is the first Sefirah is; for the reason that, the first Elohym associated to the word "**SAID**" means "**DESIRED**" in Hebrew. There is an ancient legend in Astrology that says that the Zodiac Constellations cannot move before the sixth house of the Zodiac moves first. The first decan of Virgo is called Coma, which in Hebrew is interpreted as "**DESIRED**". This cosmic law comes down through the ages without people consciously knowing why changes have come about in their lives. For example Mary Baker Eddy the Discoverer and Founder of Christian Science, writes in her book, **SCIENCE AND HEALTH: with key to the Scripture**, on the bottom of the first page of the first chapter, *"DESIRE IS PRAYER"*. William (Bill) Wilson the cofounder of Alcoholics Anonymous writes in the twelve step program, *"The only requirement for membership is a DESIRE to stop drinking"*. This spiritual concept, of course, has nothing whatsoever to do with lip-service to those saying they have **DESIRE**; though, they may truly believe they have **DESIRE**; however, subconsciously they are not truly committed to what is required of them.

The foundational search for knowledge of God and for knowledge of one's own soul is KETER and in every way the gift of the *Initiatic Visionary Experience* from God embosses that **DESIRE** resolutely upon the soul so that every move forward is a **DESIRE** to know God and this is why the 10-Sefirahs are the framework to the Kabbalistic Tree of Life: the framework or psychic pattern to all creative thought, words and/or deeds.

I believe that the LIGHT of God is continuously flowing throughout all creation: i.e. the initiate's raison d'être and this belief is founded upon the knowledge that the **MATRIX OF WISDOM** can be culled out of the two part psyche at any given time; however, the prerequisite for this spiritual event to psychically take place is for ego-consciousness to deflate itself (psychic immolation): i.e. the sun setting: i.e. the old archetypal ego-macho personality sacrificed to the realization that egocentrism is incapable of envisaging what life is all about; though, egocentrism will argue against such truths endlessly.

BETH ב **(412)** at the point of psychic immolation opens the DOOR that it was knocking upon and the breath: i.e. **SPIRIT (214)** of God flows from PEI פ (mouth of God), which is symbolic of the unconscious mind. This illustrates that ego-consciousness and the unconscious mind are now in a harmonious synchronization and then *"Elohym SAID (241), let there be LIGHT"*; for the reason that, the soul's goal is to obtain the LIGHT. These three events appear to be three different episodes within the first twenty-two words of Genesis; however, none of them could have taken place unless all three of them happened simultaneously harmoniously working together. The three events are not rehashing each other per se; rather, these three words (scriptural events) should be envisaged as continuously ongoing in the life of the initiate and are eternal everlastingly repetitive throughout the initiate's life otherwise there would be no life. The LIGHT of God had already been received in the letter **BETH** ב **(412)** per se via PEI פ inherently surrounding it and PEI פ is spelt out as PEI פ and ALEPH א, which in itself illustrates that *'Elohym (*had already*) said, let there be LIGHT'* long before the first day of creation as narrated in Genesis 1:3. In fact it can be said that the first written letter BETH ב and first hidden letter PEI פ combined as the first and only day of creation.

The DOOR that **BETH** ב **(412)** knocks on to inaugurate the **Initiatic Visionary Experience** is **DALETH** ד the fourth Hebrew letter, which has the symbolic value of DOOR. **DALETH** ד has the Gematria value of 434 and there are 434-words in the first chapter of Genesis. The entire first chapter of Genesis explains esoterically the **Initiatic Visionary Experience**; hence, the reason why it is structured as the DOOR to creation. The DOOR is Christ for Christ said, *"I am* *the DOOR"*. In other words Christ is saying, *"I am the LIGHT and in me there is no DARKNESS"*; therefore, the whole of the first chapter of Genesis is structured to give a comprehensive (not the only) explanation of the **Initiate Visionary Experience**. The first chapter of Genesis symbolizes the LIGHT culled out of the DARKNESS and the second chapter will be shown to symbolize the DARKNESS and this will be illustrated via several additional symbolic methods via the Vesica Piscis (see chapter eight), the Cycles of Divine Creation (see chapter nineteen) and the contrast between the Old and the New Testaments.

In fact the whole of the Old and New Testaments is a record of thousands of vignettes each explaining this **Initiate Visionary Experience**. It will be seen throughout this volume how there are symbolically three Torahs (see chapter three), which are in unanimity the basic generic religious paradigm in creation and, I believe, the reason for this is to illustrate that there are multiple ways (mythoi) of knocking on the DOOR to spirituality.

The reason why the first day of creation says explicitly "ELOHYM **SAID (241)**, let there be LIGHT"; rather than **BETH ב (412)** or **SPIRIT (214)** saying it is; because, neither **BETH ב (412)** nor **SPIRIT (214)** are ELOHYM per se. The **SPIRIT (214)** of ELOHYM is not ELOHYM per se; for the reason that, it's pouting (brooding) over the waters is longing for the LIGHT. All three of these episodes infer ELOHYM'S presence in their mythoi; however, the concept of ELOHYM is esoterically hidden in the mythoi of **BETH ב (412)** and **SPIRIT (214)**. The purpose of illustrating all three episodes: the powers of the Trinity (God) are to demonstrate that without the harmonious consensus of the Trinity nothing of any spiritual importance can possibly transpire in creation: i.e. in the life of the initiate. In other words without the aid of God: i.e. the spiritual forces of creation, the initiate can do nothing on his or her own volition in the material world. This is the very reason that causes the deflation of the ego to come about in the first place.

Both Yahweh (ego-consciousness: i.e. Jachin - Sun) and Elohym (unconscious mind: i.e. Boaz - Moon) are the two columns that are outside of the Masonic Temple or seen outside of Chartres Cathedral. Unless Yahweh and Elohym are mystically married they cannot enter the temple. The unanimity of these two creates the third factor, which is the WORD OF GOD: i.e. Christ; hence, the consensus of the Trinity.

Life is eternally and everlastingly redundant and this is what is being conveyed with these three episodes with **BETH ב (412)**, **SPIRIT (214)** and **SAID/desired (241)**; though, these three words are illustrating the same episode they also simultaneously are conveying that they are knocking on the DOOR eternally and everlastingly. Every time the DOOR is knocked on the LIGHT of creation flows out into the two part psyche like a tsunami; however, the DOOR immediately closes. The reason why the DOOR closes is; for the reason that the human aspect of the psyche called ego-consciousness immediately discriminates (knee jerk reaction – so-to-speak) and interprets its meaning, naming it, concretizing it into manifested creation.

This is what Jacob tried to do with the angel of God in Genesis 32:22-31 and failed; for the reason that, God cannot be soiled by the tongue of the initiate. Each time the LIGHT is conceptualized it is crucified and this will be illustrated as we go along. Living in the spiritual Garden of Eden walking with God is essentially eternally everlastingly crucifying Christ. For each time that the initiate knock on the DOOR it is like pounding on granite rock to get water out of it as Moses did in the desert at the command of God (Numbers 20:1-13). God can be envisaged as being jealous; for the reason that, He will not allow the initiate to rest on his or her laurels. The moment that the DOOR closes life begins to deteriorate (decay like a rotting corpse) and it is the responsibility of the initiate to revivify life by bringing LIGHT forward eternally and everlastingly. Each time that the DOOR of spirituality opens liken to an intuition the initiate understands God at a greater depth; however, God can never-ever be fully understood. Each time the DOOR opens larger and larger conceptual ideas can be structured textually to illustrate the WORD OF GOD: for example, going from the first letter of Genesis: BETH ב to the first word of Genesis: BERESHITH, to the first two verses of Genesis, to the six days of creation and then to the first four chapters of Genesis, etc., etc.

Every time the DOOR opens it is like having a Kundalini Serpent experience and when the DOOR closes the serpent goes back into it 3½ coiled dormant state. I want to explicitly state that nobody can really get more than one Kundalini experience in a lifetime; because, though there is a special visionary experience when the Kundalini experience (Initiatic Visionary Experience) is initially experienced that ambiance never leaves the initiate unless of course the Initiate ignores it: if that happens God will not have mercy on his or her soul. The initiate will always be able to cull out the LIGHT when he or she puts meditational contemplative thought to spiritual concepts; however, the spiritual ambiance after the initial experience will never quite be experienced the same way again. That is because the first time the spiritual experience was neither known about nor experience before; thus, it is spiritually a traumatic experience. After the first time the Initiatic Visionary Experience is experience the ambiance of God will seemingly appear to symbolize everyday thoughts, words and/or deeds; whereby, the initiate is constantly in the *know*; even if, he or she has no viable materialistic reason or logic to know it; though, when the initiate envisages it he or she knows it is true; for the reason that, God's Ambiance and the sacred scriptures tells the initiate it is true.

I will discuss the Kundalini Serpent in a few minutes. The Kundalini Serpent experience is initially a rapturous moment like a tsunami overwhelming the psyche with the sum-total of all knowledge, in a nanosecond of time. It is as if it is a download of omniscience data into an esoteric psychic database for there is no way that ego-consciousness can retain such an infinite amount of data; however, each spiritual insight after that it is like having periodic intuitional experiences, which would be liken to the Kundalini Serpent flipping in and out of the two part psyche proportional to the initiate's research schedule in acquiring knowledge of God and knowledge of his or her own soul. The DOOR will never open as long as the initiate does not put concentrated meditational contemplative thought to the sacred scriptures. Prayer is symbolic of meditational contemplative thought. The initiate that has already had the Kundalini Serpent experience is more apt to have spiritual intuitive thoughts and insights over anybody in the general population; for the reason that, he or she has already broken the hermetically sealed psychic barrier: pineal gland. It is as if the DOOR is eternally and everlastingly cracked open for the individual that has had the Kundalini Serpent experience

I want to give several materialistic examples of this inexplicable spiritual idea concerning the spiritual Initiatic Visionary Experience in an attempt at trying to convey it unfathomable meaning.

1. Trying to explain sound to a person born deaf or trying to explain sight to a person born blind are a few examples; but, not quite because neither will have the chance of ever hearing or seeing.

2. Those that had cataract eye surgery will have the experience of seeing the world in a very bright manner in which they would never believe was possible without the surgery. When the first eye has surgery done on it the patient see an extremely bright clear world as if a pane of glass was filthy dirty and then cleansed. When the other eye opens before surgery the patient closes the other eye he or she will see a yellow jaundice world as if looking through a glass of lemonade. Opening and closing both eyes like a swinging pendulum clearly shows that the patient before surgery on the one eye he or she was viewing the world through yellow jaundice eyes without knowing it. When the second eye has surgery done it the world become bright and glasses no longer have to be worn. There is no longer a yellow jaundice world.

3. Another example is drinking alcohol beverages. Those that drink alcohol for the very first time will get a strong 'beautiful sensational rush'; however, from that first time if one drinks regularly that initial 'rush' is never experienced again; though, the individual will get high or drunk as if he or she is continuously trying to experience that 'rush' again.

4. Another example of alcohol giving this alcoholic experience is found in the Roman Catholic Church's daily Eucharistic Mass when the Bread and Wine[2] are consecrated into the Body and Blood of Christ. The congregant receiving the Eucharistic host and a sip of wine would experience this alcoholic 'rush'. People that do not drink alcohol abusively nor drink alcohol at all will find the mere sip of wine to give them an alcohol 'rush', which would be symbolic of that spiritual vision that is experience by those that received the gift of the Initiatic Visionary Experience. The Roman Catholic Church having the laity sipping the Eucharist wine is an ingenious ways of conveying 'silently' the concept of the Initiatic Visionary Experience especially for those people that don't drink alcoholic beverages regularly. For each week a Catholic member of the laity that returns to Sunday Mass would experience this alcoholic 'rush'; therefore, in such a continuous weekly cadence of receiving the Eucharistic Bread and Wine the parishioner would momentary experience on a symbolic level the idea of Christ consciousness. I say that it is an ingenious idea of the laity continuously experiencing the alcoholic 'rush' because those that abuse alcoholic beverages will not continuously get the alcoholic 'rush'. This idea about the Initiatic Visionary Experience would be conveyed more fully by not explicitly explaining it; because, the parishioner would reason that such a 'rush' after sipping the wine would be a momentary experience coming directly from Christ.
5. There are another examples I can think of, which I will not explain; for the reason that, it will be offensive to some.

There are **32-paths to the Kabbalistic Tree of life**, which are broken down into four traditional categories: **10-Sefirah (Black), 7-Double Letters (Blue), 12-Elemental Letters (Green)** and **3-Mother Letters (Red).** The 32-Elohyms have been placed in a chart listing their Kabbalistic Tree of Life categories along with their places in the 32-sequential numerical count and the 31-verse count. It was obvious that these 32-Elohyms were to be placed into a cycle of 32-parts sequentially; thus, I colored coded the background and initialed each of the 32-Elohyms according to the Kabbalistic Tree of Life's four categories each Elohym belong to. There is an additional **69-group of words in the first chapter of Genesis color coded orange** and this latter will be discussed as I continue.

I created large black circular dots to designate the positions of the **10-SEFIRAHS**. How I determined this of course was via the ten times that *"Elohym said"*. What was more surprising was that eight out of the ten Sefirahs paired off into four sets; for the reason that, the **eight Sefirahs were paired off by being exactly 180° from each other. The last two Sefirahs were paired off by not being paired off.** That may seem to be coincidental until the rest of the Kabbalistic Tree of Life is evaluated. The **3-Mother letters** paired off once 180° from one another and the **12-Elementals** paired off into three sets 180° from one another. That totals to more than half (0.5625%) of the 32-Elohyms pairing off into nine sets; yet, extraordinarily, after what has just been witnessed with the other three Kabbalistic Tree of Life categories, the **7-Double letters** have no two letters pairing off 180° from one another.

The fact that the **7-Double letters** do not pair off demonstrates that the four Kabbalistic categories was deliberately structured in this manner. Mathematically, it is not possible to write a text deliberately, off the top of one's head, using the 32-Elohyms to image the Kabbalistic Tree of Life and then to synchronistically obtain this kind of precision patterning without the 7-Double letters having at the very least one set: two of them pairing off 180° from one another.

Once the Kabbalistic Tree of Life is understood and how it came about through the MATRIX OF WISDOM it is easily envisaged that the Double Letters comes from the north to the south crossing over the east-west corridor of TIME creating Christ consciousness: God's Ambiance. The Sefirahs (North) symbolize what God's said (desired) and the Double Letters (South) symbolize that God saw that it was good. The numerics of these two parts of the

---

[2] http://www.catholic.com/magazine/articles/why-grape-wine

Kabbalistic Tree of Life total to seventeen: PEI פ; whereas, the numerics of the Mother letters (East) and the Elemental letters (West) total to fifteen (15), which symbolizes the dimensions of the Holy of Holies. I find it interesting that these totals coincide with the two streets (15th St. NW and 17th St. NW) symbolizing the area of the transept that goes from the White House down, crossing the National Mall (east-west corridor of time), to the Jefferson Memorial. The number 15 + 17 = 32 / 2 = 16, which symbolizes 16th St. NW that is behind the White House inferring it symbolically slices the transept in half as if dividing the LIGHT from the DARKNESS (see chapter sixteen).

This pairing off the Sefirahs (5 pairs), Mother Letters (1 pair) and the Elements (3 pairs) is the transposition of the number 153, which symbolizes the Vesica Piscis, which per se is the Initiatic Visionary Experience.

Then there is putting the framework (10-Sefirah numbers) of the Kabbalistic Tree of Life together and then placing the other 22-Elohyms and their associate words to the Kabbalistic Tree of Life Sefirahs framework: **7-Double letters (vertical), 3-Mother letters (horizontal)** and the **12-Elemental letter (diagonal)**.

The whole of the Kabbalistic Tree of Life outlined in the first chapter of Genesis is going to be seen as coming directly from the MATRIX OF WISDOM, which actually has a graphic image of the Kabbalistic Tree of Life embossed into it. The manner in which the Sefirahs, Mother Letters and Elemental Letters are aligned is proffered directly from the MATRIX OF WISDOM.

All that which has been shown to have taken place in the first chapter of Genesis has already been expressed esoterically in the first written letter BETH ב and the first esoterically hidden letter PEI פ, which I will demonstrably illustrate later; however, the sacred scriptures continue on ad infinitum expressing the same concept: WORD OF GOD redundantly with different mythoi (this will be illustrated as this thesis continues).

BETH ב is in the MOTHER letters; for the reason that, it symbolizes 'house' and is considered ELOHYM'S TEMPLE. I, personally, will not accept modernity interpretation of the 22-Hebrew letters associate to the ARI Tree of Life. These placements of the Hebrew letters into the Kabbalistic (ARI) Tree of Life were conceived outside of spiritual esotericism. The **3-Mother letters** are the 8th, 16th and 24th positions, which is the pattern of the eight multiplication table and the word MADE, which is the associated word for Elohym in the **Mother letters** also stretches out to the thirty-second (32nd) position; though, that word MADE has no word 'Elohym' associated to it; nonetheless, the inference is that it represents a square. Ego-consciousness brings everything down to ORDER, which a square symbolizes. This pattern associated to the word MADE in the **Mother letters** is also counted off by nines. They are found in the 7th, 16th and 25th verses, which infers the 34th verse or the third verse in the second chapter of Genesis; nonetheless, another square is inferred. The ninth multiplication table reaching into the second chapter of Genesis denoting that it represents DARKNESS, which will be illustrated to be a valid interpretation later on. The eighth multiplication table stays within the confines of the first chapter of Genesis denoting the number eight (Yahweh = 26 = 8) as the LIGHT cull out of the DARKNESS. Only elements of PEI פ (80 - iconoclasm) not PEI פ (Gematria value of 81 - iconography) can be culled out of the DARKNESS into manifested creation. In other words ALEPH א, which is the second letter that spells out the Hebrew letter PEI פ, cannot be manifested into the world because ALEPH א (WORD OF GOD) is a silent letter. The initiate should see this conceptually as the primeval mystical nature of the sacred scriptures. The LIGHT concretizing into manifested creation is like ripping the spiritual sheen (ALEPH א) from the WORD OF GOD. This may well be what is meant by Adam and Eve realizing they were naked. Not naked by not having cloths; rather, it was nakedness by not being protected by the spiritual sheen of God's Ambiance.

The Mother Letters symbolizes the numbers two (2) and (7), which denotes the Ambiance of God. The eight (8) and nine (9) multiplication tables inferring these two squares symbolizes Scorpio (8) and Sagittarius (9) denoting Time (materialism - iconoclasm) and TIMELESSNESS (spirituality - iconography) respectively. Between Scorpio and Sagittarius is the Vesica Piscis symbolized by Cygnus X-3 (Northern Cross), which is created by TIMELESSNESS crossing the east-west corridor of TIME. All of this will make sense as this volume goes on.

The 3-Mother Letters will be discussed further below. I want to point out here that the 3-Mother Letter creates a cross in the design of the Kabbalistic Tree of Life and this has literally been designed artistically as the Templar's Cross around the Capitol Building grounds in Washington DC USA. I will talk more fully about this later (see chapter sixteen). I put an image below of the Capitol Building grounds positioned in the center of the Templar's Cross; amazingly, what is unique about this symbolism that is creatively designed around the Capitol Building grounds, between Constitutional Avenue and Independence Avenue and between 1st Street SW and 1st Street SE, is that the grounds are imaginatively designed in the shape of a skull with two eyes scanning the area between the White House and Jefferson Memorial. The artistic design of the skull on the Capitol Building's ground is a direct reference to the word RESH ר (esoterically codified into the first word of Genesis: BE-RESH-ITH), which symbolizes Christ consciousness' 360° spherical vision (RESH ר was already analyzed in the first chapter).

Below I do a deep contemplative mathematical analysis of the Kabbalistic Tree of Life; however, I want to say here that between the ears, inside the skull, symbolizes TIMELESSNESS (Tree of Life), which is the opposite of the outer world of the TIME/SPACE CONTINUUM (Tree of the Knowledge of Good and Evil). I am 68-years of age and I can tell you that my mind is just as sharp as a sixteen year old teenager's; though, of course in the outer world the body has aged. The city of Washington DC surrounding the Capitol Building literally places the Capitol Building as the center of the city: axis mundi (Bodhi Tree); because, all vertical streets are numbered going from north to south and going east and west all horizontal streets are alphabetized. All diagonal streets are named after the thirteen original colonies.

Those that know everything live in the material world (Tree of the Knowledge of Good and Evil); whereas, those that have Christ consciousness: God's Ambiance knows nothing, which places them in the Garden of Eden. I say that those that have Christ consciousness know nothing; for the reason that, they cannot explain to an uninitiated what they know no matter how hard they try. My writing this book, as much as I put into it, I am saying absolutely nothing; because, who, but another mystic that understands esotericism, is going to understand what I am talking about?

Also the skull around the Capitol Building is symbolic of Golgotha the place where Christ was crucified. It is symbolic of the transepts that cross the east/west corridor of Time, which is symbolized by the area that goes between 15th and 17th Streets from the White House down to Jefferson Memorial. Looking westward towards Lincoln Memorial points to Christ consciousness added to normal vision. The National Mall's artistic design symbolizes the phantasmagoria of the psyche projected outwardly upon the ethereal cinematic screen that symbolizes the blank dark-abyss of the world, which the initiate immediately lives in: i.e. Garden of Eden walking with God.

Finally, I will end this segue by saying **DA'AT** is neither a Hebrew Letter nor a Sefirah. A lot of so-called Kabbalists try to incorporate **DA'AT** into the fray of Kabbalistic thought and I see that word as a generic word for KNOWLEDGE. There is the Tree of the Knowledge of Life, which does not make it equal to the Tree of the Knowledge of Good and Evil. Yahweh Elohym in punishing Adam and Eve, he says, *"Adam is become as one of us knowing (YA-DA) good and evil (Gen. 3:22)"*. I interpret **DA'AT** and **YA-DA** as **DA'AT** symbolizing KNOWLEDGE and there can be millions of trees of knowledge **(DA'AT)**; whereas, knowing **(YA-DA)** that KNOWLEDGE **(DA'AT)** is why Adam and Eve were cast out of the Garden of Eden.

A person with Christ consciousness cannot know anything per se for every nanosecond of time a tsunami of data comes at the psyche like a tidal wave. The average person that depends solely upon iconoclastic thinking has no idea that at any given nanosecond of time he or she knows absolutely nothing; however, he or she thinks he or she does have knowledge; because, of memory (historical archival database), which is mainly dependent upon that which enamors the psyche's interest; whereas, the initiate recognizes he or she knows absolutely nothing; however, he or she will obtain knowledge when meditational contemplative thought is honed in upon a subject matter.

The **10-Sefirahs numbers (stationary)** are motionless (silence) like the Bodhi Tree. The **7-Double letters** going vertical seems to symbolize the letter/word RESH ר that crosses BETH ב the **3-Mother letters** that goes horizontally. This creates a CROSS as just discussed. The **12-Elemental letters** go diagonally, creating the concepts of the constellations of the Zodiac.

The ARI TREE OF LIFE, which is the traditional image of the Kabbalistic Tree of Life is named after Isaac (ben Solomon) Luria Ashkenazi (1534 – July 25, 1572); though, he did not conceive of it; yet, the ARI Tree of Life is a conjured up image, as far as I am concerned; for the reason that, it does not conform to the TORAH. It is possible that the ARI Tree of Life was created to contrast the GRA Tree of Life in the MATRIX OF WISDOM. As a believer in demonstrable evidence over rhetoric I tend to want verifiable evidence as to how something was developed. The ARI Tree of Life was obviously constructed by those that place DA'AT in the Tree of Life annihilating God's Ambiance in the GRA Tree of Life (iconography) throwing everything into disarray creating absolute chaos (iconoclasm).

I lean towards the GRA TREE OF LIFE that is named after *Vilniaus Gaonas*) or Elijah of Vilna, or by his Hebrew acronym HaGra ("HaGaon Rabbenu Eliyahu") or Elijah Ben Solomon, (April 23, 1720 – October 9, 1797). The GRA TREE OF LIFE is merely named after Elijah of Vilna as an honor for he certainly did not invent what existed from the dawn of the TIME/SPACE CONINUUM. The Kabbalistic Tree of Life's Natural Array is envisaged out of the MATRIX OF WISDOM. The GRA TREE OF LIFE is called the Natural Array. The mere fact that the Gra Tree of Life is called the Natural Ray is evidence enough that the ARI Tree of Life is not the original version.

My own take on the Kabbalistic Tree of Life is that it is a spiritual gift to the soul and we'll get to its original source as this paper goes on. Its directional structural aspects, I believe, represent conceptually the inexplicable and incalculable ways and means that the spiritual powers are use to bless the initiate with the **Initiatic Visionary Experience**. Directions per se have nothing to do with the spiritual process they are merely means to illustrate and psychically conceptualize via their mythoi the opposites in the material world and how the spiritual forces come at the problems of the initiates from disparate and diverse methods that are unimaginable and inexplicable to the initiate. In other words the spiritual powers can direct the initiate in any and/or all directions chaotically; but, purposefully: see the Labyrinth of Chartres Cathedral (see chapter nine).

The **12-Elemental letters** have three sets paired off from each other 180° from each other creating a Star of David. When all six points of the Star of David interrelate with each other it also produces a Cube of Space. Both the Star of David and the Cube of Space does not come out of nothing per se. They have precedence in prior texts and that will also be discussed later. I have often thought of the **12-Elemental letters** not only as the twelve zodiacal signs denoting personality traits; but, also as representing different raison d'êtres (reasons for existence). The astrological maxim *'Astrology impels it does not compel"* is **'spot on'** in this discussion. If the initiate birth sign is Gemini or any other sign then his or her character and raison d'être should align to his or her natural birth sign and to that sign's constellation's modus operandi (raison d'être). This is why no human being lives life without the celestial forces guiding or compelling him or her. To have any astrological sign compelling the psyche would suggest addiction; whereas, being impelled infer angelic guiding hands. Impelling suggest obsession. Theoretically, every human being has FREE WILL; however, I take FREE WILL to be a mythological fantasy. Every thought, word or deed each human being facilitates in his or her life is basically by rote. FREE WILL is not an option; though, FREE WILL may be thought by modernity to be an option.

FIRST CHAPTER OF GENESIS (Verses 1-13)
Hebrew Text (written right to left) & English text (written left to right)

בְּרֵאשִׁית בָּרָא אֱלֹהִים אֵת הַשָּׁמַיִם וְאֵת הָאָרֶץ: א

1 In the beginning God created the Heavens and the Earth.

וְהָאָרֶץ הָיְתָה תֹהוּ וָבֹהוּ וְחֹשֶׁךְ עַל פְּנֵי תְהוֹם וְרוּחַ אֱלֹהִים מְרַחֶפֶת עַל פְּנֵי הַמָּיִם: ב

2 The earth was without form and void and darkness was on the face of the deep
and the spirit of God moved over the face of the waters.

וַיֹּאמֶר אֱלֹהִים יְהִי אוֹר וַיְהִי אוֹר: ג

3 And God said, let there be light and there was light.

וַיַּרְא אֱלֹהִים אֶת הָאוֹר כִּי טוֹב וַיַּבְדֵּל אֱלֹהִים בֵּין הָאוֹר וּבֵין הַחֹשֶׁךְ: ד

4 And God saw the light was good and God divided the light from the darkness.

וַיִּקְרָא אֱלֹהִים לָאוֹר יוֹם וְלַחֹשֶׁךְ קָרָא לָיְלָה וַיְהִי עֶרֶב וַיְהִי בֹקֶר יוֹם אֶחָד: פ ה

5 And God called the light day and the darkness he called the night
and was evening and was morning the first day.

וַיֹּאמֶר אֱלֹהִים יְהִי רָקִיעַ בְּתוֹךְ הַמָּיִם וִיהִי מַבְדִּיל בֵּין מַיִם לָמָיִם: ו

6 And God said, let there be a firmament in the midst of the waters
and let it divide between the waters from the waters.

וַיַּעַשׂ אֱלֹהִים אֶת הָרָקִיעַ וַיַּבְדֵּל בֵּין הַמַּיִם אֲשֶׁר מִתַּחַת לָרָקִיעַ וּבֵין הַמַּיִם אֲשֶׁר מֵעַל לָרָקִיעַ וַיְהִי כֵן: ז

7 And God made the firmament to divide between the waters under the heavens
from the waters above the heavens

וַיִּקְרָא אֱלֹהִים לָרָקִיעַ שָׁמָיִם וַיְהִי עֶרֶב וַיְהִי בֹקֶר יוֹם שֵׁנִי: פ ח

8 And God called the firmament heaven and the evening and the morning the second day

וַיֹּאמֶר אֱלֹהִים יִקָּווּ הַמַּיִם מִתַּחַת הַשָּׁמַיִם אֶל מָקוֹם אֶחָד וְתֵרָאֶה הַיַּבָּשָׁה וַיְהִי כֵן: ט

9 And God said let the waters under the heavens gather onto one place
and let the dry land appear and it was so.

וַיִּקְרָא אֱלֹהִים לַיַּבָּשָׁה אֶרֶץ וּלְמִקְוֵה הַמַּיִם קָרָא יַמִּים וַיַּרְא אֱלֹהִים כִּי טוֹב: י

10 And God called the dry land earth and the gathering of the waters called he seas
And God saw that it was good.

וַיֹּאמֶר אֱלֹהִים תַּדְשֵׁא הָאָרֶץ דֶּשֶׁא עֵשֶׂב מַזְרִיעַ זֶרַע עֵץ פְּרִי עֹשֶׂה פְּרִי לְמִינוֹ אֲשֶׁר זַרְעוֹ בוֹ עַל הָאָרֶץ וַיְהִי כֵן: יא

11 And God said, Let the earth bring forth grass, the herb yielding seed and the fruit tree
yielding fruit after his kind, whose seed is in itself upon the earth: and it was so.

וַתּוֹצֵא הָאָרֶץ דֶּשֶׁא עֵשֶׂב מַזְרִיעַ זֶרַע לְמִינֵהוּ וְעֵץ עֹשֶׂה פְּרִי אֲשֶׁר זַרְעוֹ בוֹ לְמִינֵהוּ וַיַּרְא אֱלֹהִים כִּי טוֹב: יב

12 And the earth brought forth grass and herb yielding seed after his kind and the tree
yielding fruit, whose seed was in itself, after his kind: and God saw that it was good.

וַיְהִי עֶרֶב וַיְהִי בֹקֶר יוֹם שְׁלִישִׁי: פ יג

13 And the evening and the morning were the third day.

FIRST CHAPTER OF GENESIS (Verses 14-23)
Hebrew Text (written right to left) & English text (written left to right)

יד ‏וַיֹּאמֶר אֱלֹהִים יְהִי מְאֹרֹת בִּרְקִיעַ הַשָּׁמַיִם לְהַבְדִּיל בֵּין הַיּוֹם וּבֵין הַלָּיְלָה וְהָיוּ לְאֹתֹת וּלְמוֹעֲדִים וּלְיָמִים וְשָׁנִים:

14 And God said, Let there be lights in the firmament of the heaven to divide the day
from the night; and let them be for signs and for seasons and for days and years:

טו ‏וְהָיוּ לִמְאוֹרֹת בִּרְקִיעַ הַשָּׁמַיִם לְהָאִיר עַל הָאָרֶץ וַיְהִי כֵן:

15 And let them be for lights in the firmament of the heaven
to give light upon the earth: and it was so.

טז ‏וַיַּעַשׂ אֱלֹהִים אֶת שְׁנֵי הַמְּאֹרֹת הַגְּדֹלִים אֶת הַמָּאוֹר הַגָּדֹל לְמֶמְשֶׁלֶת הַיּוֹם וְאֶת הַמָּאוֹר הַקָּטֹן
לְמֶמְשֶׁלֶת הַלַּיְלָה וְאֵת הַכּוֹכָבִים:

16 And God made two great lights; the greater light to rule the day
and the lesser light to rule the night: he made the stars also.

יז ‏וַיִּתֵּן אֹתָם אֱלֹהִים בִּרְקִיעַ הַשָּׁמָיִם לְהָאִיר עַל הָאָרֶץ:

17 And God set them in the firmament of the heaven to give light upon the earth,

יח ‏וְלִמְשֹׁל בַּיּוֹם וּבַלַּיְלָה וּלְהַבְדִּיל בֵּין הָאוֹר וּבֵין הַחֹשֶׁךְ וַיַּרְא אֱלֹהִים כִּי טוֹב:

18 And to rule over the day and over the night and to divide the light from the darkness:
and God saw that it was good.

יט ‏וַיְהִי עֶרֶב וַיְהִי בֹקֶר יוֹם רְבִיעִי: פ

19 And the evening and the morning were the fourth day.

כ ‏וַיֹּאמֶר אֱלֹהִים יִשְׁרְצוּ הַמַּיִם שֶׁרֶץ נֶפֶשׁ חַיָּה וְעוֹף יְעוֹפֵף עַל הָאָרֶץ עַל פְּנֵי רְקִיעַ הַשָּׁמָיִם:

20 And God said, Let the waters bring forth abundantly the moving creature that
hath life and fowl that may fly above the earth in the open firmament of heaven.

כא ‏וַיִּבְרָא אֱלֹהִים אֶת הַתַּנִּינִם הַגְּדֹלִים וְאֵת כָּל נֶפֶשׁ הַחַיָּה הָרֹמֶשֶׂת אֲשֶׁר שָׁרְצוּ הַמַּיִם לְמִינֵהֶם וְאֵת כָּל עוֹף
כָּנָף לְמִינֵהוּ וַיַּרְא אֱלֹהִים כִּי טוֹב:

21 And God created great whales, and every living creature that moves,
which the waters brought forth abundantly, after their kind,
and every winged fowl after his kind: and God saw that it was good.

כב ‏וַיְבָרֶךְ אֹתָם אֱלֹהִים לֵאמֹר פְּרוּ וּרְבוּ וּמִלְאוּ אֶת הַמַּיִם בַּיַּמִּים וְהָעוֹף יִרֶב בָּאָרֶץ:

22 And God blessed them, saying, be fruitful, and multiply
and fill the waters in the seas and let fowl multiply in the earth.

כג ‏וַיְהִי עֶרֶב וַיְהִי בֹקֶר יוֹם חֲמִישִׁי: פ

23 And there was evening and there was morning--the fifth day.

FIRST CHAPTER OF GENESIS (Verses 24-31)
Hebrew Text (written right to left) & English text (written left to right)

כד וַיֹּאמֶר אֱלֹהִים תּוֹצֵא הָאָרֶץ נֶפֶשׁ חַיָּה לְמִינָהּ בְּהֵמָה וָרֶמֶשׂ וְחַיְתוֹ אֶרֶץ לְמִינָהּ וַיְהִי כֵן:

24 And God said, let the earth bring forth the living creature after his kind, cattle
and creeping thing and beast of the earth after his kind: and it was so.

כה וַיַּעַשׂ אֱלֹהִים אֶת חַיַּת הָאָרֶץ לְמִינָהּ וְאֶת הַבְּהֵמָה לְמִינָהּ וְאֵת כָּל רֶמֶשׂ הָאֲדָמָה לְמִינֵהוּ וַיַּרְא אֱלֹהִים כִּי טוֹב:

25 And God made the beast of the earth after his kind and cattle after their kind and
everything that creeps upon the earth after his kind: and God saw that it was good.

כו וַיֹּאמֶר אֱלֹהִים נַעֲשֶׂה אָדָם בְּצַלְמֵנוּ כִּדְמוּתֵנוּ וְיִרְדּוּ בִדְגַת הַיָּם וּבְעוֹף הַשָּׁמַיִם וּבַבְּהֵמָה וּבְכָל הָאָרֶץ וּבְכָל הָרֶמֶשׂ הָרֹמֵשׂ עַל הָאָרֶץ:

26 And God said, let us make man in our image, after our likeness: and let them have
dominion over the fish of the sea and over the fowl of the air and over the cattle
and over all the earth and over every creeping thing that creeps upon the earth.

כז וַיִּבְרָא אֱלֹהִים אֶת הָאָדָם בְּצַלְמוֹ בְּצֶלֶם אֱלֹהִים בָּרָא אֹתוֹ זָכָר וּנְקֵבָה בָּרָא אֹתָם:

27 So God created man in his own image, in the image of God created he him;
male and female created he them.

כח וַיְבָרֶךְ אֹתָם אֱלֹהִים וַיֹּאמֶר לָהֶם אֱלֹהִים פְּרוּ וּרְבוּ וּמִלְאוּ אֶת הָאָרֶץ וְכִבְשֻׁהָ וּרְדוּ בִדְגַת הַיָּם וּבְעוֹף הַשָּׁמַיִם וּבְכָל חַיָּה הָרֹמֶשֶׂת עַל הָאָרֶץ:

28 And God blessed them, and God said unto them, be fruitful, and multiply,
and replenish the earth, and subdue it: and have dominion over the fish of the sea,
and over the fowl of the air, and over every living thing that moves upon the earth.

כט וַיֹּאמֶר אֱלֹהִים הִנֵּה נָתַתִּי לָכֶם אֶת כָּל עֵשֶׂב זֹרֵעַ זֶרַע אֲשֶׁר עַל פְּנֵי כָל הָאָרֶץ וְאֶת כָּל הָעֵץ אֲשֶׁר בּוֹ פְרִי עֵץ זֹרֵעַ זָרַע לָכֶם יִהְיֶה לְאָכְלָה:

29 And God said, behold, I have given you every herb bearing seed,
which is upon the face of all the earth and every tree in the which is
the fruit of a tree yielding seed; to you it shall be for meat.

ל וּלְכָל חַיַּת הָאָרֶץ וּלְכָל עוֹף הַשָּׁמַיִם וּלְכֹל רוֹמֵשׂ עַל הָאָרֶץ אֲשֶׁר בּוֹ נֶפֶשׁ חַיָּה אֶת כָּל יֶרֶק עֵשֶׂב לְאָכְלָה וַיְהִי כֵן:

30 And to every beast of the earth and to every fowl of the air
and to everything that creeps upon the earth, wherein there is life,
I have given every green herb for meat: and it was so.

לא וַיַּרְא אלהים את כל אשר עשה והנה טוב מאד ויהי ערב ויהי בקר יום הששי: פ

31 And God saw everything that he had made, and, behold, it was very good.
And the evening and the morning were the sixth day.

32-Paths of the Kabbalistic Tree of Life			
1	Elohym Created	v1 =	Elemental - 1
2	Elohym Hovered	v2 =	Elemental - 2
3	Elohym Desired	v3 =	Sefirah - 1
4	Elohym Saw	v4 =	Double - 1
5	Elohym Divided	v4 =	Elemental - 3
6	Elohym Named	v5 =	Elemental - 4
7	Elohym Desired	v6 =	Sefirah - 2
8	Elohym Made	v7 =	Mother - 1
9	Elohym Named	v8 =	Elemental - 5
10	Elohym Desired	v9 =	Sefirah - 3
11	Elohym Named	v10 =	Elemental - 6
12	Elohym Saw	v10 =	Double - 2
13	Elohym Desired	v11 =	Sefirah - 4
14	Elohym Saw	v12 =	Double - 3
15	Elohym Desired	v14 =	Sefirah - 5
16	Elohym Made	v16 =	Mother - 2
17	Elohym Placed	v17 .=.	Elemental - 7
18	Elohym Saw	v18 =	Double - 4
19	Elohym Desired	v20 =	Sefirah - 6
20	Elohym Created	v21 =	Elemental - 8
21	Elohym Saw	v21 =	Double - 5
22	Elohym Blessed	v22 =	Elemental - 9
23	Elohym Desire	v24 =	Sefirah - 7
24	Elohym Made	v25 =	Mother - 3
25	Elohym Saw	v25 =	Double - 6
26	Elohym Desire	v26 =	Sefirah - 8
27	Elohym Created	v27 =	Elemental - 10
28	Elohym Created	v27 =	Elemental - 11
29	Elohym Blessed	v28 =	Elemental - 12
30	Elohym Desire	v28 =	Sefirah - 9
31	Elohym Desire	v29 =	Sefirah - 10
32	Elohym Saw	v31 =	Double - 7

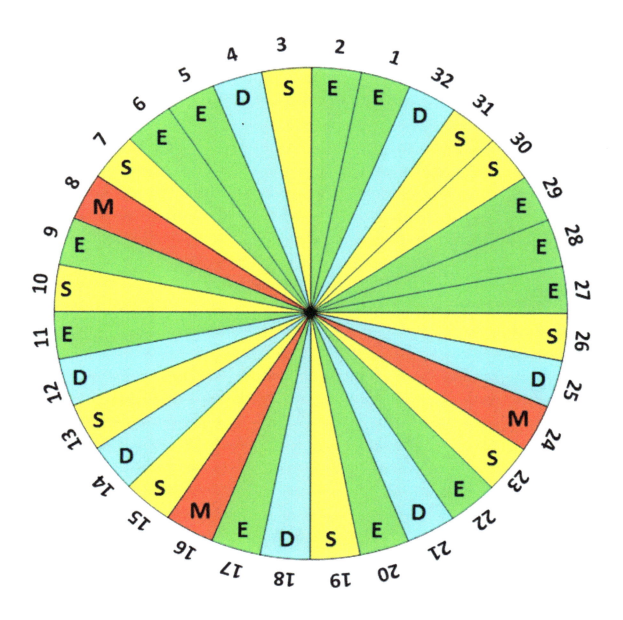

SEFIRAHS PAIRED OFF 180°

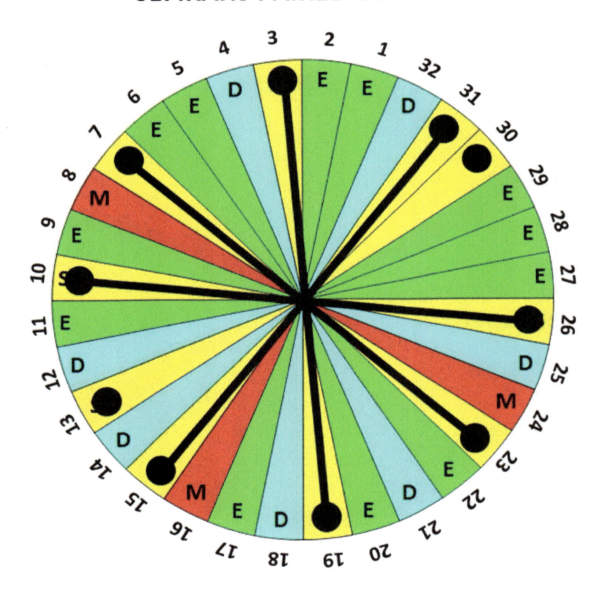

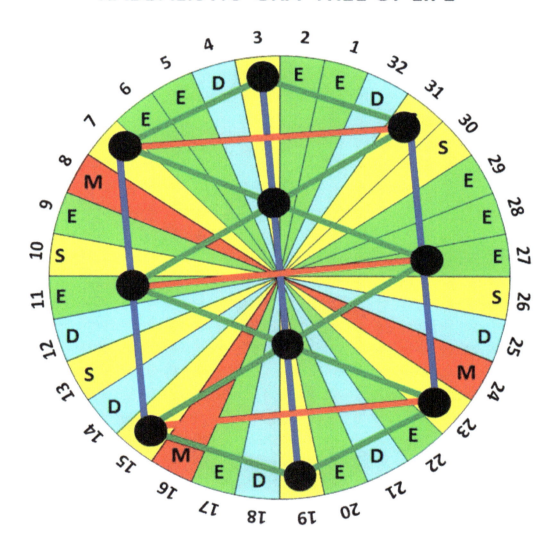

KABBALISTIC 'GRA' TREE OF LIFE

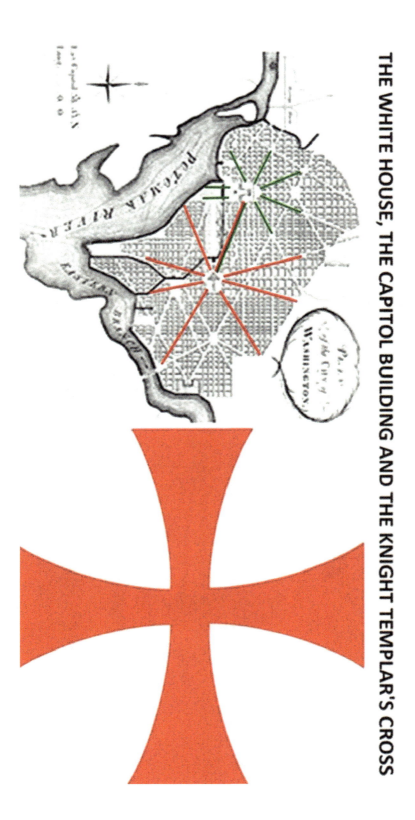

THE WHITE HOUSE, THE CAPITOL BUILDING AND THE KNIGHT TEMPLAR'S CROSS

ARI TREE OF LIFE

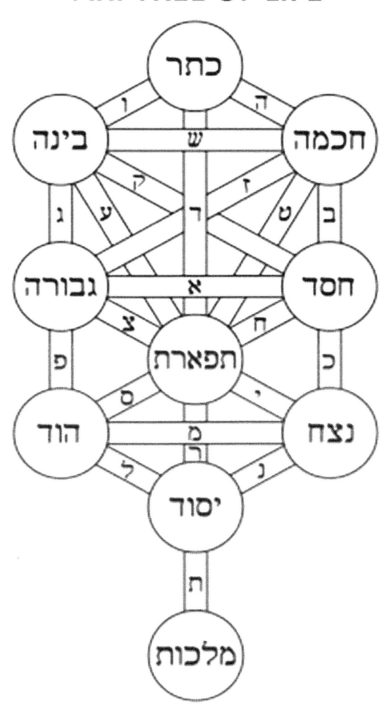

GRA TREE OF LIFE

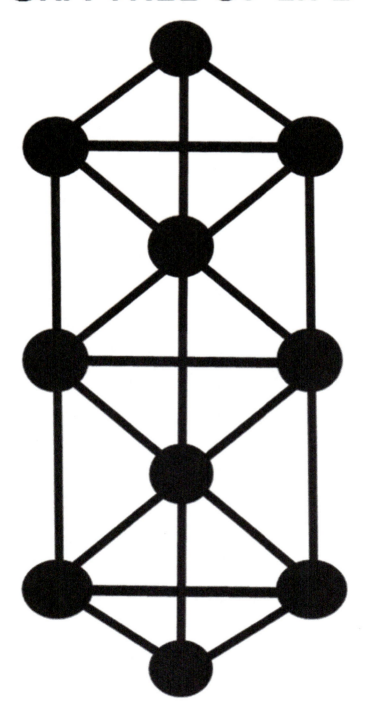

STAR OF DAVID & THE CUBE OF SPACE

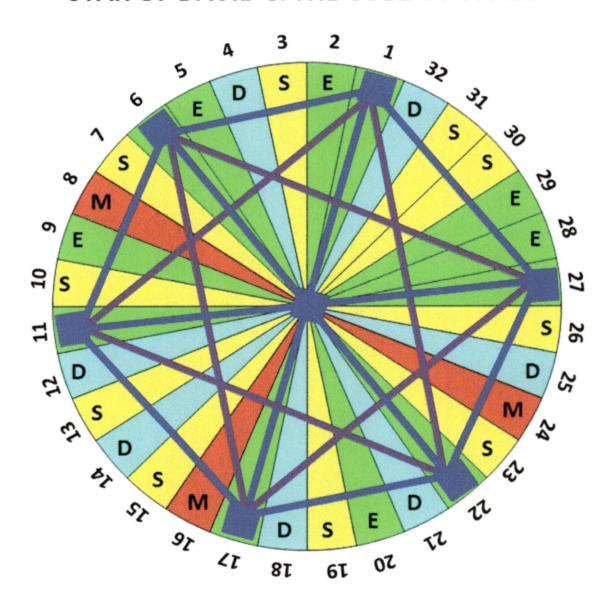

GENESIS:
Hebrew Word Count

Chapter 1		Chapter 2		Chapter 3		Chapter 4	
Vs	Words	Vs	Words	Vs	Words	Vs	Words
א	7	א	5	א	22	א	14
ב	14	ב	14	ב	8	ב	14
ג	6	ג	16	ג	15	ג	9
ד	12	ד	11	ד	7	ד	13
ה	13	ה	23	ה	14	ה	11
ו	11	ו	9	ו	21	ו	10
ז	17	ז	16	ז	13	ז	15
ח	10	ח	12	ח	18	ח	14
ט	13	ט	19	ט	8	ט	13
י	11	י	11	י	10	י	10
יא	20	יא	12	יא	15	יא	14
יב	19	יב	8	יב	12	יב	13
יג	6	יג	10	יג	12	יג	7
יד	16	יד	12	יד	23	יד	17
טו	9	טו	10	טו	15	טו	18
טז	18	טז	11	טז	16	טז	9
יז	8	יז	13	יז	23	יז	17
יח	12	יח	11	יח	8	יח	16
יט	6	יט	28	יט	17	יט	11
כ	15	כ	15	כ	10	כ	10
כא	23	כא	13	כא	8	כא	10
כב	13	כב	13	כב	22	כב	16
כג	6	כג	15	כג	11	כג	17
כד	14	כד	13	כד	18	כד	7
כה	18	כה	8			כה	22
כו	19					כו	14
כז	13						
כח	22						
כט	27						
ל	21						
לא	15						
	434		**328**		**346**		**341**

TOTALS 434 + 328 + 346 + 341 = 1449

"God divining the LIGHT from the DARKNESS"

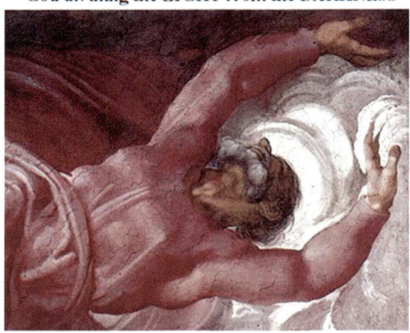

THE SISTINE CHAPEL
Michelangelo

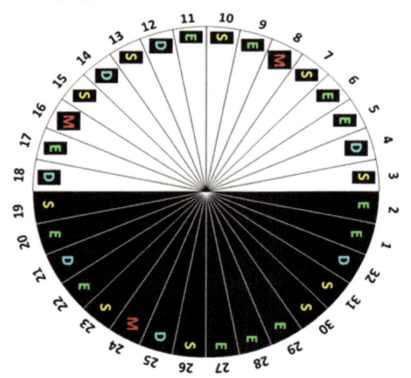

ELOHYM (Pi: 3.1415)
SEPARATING THE LIGHT FROM THE DARKNESS

MARSEILLES MAJOR ARCANA TAROT CARDS | RIDER-WAITE MAJOR ARCANA TAROT CARDS

RIDER-WAITE MAJOR & MINOR ARCANA TAROT CARDS

TAI CHI SYMBOL

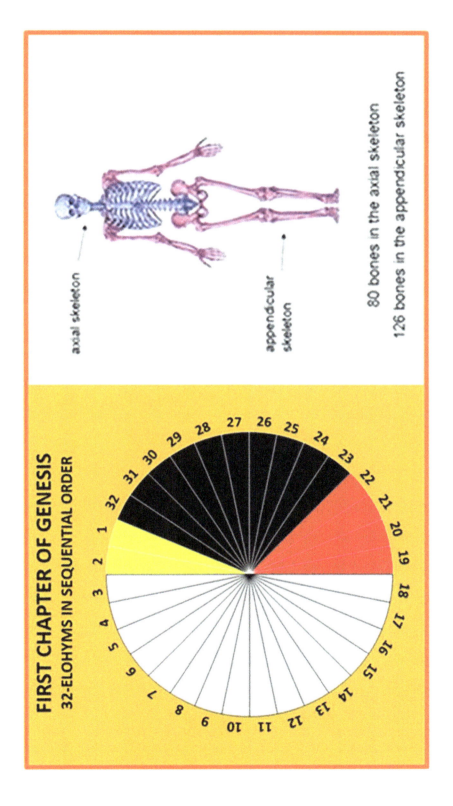

The next analysis of the 32-ELOHYMS is to study the verse count of the first chapter of Genesis in relationship to the design of the Kabbalistic Tree of Life's 32-paths. Here I omit the images of the Kabbalistic Tree of Life, the Star of David and the Cube of Space and just have a circle of the 32-ELOHYMS with the initial of the Kabbalistic Tree of Life category assign to each of the 32-positions. It is quickly learned that the first day of creation has 31-words as there are 31-verses throughout the first chapter of Genesis, which infers the cube of PI³: i.e. 31.00627...

The word ELOHYM (God) when spelt out and brought down to its letters' lowest common denominators: Aleph א (1), Lemmed ל (30 {3}), Heh ה (5), Yud י (10 {1}) and Mem (40 {4}) represents PI, by going counterclockwise from the number three: i.e. 3.1415 (short formula for Pi). This is now the second time that the first chapter of Genesis has been designated to symbolized God. If each member of the Trinity symbolizes Pi and it is calculated out to Pi x Pi x Pi the quotient is 31.00... as in 31-verses in the first chapter of Genesis or as in the first day of creation 31-words; thus, it can be envisaged that each of the 32-ELOHYMS symbolizes pi (3.1415) the diameter of its own circle: i.e. the center and circumference of its own circle. A circle of 32 ELOHYMS implies the **MATRIX OF WISDOM**: 32 x pi = 100.530...: i.e. the Vesica Piscis (153).The reader should have envisaged by now that it is not this author that has manufactured or invented the sacred scriptures' numerical data but that he has merely recognized it and expounded upon it in order to interpret the true WORD OF GOD.

The aggregate of a circle of thirty-two (32) is 528 and the diameter of said circle is 168.067... What is even more surprising is that the first day of creation has 31-words and the second day of creation has 38-words totaling 69-words. The third day of creation has 69-words and the fourth day of creation has 69-words. The first four days of creation has 3 x 69 = 207-words. The word LIGHT in the first and fourth days of creation has a Gematria value of 207 and what is envisaged from these calculations is to recognize that the sacred scriptures interprets the first four days of creation as the LIGHT culled from the DARKNESS as narrated in the first day of creation. These 207-words are symbolic of a LIGHT CHAKRA and this was determined by there being 1449-words in the first four chapters of Genesis, which calculates out to 7 x 207 = 1449 (7 LIGHT CHAKRAS); thus, this would reference 21 x 69 = 1449. There are 21-minor light chakras as seen Hindu mythology: this was all carefully thought out.

Even more surprising is the calculations culled out of the sixteen Elohym positions from #3 to #18 the aggregate is 168 or the diameter of the circle with a circumference of 528. The aggregate of the second half of the 32-ELOHYMS: #1, #2, #19 to #32 is 360 as in 360° in a circle; hence, the sacred scripture is interpreting the 32-ELOHYMS collectively as the diameter of the circumference of its own circle. The twenty-first (21st) letter of the Hebrew alphabet is SHIN ש, which has a numerical value of 300; whereas, it Gematria value is 360 as in 360° in a circle. The letter SHIN ש has the symbolic meaning of TOOTH and PEI פ symbolized the Mouth of God with 32-teeth. Meditating on this data exudes the idea that the 32-teeth symbolize the DARKNESS that the LIGHT is culled out of. The teeth imply gnawing on the Eucharistic Host (the LIGHT being the Eucharist) which is precisely how the New Testament expresses it in Greek.

Michelangelo went up to the ceiling of the Sistine Chapel to do an artistic rendition on the artworks that were already artistically worked into the mosaics of the floor and the frescoes of the lives of Christ and Moses on the walls, which included the 32-popes that circled the chapel on all four walls midway between the floor and ceiling. Michelangelo began his commentary on the ceiling by frescoing Noah and his family on the East Wall and worked his way toward the Altar Wall, which is on the West wall. Though the Drunkenness of Noah was the ninth central panel on the spine of the ceiling, which Michelangelo frescoed first he frescoed last God (symbolically Pi: 3.1415) separating the LIGHT from the DARKNESS right over the altar on the West Wall in the Sistine Chapel. In the image above illustrating the 32-segments of the circle of 32-ELOHYMS it can be seen that the first chapter of Genesis is the source of this spiritual concept. It is obvious that Michelangelo obtained his idea for this last of the nine central panels from the first chapter of Genesis.

A very interesting discovery made during the analysis of the Kabbalistic Tree of Life categories in the first four days of creation has the **SEFIRAH adding up to 48: 3, 7, 10, 13, 15** (totaling the position counts), the **DOUBLE letters add up to 48: 4, 12, 14, 18**, the **ELEMENTAL letters add up to 48: 5, 6,**

9, 11, 17 and the two **MOTHER letters total to 24: 8, 16**, which produces the pattern of the 3½ coiled Kundalini Serpent rising up the central column of the Kabbalistic Tree of Life. This is another set of calculations alluding to Hindu mythology. There is of course no doubt that the 3 x 48 + 24 also total to 168 or the hours in a seven day week: seven symbolizes complete: i.e. dormant/inactive.

In the 69-group of words colored orange in the first chapter of Genesis (see above three images), there are 142-words coupled together with 80-hyphens colored coded white. I did not color the English translation orange; for the reason that, it would have cluttered up the texts too much. I considered the hyphens to be of important when I saw that there was more than one hyphen being used several times to group words. The symbol of the hyphen is generally summarily dismissed as insignificant; however, I could not envisage the use of the hyphen unless it had an importance to the interpretation of the text otherwise, why use it? In addition there were words hyphened off that were not hyphened off in other parts of the first chapter of Genesis, which brought additional significant to the hyphens importance in the overall structuring of the first chapter of Genesis. Eighty (80) is the numerical value of PEI פ and the count of 142 is the transposition of the Gematria value of **BETH ב (412), SPIRIT (214)** and **SAID/desired (241)**. I found this latter quite extraordinary; for the reason that, **BETH ב (412)** and **SPIRIT (214)** Gematria values were in reverse of each other and now it is envisaged that **SAID/desired (241)** and the word count of **142** are in reverse order. It is as if the sacred scriptures is saying, yes, you can DESIRE spirituality now continue on setting your mind to the raison d'être God commissioned you to accomplish.

In Dante Alighieri's (1265-1321) La Divina Commedia's Mathematical System I found that Dante had obtained his esoteric knowledge from the first chapter of Genesis. Dante wrote 100-cantos (chapters) with an average of 142.33 verses, which is one of the points he lays out esoterically showing he was doing a commentary on the first chapter of Genesis (see Appendix).

Also it should be pointed out that the number sixty-nine (69) is very much like a Tai Chi symbol and also this number sixty-nine (69) reflects the symbol of CANCER, which is governed by the Moon. This 69 as Cancer's symbol denotes its equilateral designed as symbolizing equality for both sexes; whereas, ego-consciousness is 51+% preferably 100%. Cancer symbolizes the unconscious mind, which is the esoteric aspect of the psyche that denotes absolute CHAOS from ego-consciousness' patriarchal perspective; whereas, from the unconscious mind's matriarchal perspective ego-consciousness is CHAOTIC. It is ego-consciousness' responsibility to cull out LIGHT from the DARKNESS and give it ORDER so that ego-consciousness can comprehend consciously what it is envisaging. LIGHT is another word for spiritual ORDER and DARKNESS is another word for spiritual CHAOS.

The first four days of creation symbolize the LIGHT: i.e. **Earth, Air, Water and Fire** respectively; though, some would interpret the first day as FIRE and the third day as EARTH; however, this would be a false way of interpreting the texts. The LIGHT culled out of DARKNESS is instantaneously concretized and no longer the LIGHT. The LIGHT remains indispensable for as long as a nanosecond of time. Once a spiritual concept is grasp and manifested into the material world it is fully concretized into granite rock so-to-speak. Granite rock is ego-consciousness; for the reason that, spiritually conceived concepts are ego-driven: i.e. raison d'être even if they are inspired via spiritual guidance. The point is that the initiate is building the temple within the psyche and one or two concepts are not going to build an eternal cathedral. This LIGHT: **Earth, Air, Water and Fire** in the first day of creation is CHRIST and this is why the four gospels of the New Testament are based upon the four mystic elements: i.e. Zodiac's Triplicities, which are also FIXED QUADRUPLICITES: **Matthew (Air – Angel), Luke (Earth - Bull), Mark (Fire - Lion) and John (Water - Eagle).** These four mystic Elements are fixed because the moment that the LIGHT comes into the world it becomes flesh: i.e. concretized into a FIXED format, which euphemistically are called canonized scriptures. Even the gospels concretized into granite rock (DARKNESS) exude the LIGHT of Christ even though that granite rock per se was once the LIGHT culled out of DARKNESS. In the third day of creation the waters (DARKNESS) went onto one place and the dryland called earth (the culled out LIGHT) appeared. This is the reason that I interpret the first day of creation as Earth. In Egypt it is called the Creation Mastaba.

What is this DARKNESS, from which the LIGHT is culled from? When studying the images above, inferring the circle of 32-ELOHYMS, concentrate on the first two verses of Genesis along with the fifth and sixth days of creation; for the reason that, these are the sections of the first chapter of Genesis designated as DARKNESS. When it is realized the Elohyms, 1, 2 and 19-32 have a numerical aggregate of 360, in and of themselves by themselves, inferring the circle outside of the LIGHT (Elohyms 3-18): ELOHYM (Pi) that was previously culled from its DARKNESS it is easily envisaged as to why the culled LIGHT quickly becomes superfluous to the LIGHT that is yet to be culled out of the DARKKNESS. The diameter of any circle is unseen; for the reason that, the WORD OF GOD is silent as is the LIGHT in the first four days of creation. Think of the manifested and concretized LIGHT as the **REVEALED** surface texts (Trivium) of the sacred scriptures; whereas, the DARKNESS is the **COVERED** (Quadrivium – sacred geometry) beneath the surface texts and the diameter of the circle as the **HIDDEN** and inexplicable word of God that cannot be conveyed in the vernacular.

There are twenty-one (21) words in the first two verses of Genesis, fifty-seven (57) words in the fifth day of creation and one-hundred and forty-nine (149) words in the sixth day of creation.

Personally, I see the 21-words in the first two verses of Genesis as symbolizing the 21-small LIGHT CHAKRAS that spans the entirety of the first four chapters of Genesis, which infers that they are collectively the Hebrew Coder (alphabet). The first word of Genesis is created via one, two or three words depending upon how it is interpreted: *"in (the) beginning"*, *"separated six"* and *"in (the) first sign"*. I emphasize this to point out that the word BERESHITH is not the source of the twenty-second (22nd) letter of the Hebrew Coder. These 21-Hebrew letters are symbolically associated with the Major Arcana Tarot Cards, which are collectively the spiritual forces in creation. The Major Arcana Tarot Cards is the Kundalini Serpent (New Testament) and the Minor Arcana Tarot Cards is the Old Testament: i.e. 78 / 22 = 3.54... It is interesting to see that 77 (minus the Fool) divided 22 = 3.5 precisely.

THE FOOL is the 21st Major Arcana Tarot Card and if the initiate contemplatively studies the last five Major Arcana Tarot Cards: THE STAR (17 - PEI), THE MOON (18 - ALEPH), THE SUN (19 - YUD), JUDGMENT (20 - RESH) and THE WORLD (22 - TAV). It should be envisaged that these five cards are collectively missing THE FOOL (21 - SHIN) to complete the spelling of the first word of Genesis: BERESHITH.

I place images above of the complete sets of the Marseille and the Rider-Waite Major Arcana Tarot Cards. I see the Rider-Waite Major Arcana Tarot Cards as more spiritual than the Marseille Major Arcana Tarot Cards. Look at THE MAGICIAN cards in both sets. The Marseille Cards have the four mystic elements on the left side of the table entering creation and he is standing in the desert and dress and acting confusingly; whereas, THE MAGICIAN in the Rider-Waite Cards has him standing in a garden, neatly dress and acting respectfully. The mystic elements are on the right side of the table as if they are going east. These two decks of Tarot Cards I believe were created to augment each other's opposite and they should be researched in that manner.

The symbolic count of fifty-seven words, in the fifth day of creation, symbolizes the chaotic count of THE FOOL and 56-Minor Arcana Tarot Cards. THE FOOL = 21 = 3 and 57 = 12 = 3. This is why the EARTH is seen in the third day of creation as coming out of the waters just as the birds fly out of the seas in the fifth day of creation. The psychic screen that is the blank abyss is SHIN ש; for the reason that, it represents the all (360°) of DARKNESS.

The twenty-first (21st) Major Arcana Tarot Card (Fool: i.e. SHIN ש) and the fifty-six (56) Minor Arcana Tarot Cards, I believe, are to be found in the fifth day of creation. The images above illustrates the entirety of the seventy-eight (22 + 56 = 78) Rider-Waite Major and Minor Arcana Tarot Cards are in total disarray representing absolute CHAOS. The 56-Minor Arcana Tarot Cards symbolize the four mystic elements: **FIRE (Wand), EARTH (Pentacle), AIR (Sword)** and **WATER (Cup).** This is why the four gospels of the New Testament appear to be in a chaotically disarray. Each one of these four Tarot Card Suit's cards 1-10 symbolizes the ten SEFIRAHS of the Kabbalistic Tree of Life from a materialistic perspective via the KING, QUEEN, KNAVE and KNIGHT. These four Tarot Card Suits represent the LIGHT that needs to be culled out of the DARKNESS (psyche milieu), which are needed to create ORDER. The Tarot Cards emphasize that it does not matter if different people see the world in different paradigms of thought. The Tarot Cards are a great spiritual gift to all initiates; because, it helps them to cast away many biases, prejudices and preconceived notions about the world around the Garden of Eden. It matters not what other people think for what they think of others is of no spiritual consequences.

The sixth day of creation has 149-words, which is a combination of 69 + 80 and this numerical combination was seen in the 69-groups of words held together by 80-hyphens. Here in the sixth day of creation, I believe, that the scriptures are interpreting the sixth day as ORDER and the fifth day as CHAOS. The fifth and sixth days of creation have a total of two-hundred and six (206: i.e. 26 is the Gematria value of Yahweh: i.e. ego-consciousness) words, which infers the skeletal structure of the human body: Axial Skeleton (80-bones) is stationary and Appendicular Skeleton (126-bones: i.e. 126 is the transposition of 216: i.e. 6^3: Kamea of the Sun), which is active. The human skeleton symbolizes active (Appendicular: i.e. Swastika?) and passive (Axial). The fact that the fifth day of creation symbolizes CHAOS and the sixth day of creation symbolizes ORDER bringing the important of understanding the human skeleton to the fore. It is said that an Eskimo shaman neophyte has to learn all 206-bones of the human skeleton before he is accredited as a shaman.

An interesting nuance here is that the Axial skeletal 80-bones reduces down to eight (8); whereas, the Appendicular skeletal 126-bones reduces down to nine (9). Both eight and nine combined symbolize PEI פ the 17th letter of the Hebrew Coder. PEI פ as it will be seen elsewhere symbolizes the Vesica Piscis. This Vesica Piscis sits between Scorpio (8) and Sagittarius (9), which points to the Cygnus X-3: i.e. the Northern Cross (Children of the Swan) that points to the position of the galactic core center. The Axial and Appendicular skeletal structure of the Human Body has the Golden Ratio inherently codified into it: i.e. 80 / 206 = 0.388... and 126 / 206 = 0.611... These calculations could have been more precise if a bone was taken out of the Axial Skeleton (80 − 1 = 79) and place amongst the bones of the Appendicular Skeleton (126 + 1 = 127); however, that would have make the overall skeleton structure of the human framework a bit lopsided. So, I believe, the calculations are perfect in relationship to the Golden Ratio.

I want it to be understood that these nuances about the creation of the body is symbolic to the mystical teachings of the WORD OF GOD. Look at it from this perspective. The Axial Skeleton is stationary and from it the Appendicular Skeleton: i.e. arms and legs receives all the nourishment it needs to be active in the imaginary real world via the phantasmagoria of the psyche. This is symbolically analogous to meditational thought being needed to cull out the LIGHT from the DARKNESS. This concept is literally the crux of Christian theology. The entire ceiling of the Sistine Chapel is based solely upon that theology of the sculptured like personality resting (lounging around doing nothing) in contrast to the Sibyls and Prophets being psychically active in studying and researching the whys and wherefores life.

To make more sense out of all this the initiate has to realize that DARKNESS is the DOOR that Christ talked about in the New Testament, *"Ask, and it shall be given you; seek, and you shall find; knock, and it shall be opened unto you: For every one that ask receives; and he that seeks finds; and to him that knocks it shall be opened (Matthew 7:7-8)"*.

The DARKNESS is the initiate's ignorance of what he or she does not consciously know. This latter is because the Frontal Lobes of the brain symbolize Leo (ego-consciousness) and Cancer (unconscious mind): i.e. temporary reservoirs of knowledge and these nuances alone are why the initiate needs to obtain Christ consciousness to have access to all knowledge at any given time that he or she needs it (memory is a failed librarian's archival system).

Even in the material world, *"ignorance of the law is no excuse for not knowing the law"*. All knowledge is right in front of the initiate all he or she has to do is put meditational contemplative thought to it. What is behind that DOOR? It matters not what the initiate does nor how many times he or she may open that DOOR the DOOR never-ever stays open and that DOOR eternally and everlastingly has to be reopened. God does not allow anyone to rest on his or her laurels. It is very much like the mystery of the Great Pyramid on the Giza Plateau where they have found a door at the end of what is now called a star-shaft (use to be called an airshaft). Behind the door they found another door. And when they get through to that second door they will find a third door place up against granite rock. The three doors (three Torahs) symbolize the Trinity of knowledge, which symbolizes omniscience.

THE KABBALISTIC TREE OF LIFE
A DETAIL MATHEMATICAL ANALYSIS OF ITS GENERIC
MODEL CONSTRUCTED VIA THE VESICA PISCIS

There is another very interesting interpretation of the circle of 32-Elohyms splitting off into LIGHT and DARKNESS to discuss (study the image below of the Kabbalistic Tree of Life's 32-Elohyms that accompanies this discussion).

I fully understand that the following analysis of the Kabbalistic Tree of Life is not going to make much sense to the average reader; for the reason that, symbolism imbued into mathematics is an unfamiliar genre of thought; because, of the innumeracy problem that is prevalent throughout the world. Beside without a familiarity with symbolism and mathematics this is a very difficult subject matter to grasp. To the iconoclastic reader much will not make sense when precision mathematics is revealed to be embedded in a symbolic image especially when it come directly out of the texts of the sacred scriptures: i.e. the Kabbalistic Tree of Life that has been culturally known about in both Judaism and Christianity for two millennia. No religious or academic scholar has ever explicitly conducted a mathematical analysis on the Kabbalistic Tree of Life before mainly because modernity has no idea of its origins in the sacred scriptures or its original source material from which it was developed to codify into the sacred scriptures.

This of course is not to say that there are not people in modernity that do not know of this Esoteric Science. There is a secret hierarchy in both the Roman Catholic Church and Freemasonry that know of and uses this Esoteric Science in modern times. Freemasonry is presently very active in constructing this esotericism into the streets and buildings of Washington DC around the National Mall even as I write this. This will be well discussed in this book (chapter sixteen).

What I write about is my own researches that spans forty-two years, which is still ongoing and I learned it all by persistently studying and contemplatively meditating on the symbolism and mathematics via elementary mathematics: addition, subtraction, multiplication and division codified into the lettering and wording of the Judaeo Christian Scriptures and the artwork of the Roman Catholic Church. Additionally, I have researched the esotericism in many cultures' religions around the world. These four elementary mathematical genres of thought I believe symbolically represents the four mystical elements: Earth, Air, Fire and Water respectively. All other mathematical sciences are based upon them; though, the sacred scriptures do go into higher mathematics I have found that 99% of my research is based mainly upon the four elementary mathematical sciences to a precision and perfection that is unbelievable to modernity mental way of thinking.

Much of what the reader will read below will make little sense until the book is completely read and the reader begin to read and study this work again with a greater sense that it all comes together cohesively and harmoniously explaining somewhat God's Ambiance.

I want the reader to fully understand that when I first embarked upon studying the Word of God I had no idea what I was doing. I had no guides and I was totally disgusted with the rhetoric of academia and the nonsensical sermons coming from the pulpit. Looking back over that span of time that I conducted all this research I realize now that I was literally on a symbolic level searching for needles in haystacks and trying to put them together like a jigsaw puzzle; thus, the initiate has before him research materials that were not readily available to me when I first started out, like Parzival, totally ignorant of what I was venturing into as I entered the forest alone.

Previously, I when over how the five (5) sets of Sefirahs, one (1) set of Mother Letters and three (3) sets of Elementals paired off 180° from one another, using eighteen (18) Elohyms in the first chapter of Genesis to achieve that goal. I then separated out these pairing patterns of the Sefirahs, Mother Letters and Elemental Letters individually in an attempt to discern what the purpose was in creating these patterns and why none of the Double Letters 180° paired off. From the start I had a pretty good idea what was being inferred here just from the patterns of the 5-set of Sefirahs, 1-set of Mother Letters and 3-sets of Elementals; for the reason that, I realized that 153 was the numerical designate for the Vesica Piscis, which per se does not exist in the Time/Space Continuum. I will demonstrably illustrate this latter issue concerning the Vesica Piscis as I continue. The Vesica Piscis symbolizes the spiritual forces outside of creation: God.

The fact that the Kabbalistic Tree of Life illustrates that the Vesica Piscis is culled out of the DARKNESS as the LIGHT and still maintains its stability and veracity in the DARKNESS go to illustrating that the Kamea of the Sun ($6^3 = 216$) is culled out of the Kamea of the Moon ($9^3 = 729$) that leaves the quotient of 513, which is the transposition of 153 symbolizing the Vesica Piscis: i.e. see image of 32-Elohyms representing LIGHT and DARKNESS. There are many more mathematical patterns involved in this particular analysis on the Kabbalistic Tree of Life.

1. This is the mystical nature of choosing the pattern of 153: i.e. 1, 5, 3 in formulating the Kabbalistic Tree of Life in the first chapter of Genesis not only because it symbolizes the Vesica Piscis; but, it also gives the circumference of the circle's aggregate of 32-Elohyms = 528
   a. The pattern in the first four days of creation where 1-Mother Letter, 4+1-Sefirahs and 3-Elementals are position 180° from their mates in the realm of DARKNESS in the areas of the first four days of creation called the LIGHT is in contrast to those Elohyms that are not paired off 180°.
   b. These 9-Elohyms positions total to 90: 3, 6, 7, 8, 10, 11, 13, 15 and 17.
2. The Elohyms not paired off in the first four days of Creation have 1-Mother Letter, 4-Double letters and 2-Elemental. These numbers symbolized the first letter of Genesis: BETH ב, which has Gematria value of 412: i.e. Birth of Consciousness.
   a. The other 7-Elohyms not mated in the realm of LIGHT positions total to 78: 4, 5, 9, 12, 14, 16 and 18.
      i. Here I interpret the number seventy-eight (78) to symbolize the Major (22) and Minor Arcana Tarot Cards (56). This has nothing to do with fortune telling per se; though, I have to admit I made a prediction about the 2008 financial crisis via the Tower Card in April 1983 via the Major Arcana Tarot Cards symbolic patterns that are literally ethereally manifested in the world. The Tarot Cards symbolizes the symbolism that is permanently fixed into the world and this is why it is imbued in the symbolism (unpaired Elohyms in the LIGHT) of BETH ב the first letter of Genesis, which is surrounded and inundated by PEI פ. I believe that BETH has been incorporated into this mathematical nuance to illustrate that symbolism and mathematics cannot be fully comprehended until the initiate has been Born Again via the Initiatic Visionary Experience.
   b. It already has been illustrated above that the first four days of creation has positions count of 168, which is the diameter of the circumference of 528. Beside that point there are other important nuances to bring to the fore.
3. The pattern in the area of DARKNESS where the mates of the Elohyms in the area of LIGHT have the same numerical pattern of 1-Mother Letter, 5-Sefirahs and 3-Elementals.
   a. These 9-Elohyms total to 203: 1, 31, 30, 27, 26, 24, 23, 22, 19
   b. The pattern of those Elohyms not paired off 180° has 3-Double Letters, 4-Elementals, which total to 157: 2, 32, 29, 28, 25, 21 and 20.
   c. Those 18-Elohyms from both LIGHT and DARKNESS that pair off total to 293: 90 + 203. Notice that it is the 90 that is culled out of the 293. In the New Testament Christ says, *"when two (2) or three (3) are gathered together in my name there am I in the midst of them"*. The 90 symbolize Christ; because, it comes out of the DARKNESS in the form of the Vesica Piscis similar to how Tav (400), Shin (300) and Resh (200) are the first three Hebrew letters into creation and they total to 900. It will be shown how nine (9) also represents the number one (1). Also notice how 90 / 293 = 0.30..., which points to Jesus starting his ministry about 30-years of age; because, the 90 symbolizes the LIGHT culled out of the DARKNESS
4. In addition this pairing off process in the Kabbalistic Tree of Life exudes one of the most important patterns in religious symbolism: 10-Sefirahs total to 177, the 6-Elementals total to 84 and the 2-Mother Letters total to 32.

     a.   177 / 293 = 0.604…
     b.   84 / 293 = 0.286…
     c.   32 / 293 = 0.109…
          i.   It is easily seen here that 'b' and 'c' take up 0.40% of the Genesis Formula. This pattern of the Genesis Formula destroys the Golden Ratio's formula, which will be discussed throughout this work.
     d.   I want to also point out that the 135 pairing pattern is split in half otherwise the total would mystically add up to 270: 135 x 2. I point this out because 270 is the numerical count of the LIGHT: 1, 2, 3, 4, 5, 6, 7 and 8 numbers in the MATRIX OF WISDOM.

5.   The 14-Elohyms not paired off total to 235: 78 + 157, which 235 is a short pattern in the Fibonacci sequence: 1-Mother Letter totals to 16, 6-Elementals totals to 93 and 7-Double Letters totals to 126.
     a.   16 / 235 = 0.068… (Mother Letter)
     b.   93 / 235 = 0.3957… (Elementals)
     c.   126 / 235 = 0.536… (Double Letters)
     d.   Either one of these patterns just illustrated in #4 or #5 above is structured into the literature and/or architecture in religious art.
          i.   The 'a' and 'c' mirror images the ratio (0.604…) in the Sefirah.
          ii.   Notice how the paired off Elohyms mirror image those Elohyms not paired off. In other words either one of these patterns can be authentically used in the Christian or Freemasonry artwork.

6.   Finally, the last calculations I will give on the 32-Elohyms relates to the circumference of the circle: 528 relating to Dante Alighieri's (1235-1321) La Divina Commedia's Mathematical System (see Appendix): 10-Sefirahs total to 177, the 12-Elementals total to 177, the 7-Double Letters total to 126 and the 3-Mother Letters total to 48.
     a.   177 / 528 = 0.335... (Sefirahs – Stationary – silence – Bodhi Tree)
     b.   177 / 528 = 0.335… (Elementals – Diagonal – iconography: thinking outside the box)
     c.   126 / 528 = 0.2386… (Double Letters – Vertical - spiritual)
     d.   48 / 528 = 0.0909… (Mother Letters – Horizontal - iconoclasm)

7.   Dante Alighieri's La Divina Commedia has three volumes totaling 100-Cantos/Chapters, which directly relates to the MATRIX OF WISDOM and these 100-Cantos/Chapters contain 14233-verses. The three volumes are the Inferno = 4720-verses, Purgatorio = 4755-verses and Paradiso has 4755-Verses
     a.   4720 / 14233 = 0.33162… (Inferno = Double Letters and Mother Letters): calculate the Inferno by the Mother Letter percentage: i.e. 0.0909… x 4720 = 429 and it reaches out to the fourth canto/chapter 15th verse where Dante and Virgil only begin to descend into the black abyss.
     b.   4755 / 14233 = 0.33408… (Purgatorio = Elementals)
     c.   4758 / 14233 = 0.33429… (Paradiso = Sefirahs)

It can easily be envisaged by these simple calculations that Dante Alighieri did know how to break down the first chapter of Genesis to obtain the generic pattern of the Christian mythoi representing the Creation Account.

One of the most mystical and inexplicable nuances in the Fibonacci sequence is following the statements of Christ in the New Testament concerning its calculations. Christ says, ***"For where two or three are gathered together in my name, there am I in the midst of them (Matthew 18:20; KJV)."*** Every single set in the Fibonacci sequence can be reduced down to a two to three (2/3) ratio. Following the edict of the New Testament mythos as outlined by Christ the two three (2/3) ratio would have the added factor of one (1) between them: i.e. 2/1/3. This configuration is a symbolic take on the Hebrew letter RESH ר that is inserted into the letter BETH ב to create the first word of Genesis: BE-RESH-ITH ב-ראש-ית. This would change the calculations of the Golden Ratio completely on a mystical level into what I have named the Genesis Formula, which in itself is a 2/3 ratio (6/4); however, from a materialistic perspective this would not be noticeable; because, ALEPH א (Christ) is silent. This is seen in the Old Testament:

"And he said, Go forth, and stand upon the mount before the LORD. And, behold, the LORD passed by, and a great and strong wind rent the mountains, and brake in pieces the rocks before the LORD; but the LORD was not in the wind: and after the wind an earthquake; but the LORD was not in the earthquake: And after the earthquake a fire; but the LORD was not in the fire: and after the fire a still small voice (1 Kings 19: 11-12; KJV)".

RESH ר is spelt out Resh (200 = 2)-Aleph (1)-Shin (300 = 3): i.e. 213; thus, the Hebrew letter Aleph א is silent. When each of the letters in RESH ר is spelt out Resh ר (501) – Aleph א (111) – Shin שׁ (360) the total is 972, which is the transposition of the number 729: i.e. 9³ Kamea of the Moon (cubed), which the Hebrew letter PEI פ symbolizes as inundating and surround the first letter of Genesis: BETH ב. To have that kind of mystical confirmation is extraordinary.

The Gematria value of ALEPH א: Aleph א – (1) – Lemmed ל (30) – PEI פ (80) when spelt out totals to 111. The number 111 also represent the three Hebrew letters that represent the Trinity: ALEPH א (1) – YUD י (10) – QOPH ק (100). In addition when these three letters are spelt out Aleph (111) – Yud (20) – Qoph (186) they total to 317. I have not as yet discussed the GENESIS FORMULA that exudes from out of the first word of Genesis: BERESHITH, which will be discussed below. There are four additional letters that are intuited from BERESHITH to complete the Genesis Formula and they are QOPH (186) - GIMEL (73) – YUD (20) – DALETH (434) totaling to 713, which is the transposition of the number 317.

When each set of the Fibonacci sequence is studied it practically breaks down into a 2/3 ratio: not quite but almost. The second number in any of the sets in the Fibonacci sequence is always a slightly twisted numerical variation from the first number that prevents it from being an exact 2/3 ratio and it is because of that twisted numerical variation that causes the Golden Radio to be so persistent in creating itself redundantly.

Whereas, when Christ's statement is understood about the two or three coming together in his name and there is he amidst them, which brings the twisted numerical variation of the 2/3 ratio of the Fibonacci sequence out of the Golden Ratio oscillation process as if Time is psychically slowed down to a crawl; thus, the number one would have to be added to each of the sets in the Fibonacci sequence to facilitate slowing it down to align with the calculation of the Genesis Formula: for example 3/5/8 (1, 2 and 3) is a sequence in the Fibonacci sequence; however, the number one (1) has to be placed into each of these sets of calculations in the Fibonacci sequence to continuously formulate the Genesis Formula, which denote the Initiatic Visionary Experience; placing the number one (1 symbolizing the 153 = Vesica Piscis) into the two parts one half going to the heavens and the other half go to the earth, which would change the Golden Ratio and convert it to the Genesis Formula. This is not saying that the Fibonacci sequence is not in play it certainly is; however, what is being inferred via these calculations is that once the Initiatic Visionary Experience is gifted to the initiate then the Fibonacci sequence can no longer dominate the initiate psychically via the outer world by oscillating the life of the initiate. It is as if the Fibonacci sequence oscillating controls Time; whereas, once the Initiatic Visionary Experience is received Time is no longer a factor in the psyche of the initiate religiously; though, the body still ages in the real world.

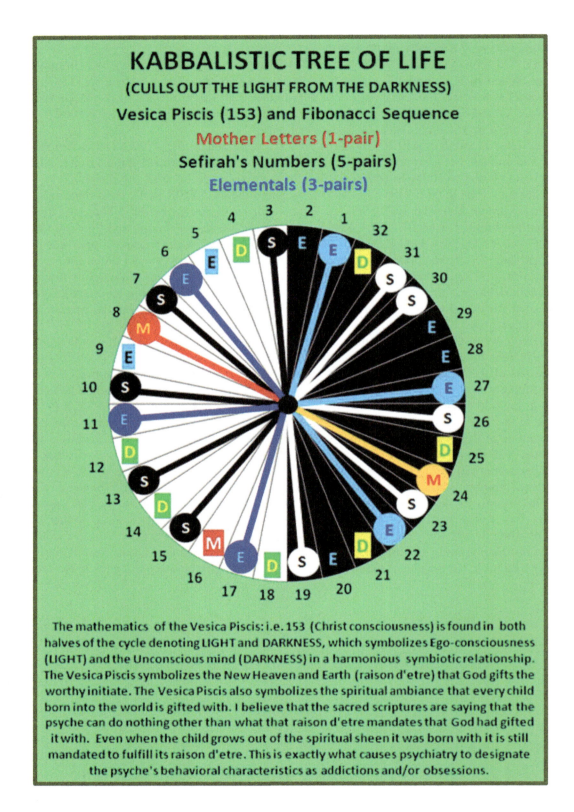

KABBALISTIC TREE OF LIFE
(CULLS OUT THE LIGHT FROM THE DARKNESS)
Vesica Piscis (153) and Fibonacci Sequence
Mother Letters (1-pair)
Sefirah's Numbers (5-pairs)
Elementals (3-pairs)

The mathematics of the Vesica Piscis: i.e. 153 (Christ consciousness) is found in both halves of the cycle denoting LIGHT and DARKNESS, which symbolizes Ego-consciousness (LIGHT) and the Unconscious mind (DARKNESS) in a harmonious symbiotic relationship. The Vesica Piscis symbolizes the New Heaven and Earth (raison d'etre) that God gifts the worthy initiate. The Vesica Piscis also symbolizes the spiritual ambiance that every child born into the world is gifted with. I believe that the sacred scriptures are saying that the psyche can do nothing other than what that raison d'etre mandates that God had gifted it with. Even when the child grows out of the spiritual sheen it was born with it is still mandated to fulfill its raison d'etre. This is exactly what causes psychiatry to designate the psyche's behavioral characteristics as addictions and/or obsessions.

CHAPTER FIVE

SOLOMON'S TEMPLE and the SISTINE CHAPEL

The Sistine Chapel is three times squared and has the same length and breadth dimensions as the original Solomon's Temple in Jerusalem. The reader should by now have realized that sacred geometry per se has little to do with the actual WORD OF GOD. Sacred Geometry is used as pictorial words to express concepts of the inexplicable nature of the WORD OF GOD that cannot be clearly expressed in any way, shape or form via the vernacular. A rectangle (Solomon's Temple) and the octagon (Christian Temple) are diametrically opposite ways of thinking iconoclastically (linear thought) opposed too iconography (outside the status quo). Not knowing how to read symbolism the laity gets caught up in iconoclastic thought and does not see the extreme difference between the two genres of thought. The whole of the Judaeo Christian Scriptures is to convey these diametrically different ways of thought; though, the average person has no idea that this problem even exist in the world at large. One of the main reasons for this is; for the reason that, the average person, including the mystic, lives his or her life in the iconoclastic world and continuously get caught up in mainstream thought and is psychically imprisoned in the rapids and the currents of time and this is why most mystics live in convents, monasteries or in a self-imposed cloistered life to get away from the nonsensical din and clamor of the world. In order for a mystic to think contemplatively he or she has to think sideways outside the stringent dogma and traditions of societal mores.

The religious life is; basically, a beheading similar to what the mythoi of John the Baptist talks about. John the Baptist's argument with King Herod was in every sense the argument of a Good Man (religious) against the satanic thoughts of ego-consciousness. This is what Freemasons do they try to make Good Men better men (Mystics). Once a 33° Mason or Christ reached 33-years of age life in the world symbolically he or she no longer has an option and a cloistered life is the only viable alternative.

The reader should have conceived by now that the number thirty-two (32) symbolizes 32°, which is, and anything below it, frozen stiff like a statue; whereas, anything above 32°: i.e. 33° plus is thawing out. This is why Dante Alighieri has Satan half frozen in ice at the bottom of Hades. In this example the reader should envisage the opposites parting ways: i.e. thawing leaving the frozen behind.

The whole of the Sistine Chapel's[1] purpose is to convey the concept that a Good Man (or Woman) needs to transform his or her psyche into that of a mystic, which thinks iconographically in order to read the WORD OF GOD properly. The Sistine Chapel ceiling displays frozen statues via 48-cherubs on 24-columns and 24-bronze figures lounging on the triangular spandrels, which are left behind by the Prophets and Sibyls which are actively studying under the guidance of divine cherubs. I see the 72-names of God symbolized as frozen statues symbolic of the LIGHT culled out of the DARKNESS concretized. Every time the LIGHT is culled out of the DARKNESS it is frozen stiff and becomes utterly useless.

When Michelangelo went into the Sistine Chapel the first 32-popes of Catholicism were already frescoed midway on the walls between the floor (earth) and the star-studded ceiling (heaven) and everything beneath the popes was also completed: i.e. the mosaics in the floor and the frescoes depicting the lives of Moses and Christ. It was Michelangelo's task to ascend to the star-studded ceiling to do a symbolic and artistic interpretation (commentary) on everything that the other artists did in the Sistine Chapel before he got there. Personally, I think Michelangelo is a synonym for the name of **Michael the Archangel**; for the reason that, Christ tells Peter that, *"Whatsoever thou shalt bind on earth shall be bound in heaven: and whatsoever thou shalt loose on earth shall be loosed in heaven (Matthew 16:19)."* Michael the Archangel (Michelangelo) went up to the ceiling of the Sistine Chapel to put into operation that mandate symbolically following the edicts of Christ. The manner in which Michelangelo executed his fresco painting on the ceiling of the Sistine Chapel was also extraordinary; because, he followed precisely, on a symbolic level, the pattern of writing (frescoing) the WORD OF GOD in the

---

[1] Here I use the Sistine Chapel as taking on the mantle of the Papacy: the Roman Catholic Church's teachings.

exact same artistic genre of thought that the sacred scriptures mandated. That alone shows that Michelangelo did nothing of his own accord; rather, he followed the guidance of his religious advisors.

The ceiling; though, slightly curbed, which goes to illustrate that Michelangelo thought has gone sideways. Everything beneath the ceiling is rectangular and Michelangelo also paints the entire ceiling fresco in a symbolically rectangular format similar to how the chapel is depicted beneath the popes and all that is symbolically formatted beneath them. This sleight of hand maneuver obscured the fact that Michelangelo actually created symbolically a circular dome to be the crown of the octagon shape that the rectangular chapel spiritually transubstantiates into. The reason that Michelangelo is frescoing the ceiling in this manner is; for the reason that, the surface textual storyline is linear thought; whereas, each and every letter in the Hebrew and Greek texts of the sacred scriptures has a symbolic meaning and alphanumeric structure in addition to Gematria being codified into it. The manner that the words created by these symbolic and alphanumeric Hebrew and Greek letters, throughout the textual storyline, esoterically obscures the sacred geometry codified to the mythoi of the texts.

People that think iconoclastically are symbolized on the ceiling of the Sistine Chapel, by Michelangelo, as stone sepulchers via the 24-bronze figures lying prone on the twelve triangular spandrels that are between the 24-columns housing 48-cherubs stone statue-like figure. These 72-figures perfectly match the pattern of the verses in Exodus 14:19-21, which are the original source material for the 72-names of God. The [Shemhamphorasch](https://en.wikipedia.org/wiki/Shemhamphorasch)[2] is derived from Exodus 14:19-21 read boustrophedonically to produce 72 names of three letters each. This is extremely interesting; for the reason that, Michelangelo explicitly conveying in this symbolism that the 72-names of God are not necessary spiritual but, rather as Christ said in the New Testament, *"Woe unto you, scribes and Pharisees, hypocrites! for ye are like unto whited sepulchres, which indeed appear beautiful outward, but are within full of dead men's bones, and of all uncleanness (Matthew 23:27)."* The reason that I point this out is; because, the spiritual forces in creation: God, cannot be named. The moment that an individual names God he or she becomes enamored by that concept and is frozen in place to that concretized thought pattern. This is why Dante Alighieri has Satan frozen at the bottom of the Inferno and it is the exact same reason that the Masonic Order has 32 + 1 degree to illustrate the contrast between the frozen-members and those that are thawed: 33° members. The 72-names of God are analogous to the LIGHT culled out of the DARKNESS concretized; because, the number seventy-two (72) is the transposition of the number 207, which is the Gematria value of the word LIGHT in the first and fourth days of creation.

The four Sibyls that occupy the four months 1, 3, 6 and 8 with 30-days create a butterfly pattern and the other eight signs create two additional butterfly patterns that reveal an ethereal Star of David in the overall ceiling fresco dead center to the Zodiac's twelve signs. This is why the Moon Calendar Year has thirteen signs; thus, Michelangelo illustrates that in his ceiling's fresco the Solar and Luna Calendars are working harmoniously together to make known the ethereal Star of David. It is not the Solar and/or the Luna Calendars that creates the Star of David; rather, it is Christ: Star of David that creates the new raison d'être in this case symbolized by the harmonious nature of the Zodiac/Calendar year; whereas, the old raison d'être would be the Shemhamphorasch that symbolizes an infinite amount of LIGHT frozen.

When the Shemhamphorasch is broken down into its 72-constituent names there are 32-Yah suffixes and 40-El suffixes; which explains what went wrong and these 72-names of God were frozen in TIME. Divide $32 / 72 = 0.444...$ and $40 / 72 = 0.555...$ This breaks down the number nine (9) into the waters of creation four (4 - feminine) and five (5 - masculine) as outlined in the **MATRIX OF WISDOM**. Even these calculations show they are frozen to the numbers four or five going out infinitely. Yah symbolizes Yahweh the Sun (5) and El symbolizes Elohym the Moon (4). For the 32-Yahs to go from male to female and 40-Els to go from female to male is SPOT ON; however, Michelangelo is showing how people get so enamored with what they conceptually conceive that they become frozen in their egocentric thought processes. There are four elements and the initiate is supposed to be flipping in and out of all four mystic elements: i.e. Fire, Earth, Air and Water eternally activating the tetrahedral forces of creation.

---

[2] https://en.wikipedia.org/wiki/Shemhamphorasch

Another extraordinarily interesting nuance that other artists, not Michelangelo, frescoed into the Sistine Chapel between the floor and the ceiling is the 32-popes aligned around the walls of the chapel. It is obvious that the Roman Catholic Church interpreted Genesis 1:1; *"Elohym separating (Bara - created) the heavens and the earth"* as "Elohym divided the LIGHT from the DARKNESS; for the reason that, all thirty-two (32) popes are positioned halfway between the ceiling (heaven) and the floor (earth) coinciding with the biblical language of the first verse of Genesis. The Church is defining all 32-Elohyms as if they all were a singular Elohym. In addition the 32-popes are the first thirty-two (32) popes in Christianity and the 32nd pope died in 314AD and that date 314 numerically coinciding with the very short formula for Pi: 3.14; thus, illustrating that the Sistine Chapel artworks is basically a commentary on the esoteric structure of the first verse of Genesis.

The battle between Emperor Constantine (CONSTANT = ORDER) and Maximinus (MAXIMUM = CHAOS) on the Milvian Bridge in the year 312AD is basically a mythological retelling of the esotericism of the first two letters of Genesis: i.e. RESH ר descending from the north vertically coming down upon BETH ב that lies prone horizontally creating the Cross of Christ. Remember that the numerics of the year 312AD are a transposition of the number 213 that symbolizes RESH ר. This is why Emperor Constantine is said to have had the dream of the Cross. Then there is the Edict of Milan in 313AD. All of this takes place in the pontificate of Pope (Saint) Melchiades the last of the 32-popes frescoed in the Sistine Chapel.

Because the West Wall was destroyed by Michelangelo in order to fresco the Last Judgment two lunettes, two windows, four popes and two frescoes were obliterated from the Sistine Chapel. Just because the Church eradicated artworks that are not now present in the Sistine Chapel does not suggest *"out of sight out of mind"*. There was a reason to have those artworks present in the beginning of decorating the Sistine Chapel with that scriptural artwork and I believe that all symbols in an artwork, past or present, are part of the entire commentary to be made on the collective artwork under analysis.

The entire plan of the Sistine Chapel was completed before the cornerstone of the building was laid; though, this may be very difficult for modernity to understand. This means that the symbolism placed on the Altar Wall/West Wall was already scheduled to be removed to fresco in the LAST JUDGMENT. The proof of this is seen in the fact that the frescoed popes are split evenly between the odd and even numbers: LIGHT and DARKNESS. These 32-popes symbolized the mantle and cowl of the papacy, with the four popes on the Altar Wall/West Wall removed as if being beheaded. The four popes symbolized the cowl of the pope's mantle. The two popes out of place: **#4 St Clement 1** and **#3 St Anacletus** symbolizes the clasp that locks the two shoulder straps of the mantle in place. In every sense the cardinal that takes on the mantle of the papacy is beheading himself like John the Baptist was beheaded.

In addition the fact that the life of Christ is symbolized on the North Wall and the life of Moses is symbolized on the South Wall is symbolic of the LIGHT (Christ) crossing the east-west corridor of Time going into the South where Moses put into play his interpretation of Christ consciousness. This I interpret to mean that Christ consciousness is being manifested in the real world into the lives of every soul; however, this means also that all of life has to be dominated by Christ consciousness otherwise the initiate returns to the iconoclastic existence that is seen on the horizon along the east-west corridor of Time. Those souls that go along the east-west corridor of Time have a false concept of God.

This concept of Christ crossing the east-west corridor of Time is symbolic of the cosmic rays from Cygnus X-3 (Northern Cross – Children of the Swan): i.e. Holy Spirit teaching the soul all things. This theme of crossing the east-west corridor of Time will be seen over and over again in this thesis via different mythoi explaining the same spiritual concepts.

SISTINE CHAPEL PRIOR TO MICHELANGELO FRESCOING THE CEILING AS COMMENTARY ON THE MOSAICS ON THE FLOOR AND WALL FRESCOES

This image faces the altar wall that was later destroy so
that Michaelangelo could fresco the LAST JUDGMENT

Michelangelo painted this fresco on the ceiling of the SISTINE CHAPEL

Take notice of the twnty-four (24) columns with two statue like cherubs on each column
and the twelve triangular spandral with the twenty-four (24) adult humans lounging on them.

Now take notice of the five Sibyl Oracles and the seven Prophets each of them is
accompanied by two cherubs as if the materistic lackadaisical have beome spiritually active.

THE SISTINE CHAPEL

ARRAY OF 32-POPES			
West Wall: Altar Wall			
31	St Eusebius	32	St Melchiades
1	St Peter	2	St Linus
4	St Clement I	3	St Anacletus
5	St Evaristus	6	St Alexander I
7	St Sixtus I	8	Telesphonus
9	St Hyginus	10	St Pius I
11	St Anicetus	12	St Soter
13	St Eleutherus	14	St Victor I
15	St Zephirinus	16	St Callistus I
17	St Urban I	18	St Pontianus
19	St Antenus	20	St Fabian
21	St Cornelius	22	St Lucius I
23	St Stephan I	24	St Sixtus II
25	St Dionysius	26	St Felix I
27	Eutychianus	28	St Caius
29	St Marcellus I	30	Marcellinus
East Wall: Entrance Wall			

SOUTH WALL (Life of Moses)

NORTH WALL (Life of Christ)

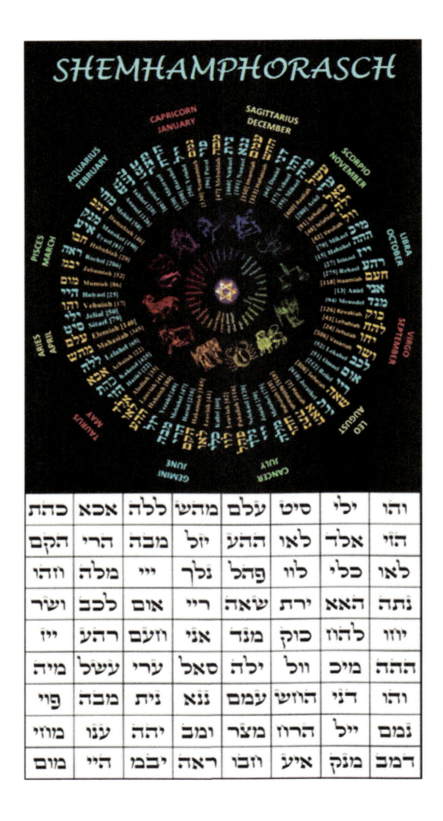

כהת	אכא	ללה	מהשׁ	עלם	סיט	ילי	והו
הקם	הרי	מבה	יזל	ההע	לאו	אלד	הזי
וזהו	מלה	ייי	נלך	פהל	לוו	כלי	לאו
ועׁר	לכב	אום	ריי	שׁאה	ירת	האא	נתה
ייז	רהעׁ	וזעם	אני	מנד	כוק	להוז	יוזו
מיה	עשׁל	ערי	סאל	ילה	ויל	מיכ	ההה
פוי	מבה	נית	גנא	עמם	הוזׁעׁ	דני	והו
מוזׁי	ענׁו	יהה	ומב	מצׁר	הרוז	ייל	גמם
מום	היי	יבמ	ראה	וזבׁו	איעׁ	מנׁק	דמב

Kircher's diagram of the 72-Names of God

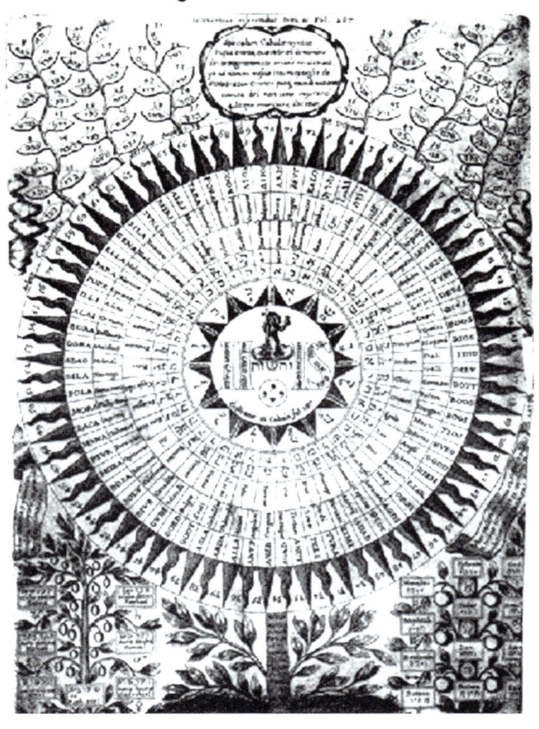

THE SISTINE CHAPEL
An Inexplicable Interpretation

The above interpretation of the artwork in the Sistine Chapel has been my basic overall interpretation of the building's architecture and the esoteric artwork expressed in the Sistine Chapel since the publication of my book and subsequent insight since. It was not until I was writing this book that the following interpretation of the Sistine Chapel ceased me via the spiritual powers that be not allowing me to continue to edit another chapter by erasing the above, which I consistently blamed on the malfunction of the computer. I would continuously try to edit this chapter and it continuously was erased; though, I always have copies of my unfinished works on the computer I was able to retrieve it and begin again and again and again. Not being able to edit three pages was bizarre. I did a number of things to correct the issue. I use the virus programs to clean the computer's software and I place the files in different memory UBS DRIVE to begin again the next day.

Apparently, I was not listening to my inner guide; because, when I began again to edit this chapter extraordinary ideas and concepts came at me like a tsunami showing me what I did not previous envisage or understand about the Sistine Chapel's artwork. The following esoteric interpretation does not eradicate the previous interpretations; rather, it emphasizes its overall validity.

I recommend very strongly that a Virtual Tour of the Sistine Chapel[3] is viewed by the reader as part of reading this commentary on the Sistine Chapel. This virtual tour is one of the most beautiful renditions of the entire chapel that I have ever seen.

1. The ceiling fresco is pattern to symbolize an architectural structure analogous to the inner temple of God.
    a. Between the twenty-four (24) columns housing the forty-eight (48) statue-like cherubs are the twelve (12) pendentives (4) and triangular spandrels (8) supporting the twenty-four (24) bronze figures that house the seven (7) Old Testament Prophets and five (5) Sibyls Oracles.
2. The thirty-six (36) pairs of mirror imaging statues are symbolically imitating God creating Adam into his own images.
    a. This mirror-imaging paradigm that goes around the chapel points to the Fibonacci sequence (symbolizing materialism) genuflecting (deflation of ego), which is more fully discussed in chapter eighteen.
    b. This ego-deflation is in sync with the initiate being prepared for the Initiatic Visionary Experience.
    c. The seventy-two (72) names of God (Shemhamphorasch) take on a higher spiritual significance.
        i. These stone sculptured statues frescoed on the ceiling of the Sistine Chapel do take on the concept of the stone statues that surround cathedrals like Chartres Cathedral, which narrates the surface storyline of the Old and New Testaments.
        ii. The seventy-two (72) names of God are divided into two parts.
            1. 40-Els (Elohyms) 40 / 72 = 0.555…
                a. Normally Elohym symbolizes the feminine not the masculine.
            2. 32-Yahs (Yahwehs): 32 / 72 = .0444…
                a. Normally Yahweh symbolizes the masculine not the feminine.
            3. This oddity is explained in a minute.
3. The 7-Prophets and 5-Sibyls points to the sunlight that comes through the windows of the cathedrals symbolically and mystically interpreting the WORD OF GOD expressed by the stone statues. The stain-glass windows in cathedrals tell the same biblical stories as that conveyed in the stone statues that are on the outer façade of cathedrals.
    a. The 7-Prophets and 5-Sibyls symbolizes the Zodiac/Calendar year.

---

[3] http://www.vatican.va/various/cappelle/sistina_vr/index.html

        i.   7-Prophets (males): 7 / 12 = 0.583…

        ii. 5-Sibyls (females): 5 / 12 = 0.416…

b. Mathematically both the Shemhamphorasch (72-names of God) and the Zodiacal/Calendar year take on the same mathematical ratios. These calculations do not take on the persona of the Fibonacci sequence; in fact, these calculations destroy the qualities inherent in the Fibonacci sequence (see chapter eighteen).

        i.   This changing male into female and female into male is mentioned in the Gospel of Thomas[4]:

> 114 *Simon Peter said to them, "Make Mary leave us, for females don't deserve life." Jesus said, "Look, I will guide her to make her male, so that she too may become a living spirit resembling you males. For every female who makes herself male will enter the kingdom of Heaven."*

        ii. This has everything to do with the New Testament (Matriarchal) being esoterically culled out of the Old Testament (Patriarchal). The outer world symbolizes the masculine and the inner world of the unconscious mind symbolizes the feminine.

4. There are three grand patterns imbued to the fresco on the ceiling of the Sistine Chapel that convey esoterically its overall commentary on the esotericism imbued into the artwork beneath the popes.

    a. **THE FIRST PATTERN** is COMIC and symbolized by the patterns in the spine (nine central panels) of the Sistine Chapel Ceiling that separates into three parts. And each one of these parts is broken up into three additional parts.

        i.   COSMIC: Creation of the World mythoi

            1. **Cosmic: Dividing the Light from the Darkness** (first panel from altar).

                a. Darkness = Spiritual forces of Creation

                b. LIGHT = Christ is the God/Man

            2. **Archetypal: Creating the Sun and the Moon** (second panel for altar).

                a. Sun = Time

                b. Moon = Timelessness

            3. **Existential: Water goes on to one place and the dryland called Earth appears** (third panel from altar).

                a. Waters symbolizes the material world

                b. Earth symbolizes the Garden of Eden

        ii. ARCHETYPAL: Adam and Eve mythoi

            1. **Cosmic: God creating Adam into his own image** (fourth panel from altar).

                a. Adam is lounging around gorging on the pleasures of materialism.

                b. God over time will make Adam into his own image.

            2. **Archetypal: The creation of Eve** (fifth panel from altar).

                a. Eve is separated out from the materialist. In the second chapter of Genesis Adam died and then a man was birthed. This Adam transformed into a female.

                b. Yahweh symbolizes societal mores tempting Eve at the very moment of her birth. Eve is coming out of the carcass of Adam.

            3. **Existential: Expulsion of Adam and Eve from the Garden of Eden** (sixth panel from altar).

                a. Adam and Eve are taking fruit from the serpent on the Tree of Life

                b. Adam and Eve are evicted from the Garden of Eden is because they ate from the wrong tree, which is seen as withered in the

---

[4] http://earlychristianwritings.com/text/thomas-scholars.html

I present this Internet site; because, it demonstrably demonstrates how academia deal with problem they do not know how to deal with. There claims that this last verse was added to the Gospel of Thomas at another time makes no sense whatsoever.

background. The angel also a serpent symbolizes Yahweh punishing Adam and Eve for obeying societal mores and not the cosmic laws.

   iii. EXISTENTIAL: Noah and his Family's mythoi

       1. **Cosmic: Noah and his family built an altar to worship Agni the God of fire** (seventh panel from altar).

           a. This altar is in the shape of the Kamea of Saturn: TIME

           b. The Kamea of Saturn is symbolically transubstantiated into TIMELESSNESS, which is what this entire Universal Cosmic, Archetypal and Existential paradigm is all about.

       2. **Archetypal: The deluge is separating the spiritual from the** material (eighth panel from altar).

           a. Noah's Ark is separating itself from the deluge. The ark literally has nine windows on the front side inferring the Kamea of the Moon and the roof infers the Kamea of Saturn, would be in the center of the Kamea of the Moon.

           b. The deluge (flood – tsunami) is the din and the clamor of the material world.

       3. **Existential: The spiritual sage judges the materialist** (ninth panel from altar).

           a. Noah's drunkenness is analogous to him gorging on the pleasures of the material world just as King Herod enjoyed himself not obeying societal mores.

           b. Ham in scolding his father (King of the family) for his behavior is very much like what John the Baptist reproached King Herod about and the reason that he was beheaded.

  b. **THE SECOND PATTERN** is ARCHETYPAL that deals with the Zodiac/Calendar year.

     i. COSMIC: is the ethereal Star of David that is esoterically symbolized in the ceiling's fresco; though, unseen by human eyes.

     ii. ARCHETYPAL: Represented by the Five Sibyl Oracles

       1. Scribes the New Testament

     iii. EXISTENTIAL: Represented by the Seven Prophets

       1. Scribes the Old Testament

  c. **THE THIRD PATTERN** is EXISTENTIAL

     i. COSMIC: There are 33-ancestors of Christ named on the ceiling of the Sistine Chapel in the lunettes. There were seven (7) other names on the altar wall's lunettes, which were wiped away when Michelangelo frescoed the Last Judgment. This number seven (7), I believe symbolizes the first letter of Genesis: BETH ב, which has the Gematria value of 412 = 7: i.e. Birth of Consciousness: *"in the beginning"*.

       1. The number thirty-three symbolizes the amount of years that Christ lived

       2. And number thirty-three (33) symbolizes the 33° Mason; thus, being made into the image and likeness of Christ.

     ii. ARCHETYPAL: The 40-Els out of the Shemhamphorasch

     iii. EXISTENTIAL: The 32-Yahs out of the Shemhamphorasch

5. There are three main patterns beneath the 32-popes that Michelangelo ascended to the ceiling of the Sistine Chapel to fresco a commentaries on. The whole purpose for Michelangelo going up to the ceiling to paint its fresco was to do a commentary on the symbolism in the mosaic in the floor and the symbolism in the frescos on the walls. Chapter fourteen gives a correlating analysis between the Zodiac/Calendar year and the twelve frescos symbolizing the Life of Moses on the South Wall and the Life of Christ on the North Wall. Every two signs of the Zodiac/Calendar year frescoed into the ceiling of the Sistine Chapel are paired off with two of the frescoes in the Life of Moses or two of the frescoes in the Life of Christ.

It must be understood that the New Testament is basically an ethereal texts; because, it cannot possibly be understood via iconoclastic thought. What is meant by this is that God (Trinity: Father, Son and Holy Spirit) are imperceptible; therefore, the activities of God cannot be expressed in the vernacular. The only way to talk about God is indirectly via a systemic system of symbolism and even then God has to be the initiate's guide.

The reader has to remember that the only four equinoctial zodiacal signs that dominate the textual storylines of the sacred scriptures are Gemini, Taurus, Aries and Pisces. All the other zodiacal signs are indiscernible. All the signs of the Zodiac are one way or another mentioned or implied in the bible; however, only Gemini, Taurus, Aries and Pisces can be outlined symbolically in the flesh of the world. Christ is made flesh via the Life of Moses or any other human being on the face of the Earth. Moses is merely a generic example of Christ birthed into the world.

The Life of Christ (Eucharist: i.e. God's Ambiance) depicted in the frescoes on the north wall of the Sistine Chapel mystically crosses the east-west corridor of Time (entrance, nave and apse) and transubstantiates into the Life of Moses on the south wall.

The twelve zodiacal signs pair off into sets of two. There are six heavenly frescoes symbolized by the Life of Christ and there are six earthly frescoes symbolized by the Life of Moses; thus, it can be envisage what Michelangelo went up to the ceiling to do a commentary on. Everything beneath the 32-popes became earthly frescoes and everything above the popes represented the heavenly frescoes. It is known that the 32-popes are symbolized being divided by pi; thus, the east-west corridor of Times symbolizes symbolically divides the heavenly frescos: i.e. Life of Christ from the earthly frescoes: i.e. Life of Moses.

The problem with the pairing of the frescoes: i.e. astrological signs is that they somewhat meld into each other as if they were one. The three sets of frescoes on the north wall in the Life of Christ mirror images the three sets of frescoes on the south wall in the Life of Moses: i.e. *as below so above*. It is the pairing and mirror imaging of frescos that creates two separate transepts that cross the east-west corridor of Time creating the Patriarchal Cross (see image below). It is the intermingling of the dynamics of the heavens and the earth (Christ transubstantiating into the earthly symbolism) that creates the tetrahedral forces in creation, which is lived out in the phantasmagoria of the psyche in the Garden of Eden. The whole of the Sistine Chapel is symbolically shaped in the image and likeness of a skull and the internal frescoes and mosaics on the floor symbolizes the brain's cerebral lobes. All of this is patterned in the rectangular shape: i.e. three squared not only to point to the east-west corridor of time (tunnel vision); but, to the fact that everything the psyche does is brought into the symbolic ORDER of the SQUARE as oppose to spiritual thought, which is symbolized by the CIRCLE or SPHERE (infinite CHAOS). Of course there is nothing wrong with that per se; however, the psyche gets so enamored by its creations that egocentrism flares up to the *"Oh, how great I am"*, mentality of an idiot.

THE FIRST PATTERN beneath the popes is COSMIC: The Life of Christ on the north wall; because, it symbolizes the WORD OF GOD, which cannot actually be conveyed via the human intellect; thus, the Life of Christ is placed upon the north wall to symbolize the heavens: i.e. Timelessness, which mystically transcend the east-west corridor of Time (entrance, nave and apse of the chapel) and transubstantiated into the manifested world, which is symbolized by the Life of Moses on the south wall, which basically could represent the life of any soul on earth. In early Christianity it is said that women sat on one side of the nave and the men sat on the other side of the nave. That practice interestingly coincides with the symbolism depicted in the Sistine Chapel by the popes symbolically separating the symbolism in the Life of Christ from the Life of Moses.

  i. COSMIC:
   1. **LAST SUPPER [SAGITTARIUS – FIRE – JUPITER/ZEUS]:** there is always the possibility of a zodiacal signs that will betray Christ. That sign symbolizes ego-consciousness, which is mandated to deflate itself; but, the initiate decides to keep its egocentrism.

Judas Iscariot, if one reads the New Testament properly, does not have an encounter with Satan until the Last Supper; though, the gospel writers mention his infamy in their early writings in their gospel. Judas Iscariot symbolizes the one thing in the world that enamors the psyche that the initiate cannot let go of. Because of that factor the twelve zodiacal signs cannot close the mystic circle; therefore, Christ has to die on the Cross of Existentialism.

This is exactly what is happening with the Roman Catholic Church: i.e. the Church is dying on the cross of Existentialism because they have turned the teachings of Christ into iconoclasm and in turn treats its laity socially and presents Catholicism globally as if it was a charitable organization. This is precisely what Judas Iscariot wanted donations for the poor. While selling Christ to the world the Church conducts its pageantries, carnivals and gambling games. This is what happens to most Mystery Schools; because, they also become social and networking clubs besides doing good works for charities. Look at what Christ say when a disciple wanted to go home and bury his father, "*Let the dead bury the dead (Luke 9:60)*."

Look at how Mary actions were ostracized for pouring oil on Christ; rather, than spending it on the poor. This is discussed in two gospels Matthew 26:6-13; 14-16; and Mark 14:3-9; 10-11. I interpret the pouring of oil anointing Jesus as Mary's (feminine symbolizing unconscious mind) meditational contemplative thought preparing Jesus for the burial. No matter what others do for spiritual purposes iconoclastic thought will find something wrong with it. A monk or nun praying or meditating, like Mary's meditational contemplation thoughts, on the WORD OF GOD would seem to iconoclastic thought to be time that should be well spent on working for the poor. The disciples said that the oil could have been sold for 300 (3) pence. Symbolically, that is the price that Judas Iscariot obtains when he soul Jesus to the high priest: 30 (3) pieces of silver.

Notice how Mathew does not mention how much the oil could have been sold for; yet, Mark mentions 300-pence could have been obtained. Then notice how Matthew mentions the amount of money Judas Iscariot gets: 30-pieces of silver; however, Mark reframes from mentioning the amount of money Judas gets. Because both the story of Mary and the oil and Judas Iscariot and the 30-pieces of silver are all connected verse-wise in both gospels they were meant to be symbolically connected. It is the masculine: i.e. ego-consciousness that concretizes thought not the feminine: unconscious mind. This is why women are more spiritual than men.

The 'Last Supper' is a sleigh of hand phrase; because, the Eucharist can only be taken once daily. It is already known that the Birth of Christ is the Death of Christ. How, therefore, can there ever be more than one meal with Christ at a given Eucharistic Mass. Often the Priest at the Holy Mass has to partake of the remains of the chalice that he serves the congregation during Holy Communion. No matter how much of the wafer host he partakes of he still only receives the benefit of one wafer host, which would be the totality of God's Ambiance.

2. GIFT OF THE KEYS [SCORPIO – WATER - MARS]: Peter is given the knowledge needed to understand the dynamics of his own psyche: ego-consciousness (Sun – golden key) and the unconscious mind (Moon – Silver Key).

The Gold and Silver keys symbolize the mystical marriage of Boaz (Moon) and Jachin (Sun). There is no male (Sun) or female (Moon) in heavens; thus, illustrating the Keys are not separate; though, the sleight of hand showing both keys would suggest otherwise. The fact that in the background the octagon gazebo (Kamea of Saturn) is clearly present illustrating that Peter had received Christ consciousness. Peter is the only one genuflecting (symbolizing ego-consciousness deflating itself) in the entire fresco before Christ and he was the only one that knew that Christ was the Messiah. All of this validates the purpose and reason for why this fresco was created.

The keys are symbolic to the 'keys to the city': i.e. Garden of Eden. The keys symbolize the raison d'etre that God gives each initiate that is worthy to receive the Initiatic Visionary Experience. Handing the keys to Peter is analogous to God declaring to all initiates that receive Christ consciousness are symbolically their own Pope. The secular 'ordained pope' is basically a prisoner in Vatican City for the rest of his life. The Pope in Vatican City is symbolically his own Pope. Every member of the Catholic laity is Christ and a priest after the Order of Melchiezidek; therefore, there is no reason that an initiate cannot be his own pope and that has nothing to do with egocentrism; though, outwardly it would appear that way. The member of the laity that has Christ consciousness either becomes a monk, nun or creates his or her own cloistered (monastic) life just to step away from the din and clamor of the world. The most beautiful gift of mysticism is silence not being annoyed by those things that use to enamor the psyche.

Sagittarius is ruled by Jupiter (Christ) that conquered Cronus/Saturn the Father of Time and it is the accomplishments of the equinoctial age of Aries ruled my Mars that allowed Christ to transcend the east-west corridor of time. Mars symbolizes the battle royale between iconoclasm and iconography (Ram - Aries in opposition to Bull - Taurus): i.e. Solomon (rectangular) Temple verses the Christian (octagon) Temple, which is envisaged in the equinoctial ages of Taurus and Gemini. This is why in the Gift of the Keys frescoed the octagon shape gazebo is first seen in the background; because, this is what the Sistine Chapel mystically looks like.

The Gift of the Keys' fresco shows the octagon gazebo in the background and the Last Supper fresco is use to illustrate the design of the octagon symbol (Kamea of Saturn) in the both the ceiling and the floor. This I believe illustrates that the Sistine Chapel symbolizes Christ consciousness, which is not affected by Time.

    ii. EXISTENTIAL:
1. SERMON ON THE MOUND [LIBRA – AIR - VENUS]: Blessings are those... Beatitudes: Matthew 5:3-11; that coincide with the Kamea of Saturn, which is symbolically the mastaba: i.e. mound of creation. Each one of these blessing points out the opposite inferring those that do not get the blessings. These pairs of opposites symbolize the Scales of Libra/Anubis.

   In order to understand what Christ is saying the initiate has to study the symbolism, numerics and alphabetic nature of the Hebrew and Greek coders. Unless the initiate understand how the New Testament was written he or she would not understand a word of the New Testament canonized texts.

2. THE CALLING OF THE DECIPLES [VIRGO – EARTH - MERCURY]: symbolizes the psychic patterns that are gifted as the raison d'etre (Initiatic Visionary Experience) given to the worthy initiate. The disciples symbolize the earthly raison d'etre that Christ is making into his image and likeness: spiritual generic paradigm. Iconoclastically these are good men (mental activities) trying to become better men.

Because of multitasking symbolism these disciples iconographically represent the spiritual generic paradigm they are not human beings per se just astrological mythoi explaining the WORD OF GOD. On a human level in the real world this would be Freemasonry initiating worthy men that follow their religious teaching and are obedient to societal mores.

iii. ARCHETYPAL:

1. TEMPTATIONS OF CHRIST [LEO – FIRE - SUN]: Satan (ego-consciousness) offers the three most important jobs in the material world. It is this quest for materialistic comfort and security that motivates most people in the outer world.

    a. ARCHETYPAL: Make bread out of rock, which is providing the initiate with any trade skill he desires.

    b. COSMIC: Become the high-priest and rule over the presiding religion. Or become a pastor of a Church.

    c. EXISTENTIAL: Become the ruler of the whole world or a politician in one's community.

2. BAPTISM OF CHRIST [CANCER – WATER - MOON]: Christ the spiritual powers of creation are imbued (Baptized in the River Jordan) into the mythoi of the Old Testament mythologies and from that milieu come the mythoi of the New Testament: i.e. new raison d'etre. It is absolutely impossible to rise above this Old Testament milieu without God's Ambiance. Remember, that Peter sunk into the waters and only could rise up again out of the water via the aid of Christ: i.e. God's Ambiance.

    Baptism (family, religious and societal mores) is the tsunami that comes at the initiate like a tidal wave of confusing knowledge, which he or she has to assimilate into a reasonable and logical way of life. Very few people are pulled out of these waters via God's guidance.

    a. ARCHETYPAL: This is analogous to a child born into the world and being baptized into family mores.

    b. EXISTENTIAL: Societal mores.

    c. COSMIC: Religious dogma and traditions.

b. **THE SECOND PATTERN is ARCHETYPE,** which has everything to do with the east-west corridor of Time. What most people do not understand is that when they walk into a religious Church, Temple, Cathedral, etc., etc. they are walking symbolically from TIME to TIMELESSNESS: i.e. symbolically the east and west walls are one and the same wall as are the north and south walls one wall: i.e. ethereally they all symbolize less than a nanosecond of time: i.e. ethereally and esoterically there is no time or space in a sacred space; thus, the Sistine Chapel symbolizes the Garden of Eden: i.e. God's Ambiance: from a spiritual perspective wherever the initiate stands stationary symbolically there are no directions. In the material world the materialist is always facing the North and that is because he or she is always facing the horizon: i.e. the east-west corridor of Time. Ego-consciousness symbolizes the SUN going along the elliptic, which is always going towards the west. The Sistine Chapel symbolizes exactly what Zachariah speaks of concerning Mount Olive in the fourteenth chapter of his work in the Old Testament. Is it not quite synchronistic that Zachariah is the first prophet frescoed into ceiling above the east entrance door symbolizing TIME?

> *"And his feet shall stand in that day upon the mount of Olives, which is before Jerusalem on the east, and the mount of Olives shall cleave in the midst thereof toward the east and toward the west, and there shall be a very great valley; and*

> *half of the mountain shall remove toward the north, and half of it toward the south (Zachariah 14:4)."*

i. **ARCHETYPAL:** The six large circular mosaic patterns on the floor of the Sistine Chapel at the entrance door (see image below) is symbolic of the first word of Genesis: BERESHITH: i.e. *"In the beginning"*, which has already been discussed. It symbolizes the whole Initiatic Visionary Experience that is laid out via the Archetypal, Existential and Comic letters of the indigenous language representing the spiritual forces of creation. The reasons these six circles are patterned on the floor of the Sistine Chapel is because they symbolize along with the Kamea of Saturn the foundations of God's Ambiance: Christ consciousness. These six circles go from Time, which is just outside the east-door of the Sistine Chapel, where the first circle starts, into Timelessness that is symbolically represented by the center of the chapel partitioned off by a screened barrier.

ii. **EXISTENTIAL:** Symbolized the pattern of the Kamea of Saturn mosaic in the floor of the Sistine Chapel that symbolizes Earth (mastaba – creation mound), which the barrier in the center of the chapel separated from the heavens (Vesica Piscis), which is the invisible barrier. The Kamea of Saturn is the area where the altar is in the Sistine Chapel. Coming into the chapel from the din and the clamor of the world and worshiping God on the Kamea of Saturn is analogous to Noah and his family coming out of the deluge and then building the altar in the shape of the Kamea of Saturn cubed: i.e. Holy of Holies. It is also the generic patterned Michelangelo designed into the nine central panels of the ceiling.

iii. **COSMIC:** represents the barrier in the center of the Sistine Chapel; however, the Vesica Piscis literally symbolizes the whole of the chapel.

    1. Each letter of the Hebrew coder is the Vesica Piscis that separates the numerics from the alphabetic nature of the Hebrew letter. The Vesica Piscis is the transept that symbolically crosses the east-west corridor of time, which does not exist in the Sistine Chapel overtly; however, it is symbolized here by the marble screen barrier to represent the nature of each spiritual powers of creation. Not that any of the letters are more important than any of the others. All letters contain infinite knowledge; however, the spiritual powers of creation are mystically broken up in the world of time and space so that the human intellect can somewhat understand what is being conveyed. This discussion on the 22-letters of the Hebrew coder is well laid out on the National Mall in Washington DC (see chapter sixteen).

        a. The entire area between the east and west walls symbolically does not exist in the Time Space continuum.

        b. This six concentric circles symbolizing BERESHITH symbolizes the first two verse of Genesis: predominantly discussing the dynamics of the letter/word RESH, which symbolizes:

            i. Gen. 1:1; *"In the beginning God separated **the beginning and ends** of the heavens and **the beginning and ends** of the earth:* RESH (Heaven Bereshith) – ALEPH (God) – SHIN (Earth – Kamea of Saturn): i.e. God separates the heavens and the earth.

            ii. Gen. 1:2; *"The earth (Kamea of Saturn) was without form and void and darkness was on the face of the deep".*

THE SISTINE CHAPEL
TRANSUBSTANTIATING
The LIFE OF CHRIST into the LIFE OF MOSES

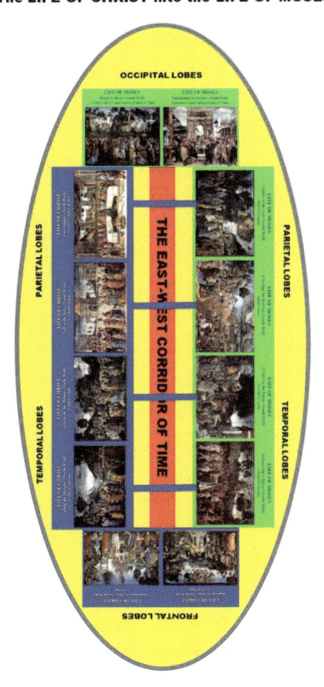

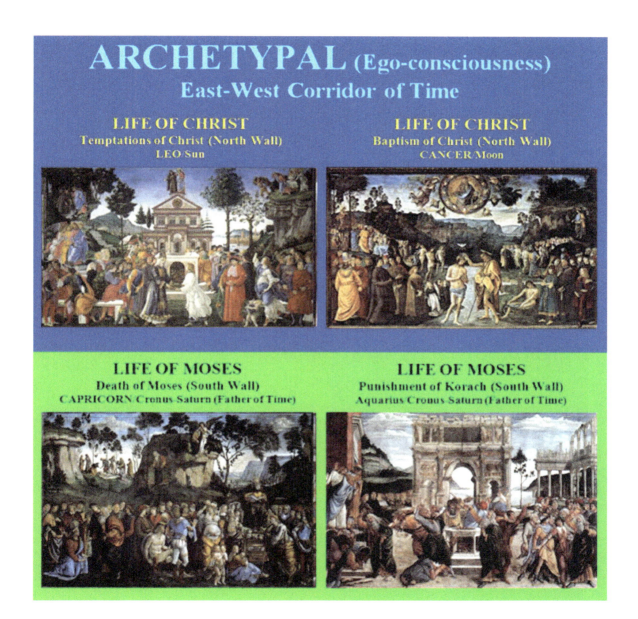

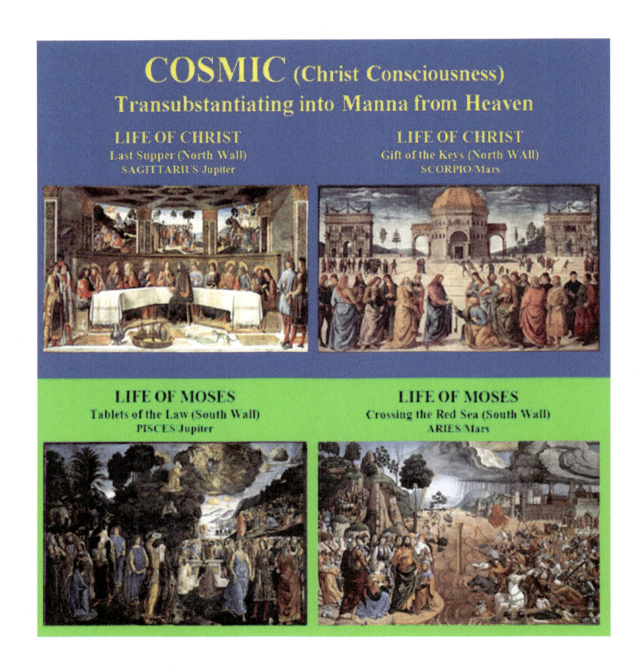

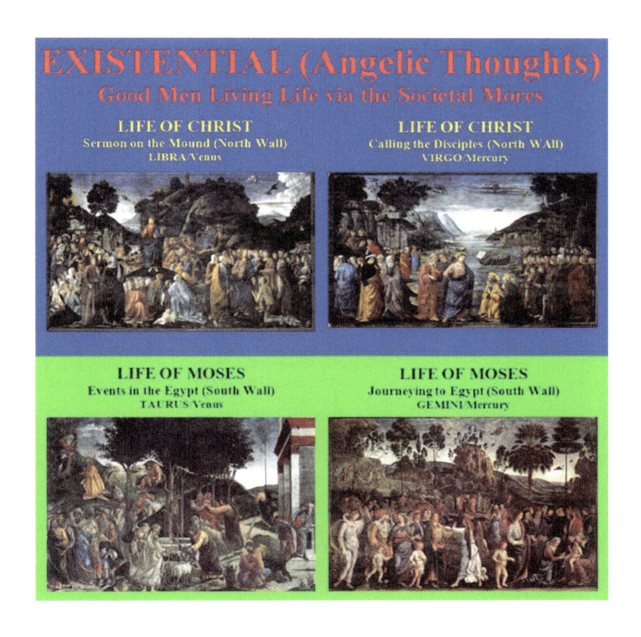

2. Both the east and west walls are symbolically one wall.
   a. The west wall, prior to Michelangelo frescoing the Last Judgment had two nativity frescoes that aligned with the frescoes in the Life of Moses and the Life of Christ; thus, again the phrase, *"In the beginning"* is envisage again via these birth scenes (see images below).
   b. Also before Michelangelo destroyed the west wall, there were 32-popes around the four walls interlacing with sixteen windows. The four popes that were wiped off the west wall were the first two popes and the last two popes pointing to the Alpha and the Omega. Jesus Christ is called the Alpha and the Omega (beginning and end). The 32-popes symbolized the 32-Elohyms in the first chapter of Genesis analogous to the 32-paths of the Kabbalistic Tree of Life, which represents the numerics and the alphabetic nature of the Hebrew Alphabet in both the heavens and the earth. It is through the transept that each letter of the alphabet represents the heavens and the earth that are separated by God: spiritual forces of creation.
   c. There were two windows and two lunettes also erased from the wall that, I believe, augment each other.
      i. The two lunettes had seven of the ancestors of Christ in their fold that points to the birth of consciousness just the first letter of Genesis: BETH ב, which has the Gematria value of 412, which totals to seven (7) and that again points to the beginning. These seven ancestors of Christ added to the thirty-three (33) others totals to forty (40), which symbolizes the waters of creation that the soul has to rise above.
      ii. The two (2) windows symbolizes the beheading of BETH ב, which the number two (2) symbolizes ego-consciousness. That leaves fourteen other windows that points to the fourteenth Hebrew letter NUN נ[5], which symbolizes that a cardinal becomes 'a faithful servant' when he is elected to be the pope; however, all sixteen windows pouring in the sunlight points to the sixteenth letter of the Hebrew coder called AYIN ע[6], which points to vision that is well symbolized on the National Mall in Washington DC (chapter sixteen). The light shining through the sixteen windows symbolizes the vision that separates the heavens and the earth. The LIGHT coming out of the DARKNESS through the sixteen windows symbolizes God's Ambiance: Christ consciousness.
   d. The east walls have two frescos that depict the Ascent of Christ from the dead and the battle over the body of Moses.
      i. There can be no battle over the body of Christ; because, it is ethereal. The Eucharist is not a wafer host; rather, it is the Ambiance of God that is entertained in experience of a spiritually contented life; however, the life of Christ cannot be clung to as if one is eternally connected to it. The initiate has to daily partake of the Eucharist to maintain his or her

---

[5] https://www.youtube.com/watch?v=MynXTRENj70
[6] https://thehebrewclub.wordpress.com/2013/01/02/ayin-the-16th-hebrew-letter/

spiritually contented life. Symbolically, showering and putting on clean cloths daily or cleaning the house daily is analogous to continuously searching for knowledge of God.

    1. Christ can never die per se; however, when ego-consciousness raises its ugly head as in the case of Judas Iscariot Christ dies in that psyche insofar as his spiritual forces, symbolized by the Quadrivium is buried beneath the alphabetic of the Torah. Until the mastaba (Earth – creation mound) returns on the third day of creation (on the third day of creation in the first chapter of Genesis Christ rose again from the dead) Christ cannot rise from the dead in the psyche of that individual. Rising from the dead Christ returns to his throne in the Vesica Piscis.

    ii. The battle over the body of Moses is the continuous encounter with good and evil (devil on one shoulder and an angel on the other). The death of Moses is not physical death it is the death of ego-consciousness and the birth of Christ consciousness. The three temptations that those that obtain Christ consciousness endure persist throughout the duration of life.

e. THE LAST JUDGMENT has its own Alpha and Omega symbolism and that is envisaged in the spaces where the two lunettes use to harbor the seven ancestors of Christ. The lunette on the northeast side has a 'column' being escorted into heaven that, I believe, symbolizes the mystical marriage of Boaz and Jachin, which would be "the beginning". The second lunette area in the southwest area symbolizes the ascent of the cross; thus, the 'column' and the 'cross' symbolizes the "Alpha and the Omega".

Symbolically, the Last Judgment is essentially asking the same question that all the other three walls are asking. How do you believe in God? From a worldly perspective that is a rhetorical question; because, it cannot be answered verbally in the vernacular. It is answered in how the initiate lives out his or her life in thought, word and deed. Literally, that is precisely how the initiate prays to God through his or her thoughts, words and deeds.

    i. **LUNETTES**: do you believe in God through the ancestor of Christ?

    ii. **POPES**: do you believe in God through the mythoi of Mary, Jesus and the communion of saints?

    iii. **WINDOWS**: do you believe in God through nature?

    iv. **FRESCOS**: do you believe in God through guru and the fabrication of history or the exhortations of heroes and great men or are you enamored by any philosophy imaginable?

    v. **GRAVES AND DESENT INTO HELL**: do you believe in ghost and spirits and all kinds of superstitions?

    vi. **OR DO YOU GO DIRECTLY TO GOD FOR GUIDANCE?**

MICHELANGELO descent from frescoing the ceiling of the Sistine Chapel to paint the LAST JUDGMENT was because he had frescoed a commentary on the ceiling that was symbolically symbolized below the popes. Michelangelo mirror imaged the ceiling in the image and likeness of what was below similar to how God mystically created Adam into His own image and likeness. The Last Judgment is obviously a reemphasizing and clarification of what the walls were mystically conveying.

The mosaics in the floor of the Sistine Chapel were laid out as the foundation to the basic overall theme of what was to become the symbolism frescoed on the four walls and ceiling. The Church's artists had perfectly laid out the foundational plan to the overall symbolic design in the symbolism of the floor as to how they were to accomplish their task. It will be difficult for modernity to consider that the symbolism in the mosaics of the floor of the Sistine Chapel is the keys to understanding the esotericism of the entire chapel. The fresco on the north wall depicting the Gift of the Keys to Peter symbolizing Scorpio, which represents the first verse of Genesis especially the first word of Genesis: BERESHITH and in the background of that fresco, is the gazebo symbolizing the mystically hidden Sistine Chapel in an octagon shape. The Gift of the Keys symbolizes the keys to understanding the overall symbolism of the chapel. The six cycles on the floor leading up to half the chapel symbolizes the word BERESHITH (in the beginning), which represents the Golden Key (Sun) and the nine cycles in the second half of the Sistine Chapel's mosaics on the floor symbolizes the Kamea of Saturn represents the Silver Key (Moon). These two images per se symbolize the Vesica Piscis: i.e. the confluence of spirituality and materiality: God/Man Christ. This will be discussed further below.

The Kamea of Saturn (earth) discussed in the second verse of Genesis is without form and void and this is the prototypical generic paradigm, which was initially define in the first word of Genesis: BERESHITH (six concentric circles). The entire Sistine Chapel's building and artwork rises and is conceptually based upon this foundational generic paradigm, which is laid out in the first word of Genesis: BERESHITH. The reason that the word "moved' is used in the second verses of Genesis is also translated as "pouted or brooded" is; for the reason that, the moment that the mastaba (mound of Creation - earth – Kamea of Saturn) enters the TIME/SPACE continuum it is concretized and Time has passed it by; thus, the mourning process (pouting, brooding) begins; because, the initiate is again seeking LIGHT. The initiate cannot live life without seeking the LIGHT. There is no resting upon one's laurels.

1. First two days of creation symbolizes the TIME/SPACE CONTINUUM and this is why the first two days of creation are symbolized as Capricorn and Aquarius, which is governed by Saturn: Father of Time; for the reason that there can be no time without space nor space without time.
   a. Gen. 1:3-5; this first day of creation is all about TIME: "dividing the LIGHT from the DARKNESS".
   b. Gen. 1:6-8; this second day of creation is all about SPACE: "separating the waters above (Time/Space) the 'firmament (Vesica Piscis – Garden of Eden)' from the waters beneath (phantasmagoria of the psyche) the firmament".
   c. These two days of creation are shown to symbolize a single Minor LIGHT Chakra; because it has sixty-nine (69) words.
2. The mastaba: mound of creation (Earth):
   a. Gen. 1:9-13; this third day of creation is about the Vesica Piscis (Garden of Eden), which rose up out of the waters above the heavens from the waters beneath the heavens.
   b. This third day of creation has sixty-nine (69) words: one Minor LIGHT Chakra
3. Two great luminaries give LIGHT to the Earth (this is another sleight of hand maneuver: i.e. wording); for the reason that, the Sun per se and the Moon per se are not the two great luminaries that give LIGHT to the Earth. Neither the Sun (ego-consciousness - Jachin) nor the Moon (unconscious mind - Boaz) have the autonomous power to give spiritual LIGHT to the soul (soul). Boaz and Jachin have to be mystically married (Christ consciousness) to obtain the spiritual ability to do that.

   Earth symbolizes the Soul: it is not the psyche per se; though, when it becomes ego-centric it splits into the psyche: ego-consciousness (Sun) and the unconscious mind (Moon) and this is why they are not allowed to enter the Church: sacred space until they are mystically married.

Ego-consciousness (Sun - Jachin) and the unconscious mind (Moon - Boaz) not being mystically married would be analogous to the brain splitting in half where only one half controls the entire life of the initiate. Existentially that is what is going on in modernity; for the reason that, 99.999...% of the population of the world does not know of the unconscious mind; thus, only egocentrism reigns supreme as the world's tyrannical dictator.

  a. Gen. 1:14-18; this fourth day of creation is all about God and the Trinity. God per se cannot come into manifested creation; however, when the spiritual forces (God) outside of creation it does cross the east-west corridor of time: i.e. His son Christ instantaneously transubstantiates into the psychic life: ego-consciousness and the unconscious mind of a worthy initiate (Good Man), which per se become Christ via the Trinity.

    i. COSMIC: Christ consciousness: mystical union (marriage) of ego-consciousness (Kamea of the Sun cubed: $6^3 = 216$) and the unconscious mind (Kamea of the Moon cubed: $9^3 = 729$):

      1. When the Kamea of the Sun is subtracted from the Kamea of the Moon the quotient is 513, which is the transposition of 153: Vesica Piscis: thus, momentary nanosecond by nanosecond the Vesica Piscis is in play and this is why the culling out of the spiritual LIGHT from the DARKNESS is never-ending and it is called ETERNAL LIFE.

    ii. ARCHETYPAL: Unconscious Mind mystically married (greater luminary to rule the day):

      1. Kamea of the Moon cubed: $9^3 = 729$, which harbors all other Magic Squares. Moon Light is permanent; because, it symbolizes all creation.

    iii. EXISTENTIAL: Ego-consciousness mystically married (lesser to rule the night) (lesser luminary to rule the night):

      1. Kamea of the Sun cubed: $6^3 = 216$, which is the LIGHT culled out of the DARKNESS. Sun Light is temporary; because, it is separated by the Earth's terminator illustrating how transitory sunlight is.

    iv. This fourth day of creation has sixty-nine (69) words: one Minor LIGHT Chakra.

  b. The first four days of creation have three Minor LIGHT Chakras, which totals to two-hundred and seven (207) words, which is the Gematria value of the word 'LIGHT' in both the first and fourth days of creation. The seven LIGHT Chakras will be discussed later in the work.

  c. From an iconoclastic perspective these dynamics of the Sun and Moon would appear to be pagans worshipping the Sun or the Moon. This is brought out to give an example of why iconoclastic thought is limited to bare assumptions.

Before continuing on to the EXISTENTIAL pattern in the Sistine Chapel's overall plan it must be fully understood that the frescoes depicting the Life of Christ and the Life of Moses were deliberately set up to mirror-image each other. Christ the LIGHT of God crosses the east-west corridor of Time and then that LIGHT: Eucharist (wafer host) is transubstantiated into the life of the initiate. In fact I provided the images of the Nativity of Jesus Christ and the Finding of Moses and both these images have a comment, from the Vatican, explaining what their purpose was to provide an Old Testament or New Testament to the other side of the Altar Wall. Inferentially these first two, lost frescoes, can be used logically to reason that the frescoing paradigm continues to ensue throughout the remainder of the frescoes on the north and south walls; however, that is another sleight of hand maneuver via artwork. Both the lost frescoes that were on the west wall depicting the nativities of Jesus and Moses and the two frescoes on the east wall are aligned to each other it is only reasonably logical from an iconoclastic point of view, without even thinking about it, that the other six frescoes in the Life of Christ and the Life of Moses would also be aligned to each other. This of course from iconography's point of view is totally illogical; for the reason that, the east-west corridor of Time, which the east and west walls and the nave and the apse of the Sistine

Chapel symbolize, have nothing whatsoever to do with the Life of Christ on the north wall crossing the east-west corridor of Time transubstantiating into the Life of Moses.

Because the Sistine Chapel is built according to the measurements of Solomon's Temple in an elongated rectangular format: three squared it literally skews the alignment of the frescoes on the north and south walls to an iconoclastic way of thinking. Like the panel in the ceiling depicting God Creating Adam into His Image: God coming down from on high to Adam that is on a slanted hill. It is as if that slanted fresco scene appears to be as if the Scales of Libra/Anubis symbolically illustrates that materialism: Life of Moses outweighs spirituality: Life of Christ. The frescoes on the north and south walls seem to have been set up to mirror-image that slanted idea: i.e. God coming down from on high to the south where Adam is lounging.

However, realistically the entire chapel is ethereally set up in the circular pattern of Astrology: i.e. twelve (12) zodiacal signs, which aligns each of the frescos in the Life of Christ with those frescoes depicting the Life of Moses. The Zodiac is a symbolic image of the brain and its four cerebral lobes (see chapter fourteen). It is as if, and it is what mostly likely did transpire over time, the ancient sages in their mystical artistic endeavors canonized their knowledge of the mystical universe by creating and using the zodiacal images to symbolically represent the cerebral lobes.

If the initiate was to go online to the Internet sites that give information on the cerebral lobes and the pineal gland and obtain a basic understanding of the dynamics of the brain he or she will have a greater confidence in obtaining validation to his or her research. I believe that the pineal gland is what develops the brain in the universal manner it is structured. Think about that for a moment.

Apparently a non-intelligent spiritual being is about to be placed into the phantasmagoria of a sentient psyche it knows, absolutely, nothing about. It is born of parents that are going through the same life cycle's process; however, the parents know nothing whatsoever about the world they live in and they do not know they should be explaining the dynamics of the world to their child. To accompany this chaos the brain of the baby is literally programmed to teach the new born baby about the spiritual powers (God) of the universe and the child does not know anything whatsoever about that systemic educational system that is available to him or her if he or she could only find out where it is located. In addition to this milieu the world seems to be completely separate from the individual and the child has no idea that it is his or her psyche that projects the universe into existence based solely upon the structure of its own brain and the child knows utterly nothing of this psychic phenomenon. This projecting the universe onto the blank abyss of the cinematic screen of the psyche inferentially is saying that the psyche does know everything about the process of the creation of the universe; yet, another part of the psyche is inferentially saying it knows nothing about it whatsoever.

In addition to all this those ancient sages in antiquity that have discovered the truth about the psyche's universal generic paradigm codified it into the dynamics of their literature, artworks and architecture in all times and climes without telling anybody what they did. In every sense the individual (BETH ב) that is completely ignorant of his surrounding is literally inundated and surrounded by PEI פ (Mouth of God). It is as if the individual is eternally a child that never-ever grows out of his or her adolescence years (archetypal) until he begins to seek the answers to life (existential) and only becomes an adult when he or she gains Christ consciousness.

If I am interpreting life properly, the Frontal Lobes, which symbolize absolute ignorance. That limitation is necessary to codify the LIGHT into the outer world otherwise the LIGHT would be an utter tsunami causing insanity. Over the course of Time and the accumulation of truthful knowledge about the WORD OF GOD Christ consciousness will harmoniously sync the psyche into a mystical marriage.

The ancients learned that the soul lives out its entire life between the ears. This is inferred in the symbolism codified to their sacred scriptures, literature, artworks, monuments and architecture. Life is not live out beyond the skin enveloped for there is nothing beyond it especially not the body or the skin envelope. The psyche radiates its thought: i.e. psychic life onto the blank abyss analogous to a cinematic screen. The whole world is a projection of the phantasmagoria of the psyche, which is essentially the soul learning about its own psyche and what the principles (spiritual laws, rules and regulation) are that governs the dynamics of its activities.

It is in viewing the Sistine Chapel by studying its artwork through the lenses of Astrology and the Cerebral Lobes that the initiate will obtain much more clarity about his soul and psyche in relationship to God's Ambiance. Think of the Sistine Chapel in a circular mode as Golgotha (place of the skull). The whole chapel's four walls symbolize the skull and how its internal dynamics work. In other words the Sistine Chapel symbolizes the internal Temple of God. This is precisely how the Capitol Building in Washington DC is setup to represent Golgotha (see chapter sixteen). Freemasonry uses different symbolism than the Roman Catholic Church; however, both their artistic endeavors illustrates that they are conveying the same mystical concept.

The reader should study all of the fresco images in detail. There is a beautiful online site: Sistine Chapel Art Walk[7] that will list all the events taking place in each fresco and below there is an image that the reader should study called the PARTRIARCHAL CROSS[8] to see the correlation between the frescoes on the north wall aligning with the frescos on the south wall in relationship to Astrology and the Cerebral Lobes. This may appear to be too intellectual to understand; however, it is only one science's symbolic way of thought mirror-imaged into other symbolism and mythologies. These disparate ways of expressing the divine WORD OF GOD is so that the esoteric science, which cloths the WORD OF GOD will be greatly simplified and clarified through a number of examples. The more the mystical generic paradigm of mythology is understood the easier it is to read it in other cultures and in one's daily activities.

Most people do not sacrifice their Time out of their fully scheduled day to do this kind of religious research. Those that do sacrifice their Time on the altar of the Existential Cross or the Cosmic Cross will come to realize that they will benefit immensely through the gifts of blessings in many ways. By sacrificing their precious Time in searching for knowledge of God initiates will benefit in ways they could never possibly imagine or obtain financially from their employer or through any other means via their own volition. This may sound ridiculous and nonsensical; nonetheless, it is what it is. The spiritual search for God allows for the worthy initiate to become content with life for he or she will have what they need not necessarily what they want. There is no greater gift then a contented life.

The next pattern to be discussed will connect the Life of Christ through the zodiacal signs and the Sun Signs of Astrology with the Life of Moses by demonstrating how Christ consciousness crossing the east-west corridor of time transubstantiates into the Life of Moses.

The mythologies of other cultures, I believe, were deliberately used to create the mythoi of Christianity; for the reason that, they serve a dual purpose: i.e. one is to explain explicitly the esoteric nature of the Christian teachings and the second purpose is to create biases, prejudices and preconceive notions with those that have attention deficit disorder, which is practically 99.999…% of the laity. Why give the laity false information? For the reason that, those that have attention deficit disorder really do not care about anything other than their own ego-centrism. People with attention deficit disorder are willing to accept and/or believe anything from the charismatic religious or academic lecturer or half-truths from news reporter or the idiocy that comes out of the mouths of radio or television commentators, etc., etc. Believe it or not the Supreme Court of the United States calls this insanity: i.e. Satire.

History is a fantasy for it is written by people that have certain religious, political or personal agendas, which are preciously housed in library of books full of biases, prejudices and preconceived notions. How is anybody to rise above that tsunami of such nonsense? More than three and a half decades ago I, personally, came to the conclusion that the only way to read history was as if it was mythology written esoterically to tell religious truths. I personally dismiss recent history going back two hundred or more years; because, so much of it has to endure the test of time and then treated as if it is mythology.

Astrology is condemned by the Roman Catholic Church or so they broadcast globally as loud as they can; but, secretly and esoterically Catholicism is all about astrology. Mythological disinformation is not a religious lie. It may be a secular materialistic lie; but, not a lie against the WORD OF GOD.

---

[7] http://triggerpit.com/2010/11/21/sistine-chapel-incredible-christian-art-walk-through/
[8] https://en.wikipedia.org/wiki/Patriarchal_cross

Just as symbols, numbers and the alphabet are tools for writing Astrology's zodiacal signs and sun signs are graphic pictorial tools that bring up visions of whole mythologies that would take volumes to regurgitate. The twelve zodiacal signs pair off into six sets and they are mated throughout; however, each set is additionally mated to a zodiacal sign across the east-west corridor of Time: ARCHETYPAL: going from east to west creating the Hebrew letter BETH ב as does COSMIC: going from north across the east-west corridor of Time to the south also confined in the Hebrew letter BETH ב and then there is EXISTENTIAL: going south across the east-west corridor of Time to the north again in the Hebrew letter BETH ב. The first two chapters discussed the letters PEI פ and BETH ב and how PEIפ continuously releases (not chase) Sun across the elliptic. What this symbolism demonstrably demonstrates is that culling out of the LIGHT whether it is Cosmic, Existential or Archetypal the Sun (ego-consciousness) continuously writes the Book of Life for the soul and this is why the Hebrew writing goes from east to west; because, writing symbolizes the east-west corridor of Time: symbolically Antiquity's Hall of Records.

    c. **THE THIRD PATERN is EXISTENTIAL,** which is about the Life of Moses laid out in the six frescos on the south wall. This pattern also breaks up into the three distinct prototypes denoting the Cosmic, Archetypal and the Existential way of life.

        i. ARCHETYPAL

            1. Moses Testament and Death (Capricorn - Earth)

                a. Capricorn symbolizes the Father of Time: i.e. Saturn and the moment LIGHT (Archetypal) comes into the world it is concretized (eaten and devoured). In other words Time destroys that LIGHT (Fire) by concretizing it via Earth: Kamea of Saturn (mastaba – mound of creation). The new LIGHT has to be continuously culled out of the DARKNESS. Jupiter ends up defeating Cronus/Saturn not by continuously coming into the world, which is a given; but, rather it defeat Time by pulling the initiate into the milieu of God's Ambiance.

                    The psyche is eternally young and never-ever ages; however, this is not what is being discussed here. In the outer world the body ages and so does memory. When a normal person researches it takes him or her enormous amounts of time to acclimate to a subject matter; however, those that have obtained Christ consciousness are literally given information about subject matters from the Holy Spirit he or she knows nothing about. Even those subjects that are not known about; but, if data needs to be studied such subjects (or information out of those subjects) are almost instantaneously understood with a minimal amount of research.

                b. This fresco correlates with Leo – Fire: i.e. Three Temptations of Christ (Frontal lobe): i.e. the Burning Bush; though, the Burning Bush (Bereshith) is in the fresco depicting the Scenes in the Life of Moses. The Burning Bush symbolizes the Initiatic Visionary Experience, which makes a Good Man into a Better Man. This is the materialistic death of Moses and his spiritual birth: *"in the beginning"*.

                    i. Leo (Moses) symbolizes ego-consciousness taking off his shoes; because, he is on sacred ground (mastaba – creation mound) showing respect to God, which would be the same as genuflecting in the Roman Catholic Church.

                c. Capricorn symbolizing Time that feeds the Gods; because, Time allows the psyche via the occipital lobes to envisage its own thoughts through images. Capricorn down to Leo symbolizes one-half of the east-west-corridor of Time: i.e. status quo.

2. Punishment of Korach (Aquarius - Air)

    a. Korach (Occipital lobe) also represent the Father of Time Cronus/Saturn via space; however, in this respect Korach symbolizes the unconscious mind: i.e. trying to defeat the status quo.

    b. Punishment of Korach aligns to Cancer – Water (Frontal lobe): i.e. unconscious mind: i.e. The Baptism of Christ, which is the second-half of the east-west-corridor of time.

        In the fresco of the Punishment of Korach is a Baptismal Fount, which is in the shape of an octagon: Kamea of Saturn, which is the altar of Time. In fact this is the image of the Baptismal Fount in Christian Churches symbolizes in the mosaics on the floor as the Kamea of Saturn in the second half of the Sistine Chapel.

        Baptism symbolizes collectively the family, religious and societal mores that the child is subject to be educated into or baptized into the ways of the world. Notice how most godfathers and godmothers at Baptisms rarely if ever teach their godchildren religion. Actually, religious teachings are left to the godchildren's true godfathers (Holy Spirit) and godmothers (angelic thoughts).

        The sands of the deserts is liken to an ocean of water and for Korach to be buried in the sands is analogous to the unconscious mind sinking (returning) back to its proper level. The content of the unconscious mind cannot become conscious unless the initiate (Korach) can rise up above the din and clamor of the world. Most people do not have the religious stamina to do so.

    c. A mistaken interpretation would be to think because there is a Roman arch in the fresco of the Punishment of Korach that it aligns to the Gift of the Keys directly across the room on the north wall, which has two Roman arches. The gazebo octagon temple in the Gift of the Keys symbolizes the Initiatic Visionary Experience destroying the east-west (both arches) corridor of time. Sleigh of Hands maneuvers like this will tend to bring about false interpretations: misdirecting the lackadaisical: people with attention deficit disorder.

    d. Water like the deluge (tsunami) in Noah age will put out the Burning Bush if one allows it. This is the problem with Baptism. Baptism is not a sprinkling of water on an infant's brow. True Baptism is to have your psyche inundated and surrounded by all the teachings of one religion and that onslaught of knowledge is truly equal to that of a tsunami; for the reason that, a great deal of the laity do not sacrifices their *whole hearts, minds, time, finances and resources* in trying to understanding what those teachings are saying; rather, they prefer to listen to the 'charismatic know nothing experts' that lectures year after year from the pulpit never-ever saying anything whatsoever that is worthwhile listening to. True spirituality comes through self-study with the guidance of God.

    The east-west corridor of Time can continue on for the entire duration of life without any benefits whatsoever received from the spiritual forces of creations. The souls that endure these trials and tribulations in life have no idea that such spiritual benefits are at all possible. Capricorn and Aquarius are governed by the Sun Sign Saturn, which creates a container outside the Holy of Holies: Temple of God and each one of these signs flank the corridor of Time down to their corresponding zodiacal signs (not

Sun Signs: Sun and Moon) Sun and Moon: Leo and Cancer respectively. This gets confusing because the Sun and Moon zodiacal signs are governed by the Sun Signs Sun and Moon respectively. Notice that zodiacal signs of the Sun and Moon: Leo (Jachin) and Cancer (Boaz) respectively are outside of the Temple of God; for the reason that, they are eternally at odds with each other: ego-consciousness (Sun) and the unconscious mind (Moon) are eternally at war with each other. Both of these warring factions via their biases, prejudices and preconceived notions build up flanking walls creating tunnel vision that prevent them from every knowing that there are spiritual forces in creation. They are both totally oblivious of that fact; thus, PEI פ is everlastingly releasing the Sun along the elliptic, which writes a true unambiguous message about the psychic conditions of a soul's life to the spiritual forces of creation.

Boaz (Moon) and Jachin (Sun) are columns or towers (Chartres Cathedral) outside the Temple of God; because, they exist in Time (Cronus/Saturn: Father of Time); thus, illustrating that Boaz and Jachin and TIME are one and the same. Now go inside the Sistine Chapel where Boaz (Cancer) and Jachin (Leo) are mystically married and are symbolized on the west (altar) wall; whereas, Aquarius and Capricorn are on the west (entrance) wall governed by Cronus/Saturn, which illustrates that the east and west wall symbolically represent the same space; but, on a mystical level where there is neither Time nor Space: i.e. TIMELESSNESS.

Do not misinterpret what I am saying here. The twelve signs of the Zodiac and the seven Sun Sign are not disparate categories completely isolated from each other. All twelve signs of the Zodiac and seven Sun Signs tell portions of the missive God commissioned them to convey concerning the Initiatic Visionary Experience and they work harmoniously together to ensure that that experience is maintained. For example when the individual goes down the corridor of Time with his tunnel vision blinders on it is Mercury the messenger of the Gods that transmits the soul's missive to the spiritual forces of creation: i.e. God. Basically, going down the corridor of Time towards the west wall where the Last Judgment is house is essentially the soul judging itself every moment of its existence.

These three patterns symbolize Heaven (Cosmic), Purgatory (Existential) and Hell (Archetypal). A person can live in the realm of the Archetypal obeying societal mores and abiding by his or her religious beliefs for his or her entire life; however, this does not make that person a 'Good Man' that Freemasonry would want to make a 'Better Man'. What the east-west corridor of Time is saying via the Baptism of Christ (Cancer) and the Temptations of Christ (Leo) is that each soul coming into the world is going to be drown in societal mores: family, religious and secular rules and regulation and during that time that person will be tested as to his or her true aspiration in life. Not many people can past the test of Satan: ego-consciousness. The Temptations of Christ pretty well laid out the entire human perspective as to Job Skills, being a Religious Leader or a Ruler of the World. That pretty well tempts all mankind collectively or individually as to what he or she would want to do in life; however, Christ's answer to Satan explicitly points out that there is a higher purpose for life. Notice it was not until Christ rose out of the waters of Jordan that God declared Jesus to be his Beloved Son. It is written that Abraham Lincoln said, *the best way to test a man's character is to give him power*. The fact that Jesus Christ rose up out of the waters of Jordan and passed the test of Satan this indicates that someone (generic paradigmatic human) in the archetypal realm received the Initiatic Visionary Experience and he or she was not founding wanting.

The Sistine Chapel is all about the dawn of the Initiatic Visionary Experience and what the initiate can and should learn about it. There is so much more to these four zodiacal signs: Capricorn, Aquarius, Leo and Cancer. The artwork in the Sistine Chapel is spiritually and perfectly frescoed on an esoteric level via iconography (symbolism); however, the frescoes per se speak the language of exotericism: iconoclasm (history: i.e. literal minded thinking). It is because of iconoclasm that the laity cannot envisage astrology in the artwork laid out in the Sistine Chapel.

In normal everyday life the average person walks down the corridor of Time with tunnel vision: i.e. biases, prejudices and preconceived notions and that person's peripheral vision is confined to his or her tunnel vision. Essentially, the average person is saying through his or her own thoughts, words and deeds, *"my way or the highway"*: ego-consciousness reigns supreme.

Remember that the Sistine Chapel is esoterically symbolized in a zodiacal cycle; thus, its easily envisaged that Capricorn and Aquarius (Occipital lobes), which represents the dawn of Time goes straight down the corridor of Time to align with Cancer and Leo (Frontal lobes). The west-wall is symbolically the outer world and Leo (Sun – ego-consciousness) and Cancer (Moon – unconscious mind) are symbolic of the two windows that Michelangelo took off the altar wall. In fact Leo and Cancer symbolically are represented by the eyes of the skull. It is only through the psyche: ego-consciousness and the unconscious mind that the individual has the power to envisage his own thoughts, words and deeds. It is the occipital lobes that give the psyche the power to see; however, if ego-consciousness and the unconscious mind are not in synch working harmoniously together entering a sacred space then they would merely be living life iconoclastically. From this perspective Boaz (Moon) and Jachin (Sun) the two columns outside the Masonic Order Temple would not be mystically married; thus, they would not be allowed into the Temple.

Another very important nuance that comes out of the frescoes in the Life of Christ mirror-imaging the frescoes in the Life of Moses is that the mirror-imaging process, which is more clearly shown on the Sistine Chapel's ceiling fresco in God creating Adam in his own image, the 48-cherubs are paired off mirror-imaging each other and the 24-bronze figures are paired off mirror-imaging each other, inaugurates the Initiatic Visionary Experience. Without this mirror-imaging process Christ consciousness cannot be achieved. This mirror-imaging process will be discussed later when it is shown how the first word of Genesis: BERESHITH was created in relationship to the development of the Genesis Formula.

Whereas, when the initiate receives the Initiatic Visionary Experience he or she obtains another set of eyes, which symbolizes the third eye: i.e. Christ consciousness. This is beautifully illustrated in the symbolism in Washington DC. Right on the westside of the Capitol Building on 1st street NW there are two circular monuments: Peace Monument[9] and Garfield Monument[10] and that look like eyeballs looking down Pennsylvania and Maryland Avenues inferring peripheral vision beyond the limited scopes of tunnel vision symbolized by the National Mall. These two monuments symbolize the harmonious relationship between the unconscious mind and ego-consciousness: third eye – mystical vision: living in the Garden of Eden. President Garfield was a general in the Civil War and he was adamantly against slavery; whereas, on the other side of the Lincoln Memorial there are two other monuments: The Arts of War and the Arts of Peace[11], which I believe symbolizes physical vision in the material world eternally at odd with each other: i.e. multiple arts of war and multiple arts of peace. I discuss this in chapter sixteen; however, I speak about these two sets of monuments here to emphasize that both tunnel vision (iconoclasm) and Christ consciousness (iconography) are two diametrically opposite ways of consciously viewing the world.

There are two transepts that cross the east-west corridor of time, which changes the initiate's whole outlook on life: Cosmic and Existential. Actually, it could be a number of transepts to elucidate a number of ideas and/or concepts. In Washington DC; though, there is one transept, the inference is that there are twenty-two symbolizing all the letters of the Hebrew coder.

The first transept in the Sistine Chapel that crosses over the east-west corridor of Time symbolizes Christ consciousness: i.e. walking in the Garden of Eden with God as the initiate's only confidant. The second transept is the Existential where the Good Man is worthy to receive the Initiatic Visionary Experience opposing those that are determined to maintain the status quo; however, these two transepts are basically one and the same seeing that realistically the WORD OF GOD first transept cannot be envisaged in the materialistic world. These two transepts symbolize the Vesica Piscis: the God/Man Christ, which is the harmonious relationship between the material and the spiritual. This is why the Patriarchal Cross cannot be envisage and only the elongated cross is viewed throughout the Church's symbolism.

The first two days of creation make no sense unless the reader understands that "God was creating Hell before He separated the beginning and ends of the heavens and the beginning and ends of the earth (Saint Augustine: i.e. Confessions)". I say this because I am about to introduce Virgo holding the Scales

---

[9] http://www.aoc.gov/capitol-grounds/peace-monument
[10] http://www.aoc.gov/capitol-grounds/garfield-monument
[11] https://en.wikipedia.org/wiki/The_Arts_of_War_and_The_Arts_of_Peace

of Libra. In the first two chapters of Genesis Virgo mystically holds the Scales of Libra (see chapter nineteen).

    ii. EXISTENTIAL

        1. Events in the life of Moses (Taurus - Earth)

            a. These fresco scenes show Moses as an ego-centric individual.

                i. Moses kills the Egyptian and then buried him, which, I believe, symbolizes the Sphinx, which is analogous and symbolic to the Egyptian religion. Burying the Sphinx is similar to burying the symbols and numerics of the lettering of the sacred scriptures. Yes, the head of the letter is visible on the surface storyline; however the blood (symbols) and water (numerics) that came out of the side of Jesus when he was pierced in the side, while on the CROSS, was soaked up and summarily dismissed by the iconoclastic mentality if they even knew of the existence of the symbolism and the numerics that are in the Hebrew coder.

                    The Israelites could not acclimate to the Egyptian's religious way of life because of egocentrism; thus, Moses became the personification of all the Israelites; though, the Israelites knew how to become religious. This is interpreted from Joseph reign as the overlord of Egypt. It is as if that knowledge, that allowed Joseph to reign over the Egyptian Empire, was handed down to the Israelites from Abraham that came out of the land of Ur, whom religion was similar to the Egyptians.

                ii. Look at a map of where the land of Midian is and the great distance Moses had to travel to get there. Moses crossed the Red Sea, traversed the entire land of the Sinai Peninsula and then cross the Gulf of Aqaba to get to the land of Midian (modern day Saudi Arabia). It is as if Moses had an agenda in mind long before he killed the Egyptian (Sphinx) and started out on his forty-year quest. This was the time that his ego-centrism was driving him.

                iii. Moses' egocentric ways in this fresco chases away the Shepherds that were harassing the daughter of Jethro. This is very much how a Bull (Taurus) like the Minotaur[12] acts when it sees something moving (changing). Egocentrism is about the status quo. This is what the maze[13] (religious and societal mores) that the Minotaur is imprisoned in symbolizes: a multipath or numerous choices to be made: i.e. being self-centered independent. A maze is not a labyrinth[14] (one-way path) to the goal: i.e. symbolic of slavery.

                iv. Moses marries a daughter of Jethro. Shortly after this marriage Moses has the incident with the Burning Bush and takes his shoes off; because, it is on sacred ground. Taking off his shoe shows Moses has learned to deflate his ego-

---

[12] http://www.history.com/topics/ancient-history/greek-mythology/videos/origins-of-the-minotaur
[13] https://en.wikipedia.org/wiki/Maze
[14] https://en.wikipedia.org/wiki/Labyrinth

centrism. This is most likely because of the marriage and the teachings of Jethro the priest of Midian.

    v. This fresco lineup with the Sermon on the Mound; because, Christ is pointing out who gets the blessings; whereas, across the east-west corridor of time Moses would not get a blessing in the state of ego-centrism. In the Sermon on Mound in his discussing the beatitudes Christ is esoterically imitating Virgo holding up the Scales of Libra: i.e. Blessing on one scale and ego-centrism on the other scale.

2. Moses journeying to Egypt (Gemini - Air)

    a. These scenes in the Life of Moses show him focused on the mission that God gave him.

        i. It would appear as if this fresco was put in the wrong position on the south wall seeing that the Journey to Egypt was after the earlier life scenes in Moses' life.

        ii. While journeying into Egypt Moses would want to find companions that would work with him to accomplish his mission; this fresco in the Life of Moses mystically lines up with the fresco in the Life of Christ on the north wall: i.e. Calling of the Disciples; whereas, Moses would be choosing Good Men and then trying to make them Better Men; whereas, Christ takes those Better Men and gives them the Initiatic Visionary Experience.

The Life of Moses in the Sistine Chapel are interesting frescoes; for the reason that, iconoclastic priests that knows nothing about the esotericism imbued into their religion teachings or literal-minded art historians interpret the frescoes in the Life of Moses[15] according to the frescoes in the Life of Christ that are directly on the opposite south wall. It has already been demonstrably demonstrated that both sets of frescoes are misaligned on the north and south walls; because, the chapel is built in a rectangular shape rather than in a zodiacal cycle.

    iii. COSMIC

        1. Crossing the Red Sea (Aries - Fire)

            a. Moses crossing the Red Sea mystically syncs with the Gift to the Keys to Peter in the life of Christ. The layout of the fresco of Christ giving the Keys to Peter shows them in the center of the plaza showing the pattern aligned to the octagon gazebo (Christian Church) located in the background. That pattern goes right down to the Church with the two arches separating from the gazebo indicates that pathway is symbolically the Red Sea.

            b. Peter is on his knees genuflecting before Christ indicating that he has become a sheep that is willing to follow Christ.

            c. The Israelite people were led by a pillar of fire (in the center of the Red Sea) during the day and a cloud by night, which symbolizes the two great luminaries that were placed in the firmament of the heavens that symbolized the Sun and the Moon that rules the day and rules the night.

            d. Peter on the north wall has Christ giving him the gold and silver keys, which symbolizes the Sun and Moon.

---

[15] http://www.artbible.info/art/sistine-chapel.html This Internet site lists the fresco of the Life of Christ and the Life of Moses linking them individually to their own sites.

    e. This fresco of Moses Crossing the Red Sea is the second scale of Virgo holding the Scales of Libra. Here you have Peter acting on his knees like a sheep (ram).

    f. Moses would not have been able to cross the Red Sea if he was not worthy to receive the two tablets of law.

    g. It is the mindset of the initiate that received the tablets of law: i.e. Better Man that receives the Initiatic Visionary Experience: i.e. Christ consciousness. This is why Scorpio and Aries symbolize half of the cosmic aspects of this transept.

2. Moses and the Tablets of the Law (Pisces - Water)

    a. This fresco shows God giving Moses two tablets of laws, which he could only have, receive if he crossed the Red Sea; thus, he now has manna coming from heaven to feed the people just as the Last Supper has the disciples feeding on the Eucharist (Manna from heaven).

        i. Moses crossed the Red Sea once in his journey to Midian; however, he like most Christians entering the Sistine Chapel did not know God's Ambiance; thus, at the Time sacred space meant nothing to him.

    b. Moses comes down from the Mount Sinai with the two tablets and encounters the people that created a Golden Calf, which is a perfect artistic manner of creating and symbolizing ego-centrism. Just as Judas Iscariot was tempted by Satan: i.e. ego-consciousness at the Last Supper.

        i. Judas Iscariot is sitting on the other side of the table from Christ in the Last Supper fresco just as the people that created the Golden Calf are divided from Moses and his supporters.

    c. There can be no doubt that Moses symbolizes Christ in the New Testament using different and more materialistic minded symbols to express the same conceptual spiritual ideas.

The artistic manner that symbolism was codified into the artwork of the Sistine Chapel below the thirty-two (32) popes seems to be commemorating the Hebrew Coder.

1. The twelve (12) zodiacal signs symbolize the twelve (12) Elemental letters.

2. The seven (7) sun signs of Astrology symbolize the seven (7) double letters.

3. The Patriarchal Cross symbolizes the three (3) Mother letters. These Mother letters give off an image of an equilateral cross and an elongated cross, which looks like two squares.

Below view the Kabbalistic Tree of Life harboring the twelve zodiacal signs and take notice of the numerics of each of the signs. Pisces (12) and Sagittarius (9) represent Jupiter/Zeus, which totals to twenty-one (21) and Capricorn (10) and Aquarius (11) represent Cronus/Saturn, which also totals to twenty-one (21); thus, it is these four zodiacal houses in Olympus that writes the first two verses of Genesis, which is symbolized in the mosaics of the floor: i.e. six concentric circles symbolizing BERESHITH and the nine circles squared forming the Kamea of Saturn. The first two verses of Genesis is a commentary on the six letters of BERESHITH, which is the impetus for the symbolism in the mosaics in the floor of the Sistine Chapel.

> *In the beginning Elohym (God) separated (Bara) 'the beginning and ends (את)' of the heavens and 'the beginning and ends (את)' of the earth (Gen. 1:1).*

> *And the earth was without form and void and darkness was on the face of the deep and the spirit of Elohym moved over the face of the waters (Gen. 1:2).*

The Hebrew word 'את' is not translated; though, it is used 26-times in just the first chapter of Genesis. There are twenty-one (21) words in the first two verses of Genesis and this is symbolizing the numerics of Cronus/Saturn and Jupiter for these 21-words symbolize the 'beginning and ends (את)' of the Hebrew coder. There are twenty-two (22) letters in the Hebrew coder. To find the other letter the numerics of the other eight (8) zodiacal signs have to be totaled. The zodiacal signs from Aries around to Scorpio total to thirty six (36). These eight (8) zodiacal signs pair off into the first eight numbers (1-8) symbolizing the Sun Signs of Astrology (Mars, Venus, Mercury, Sun and Moon) that exist below Mount Olympus. When the numerics of Capricorn (10) and Aquarius (9) twenty-one (21) are added to the thirty-six (36) they total to fifty-seven (57), which is the exact amount of words in the fifth day of creation; therefore, the numerics of the twelve (12) zodiacal signs symbolizes the amount of cards in the Major and Minor Arcana Tarot Cards. The twenty-second (22nd) Hebrew letter that is represented in the first verse of Genesis is BETH ב that symbolizes the spirit of Elohym that moved over the face of the waters. BETH ב is Adam, which Elohym: i.e. God makes into his image and likeness: i.e. Eve[16]. The 'Spirit of Elohym' symbolizes the image and likeness of Elohym (Eve) not Elohym per se. I say this; for the reason that, Elohym (God) cannot move for He cannot per se exist in Time. That movement *"the spirit of Elohym moved over the face of the waters"* infers the introduction of Time; hence, the Kamea of Saturn in the mosaics on the Sistine Chapel floor. There is neither Space without Time nor Time without Space; thus, there can be no movement without Time and Space.

BETH ב moving over the face of the waters symbolizes 'spirit of Elohym (Eve)' rising up out of the abysmal waters to live on the earth just as the birds coming out of the sea in the fifth day of creation went to live on the earth. Because the four suits of the Tarot Cards symbolizes the four mystic elements: Fire, Earth, Air and Water and the four directions I interpret the other twenty (20) from the twenty-one coming from Capricorn (11) and Aquarius (10) to symbolize the twenty (20) angels from The Chief Angel Princes of the Altitudes (the Four Cardinal Points) listed in Gustav Davidson's work A DICTIONARY OF ANGELS[17] (pg. 348), which also list on the same page The (ten - 10) Archangels of the Holy Sefiroth[18].

The Roman Catholic Church saw in the medieval times and in the Renaissance and Baroque periods that the Kings and Queens of Europe were divinely chosen by God. I believe that the five (5) court cards in each of the four suits (4 x 5 = 20 Ignudis) of the Tarot Cards symbolize this kind of secular government for they have risen to power in the secular materialistic world: i.e. KING (Sun - Prophet), QUEEN (Moon - Sibyl), KNIGHT (Mercury – Angel Cherub), KNAVE (Venus – Demon Cherub) and the tenth (minor official) in the Minor Arcana Tarot Cards. The nine lower cards in the Minor Arcana Tarot Cards' suits symbolize the general population that is governed by the same Cosmic Laws as the Court Cards. This is why the Kamea of Saturn can enumerate the nine cells from each of the four directions in precisely the same manner as the other three directions; though, it may initially appear to be a different way of enumerating the 3 x 3 magic square: Kamea of Saturn. There is only one way to enumerate the Kamea of Saturn into a perfect magic square via the Sigil (signature) of Saturn (see images below) no matter what direction is used to position the nine archetypal numbers into the Kamea of Saturn.

I mention these two groups of angels; for the reason that, they have everything to do with what Michelangelo did on the ceiling of the Sistine Chapel by frescoing ten (10) medallions[19] and twenty (20) Ignudis[20]. Notice that each of the nine central panels of the Sistine Chapel ceiling is enumerated via numbers one through nine (1-9, see image below). The medallions and the Ignudis are flanking only the odd number panels. This is because the even numbers symbolizes the unconscious mind and cannot become manifested into the world; whereas, the odd numbers symbolizes ego-consciousness, which becomes a firm conceptual idea forming a CROSS. From an earthly perspective ego-consciousness uses reason and logic and everything thing coming out of ego-consciousness is considered ORDER; whereas, anything in the unconscious mind is considered CHAOS. The unconscious mind is only considered

---

[16] I show the calculation for this interpretation in chapter fourteen.

[17] https://www.amazon.com/Dictionary-Angels-Including-Fallen/dp/002907052X/ref=sr_1_1?s=books&ie=UTF8&qid=1470144925&sr=1-1&keywords=angel+dictionary

[18] This is another spelling for the Ten Sefirahs (numbers) in the Kabbalistic Tree of Life

[19] http://www.wga.hu/html_m/m/michelan/3sistina/8medalli/index.html

[20] http://www.wga.hu/html_m/m/michelan/3sistina/2ignudi/index.html

CHAOS from ego-consciousness' perspective; however, CHAOS has absolute ORDER from a spiritual perspective no matter what the materialistic ego-consciousness has to say about it; because, LIGHT could not be culled out of the DARKNESS if the DARKNESS did not have absolute ORDER.

The Chief Angel Princes of the Altitudes (the Four Cardinal Points – twenty Ignudis) and the Archangels of the Holy Sefiroth (ten medallions) are not envisaged via the physical eye beneath the 32-popes that divide the heavenly fresco from the earthly frescoes. This is because the WORD OF GOD is actually invisible to the normal human intellect (iconoclasm). The only way to envisage this additional data is to cull it out of the esoteric data already culled out of the DARKNESS. In the case of the ten medallions (Sefirah) and the twenty Chief Angel Princes of the Altitudes the initiate would have to know the 32-popes symbolizes the Kabbalistic Tree of Life, which houses the twelve signs of the zodiac and the initiate would have to know that the Sun Signs were associated to Astrology. The task is for the initiate to conduct a detail comparative analysis on the esotericism in the many different and diverse mythologies, not necessarily a comparative analysis of other religions, which of course is an obvious factor in one's researches.

The initiate has to cull out the data and nuances out of a number of generic paradigmatic modes of thought that conveys spiritual ideas: i.e. WORD OF GOD. It is extremely difficult, if not impossible, for one paradigmatic mode of thought to express transparently the entire generic spiritual religious paradigm that expresses the WORD OF GOD. This is because of the initiate when initially entering the black abyss (forest) like Parzival is totally ignorant of what lays ahead; besides, there are the innumerable biases, prejudices and preconceive notions that are barriers that were instinctually and unwittingly set up throughout life to protect the psyche against the onslaught (tsunami) of spirituality. This is why the culling out of the disparate nuances from multiple spiritual genres of thought: sacred scriptures, the Hebrew coder, symbolism, numerics, cerebral lobes, Astrology, Tarot Cards, different religions' mythologies, multiple artworks, architecture, sculptures, etc., etc. are all extremely necessary for the initiate to conduct his or her meditational contemplative thought to obtain a comprehensive understanding of the WORD OF GOD conceptually and also by envisaging incalculable redundant examples of the WORD OF GOD throughout creation. It is those innumerable examples of redundancy that are envisaged throughout creation that validates and encourages the initiate into knowing that he or she is on the right path of spirituality. These innumerable examples also exude additional nuances not originally envisage that will widen the researcher's perspective as to how to continue to meditate contemplatively on his or her researches. This is why it takes decades to understand symbolism that expresses the WORD OF GOD for the initiate has to educate him or herself in the numerous genres of thought that will aid him or her into deciphering the WORD OF GOD. The correlation of all these genres of thought illustrate not only to the initiate; but, to the world at large that these ideas are not conjured up by the lone initiate; but, are inherently universally understood by all cultures in all times and climes in a worldwide systemic system of thought. Without this kind of substantiating principle inherent in esotericism the work that the initiate does will appear outwardly to be of the occult or new age philosophies.

An example of ORDER and CHAOS can be envisioned in the fact that the first chapter of Genesis has 434-words and is read in a manner of a few minutes by the materialist and a lifetime by a mystic. In those few minutes that the materialist (iconoclastic individual) reads the first chapter of Genesis he or she will not see the Kabbalistic Tree of Life codified to the texts via the symbolism and numerics of its alphabetic letters. What ego-consciousness envisages is what it considers ORDER and what it does not understand it considers CHAOS; contrarily, from the opposite perspective CHAOS, which is unknown to ego-consciousness sees its hidden data as ORDER and see ego-consciousness as CHAOS.

These nine central panels in the Sistine Chapel are numbered based upon the days of creation and the other chapters in the book of Genesis up to Noah and his family. The odd numbers literally creates sacred geometry that symbolizes the CROSS in the center of the Kamea of Saturn, which infers that spirituality comes from the north (9, 5 and 1) and go across the east-west corridor of Time (7, 5 and 3) to transubstantiate to the south. This is why the 32-popes in the Sistine Chapel are divided and numbered via odd numbered popes on the south wall and the even numbered popes on the north wall. Take the odd and even numbers out of the Kamea of Saturn and the even numbers total to 20 (2); whereas, the odd total to

25 (7), which are numbers that symbolize the LIGHT (207). Also two (2) divided into seven (7) is the three and a half (3½) coiled Kundalini Serpent inferring that the CROSS is the DARKNESS that the LIGHT is culled from. Also the Kamea of Saturn's nine numbers (1-9) totals to forty-five (45), which is the Gematria value of the word 'ADAM'. When Eve is taken out of ADAM her Gematria value is nineteen (19) and what was left was twenty-six (26), which symbolizes the numerics of the word YAHWEH; whereas, Yahweh symbolized the spiritual secular and religious societal mores that the initiate has to become inundated (Baptized) and acclimated to. In looking at Michelangelo's frescoed panel of the Birth of Eve when she is seen coming out of the carcass of the old Adam she is immediately confronted by YAHWEH. The numerics of the Kamea of Saturn even numbers equals 20 and odd numbers equals 25 appears initially to be the same as Eve's Gematria value being 19 and Yahweh's Gematria value being 26; however, this is misleading because Adam split 20 (female 0.444...) and 25 (male 0.555...) symbolically inferring a patriarchal culture; whereas, Eve 19 and Yahweh 26 points to no male and female in heaven nor a patriarchal or matriarchal culture. This idea will be further explored in another chapter.

The CROSS per se merely symbolizes DARKNESS (spirituality) harmoniously syncing to the life of the initiate whatever, his or her skill, religious belief system or endeavors in life are about and then that soul head to the south: i.e. Garden of Eden. The Kamea of Saturn is the Holy of Holies; for the reason that every column, row and diagonal in the 3 x 3 Magic Square: i.e. Kamea of Saturn totals to fifteen (15) and the Holy of Holies has the same dimensions: i.e. 15^3. There can be no doubt that the Earth is symbolically a symbol for the soul living in Time; for the reason that, Time concretizes everything that comes into the manifested creation. All seven (7) magic squares come out of the MATRIX OF WISDOM (see chapter seventeen). All that comes out of the MATRIX OF WISDOM are the Sun Signs of Astrology, which symbolized these seven magic squares. These magic squares are also symbolized as the double letters in the Kabbalistic Tree of Life symbolized as coming down from the north from the heavens.

UNIVERSAL COSMIC, ARCHETYPAL AND EXISTENTIAL PARADIGM

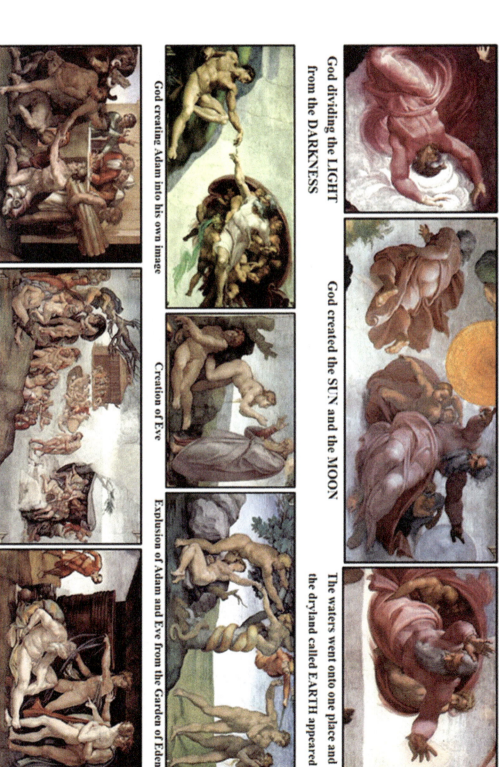

God dividing the LIGHT from the DARKNESS

God created the SUN and the MOON

The waters went onto one place and the dryland called EARTH appeared

God creating Adam into his own image

Creation of Eve

Explusion of Adam and Eve from the Garden of Eden

Noah and Family built an altar to worship God

Noah's Ark rising above the deluge (flood)

Drunkeness of Noah

SISTINE CHAPEL - CEILING PLAN

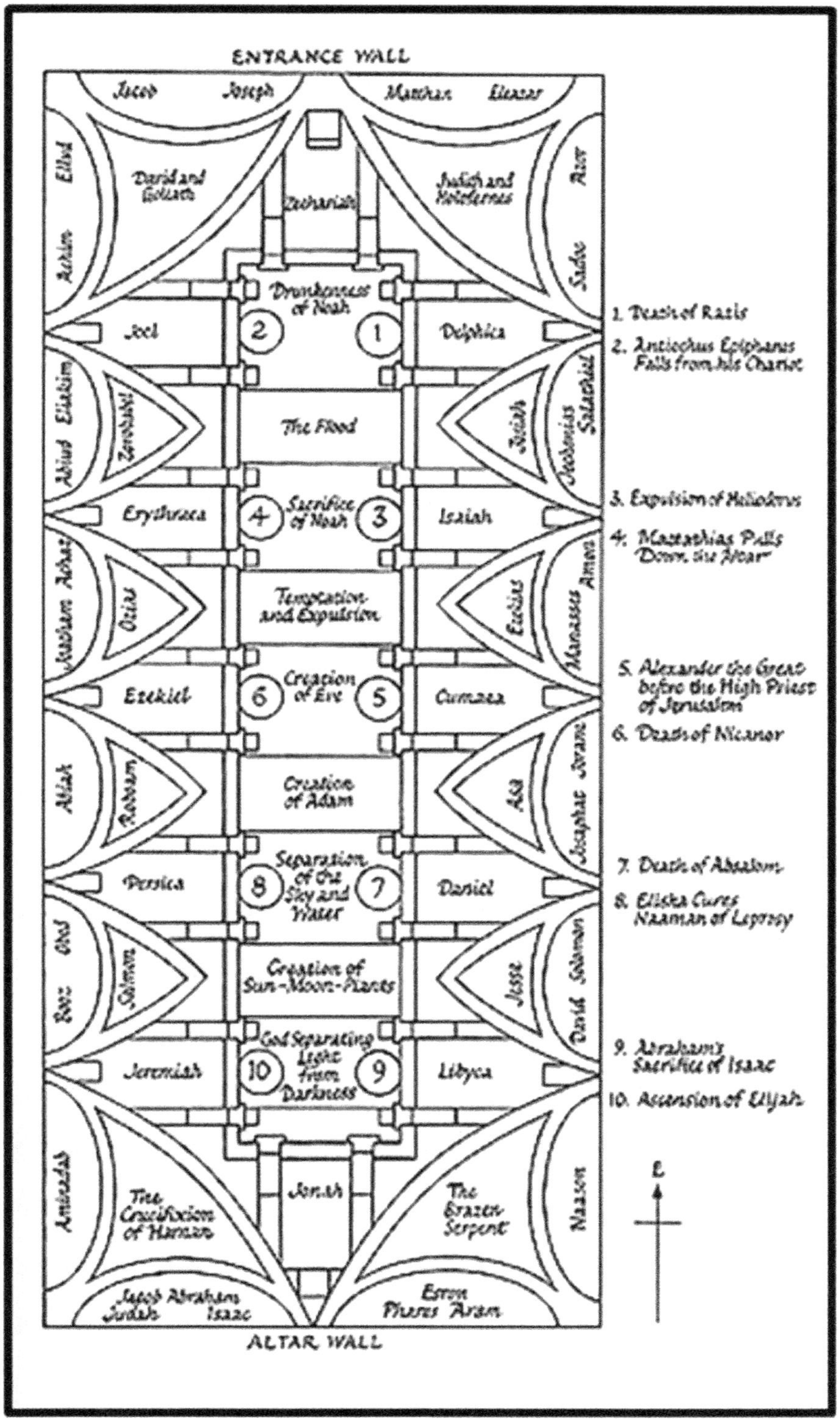

SISTINE CHAPEL - FLOOR PLAN

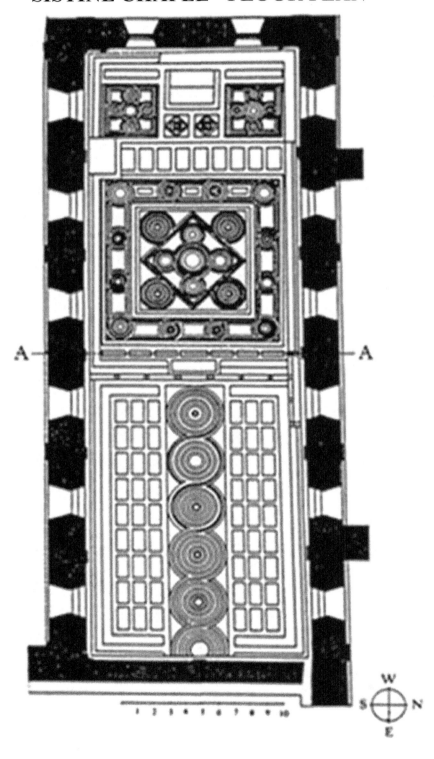

SISTINE CHAPEL: LAST JUDGMENT: ALTAR WALL

THE SISTINE CHAPEL (Lost Frescos): Altar Wall - West Wall

Artist: Perugino , Dates: 1480s
FINDING OF MOSES
Location: Altar wall of Sistine Chapel
(now Lost)
Purpose: To provide an Old Testament //
to the Nativity of Christ on the
other side of the Altar wall

Artist: Perugino Dates: 1480s
NATIVITY OF CHRIST
Location: Altar wall of Sistine chapel
(now lost)
Purpose: to provide a New Testament //
to the finding of Moses on the other side of the Altar wall

https://quizlet.com/9956031/renaissance-art-flash-cards/

THE SISTINE CHAPEL: EAST WALL

FIGHT OVER THE BODY OF MOSES

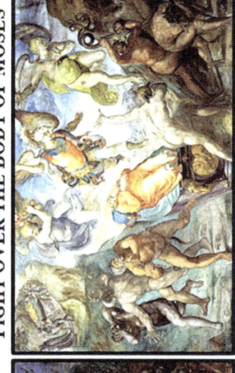

ASCENTION OF CHRIST

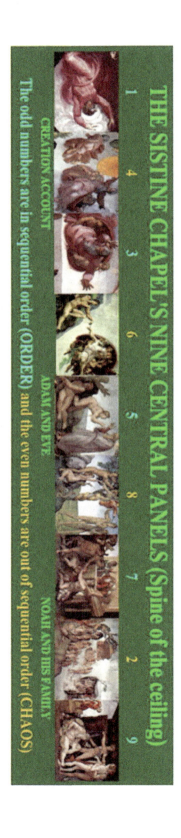

THE SISTINE CHAPEL'S NINE CENTRAL PANELS (Spine of the ceiling)

CREATION ACCOUNT

ADAM AND EVE

NOAH AND HIS FAMILY

The odd numbers are in sequential order (ORDER) and the even numbers are out of sequential order (CHAOS)

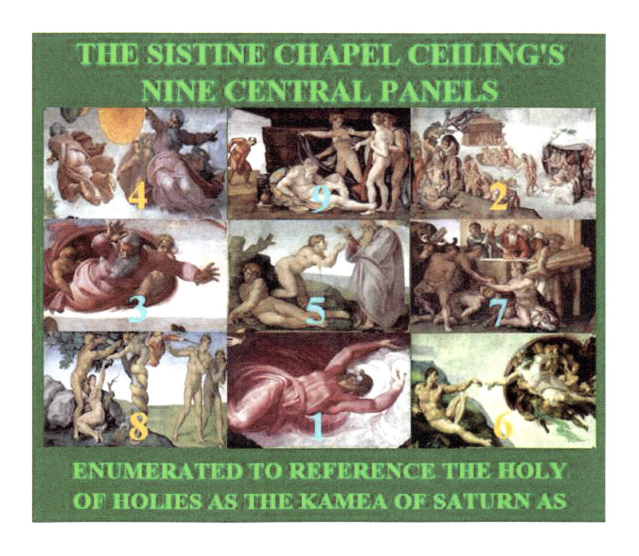

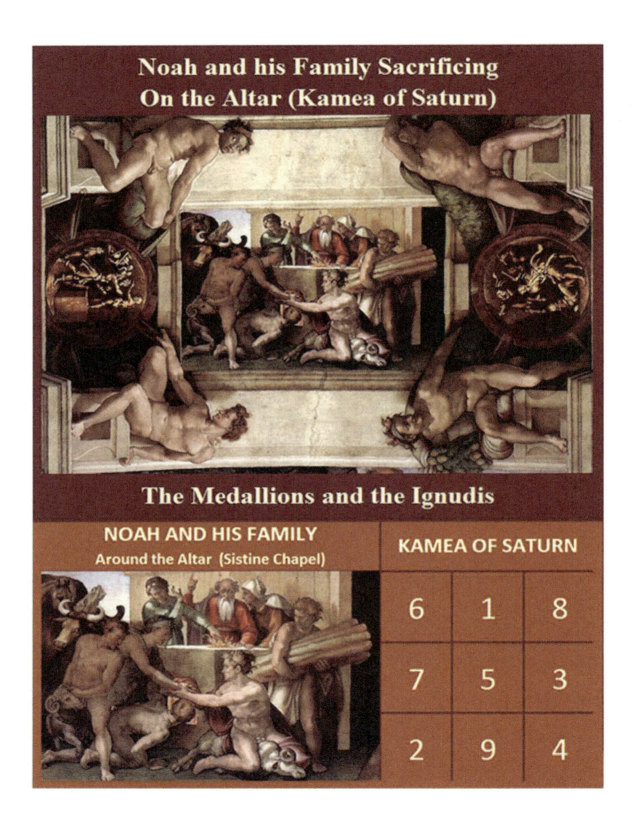

Noah and his Family Sacrificing On the Altar (Kamea of Saturn)

The Medallions and the Ignudis

NOAH AND HIS FAMILY
Around the Altar (Sistine Chapel)

KAMEA OF SATURN

6	1	8
7	5	3
2	9	4

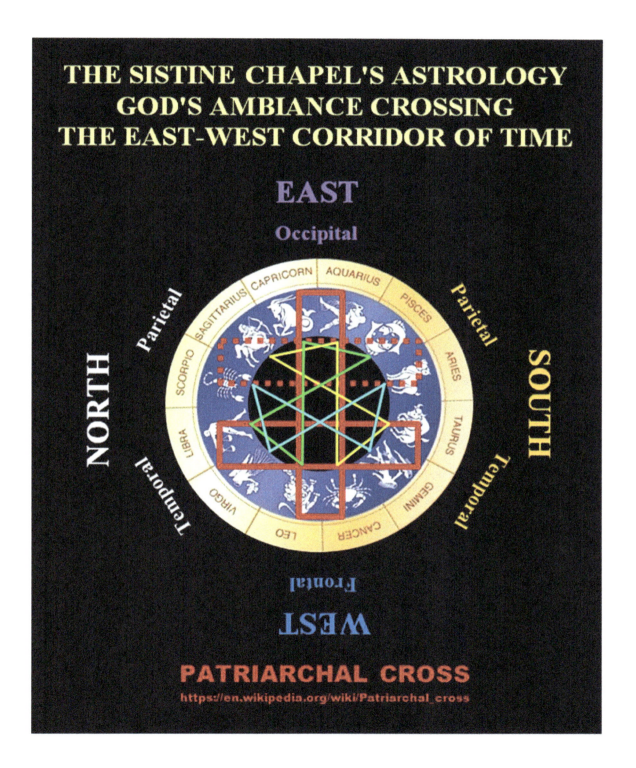

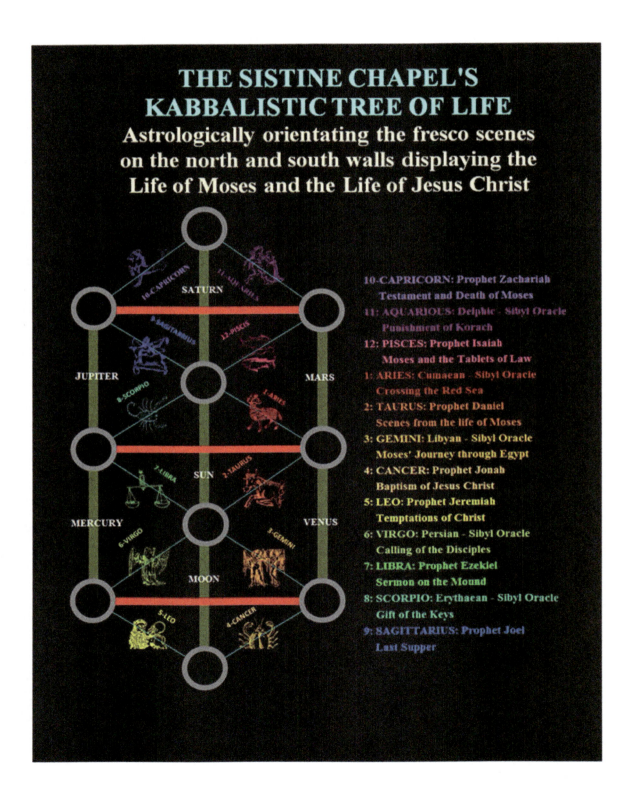

THE SISTINE CHAPEL'S
KABBALISTIC TREE OF LIFE
Astrologically orientating the fresco scenes
on the north and south walls displaying the
Life of Moses and the Life of Jesus Christ

10-CAPRICORN: Prophet Zachariah
Testament and Death of Moses
11: AQUARIOUS: Delphic - Sibyl Oracle
Punishment of Korach
12: PISCES: Prophet Isaiah
Moses and the Tablets of Law
1: ARIES: Cumaean - Sibyl Oracle
Crossing the Red Sea
2: TAURUS: Prophet Daniel
Scenes from the life of Moses
3: GEMINI: Libyan - Sibyl Oracle
Moses' Journey through Egypt
4: CANCER: Prophet Jonah
Baptism of Jesus Christ
5: LEO: Prophet Jeremiah
Temptations of Christ
6: VIRGO: Persian - Sibyl Oracle
Calling of the Disciples
7: LIBRA: Prophet Ezekiel
Sermon on the Mound
8: SCORPIO: Erythaean - Sibyl Oracle
Gift of the Keys
9: SAGITTARIUS: Prophet Joel
Last Supper

CHAPTER SIX

THE BIRTHS OF ADAM AND EVE

ADAM (Gematria value 45) in the second chapter of Genesis is created from the DUST (Gematria value 270) of the ground; thus, GROUND has to be another symbol for DARKNESS. The **MATRIX OF WISDOM** has a total numerical count of six-hundred and thirty (630): i.e. all numbers 1s, 2s, 3s, 4s, 5s, 6s, 7s, and 8s collectively total to two-hundred and seventy (270); whereas, the forty nines (40 x 9) total to three-hundred and sixty (360) or the degrees in a circle, which has already been illustrate symbolizes DARKNESS. The DUST (270) of the ground is the LIGHT culled out of the DARKNESS and 270 is a transposition of the Gematria value of LIGHT (207). The breakdown of the **MATRIX OF WISDOM** into 270 + 360: a three to four (3 to 4) ratio symbolizes the SEVEN LIBERAL ARTS: Trivium (three Grammatical Arts) and the Quadrivium (four Mathematical Sciences). The **MATRIX OF WISDOM** is clearly defining why humans are earthbound. The Trivium is earthbound knowledge; whereas, the Quadrivium for the most part is inexplicable abstract knowledge. Most humans have innumeracy problems. All that humans cull out of the DARKNESS (40-nines) is reduced down to the four mystic elements or the Sun Signs of Astrology or Chess pieces, which individually and collectively symbolizes the LIGHT of creation: **1 & 8 (Fire or Mars - Rooks), 2 & 7 (Earth or Venus - Bishops), 3 & 6 (Air or Mercury - Knights) and 4 & 5 (Water or Moon and Sun – Queen and King).** This reducing the DARKNESS down into a recognizable order is an intelligible ways of explaining conceptually how the psyche's ego-consciousness take the CHAOS of the psyche's unconscious mind and put it into limitless intelligible and comprehensible formats; yet, from a materialistic standpoint the four nuclear forces also coincide with the four mystic elements. Think of the rain, which is a moment of DARKNESS and out of it, comes the rainbow: circle of colors. Everything in the outer real 'concretized' world reflects the dynamics of the tetrahedral forces of the psyche.

When considering the **MATRIX OF WISDOM** as the foundation of the integration of the Trivium and Quadrivium it has to be realized not only do humans live their lives in these mystical nuances; but, the sacred scriptures are written in this secret sacred and esoteric manner. The Trivium is the surface textual mythoi storylines; whereas, the Quadrivium represents the symbolic, numerical and Gematria value of letters. Much of the Roman Catholic Church's hierarchy and the average member of the laity reading the bible have absolutely no idea that such a clandestine way of writing the sacred scriptures is at all possible. I have spoken too many priests and to many members of the Catholic laity about symbolism and, for the most part, with an ocean of symbolism (like a tsunami rushing in surrounding and engulfing them very much like PEI פ inundates and surrounds BETH ב) codified into Catholicism's artwork most of the priests and laity have absolutely no idea that symbolism is the crucial aspects of the Roman Catholic Church's teachings. The mystical and disparate aspects of iconoclasm and iconography is mind boggling to understand and to see an ocean of ignorant surrounding oneself as if the mystic stands on the mastaba of creation all alone in the Garden of Eden with God as his or her only confidant.

Every thought, word and deed is symbolic of psychic activity. The general population, for the most part, has no idea that the very words out of their mouth are ethereally symbolic of the thoughts they are trying to express. How do the spiritual forces of creation reach the intellectually dyslexic psyches of the populace? It is difficult for an uninitiated to understand that language is merely the gaga prattle of a new born baby. Think about how language came about. There are hundreds of languages around the world and thousands of dialects of those languages. Language begins from a very primitive state and developed over time. Grunts and Guttural sounds became meaningful expressions that conveyed symbolic needs and idea; hence, how language was birthed into the antediluvian times. Today in modernity a culture's general population would not recognize their language as a variation on the primitive grunts and guttural sounds of their ancestors; nevertheless, they are synonymously the same language.

In contrast the Esoteric Science used to write the WORD OF GOD via the SEVEN LIBERAL ARTS were taught to the spirituality attentive and that language has nothing whatsoever to do with the ways of the world; though, the mythoi of the world is used to package and store the WORD OF GOD for those worthy of understanding it.

The word DARKNESS has a Gematria value of three-hundred and twenty-eight (328) and the second chapter of Genesis has a Hebrew word count of 328 and the word SERPENT has a Gematria value of 328. The laity of Judaism, Christianity and Islam is not taught to read the sacred scriptures letter by letter no less via each letters symbolic, numerical and Gematria value. Nobody birthed into the materialistic world was promised a ROSE GARDEN. That Garden of Eden has to be earned.

Personally, I don't see how the first four chapters of Genesis can be interpreted without this knowledge relating to the number 328 representing DARKNESS symbolically. The number 328 (5/8) is symbolically a set in the Fibonacci sequence and Yahweh (26 = 8) and Elohym (86 = 14 = 5) represent that set in the Fibonacci sequence with Christ amidst them: called Yahweh Elohym.

I like telling the story of the 535-members of the House of Representative (435) and the Senate (100). Theoretically this is 434 + 1 (Bereshith being two words "separated six" and 435 is the aggregate of 29 symbolic of Saturn) the amount of words in the first chapter of Genesis and 100 is the amount of cells in the MATRIX OF WISDOM. The number 535 is an amalgamation of 207 (LIGHT) and 328 (DARKNESS). It cannot be coincidental that Congress is esoterically structured that way. USA voters get precisely what they pay for: i.e. vote for: voters get the inherent nature of their psyches. The MATRIX OF WISDOM numerics total to 630 and the 270 = LIGHT: 1s, 2s, 3s, 4s, 5s, 6s, 7, and 8s. That 270-sync with the 270-Electoral College voted needed for a candidate to win the US Presidency.

I believe Freemasonry when they setup the United States Government they presented the psyche in a perfect manner; for the reason that, the government is the psyche of the general population: i.e. Democracy is equivalent of mob rules (absolute CHAOS for only greed for materialism reigns supreme and this is why there is so much Corporate Greed in the world). The public gets exactly what it psychically and materialistically desires. Seeing the rich and powerful stomping upon the poor and downtrodden enamors the psyche of the general population; for the reason that, it declares plainly very much like the lottery ticket that there is a smidgen of hope for the poor and downtrodden to rise above the fray. Freemasonry will probably finish their symbolic construct of the United States by the end of the year 2799AD or as close to that date as possible. It is not unprecedented for a religious organization to deliberately take a long time in finishing a particular sacred building. The Catholic Church took 816-years (1836AD) to finish Chartres Cathedral begun in 1020AD and there is a very spiritual reason for that. That date alone illustrates that there is still a secret hierarchy that understands the esotericism of the sacred scriptures.

The second chapter of Genesis speaks of Adam being created from the dust of the ground and then God breathing into his nostrils: i.e. two part psyche: ego-consciousness and the unconscious mind *"the breath of divine inspiration of life"* goes to illustrating what the second verse of Genesis is talking about. The second chapter of Genesis is not a new or an alternative creation account; rather, it is a commentary on the first two verses of Genesis. The second chapter of Genesis is rehashing in a more detail and mystical and mythological manner what is transpiring in the first two verses of Genesis.

The nostrils and the two-part psyche symbolize the world of materialistic opposites. This is why the human body is created in segments of opposites: two eyes, two ears, two nostrils, two arms, two hands, two feet (even the fingers and toes have opposites) and two legs. Most of all the body symbolizes the synchronicity of the opposites into a harmonious interplay.

The Gematria value of DARKNESS literally interprets itself. In the number three-hundred and twenty-eight (328) is a division of 5/8. The two and three total to five and 5/8 is a set in the Fibonacci sequence: i.e. Golden Ratio. That could be a coincidence until it is learned that the opposite LIGHT (207) and DARKNESS (328) calculates out to DARKNESS 328 / 535 = 0.613…, which is extremely close to the formula of the Golden Ratio: 0.618034. This very same mathematical scenario is played out in the landscape of Washington DC and the Potomac River. I'll get to that later; but, it is curious that Freemasonry designated the seat of the United States Government to be permanent and absolute

DARKNESS and one can envisage how this works out. It is known that the Fibonacci sequence goes on infinitely and what was previously DARKNESS becomes the LIGHT; however, DARKNESS, like the United States Government, continuously grows larger and larger; however, the DARKNESS always becomes the LIGHT: i.e. trickles down mystical economics to the poor and downtrodden. It is via the harmonious interplay of the Golden Ratio formula that all life exists in the world. What was evil yesterday is sanctioned today. Remember the people that were arrested and jailed for selling alcohol and drugs or being homosexual and now all those acts that were once crimes are now civilly accepted into the United States societal mores. It is as if the spiritual forces of creation are forcing upon the general population the truth about what humans think are good and evil, which are merely opinions and really don't mean anything on a spiritual level. SIN is false belief about God and his creation. Sin has nothing to do with violating morality, ethics or penal and civil laws. These are not God's laws they are manmade control systems to create a decent society to live in: to make them into 'Good Men'.

Now the Lord God (Christ) seeing that Adam is without a mate creates beast and all sorts of animals from the ground. Notice that Genesis 2:19; does not say that the animals came from the "dust of the ground" indicating that the animals were raw archetypal beings from the stellar universe, which I believe symbolized the zodiacal cycle of animals. Carl G. Jung (1875-1961) would call these the Archetypes of the Collective Unconscious[1]. Personally, I don't believe that there is a Collective Unconscious; rather, there is the **MATRIX OF WISDOM**, which each human being possesses as his or her psyche autonomously and this **MATRIX OF WISDOM** is a personal raison d'être, it is not a Collective Unconscious; though, it may well have appeared that way to Carl G. Jung's in his evaluation of his empirical researches. What I mean by calling the animals raw archetypal beings is that the nines (9s) in the **MATRIX OF WISDOM** are not being dissected into the four mystic elements: **1 & 8 (Fire or Mars - Rooks), 2 & 7 (Earth or Venus - Bishops), 3 & 6 (Air or Mercury - Knights)** and **4 & 5 (Water or Moon and Sun – Queen and King)**. The four mystic elements give the sense that Adam was cultivated and civilized into understanding and naming the animals. There is no doubt in my mind that the raw archetypal beings are humans behaving like animals; for the reason that, they lost their spiritual sheen: i.e. *"divine inspiration of life"* that God breathed into them before birth. When it says the Lord God (Yahweh Elohym) created the animals from the ground this is referring to Yahweh: i.e. ego-consciousness venturing out on its own trying to solve his own problems. Reading the first part of the second chapter of Genesis where it says Yahweh Elohym formed Adam from the dust of the ground and then placed him in the Garden of Eden. How did Adam loose that *"divine inspiration of life"* that was breathed into his nostrils? The four rivers are indicative to the four mystic elements, which should have sustained Adam stay in the Garden of Eden. The fact that Adam did not have a mate infers that he was not conversing with the spiritual powers that be (God); thus, he was without a mate. For that reason Adam became per se the archetypal being that Yahweh Elohym made from out of the ground, which points to the fact that he no longer possess the four mystic elements: the LIGHT that was culled out of the DARKNESS. The LIGHT completely vanished out of his life; however, going through the task of trying to understand the animals he could not on his own volition obtain a mate. That fact along showed that Adam understood he was not the end all and be all of creation and he had to deflate his ego

Adam was not momentarily conversing with Yahweh Elohym (LIGHT); rather, he was conversing with the outer world and not breaking the DARKNESS (9s) down into LIGHT: i.e. 1 and 8, 2 and 7, 3 and 6 and 4 and 5. Expelling Adam and Eve out of the Garden of Eden is suppose to be a momentary event in the psyche of the initiate not a permanent expulsion The sacred scriptures is giving momentary ethereal vignettes symbolizing ongoing events in the psyche of the initiate.

Adam did not have a mate so Yahweh Elohym tells him to name the animals, which I believe represent the zodiacal signs of astrology; however, that also represents the animal instincts of every human being on earth; thus, Adam was expected to know his own inner self: i.e. his inner weakness in relationship to societal mores: family, religion and secular rules and regulations. Adam himself after

---

[1] http://www.amazon.com/Archetypes-Collective-Unconscious-Collected-Works/dp/0691018332/ref=sr_1_1?ie=UTF8&qid=1462977542&sr=8-1&keywords=archetypes+of+the+collective+unconscious

doing what Yahweh Elohym expected him to do still had no help-mate. It is because Adam obeyed the edicts of Yahweh Elohym that he, through the auspices Yahweh Elohym (Christ consciousness), was able to cull out the LIGHT (Eve) from the DARKNESS. Adam per se is the DARKNESS as is every initiate is his or her own DARKNESS. Breaking the DARKNESS (Chaos) down into LIGHT (Order: i.e. 1 and 8, 2 and 7, 3 and 6 and 4 and 5) is culling Eve out of the DARKNESS and because of Adam changes into MAN he is no longer the Adam that existed moments ago. This prototypical example of Adam naming the animals: i.e. 'earthly conditions via one's own raison d'etre' conceptually has to be repeated continuously ad nauseam.

An example of this pivotal prototypical generic paradigmatic example is a person that has Christ consciousness and while he or she is religiously studying the WORD OF GOD he or she is in the Garden of Eden culling out the LIGHT. Now that person has to go about his or her earthly responsibility and obligation to his or her societal mores and that individual will momentarily lose Christ consciousness; however, the moment that initiate returns to his or her religious studies Christ consciousness returns. Christ consciousness is Eve the LIGHT culled out of the DARKNESS.

In the third chapter of Genesis another altogether different conceptual vignette is being conveyed. It is obvious, at least to me that the serpent per se is 'reason and logic'; for the reason that, it is the subtlest of all the beast of creation. There is per se nothing wrong with 'reason and logic'; however, if the initiate defies the edicts of Yahweh Elohym than 'reason and logic' becomes extremely subtle and satanic. A perfect example of this in modernity is found in Flint Michigan's Water Crisis. There is no doubt in my mind that in the minds of the State and Local officials their decisions that brought about the crisis were reasonable and logical; however, these decisions were based upon numerous other like decision like selling off parks and children's recreational playgrounds to Greedy Corporate America and other activities, which there were actually no viable complaints about. Especially when the news media is controlled by the State and Local officials unless of course the news goes viral by other means and then it fair-game for all news reporters get to hype it out.

Adam and Eve had the same problem; because, Yahweh Elohym gave Adam a directive not to eat from the Tree of the Knowledge of Good and Evil (Gen. 2:9). The serpent in the third chapter begins the conversation by splitting up the commandment of Yahweh Elohym (Gen. 2:16-17) into "Elohym said (Gen. 3:1)", which infers that Yahweh said something else. It matters not how, through reason and logic, a law is put into legislation what matters is that the law is the end product and should be obeyed. Yahweh and/or Elohym had nothing to do with creating this edict Yahweh Elohym created. Yahweh Elohym is not a combination of Yahweh and Elohym; though, that is the sleight of hand that is proffered.

Remember that the entire second chapter of Genesis has 328-words, which symbolizes that the number 328 represents total absolute DARKNESS, which means that there is no LIGHT. From a zodiacal point of view the second chapter of Genesis symbolizes Cancer and Leo; but, also symbolically the Kamea of the Moon (PEI פ) is blocking out the LIGHT: of the spiritual Sun: i.e. Kamea of the Sun as in the total eclipse of the Sun. Cancer is the fourth (4) zodiacal sign and Leo is the fifth (5) zodiacal sign. By the Moon totally eclipsing the Sun comes the Gematria value of Adam = 4 and 5 = 45, which symbolizes the waters of creation like a tsunami overwhelming ego-consciousness. Now that Adam's ego (sun setting or eclipsed) is deflated he is eligible to be Born Again. The deflation of ego-consciousness is already the death of the old heaven and the old earth. Eve (Gematria value of 19) has already been taken out of Adam (45) via the deflation of ego-consciousness leaving 26 behind, which is the Gematria value of Yahweh: i.e. ego-consciousness setting into the west. The old sun-god is dead. This is not being disrespectful to the name of God: i.e. Yahweh is considered Christ consciousness in the flesh; however, without that spiritual sheen Yahweh as ego-consciousness is Satan.

Yahweh Elohym taking a rib out of Adam is symbolic of removing Eve from Adam. The mythos of the rib is just a recapitulation of what has already transpired. That is how the sacred scripture is written; though, it appears to be a continuous linear storyline. Taking a rib out of Adam is symbolic of taking a bone out of the skeleton housed in DARKNESS as first noticed in the fifth and sixth days of creation. The rib comes from the axial Skeleton, which is stationary, which dominated Adam's movements with the appendicular skeleton. Then Eve: i.e. the new spiritual sun is built from the rib. It is not the Full Moon;

for the reason that, it was eclipsing the spiritual sun; rather it was a New Moon that blocked the sun. When Eve (19) was taken out of ADAM (45), he, for all intent and purpose, died and the proof of that is found in Genesis 2: 23; where the last word is MAN שיא, which has a Gematria value of 311. Consider that before Eve is taken out of Adam (45) he is both male (5 = ego = Sun) and female (4 = unconscious mind = moon) and when the moon is taken out of Adam, which he then into turns to a man 311 = 5, this takes the 9 x 9 (81) Matrix of the Moon and adds Eve (19) to it creating the MATRIX OF WISDOM (10^2).

That Gematria value of Man 311 become exceedingly important when you realized that Eve (19) is brought to Man and the two become one; hence, 311 + 19 = 330: is this the root of 33°?. Let me first say that Eve with the Gematria value of 19 is one of the most spiritual symbols in the whole of the bible and I will discuss that as we continue. Adding QOPH the 19th letter of the Hebrew coder to the Gematria value of 311 literally creates the second half of what I call the GENESIS FORMULA. Both Yud and Aleph was with Shin in the spelling of MAN. Yud (Yahweh) and Aleph (Elohym) symbolize two aspects of the Trinity and Qoph is the third and final aspect of the Trinity. All this is worked out in the first word of Genesis: BERESHITH that will be discuss shortly. MAN 311 + Eve 19 totaling 330 from another perspective point to SHIN and Lemmed ל (30) the twelfth letter of the Hebrew coder is said to be *"the heart of Eve"*. Lemmed is also said to be the center of the Hebrew Coder. The 330 can also symbolize two SHINS שש spelt out, which would symbolize two concentric circles, which in antiquity symbolized the womb or fertility, which again points to Eve being BORN AGAIN.

In the image below of Michelangelo's fresco painting God creating Adam it can be seen that God is in a head (RESH ר): i.e. the brain as if God is symbolic of the Pineal Gland coming down vertically upon Adam lounging horizontally. In every sense God is creating the cross and that also will be discussed shortly. Catholicism artwork is an esoteric commentary on the Genesis Creation Account. The laity does not understand symbolism because they are not trained to understand it. Adam in the prone position is very much like Noah lounging on his couch drunk. This is the same as the 24-human bronze figures lounging upon the triangular spandrels. They are basically prone statues not energetic at all. Adam and Noah and the 24-bronze figures total to 26, the Gematria value of Yahweh as symbolizing collectively the frozen stone statues lounging lackadaisically. I envisage these 26-prone figures lounging on a slanted diagonal pyramidal incline suggestive of the slanted tunnel vision that takes place psychically when egocentrism's ignorance tries to grasp on its own volition what it does not understand. This is symbolically what takes place beneath the 32-popes when the circle (sphere or octagon shape) is transformed into a rectangular shape denoting tunnel vision. This is how the Life of Christ and the Life of Moses were repositioned on the north and south sides respectively to flank the east-west corridor of time: the pathway from the entrance door down the nave to the apse.

The next fresco panel in the nine central panels on the ceiling of the Sistine Chapel is the birth of Eve. This shows exactly what takes place in the second chapter of Genesis. A new MAN is about to be birthed. Notice that Michelangelo has Yahweh: i.e. ego-consciousness standing right there at the moment of Eve's birth ready to introduce (concretize, name) her into societal mores: three temptations of Christ. Remember Yahweh Elohym's (Christ's) command to Adam not to eat of the Tree of the Knowledge of Good and Evil. In all respects Yahweh standing there waiting for Eve is Satan ready to tempt her. Eve already had her cabal so to speak with Yahweh Elohym and herself symbolizing collectively the Trinity. For Eve to speak to or about a dead god (sun - Yahweh) would be in every sense eating from the forbidden tree: i.e. *"thou shalt not have any other gods before me"*. Eve did not need information or knowledge from the serpent (328); for the reason that, she was just culled out of the DARKNESS (328). In 1 John 1:5; Saint John says speaking of Christ, *"in him was no darkness"*. Eve had taken on the mantle of LIGHT and to have been speaking to the serpent shows she was enamored by the Tree of the Knowledge of Good and Evil. The only way that Eve could have been speaking to the Serpent is if the MAN that was named Adam a few verses later became the archetypal beast (Serpent: i.e. DARKNESS): ego-consciousness. If Adam was not the Serpent than why did he accept the fruit from the forbidden tree? Adam would have known the personality traits of the Serpent having previously named all the animals. If the confusing conversation that Eve had with the serpent is studied it will be seen how the Serpent treated

Elohym as a competitor rather than part of a unified Trinity, which would have resulted in a harmonious interplay. It that happened there would have been no need for the sacred scriptures to have been written.

I highly recommend for those truly interested the Hebrew alphabet and the words of the bible to get a copy of The Interlinear Hebrew-Greek-English Bible, One-Volume Edition[2]. I have already mentioned Rabbi Ginsburgh work on THE HEBREW LETTERS; but, I also recommend the volume The New Strong's Expanded Exhaustive Concordance of the Bible, with Hebrew and Greek Dictionaries[3]. These three books are all any biblical student needs if he or she truly wants to know how to read the bible letter by letter. Learn each Hebrew letter's symbolic, numerical and Gematria values and commence researching the Hebrew texts from there.

BERESHITH בראשית is the first word of Genesis and it is the single most important word in the whole of the sacred scriptures; for the reason that, the entire Old and New Testaments are commentaries on its infinite fount of knowledge. Actually, every word of the sacred scriptures has an infinite fount of knowledge and any initiate can cull out from any word the same database of knowledge: i.e. the WORD OF GOD if he or she puts her *whole heart, mind, soul, time, finances and resources* into obtaining it. I have dedicated my life, since August 1974, to knowing the WORD OF GOD and somehow I have been enamored to basically studying this one word in relationship to the entire Old and New Testaments and the creation of the manifested world at large.

I have discussed above some of the mysteries of the first written Hebrew letter of Genesis: BETH ב and the first esoteric (hidden) letter PEI פ. The first word of Genesis **BERESHITH** בראשית is actually a recapitulation of that discussion in a more detailed format and much is esoterically (hidden) codified into this word **BERESHITH** בראשית that is already codified into BETH ב and PEI פ, which in point of fact is the manifestations of the first two letters of Genesis from letters: **BETH** ב and **RESH** ר into what appears to be these letters/word spelt out amalgamating and formatting the word **BERESHITH** בראשית.

The letter/word **RESH** ר literally symbolizes the commencement of the **Initiatic Visionary Experience**, which destroys the old heaven and earth symbolized by BETH ב and brings forth a new heaven and earth that symbolizes Christ consciousness. The letters YUD י and TAV ת in the spelling out of the letter/word BETH ב symbolize the old sky god YAHWEH (sun) setting in the west as if the sun is sinking into the vastness of the ocean symbolically similar to the picture above of the angel sinking into the ocean to live in the sunken Atlantis, which had succumbed to the tsunami of the unconscious mind (ocean). We know of course the sun doesn't sink into the ocean; nonetheless, it gives the symbolic appearance of doing so, which most religious cultures in antiquity understood iconographically or even iconoclastically that the sun god died each night rising from the dead each morning. Those that are iconoclastic and know nothing of symbolism will envisage this kind of interpretation of the Judaeo Christian scriptures as paganism.

RESH ר symbolizes Christ in the flesh; however, the first thing that Christ had to do before he began his ministry was to be baptized into the world and this means that Christ had to come through the conduit of **BETH** ב in order to come into the world in the flesh. This symbolizes the mythoi of John the Baptist baptizing Christ in the Jordon River. This is not just saying Christ is birthed into Judaism; rather, this baptizing is a generic concept relating to all the spiritual religious cultures around the world. This is symbolically the same process as what Yahweh Elohym (Christ) did to Adam in the second chapter of Genesis by taking a rib from him and developing a woman (Eve) from that one rib, not from the entire skeleton of the body. This is why after the total eclipse of the sun the sun initially appears as a rib in the heavens as the New Moon (ocean – unconscious mind) moves to the side as the whole of the sun appears, which is symbolically similar to the waters in the third day of creation moving unto one place and the

---

[2]http://www.christianbook.com/interlinear-hebrew-english-bible-volume-edition/9781565639775/pd/639774?dv=c&en=google&event=SHOP&kw=academic-20-40|639774&p=1179710&gclid=CPyIgrDE08wCFUEfhgodcpcE-Q
[3]http://www.amazon.com/Strongs-Expanded-Exhaustive-Concordance-Bible/dp/1418541680?ie=UTF8&keywords=strong%27s%20exhaustive%20concordance%20of%20the%20bible%20with%20greek%20and%20hebrew%20dictionaries&qid=1463021981&ref_=sr_1_1&s=books&sr=1-1

dryland Earth appearing. Christ is baptized into is the psychic materialistic waters that enamors the soul of the initiate that is to be spiritually regenerated and revitalized via the Initiatic Visionary Experience.

To understand conceptually how Christ is baptized (manifested) into the world's domains: i.e. religious cultures the spiritual forces of creation: Christ (Tao, Buddha, Krishna, Horus, etc.). I have to tell the story of the Hebrew alphabet narrated in the prologue of the Zohar (Jewish Kabbalistic writings)[4] coming before the Lord of Creation: i.e. Yahweh to petition him to choose one of them as the conduit that would bring forth manifested creation. Ironically, it is Christ himself that initiates this process. The last four letters of the Hebrew Coder: ***TAV (400), SHIN (300), RESH (200) and QOPH (100) spell out the word Christ (krst) in Greek using Hebrew letters***. I myself did not come up with this about the last four letters of the Hebrew Coder representing Christ; Robert M. Hoffstein, a Jewish scholar speaks of this in the introduction of his work: A Mystical Key to the English Language[5]; nonetheless, this perfectly coincides with the prologue of John's gospel in the New Testament.

In the prologue of the Zohar the Hebrew alphabet from the last letter: TAV ת of the Hebrew Coder to the first letter: ALEPH א parades before the Lord of the World petitioning him to make one of them the conduit for creation. For one reason or another Yahweh would declare each of the letters too good or too bad to be the conduit of creation until the second letter: BETH ב appeared before him and ALEPH א never did obtained an audience before Yahweh to make his case. As each of the other letters were rejected they when back out of creation. **BERESHITH** בראשית as it is envisaged now it is actually the second time that the Hebrew alphabet can be conceptually envisaged as having come back into creation. This is easily determined because **ALEPH א** and **BETH ב** are on their way out of creation and **TAV ת, SHIN ש** and **RESH ר** have returned.

It can conceptually be understood this returning of the Hebrew alphabet back into creation is the Second Coming of Christ. It was about this time that I took another suggestion from the Zohar. The Zohar says BERESHITH symbolizes the six ordinal directions. That is all the texts say about that particular nuance concerning Bereshith. That textual nuance in the Zohar doesn't say that Bereshith was made up of six Hebrew letters; however, I already was aware of that so instantly I got the idea of carrying out the mathematics as if the word **BERESHITH** בראשית was a sphere and/or a cube.

BETH ב being the conduit of creation would have all the letters in its world reduced to the number two (2) in one form or another. BETH ב was most likely chosen because it was the smallest digit numerically that can be envisaged in the world of TIME since ALEPH א symbolizes the word of God it is not visible and it symbolizes TIMELESSNESS. Anything coming through BETH is compressed symbolically into the form of BETH ב creating the east-west corridor of time. Think about how metal is compressed into streams of wire.

In the word **BERESHITH** בראשית the letter BETH ב (2) is at the far right designating it as being in the EAST; whereas, TAV ת is at the far left designating it as being in the WEST. This would make BETH ב the radius of the circle; whereas, BETH ב and TAV ת combined represented the diameter (east-west corridor of time) of the circle: i.e. four (4). RESH ר is the head or the beginning and like Michelangelo's fresco painting of "God creating Adam" coming from on high: i.e. NORTH; whereas, SHIN ש would symbolize the SOUTH. YUD י symbolizing the setting sun would represent DOWN and ALEPH א symbolizes the moon rising, which would symbolize UP. This moon rising is precisely why each of the six days of creation says, ***"It was the evening and the morning"***. This is also why the second chapter of Genesis symbolizes DARKNESS depicting the total eclipse of the sun. Surprisingly, the center of said cycle screamed of another letter; for the reason that, the center cannot be summarily dismissed. QOPH ק was the next letter and only it could be the third aspect of the Trinity and only it could symbolize the galactic core: the center of all creation and without QOPH ק creation could not RESET so to speak. This concept of resetting creation while an initiate is actually living in the material world would seem

---

[4] http://www.amazon.com/Zohar-Volumes-Shimon-Bar-Yohai/dp/1571892397/ref=sr_1_13?ie=UTF8&qid=1463073470&sr=8-13&keywords=zohar

[5] http://www.amazon.com/Mystical-Key-English-Language/dp/0892813091/ref=sr_1_2?ie=UTF8&qid=1463072712&sr=8-2&keywords=hoffstein

ridiculous and or imaginatively made-up; yet, that is precisely what takes place spiritually while everybody around the initiate would not know any difference. Even the initiate himself may not know immediately the changes have been made.

The calculation for the surface area of the sphere would be the diameter: 4 x pi = 12.566… x 4 = 50.265… That was curious because the bible only has whole letters, words, verses, chapters and books; thus, there are only 50-chapters in the book of Genesis and this I thought initially could be a coincidence. So I did the calculation on the volume of said sphere and came up with 33.51… Now that was astonishing piece of evidence; because, 3351 (removing the decimal) was the reverse of 1533, which is the precise amount of verses in the book of Genesis. Now that cannot be a coincidence at all; for the reason that, this calculating out the word BERESHITH into a sphere produced the amount of chapters and verses in the book of Genesis. I had learned from Richard C. Hoagland videos and website about an important discovery made by the two Voyager probes sent out by NASA in 1977[6]. The probes discovered that about 19.5° of the axis poles of all planetary orbs: i.e. sun, moons, planets and even on earth there is an upwelling of forces that create scarring on the surfaces of the orbs or vortexes, sunspots and volcanoes on Earth. These are known as the tetrahedral forces in creation. It is interesting that this diagram (below) of the tetrahedral forces matches the diagram made out of word BERESHITH.

Knowing that the word BERESHITH interprets the book of Genesis as a sphere I tested this theory of the 19.5° out on its 1533 verses x 0.195 = 298.935 (299) to see what would happen. I know that degrees are not equivalent to percentages; however, I believe the bible works with the numerics inferring whatever nuance it needs to convey its ideas. The 299th verse of Genesis is the last verse of the eleventh (11th) chapter of Genesis; therefore, the first verse of the twelfth chapter of Genesis would point to the upwelling of forces in the Genesis texts, which was Yahweh calling Abram out of the land of his father. How did the ancient scribes know about this cosmic law in the manifested universe? The first eleven chapters of Genesis are known as the antediluvian times (Goddess: Matriarchal) and anything after that is considered modern times (Patriarchal).

Actually, this universal materialistic law symbolizing the tetrahedral forces in creation is codified into the first letter of Genesis: BETH ב (2) inundated and surrounded by PEI פ (80 = 8) and from this perspective BETH ב would be 20% and PEI פ would represent 80% when (2 and 80 are reduced to their lowest common denominators: i.e. 2/8). The bible can only work with whole number, whole letters, whole words, etc., etc. As the mythoi of the sacred scriptures get larger, like a ripple in a pond, the precision of the mathematics become more precise. I believe that the Hebrew letter Qoph ק symbolizes the pineal gland and when it is activated it creates the spiritual tetrahedral forces in the psyche of the initiate. This is what initiates the **Initiatic Visionary Experience**. This is not an initiation ritual this is actually what happens in the psyche of the individual in the real world and it is not a theatrical ceremony played out by the members of a secret society to politically elevate the social status of one or more of its members. The **Initiatic Visionary Experience** is a spiritually spontaneous event in the psyche of the individual and no one can possibly know when it will descend upon the psyche of an initiate.

It is by my noticing the skip pattern sequence of the cosmic letters: **TAV ת (400), SHIN ש (300) and RESH ר (200)** in the word **BERESHITH** בראשית as seen in the image below that gave me the idea of taking the complete Hebrew alphabet coming into creation and the complete Hebrew alphabet going out of creation and then I reduced the alphabet down to ten letters when I saw that both ends of the pattern were equal. I called this ten letter pattern the GENESIS FORMULA.

The bible is mostly vignettes, which are the product of the sleight of hand. The reader is constantly placed before an expert magician that is showing the initiate the outer magic; but, hiding the truth behind his actions. In every sense the concept of the Hebrew alphabet going into and then out of creation got me this far in developing sacred geometry out of the mythoi of the texts; however, once the rest of the alphabet coming into and going out of creation were wiped away they no longer had a direct part in the interpretive process of the GENESIS FORMULA. What exactly is the GENESIS FORMULA saying? It was almost instantly that I envisaged the four ones: **YUD י, ALEPH א, QOPH ק and YUD י** as

---

[6] https://en.wikipedia.org/wiki/Voyager_program

developing the sacred geometry of the Vesica Piscis. The Vesica Piscis is the harmonious interrelationship between the spiritual and the material where each is equal to the other; for the reason that, they both in unanimity create a spiritual ambiance (a contented sacred space: i.e. Garden of Eden) that is unparalleled in the outer materialistic 'real' world. With that psychic contented atmosphere the initiate would want no part of the outer materialistic world. Just because an initiate lives in the materialistic world does not mean that he or she is living iconoclastically 100% of the time; to a certain extent, it is most likely that he or she is living it 50%/50%.

Previously, I discussed the Golden Ratio in regards to the relationship between LIGHT (207) and DARKNESS (328): with DARKNESS 328 / 535 = 0.613... I reiterate this here to point out that the number 613 per se infers simultaneously the Golden Ratio plus the inference of the 613-laws that are culled out of the Ten Commandments: 365-thou shalt nots and 248-thou shalts[7]. Even these figures come very close to the calculations of the Golden Ratio especially when considering that the sacred scriptures are using symbols to multi-task. Admittedly, it is not perfect with finite numbers; however, in this case 365 infers days in a year, which is most likely why it was chosen; because, 365-days inferred the circle: 360 = SHIN ש: i.e. DARKNESS.

Here in the GENESIS FORMULA the split between the ten letters' pattern into 4/6: TRINITY/EMPYREAN and BERESHITH respectively goes to illustrating another example of the Golden Ratio and the ten letters infers the Ten Commandments; however, confusingly it would appear from the calculations that the DARKNESS was called out of the LIGHT. Of course I beg to differ; for the reason that BERESHITH is the LIGHT cull out of the DARKNESS with the immediate codicil that that LIGHT: i.e. BERESHITH instantaneously turns into DARKNESS just as it turned to DARKNESS when Christ was crucified on the cross in the New Testament, which BERESHITH has everything to do with narrating that spiritual nuance.

BERESHITH, actually, speaks only to the RESH ר part of the word; for the reason that psychically the old ego-consciousness (the sun sets and died) and unconscious mind (moon: i.e. PEI פ): old heaven and earth had passed away and the new heaven and earth RESH ר has come into manifested creation. This is known about this word RESH ר for many reasons; however, the most important one is its Gematria value of **501: RESH (200), ALEPH (1) and SHIN (300).** BETH ב Gematria value has already been established as 412 reduced from 501 leaves 89 = 17 or the 17th letter of the Hebrew Coder: i.e. PEI פ; thus, it can be envisaged that RESH ר with the Gematria value of 501 symbolizes the harmonious interplay of BETH ב and PEI פ. What is also interesting here is the combined totals of the Gematria values of each letter spelt out in the letter/word RESH ר: RESH (501), ALEPH (111) and SHIN (360) = 972 = 18, which is the transposition of the number **81: 9 x 9 = KAMEA OF THE MOON.** There is a lot more to this; however, much of it is redundant to what has already been discussed.

Equidistance between the letters RESH ר and SHIN ש in the letter/word RESH ר is ALEPH א, which the Zohar says represent ELOHYM previously established as the formula for Pi: 3.1415. Any part of the Trinity represents Pi: 3.1415 as envisaged in the image below illustrating BERESHITH representing a sphere. **YUD י represents Yahweh. ALEPH א multitask also when it is spelt out: ALEPH א (1), LEMMED ל (30) and PEI פ (80) totaling 111.** Notice how LEMMED ל (30) is positioned equidistance between ALEPH א (1) and PEI פ (80), which is known as the transposition of the spelling of Gematria value of PEI פ (81: 9 x 9, KAMEA OF THE MOON). Previously, it was seen that Eve (19) symbolizing QOPH ק the 19th letter of the Hebrew Coder was mated with MAN that has the Gematria value of 311; thus, when 19: was added to 11: Aleph א (1) and Yud י (10) totaled to 30: i.e. LEMMED ל, which has a Gematria value of 30 and as a result the KAMEA OF THE MOON is imbued with the "HEART OF EVE". Remember that Yahweh Elohym (Christ) took a rib out of Adam and built a woman from it that, I believe, symbolizes the **MATRIX OF WISDOM**, which I will illustrate later how it was built as a commentary on the MONAD.

ALEPH א also symbolizes the Trinity from another perspective: ALEPH א (1), LEMMED ל (30) and PEI פ (80) = 111, which LEMMED ל (30) symbolically represented Aleph א (1), Yud י (10) and Qoph ק

---

[7] https://en.wikipedia.org/wiki/613_commandments

(100); thus, when it is read in the New Testament that *"Now when all the people were baptized, it came to pass, that Jesus also being baptized, and praying, the heaven was opened, And the Holy Ghost descended in a bodily shape like a dove upon him [Cygnus X-3: i.e. the Swan?], and a voice came from heaven, which said, Thou art my beloved Son; in thee I am well pleased. And Jesus himself began to be about thirty years of age, being (as was supposed) the son of Joseph, which was the son of Heli, (Luke 3:21-23)"* it can be understood that even the New Testament takes on the tradition that at the age of thirty **(30: LEMMED ל)** the Trinity comes together in unanimity. This is an example of how the New Testament was written from the interpretation of the systemic Esoteric Science codified to the Old Testament. **ALEPH א** per se symbolizes the **MATIX OF WISDOM** cubed (10³) for a large **ALEPH א** is 1000. **ALEPH א** symbolizing ELOHYM represents *"the spirit of Elohym hovering (moving) over the face of the waters"* in the second verse of Genesis. Elohym split into **ELOH–YM אלה-ים** and this hovering over the waters is just before Christ is baptized in the Jordon River. The **YUD** and **F-MEM** symbolize all the people baptized into the religious teachings of Judaism; whereas, **ALEPH א (1)**, **LEMMED ל (30 {3}), HEH ה (5)**, which is a transposition of the number 153, which is the aggregate of 17 or the 17ᵗʰ letter of the Hebrew Coder: i.e. PEI פ. I see the KAMEA OF THE MOON as the initiate's raison d'être that is gifted to him or her when he or she is blessed with **Initiatic Visionary Experience**. The old raison d'être: Kamea of the Moon is destroyed when the old heaven and earth passed away and instantaneously a new heaven and a new earth: i.e. raison d'être (Kamea of the Moon) is gifted, already worked out to the finest of details, to the initiate.

God the Father and the Holy Spirit coming down when Christ is baptized saying, *"this is my beloved son"*, is point to the average initiate rising to the status of Christ. God the Father is speaking about the average person that has risen above the din and clamor of the world, which the waters of Jordan symbolized to become God's beloved son.

Another nuance that comes out of the Genesis Formula showing how the New Testament is written via the systemic Esoteric Science is to view the Hebrew Coder going in and out of creation again. Notice how **Ghimmel ג (3 - camel)** has gone out of manifested creation before BETH ב (2). In the New Testament Jesus says, *"It is easier for a camel to go through the eye of a needle, than for a rich man to enter into the kingdom of God"*. The rich man is of course **BETH ב**: ego-consciousness that refuses to deflate itself. **Ghimmel ג (3 - camel)** the camel had to hunch itself down to get into the gates of the cities of antiquity. Here in the Genesis Formula **Ghimmel ג (3 - camel)** the camel is envisaged as having already gone through Qoph ק (19 - needle) the eye of the needle and the rich man: ego-consciousness is too proud to genuflect to get through the eye of the needle. This is where, I believe, the tradition of genuflecting before the altar in the Roman Catholic Church originated. Any Hebrew texts of the Torah will have the first written letter BETH ב scribed as the largest single letter of the entire Torah. The nuance here of course is that coming into manifested creation one can come in walking standing up proudly; whereas, in order for the initiate to enter the Kingdom of God the initiate has to first deflate ego-consciousness: i.e. genuflect.

Additionally, **ALEPH א spelt out ALEPH א (1), LEMMED ל (30 {3})** and **PEI פ (80 {8})** and its numbers reduced to their lowest common denominator 1, 3, 8 is the transposition of 318, which is the Gematria value of the Greek word CROSS and this has a great deal to do what is to be discussed about **RESH ר** as we continue.

One of the most mystical and enigmatic discoveries cull from out of the Genesis Formula is that when its ten Hebrew letters are placed into circular format mini-images of the Kabbalistic Tree of Life, the Star of David and the Crown of Creation (Keter) are literally forced upon the initiate. As the reader can see I made this discover after I had done the research on the larger versions of the Kabbalistic Tree of Life and the Star of David laid out in the texts of the first chapter of Genesis. It is as if the first word of Genesis: BERESHITH was predestine to validate that research; however, what this discovery also illustrates is that all of creation emanates out of just a small amount of data. In addition it will be learned that these images of the Kabbalistic Tree of Life and the Star of David did not originate with the Judaeo Christian Scripture they originated with the **MATRIX OF WISDOM**.

GOD CREATING ADM INTO HIS OWN IMAGE

NOTICE HOW ADAM IS PRONE

EVE BIRTHED FROM THE DEAD CARCASS OF ADAM

EVE RISES VERTICALLY FROM ADAM'S CORPSE

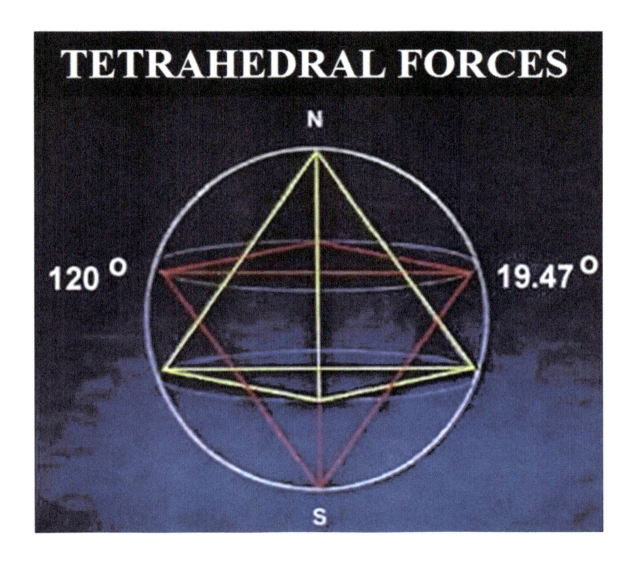

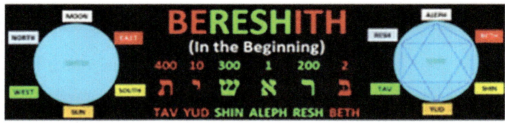

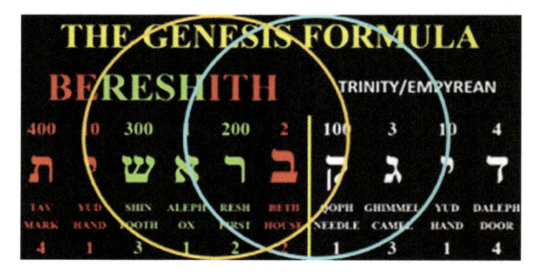

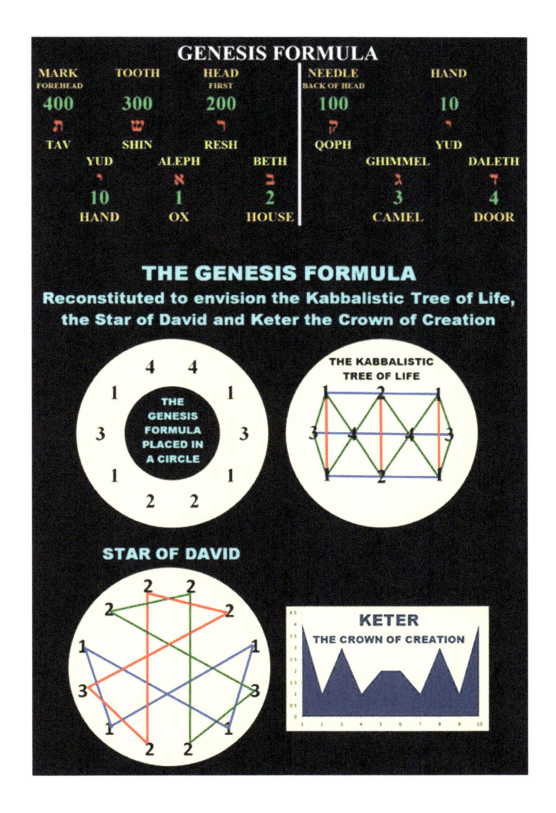

CHAPTER SEVEN

ADAM AND EVE IN THE GARDEN OF EDEN

BERESHITH בראשית symbolizes the **TRINITY/EMPYREAN** קראשית; however, this is not envisaged by the uninitiated; for the reason that, the Hebrew letter **PEI** פ that inundates and surrounds **BETH** ב is not visible to the naked and iconoclastic eye.

In essence, the Trinity/Empyrean aspects of the Genesis Formula are, for all intent and purpose, the New Heaven and Earth: i.e. new raison d'être that God gifted the initiate with. The letter QOPH ק and YUD י in the Trinity/Empyrean symbolize two parts of the three part Trinity; whereas, **Ghimmel** ג and **DALETH** ד combined represent the Christ aspect of the Trinity. **Ghimmel** ג symbolizes the deflated ego-consciousness and it represents the materialistic aspect of the God/Man Christ; whereas, DALETH ד symbolizes the DOOR (numerical count of 434-word in the first chapter of Genesis), which in itself symbolizes Christ that represents the spiritual aspect of the God/Man Christ: i.e. three and four total to seven, which is the septenary that symbolizes the Birth of Christ Consciousness. Three (3) symbolizes the Trivium (three Grammatical Arts) and four (4) symbolizes the Quadrivium (four Mathematical Sciences): i.e. THE SEVEN LIBERAL ARTS. **Ghimmel** ג in the Trinity/Empyrean infers the initiate taking on the Camel's burden; for the reason that, learning the Esoteric Science (Hermeticism) is no easy task.

The Trinity is clearly envisaged in the Trinity/Empyrean aspect of the Genesis Formula. This goes to symbolically illustrate the **REVEALED** (BERESHITH) and **COVERED** (Trinity/Empyrean) Torahs; for the reason that both these parts of the Genesis Formula reflect each other as if they were looking at each other in a mirror: i.e. mirror-imaging process. This means that BERESHITH has the Trinity codified also into its half of the Genesis Formula. Contemplative thought will bring to mind the old occult maxim **"as above so below"**: however, true Hermeticism is diametrically opposite to that. It should be read **"as below so above"** for this is the pivotal reason that Michelangelo went up to the ceiling of the Sistine Chapel to fresco a commentary on all the artwork below codified into the mosaics of the floor and into the frescoes on the walls. The reason that both sides of the GENESIS FORMULA are essentially equal is; for the reason that, whatever the spiritualized ego culls out of the DARKNESS (Trinity/Empyrean) would reflect the initiate's real world character and personality below: i.e. raison d'être; thus, both sides are eternally the same.

BETH ב and RESH ר are positioned inside the Vesica Piscis and these two Hebrew letters symbolize the God/Man Christ: Christ consciousness. BETH ב symbolizes the archetypal letter (beast) civilized (calmed) by the spiritual cosmic Hebrew letter RESH ר that symbolizes Christ. RESH ר has already been interpreted as PEI פ and BETH ב. What I find extraordinarily interesting here is that each of the four comic Hebrew letters making up the word **CHRIST: TAV** ת, **SHIN** ש, **RESH** ר **and QOPH** ק are essentially conveying the same mystic message. **QOPH** ק: **BETH** ב and **PEI** פ combined, **RESH** ר: is seen also as **BETH** ב and **PEI** פ, **SHIN** ש is seen as the combination of **Qoph** ק, **Aleph** א and **Yud** י: i.e. Trinity dominating all creation (360° circle) and **TAV** ת is symbolic of the Kundalini Serpent rising up out of the forehead.

The two part GENESIS FORMULA is symbolic of the two part psyche; though, they are in actual fact equal; however, they are symbolic of the formula for the Golden Ratio. BERESHITH בראשית aspect of the Genesis Formula symbolizes the product of ego-consciousness: i.e. masculine (number two - 2); where, the **TRINITY/ EMPYREAN** קראש aspect of the Genesis Formula symbolizes the product of the unconscious mind: i.e. feminine (number three - 3).

Jesus says, in the New Testament, ***"And I tell you that you are Peter, and on this rock I will build my church, and the gates of Hades will not prevail against it. I will give you the keys of the kingdom of heaven. Whatever you bind on the earth will be bound in heaven, and whatever*** *you loose on earth will be loosed in heaven (Matthew 16:18-19)."* And *"Again I say unto you, that if two of you shall agree on earth as touching anything that they shall ask, it shall be done for them of my Father which is in heaven. For where two or three are gathered together in my name, there am I in the midst of them (Matthew 18:19-20)."*

Matthew 16:19; basically says the same thing as Matthew 18:18. I believe that this is mentioned twice in Matthew's gospel; for the reason that Jesus was saying something to Peter on a personal level; for the reason that, he envisaged Jesus as the Christ, who symbolizes the Pope, which is analogously symbolic to every soul that communicates with Christ; but, Jesus also in Matthew gospel was talking to the general public. The reason I point this out is that Matthew's 16th chapter verse 18th, I believe, is deliberately pointing out the short formula for the Golden Ratio: i.e. 1.618 and these verses in Matthew gospel's two sections is a commentary on the Genesis Formula, which is ten words split into two section 4/6 reduced down to 2/3.

When Jesus said, *"For where two or three are gathered together in my name, there am I in the midst of them (Matthew 18:20)."* Jesus was referring to the Hebrew letter **RESH: Resh (2), Aleph (1)** and **Shin (3): i.e. 213**. Aleph (1) that would symbolize the Vesica Piscis between the heavens and the earth as envisaged in the Genesis Formula.

However, the general population uses ego-consciousness (2) and the unconscious mind (3) in the everyday normal activities of life when individually the average person does not have Christ consciousness. In other words at this point the Genesis Formula is not created yet. Basically the Golden Ratio (Fibonacci sequence) is maintaining the status quo of a person's character and personality; thus, if a person has an addiction it will only get worse just as analogously the aging process builds to the crescendo of death. This is very much like a person philosophy on life will become stauncher as the years go by similar to how concrete in a dam get harden as the years go by.

When the Genesis Formula was created as the Garden of Eden, for all intent and purpose, this is why Yahweh Elohym (Christ) told Adam not to eat from the **TREE OF THE KNOWLEDGE OF GOOD AND EVIL**. This Tree of the Knowledge of Good and Evil is in point of fact not the two part Genesis Formula. Yes, each side of the Genesis Formula has Trinity aspects put together perfectly and this is why the Genesis Formula was created; for the reason that, the Trinity created the two part Genesis Formula to bring forth the Vesica Piscis: i.e. Garden of Eden. The **TREE OF THE KNOWLEDGE OF GOOD AND EVIL** is literally created by ego-consciousness; for the reason that, **BERESHITH** and the **Trinity/Empyrean** become superfluous once the Vesica Piscis (Garden of Eden) is in use. The fact that both parts of the Genesis Formula have become equal to one another is the reason that the spiritual and the material combine to create the God/Man Christ.

This Trinity equality found on each side of the Genesis Formula is precisely why the Kabbalistic Tree of Life radiated out from both the LIGHT and the DARKNESS the Vesica Piscis via the 1, 5, 3 pattern.

For Adam and Eve eating from the **TREE OF THE KNOWLEDGE OF GOOD AND EVIL** would destroy Christ consciousness (Vesica Piscis). Adam had to first revert back into an archetypal beast in order for him to turn into the serpent that spoke to Eve. And when the initiate studies the command that Yahweh Elohym (Christ) gave to Adam concerning not eating from the **TREE OF THE KNOWLEDGE OF GOOD AND EVIL** in relationship to the discussion Eve has with the serpent the misunderstanding; between, Christ's edict and Eve and the Serpent's discussion is seemingly a chaotically confusing.

"Then the Lord God (Christ) took the Adam and put him into the Garden of Eden to cultivate it and keep it. The Lord God commanded Adam, saying, from any tree of the garden you may eat freely; but, from the tree of the knowledge of good and evil you shall not eat, for in the day that you eat from it you will surely die (Genesis 2:15-17)."

It is important here to notice that the deity's name in the second chapter of Genesis is Yahweh Elohym (Lord God). These are the two deities of the Old Testament; however, when they unite they represent the Garden of Eden (Vesica Piscis), which symbolizes the God/Man Christ. In every sense this is the two part Genesis Formula coming together to create the Garden of Eden: amalgamation of the spiritual (Elohym) and the material (Yahweh). It is the spiritual unconscious mind (Kamea of the Moon) making ego-consciousness (sun) into the spiritual Christ (Kamea of the Sun) and this is why BERESHITH'S six letters symbolizes the Kamea of the Sun (6^3), which in Christianity is symbolized as Christ: i.e. the Spiritual Sun. From this perspective neither parts of the Genesis Formula that does not make up part of the Vesica Piscis cannot be consider the Garden of Eden for the simple fact that Christ consciousness in neither a compromise nor a negotiation; to a certain extent, it is an ambiance of the two coming together. Those parts of the two circles: material and spiritual in the Genesis Formula that are not part of the Vesica Piscis (Garden of Eden) represent the TREE OF THE KNOWLEDGE OF GOOD AND EVIL; for the reason that, the remaining part of BERESHITH represent the LIGHT being concretized (evil); whereas, the remaining part of the TRINITY/EMPYREAN would symbolize the highest possible good in creation.

"Now the serpent was more subtle than any beast of the field which the Lord God had made. And he said unto the woman, Yea, hath God said, Ye shall not eat of every tree of the garden? And the woman said unto the serpent, we may eat of the fruit of the trees of the garden: But of the fruit of the tree which is in the midst of the garden, God hath said, Ye shall not eat of it, neither shall ye touch it, lest ye die. And the serpent said unto the woman, Ye shall not surely die: For God doth know that in the day ye eat thereof, then your eyes shall be opened, and ye shall be as gods, knowing good and evil. And when the woman saw that the tree was good for food, and that it was pleasant to the eyes, and a tree to be desired to make one wise, she took of the fruit thereof, and did eat, and gave also unto her husband with her; and he did eat. And the eyes of them both were opened, and they knew that they were naked; and they sewed fig leaves together, and made themselves aprons (Genesis 3:1-7)."

The subtlety of the serpent is lies: half truths that may even be thought to be the truth. The serpent begins the conversation with Eve saying, "Yea, hath God (Elohym) said." The answer is of course, no, God (Elohym) did not say it. Once the serpent (Adam) got Eve speaking about her deity as God (Elohym) and not YAHWEH ELOHYM (Lord God) confusing her as to which deity said what, the serpent wins the argument; because, neither Eve nor the serpent is referring to what Yahweh Elohym said. It should be realized that neither Yahweh nor Elohym represents Yahweh Elohym (Christ) in any way for neither one of them individually adheres to what the other has to say. Yahweh Elohym is spiritually a harmonious seamless relationship. Remember that the old god Yahweh (sun) and the old god Elohym (moon) past away. The fact that Adam step out of his role as the spiritual sun: Christ and became the archetypal serpent beast Eve had nobody else but the serpent to keep her occupied so she wanders off as most women do in the world when their man takes them for granted and treat them complacently. For both Adam and Eve to be speaking about the dead god Elohym (God) illustrates that they had both reverted back to their old way of life. This would be like an alcoholic or drug addict having been healed of their addiction and then reverting back to that old addiction. We see this in the world where an alcoholic sobers up and gets a job, home and then marries and has a few children and he starts drinking again. He ends up losing his job, his home and his family and this is basically from a materialistic perspective being kicked out of the Garden of Eden. The finishing stroke in all of this is Adam and Eve *"knew that they were naked; and they sewed fig leaves together, and made themselves aprons"*. Think about a couple having sex. During that blissful experience neither one of them knows that they are consciously naked; yet, moments after the sexual experience they put on cloths and resume their mythological rolls in life. Adam and Eve finally realized they were naked in the Garden of Eden; for the reason that, neither ego-consciousness nor the unconscious mind were allowed in the Garden of Eden (internal psychic temple) to discriminate and cloth the WORD OF GOD. Once Adam and Eve were introduced to ego-consciousness (Sun - Jachin) and the unconscious mind (Moon - Boaz) again they made aprons, which is, as far as I am concern, a direct reference to the Masonic Order or other Mystery Schools. What I mean by this is that just because someone knows the secrets of the Esoteric Science (Hermeticism) does not mean in any way, shape or form he or she understands conceptually and/or spiritually the WORD OF GOD and this last in emphasized by Yahweh Elohym (Christ) tossing Adam and Eve out of the Garden of Eden. Adam and Eve sewing the fig-leaves together is a negotiation or compromise process it is not a seamless spiritual relationship. I get a kick out of the fact that Father Robert Barron of Chicago, Illinois were ordained an auxiliary bishop to the archdiocese of Los Angeles, California and the first thing he did was to create an apron: Coat of Arms[1] with his own symbols on it.

Eve was birthed from the dead carcass of Adam and the word ADAM has a Gematria value of 45 and the numbers 4 (Moon – unconscious mind) and 5 (Sun – ego-consciousness) in the **MATRIX OF WISDOM** symbolizes the waters of creation. Eve has Gematria value of 19 taken from 45 reduces down to 26, which is the Gematria value of Yahweh: i.e. the non-spiritual Sun: i.e. Satan: ego-consciousness. Michelangelo depicts Eve rising from the dead carcass of Adam to immediately be confronted by Yahweh. Remember that when Eve was birthed it is said she was taken out of MAN (Genesis 2:23) not Adam. This also goes to Cain's birth being Yahweh gave Eve a MAN (Genesis 4:1); whereas, Seth is called a seed given to her by Elohym (Genesis 4:25) to replace Abel. The wording and the Gematria value of words in the scriptural texts explains the separate and/or diametrically opposite functions of other words like Yahweh and Elohym. Few people take the trivial translations as fact and look up the more detail interpretation of the texts via numerical and Gematria value of letters and words. This was discussed to point out Eve was symbolic of the Spirit of Elohym moving over the face of the waters (Genesis 1:2) similar to Christ being baptized and coming out of the Jordan River and immediately going into the desert and being tempted by the serpent as Eve is immediately after birth tempted by Yahweh the serpent. It is my contention that Eve as well as Christ in the New Testament was being recruited to join a Mystery School or guild, which would provide a trade (food from the rock), hierarchal status in a religion or a hierarchal status in the secular government (three temptations of Christ) and Eve failed in the spiritual testing process altogether by eating of the fruit of the forbidden tree; thus, though the Mystery Schools know the secrets of the Esoteric Science that knowledge does not illustrate that they have had the *Initiatic Visionary Experience*. All the evidence such as the birth of Eve and the Sewing of Aprons and the Gematria value of words comes directly from the texts of the sacred scriptures. Adam and Eve finding they are naked is very much like finding they had no network of friends and companions that would aid them in their life struggles as is guaranteed in the membership of the Masonic Order and other Mystery Schools and College Frat Houses: Fraternities. Sewing aprons in the Masonic Order is a tradition that all members have to go through in achieving different degree status in the Secret Brotherhood. Adam and Eve finding they are naked and sewing themselves aprons is because they had lost the LIGHT of God that protected them in the world. Adam and Eve knowing they were naked points to them knowing nothing about spirituality. When Adam and Eve had the LIGHT of God embracing them they did not need that fount of knowledge because the Holy Spirit gave it to them as they needed it. This is why throughout the secular world every profession has a different uniform to put on that cloth and identifies them in their chosen profession indicating they are well versed and educated in their academic professions or trade skills: i.e. the different animals that Yahweh Elohym (Christ) had Adam name.

---

[1] https://www.youtube.com/watch?v=8zomejCz53A

Every set in the Fibonacci Sequence
Reduces down to a 2/3 Ratio

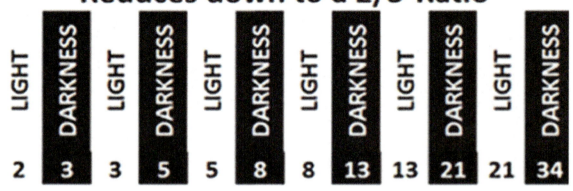

DARKNESS turns into LIGHT

CHAPTER EIGHT

THE VESICA PISCIS IN VARIOUS ARTISTIC FORMS

The next twelve (12) images speak somewhat to how the Vesica Piscis (Christ, Buddha, Krishna, Tao, etc.) is artistically expressed and formatted in art around the world.

The first image shows how the Vesica Piscis is calculated out in sacred geometry; for the reason that the Vesica Piscis is form by two circles coming together and its edges touching each other's center. The space between these two centers is called the Vesica Piscis.

The second image shows conceptually the dynamics of the tetrahedral forces of the psyche when the two diametrically different concentric circles come together. As it can be seen the concentric circles are not envisaged as going diametrically opposite to one another: i.e. clockwise and counterclockwise; however, I will get to that concept later; nonetheless, when these two opposites ORDER and CHAOS: both from their own perspective are perfectly ordered, they create the dynamics of the tetrahedral forces in creation (psyche), which was discussed above in regards to the discovery made by NASA'S Voyager Program.

The third and fourth images are quite unique; for the reason that this Vesica Piscis was created within the last decade. The Washington Monument in Washington DC initially had a gigantic circle surrounding it in 2003 and between the years 2003 and 2007 that these images presented was taken. Metal scaffolding was erected around Washington Monument ostensibly to clean the outer façade of the monument, which I believe was the magician's sleight of hand in order for the Masonic Order to landscape around the monument to insert the Vesica Piscis image. This image is a rehashing somewhat of the image in Bernini Square at Saint Peter's Basilica in Vatican City. It will be seen below how from 2000 to the present date Freemasonry has been working quite steadily in developing the esotericism on the National Mall in Washington DC.

The fifth image is a depiction of Bernini Square at Saint Peter's Basilica in Vatican City. Notice that two circles can be drawn around the obelisk from the two flanking fountains to create a Vesica Piscis just like Washington's Monument. What validates that the obelisk and the fountains symbolize the Vesica Piscis is the 140-statues on top of Bernini colonnades and the thirteen additional statues on the roof of Saint Peter's Basilica, which totals to 153-statues: 153 is the aggregate of 17th symbolizing PEI פ (Kamea of the Moon). What biblically validate this is found in the New Testament.

"*But when the morning was now come, Jesus stood on the shore: but the disciples knew not that it was Jesus. Then Jesus saith unto them, Children, have ye any meat? They answered him, No. And he said unto them, Cast the net on the right side of the ship, and ye shall find. They cast therefore, and now they were not able to draw it for the multitude of fishes. Therefore that disciple whom Jesus loved saith unto Peter, It is the Lord. Now when Simon Peter heard that it was the Lord, he girt his fisher's coat unto him, (for he was naked,) and did cast himself into the sea. And the other disciples came in a little ship; (for they were not far from land, but as it were two hundred cubits,) dragging the net with fishes. As soon then as they were come to land, they saw a fire of coals there, and fish laid thereon, and bread. Jesus saith to them bring of the fish which ye have now caught. Simon Peter went up, and drew the net to land full of great fishes, an hundred and fifty and three: and for all there were so many, yet was not the net broken (John 21:4-11).*

The sixth image is Christ on the cross between two thieves, which is a perfect image of the Vesica Piscis. I, personally, believe the image of Christ crucified between two thieves is the image that Catholicism should be depicting throughout Christendom. This image is somewhat analogous to the Vesica Piscis found in the first chapter of Genesis. The LIGHT in the first chapter of Genesis represented the Vesica Piscis: i.e. Christ. The repentant thief is told by Christ that he would be in heaven with Him. This penitent thief in every sense deflated his ego and this is why only one cycle is envisaged in the first chapter of Genesis.

The seventh image shows Michelangelo's rendition of the Temptation and Expulsion of Adam and Eve from the Garden of Eden. It is a beautiful depiction of the Vesica Piscis; for the reason that, it shows two serpents wrapped around the tree. For centuries this panel in the ceiling of the Sistine Chapel was thought by most visitors to represent one serpent; however, if the reader follows the tail of the serpent up and around the tree it will be seen that there is enough serpent left around the tree to represent a second serpent: i.e. the angel. The angel with cloths symbolizes Yahweh (civilized societal mores); whereas, the naked serpent symbolized Elohym unfettered by societal mores. The Tree symbolizes the Bodhi Tree (axis mundi - center of creation).

The eighth image is Mercury's Caduceus, which like Michelangelo depiction of the Temptation and Expulsion of Adam and Eve has two serpents wrapped around a central staff: i.e. axis mundi. Mercury represents the "messenger of the Gods" it is not difficult to envisage the Caduceus as an image of the Vesica Piscis.

The ninth image is the Churning of the Milky Ocean in Hindu artwork. This image goes to show more about the sacred space in the center. Both sides of the Vesica Piscis are struggling against each other while Krishna is motionless in the center. The turtle that Krishna stands on symbolizes creation motionless.

The tenth image is the School of Athens by Raphael Santi. Plato is pointing upwards towards heaven and Aristotle symbolically is pointing downward toward earth and they are walking down the corridor of Time side by side. The corridor of Time is depicted as the three archways, with the archways' ceilings having a pattern of $56 \times 3 = 168$ or the hours in a week. I think that Raphael is saying symbolically Plato and Aristotle teachings have survive the ravages of Time and that is why they are use prevalently depicted in the Roman Catholic Church teachings.

Plato and Aristotle represented two diametrically opposite philosophies that took on both the four mathematical sciences (Quadrivium) and the three grammatical arts (Trivium). Aristotle was considered the first scientist; therefore, he lean more towards the Quadrivium and Plato lean more towards the Trivium. What is interesting about this fresco is that Plato and Aristotle appears as if they would fit inside a Vesica Piscis; but, that would be a wrong assessment; for the reason that, they are both walking down the corridor of Time; whereas, each of the three archways has a transept crossing the corridor of Time. On the last transept in the forefront (south side) are people writing (Trivium); whereas, on the right (north side) people are creating images of geometry; however, I see that the entire transept symbolizes both sides of the transept have Christ consciousness. Both sides of the transept seem to have both the Quadrivium and the Trivium; though, each side leans more towards one than the other as if one side lives more by the left hemisphere of the brain and the other side lives more towards the right hemisphere of the brain. Almost at the end of this work the multiple transepts crossing the corridor of Time will be shown to be a prerequisite in creating the Genesis Formula: i.e. the Initiatic Visionary Experience.

The eleventh image shows the Vesica Piscis above the central door of the West Façade (Royal Portal) of Chartres Cathedral. This eleventh image showing the four fixed signs of the Zodiac: Angel (Matthew - Air), Bull (Luke - Earth), Lion (Mark - Fire) and Eagle (John - Water); though, they represent Christ as LIGHT: Christ per se is not a fixed image; for the reason that Christ symbolizes the dynamic tetrahedral forces of creation. This image of Christ sitting in the center of the Vesica Piscis on his throne literally states that Christ has nothing to do with Astrology; though, Astrology is use to mythologize the WORD OF GOD. Astrology is merely the swaddling clothing (Masonic Aprons or societal mores garment) that Christ is wrapped in.

The twelfth image shows again the Vesica Piscis in the Genesis Formula to illustrate how the image in Chartres Cathedral came about. The four beasts: lion, eagle, angel and the bull symbolizes the Fixed Triplicities of Astrology: LIGHT culled out of the first four days of creation symbolizing the four gospels of the New Testament. Unless these four gospels are systemically united into a cohesive whole Christ consciousness cannot be gifted to the initiate.

VESICA PISCIS

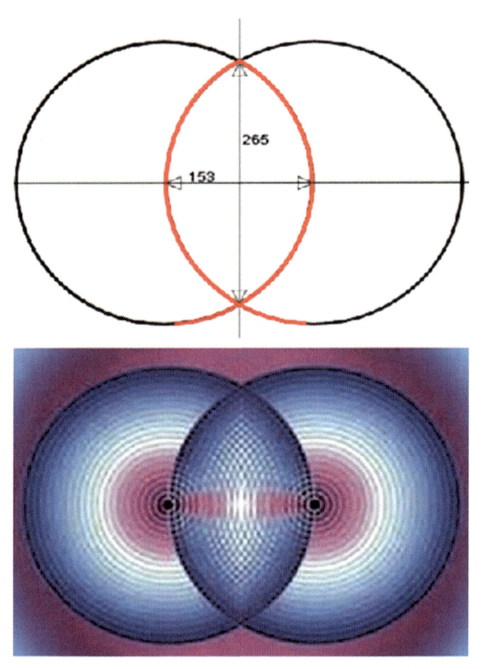

VESICA PISCIS & TETRAHEDRAL FORCES

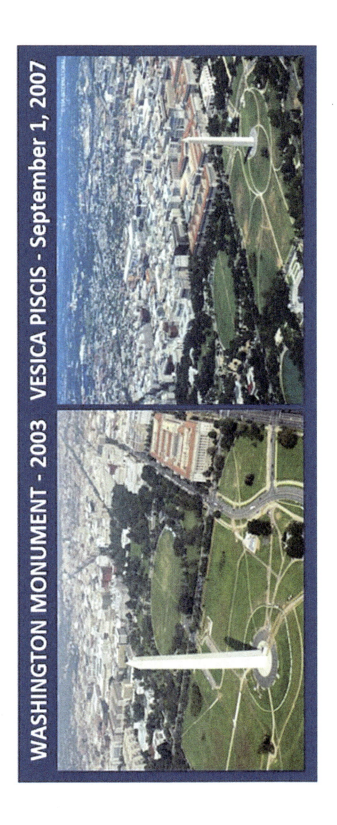

SAINT PETER'S BASILICA

CRUCIFIXION OF CHRIST

THE TEMPTATION AND EXPLUSION OF ADAM AND EVE

TWO SERPENTS WRAPPED AROUND THE TREE

CADUCEUS

CHURNING OF THE MILKY OCEAN

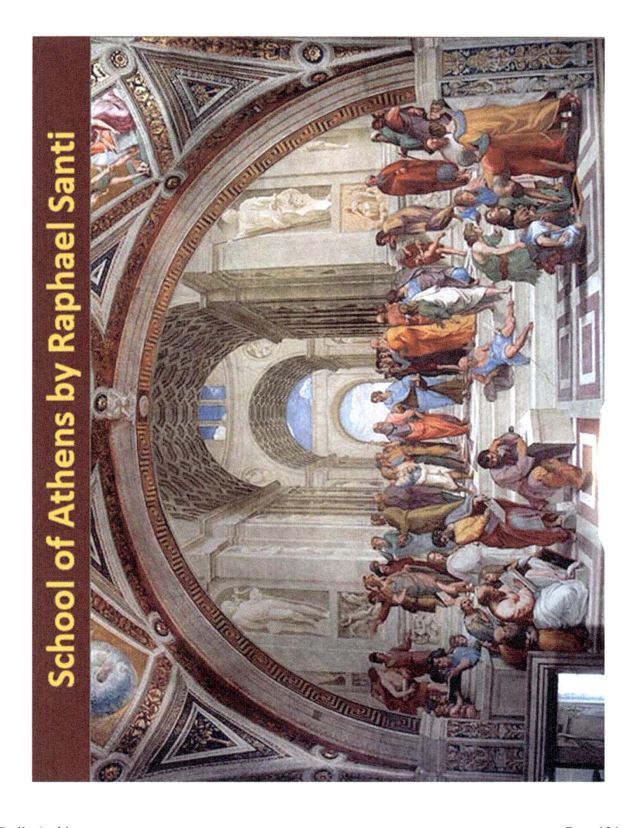

School of Athens by Raphael Santi

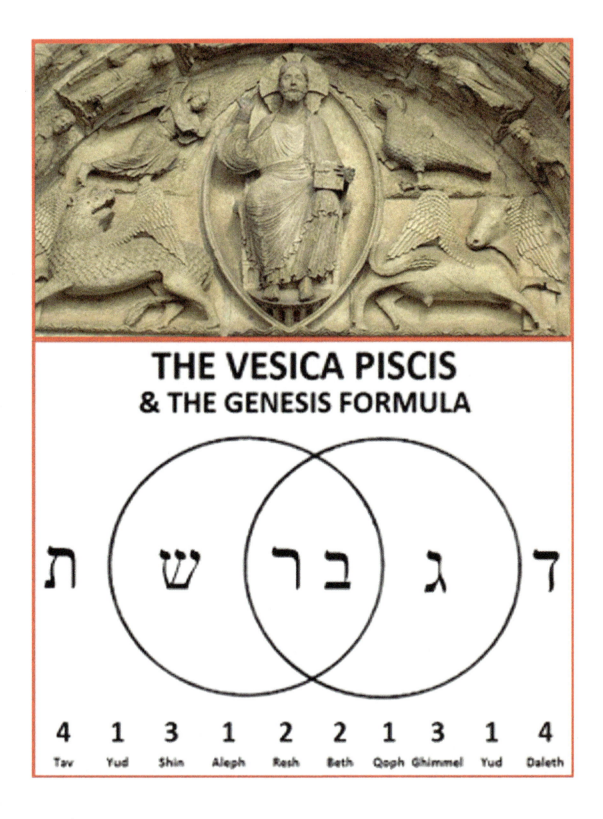

CHAPTER NINE
SOME MYSTERIES OF CHARTRES CATHEDRAL

Chartres Cathedral has an amazing background story that most of the Roman Catholic laity knows nothing about; for the reason that, the hierarchy of true Catholicism believes, and rightly so, that each member of the laity owes his or her *whole heart, mind, soul, time, finances and resources* to his or her search for the knowledge of God.

I happen to be born in a most advantageous and opportune time; though, I am not a rich man and have not traveled the world to visit the religious sites I write about; rather, I have a library of books, cds and DVDs and the Internet to research the detail nuances of the bible and my religion: the Roman Catholic Church. The numerous personal discoveries I have made from out of the bible and from many of those books and religious sites would be classified as armchair contemplative meditational thought. I am proud not to be an academic scholar frozen into a closed mindset. I am free to think as I please, outside the box, unhampered by the restrictions of what is classified academically as **"discipline"**, which I give the nomenclature **"frozen antiquated thought"** no more different than Satan frozen in the glacier in the lowest realm of hell as narrated by Dante Alighieri in his La Divina Commedia. Do not get me wrong academia is needed as curators (museum curators) of knowledge in lower and higher educational system and no matter how new the knowledge is that is culled from the DARKNESS it is still academically restrictive. I will say that the battle between academia and the pioneer researcher is essentially and mythologically the same as the battle between LIGHT and DARKNESS.

I love pointing out the fact that a 33° Mason is no longer a member of the Masonic Order; though, that degree is considered the highest degree in that Mystery School. The first 32° symbolize that which is frozen and the 33° is the beginning of the thawing of that glacier of knowledge Masons, religious hierarchies and academic are frozen in. That itself is the mystery behind the 32-tablets of knowledge that Atlantis is said mythologically to have hidden in three archives in antiquity's Halls of Records.

Bishop Fulbert and his religious cabal began constructing the Romanesque Chartres Cathedral after the previous Carolingian church burnt down back in 1020AD, which that date, I believe, is symbolic of the large **ALEPH** א, which represents the **MATRIX OF WISDOM** cubed (10^3) with the Crown of Creation (Keter) added to it symbolized by the eleventh Hebrew letter **KHAF** כ **(20)** indicating the discovery of sacred geometry in the sacred scriptures. Previous to the Carolingian Church was the Merovingian Church (both Catholic) and before that the Roman pagan church and they all burnt down. These fires are important to remember; for the reason that, these and subsequent fires are essential to understanding this commentary on Chartres Cathedral.

The year 1020AD is a pivotal year in the mythological history of Chartres Cathedral; because, it symbolizes the book of Genesis. The first eleven chapters of Genesis symbolizes the antediluvian times: i.e. the times of the Matriarchal Society. This period of time in the first eleven chapters of Genesis is designated as the Keter the Crown of Creation; because, it has 299-verses, which total to twenty (299 = 2+9+9 = 20) and the rest of the book of Genesis has 1234-verses that symbolizes a Tetractys or a large **ALEPH** א.

The first eleven chapters of Genesis symbolizes the Vesica Piscis; because, the first thirty-five uses of the word ELOHYM is broken up into two parts 32-Elohyms in the first chapter of Genesis and 3-Elohym in the first three verses of the second chapter of Genesis and then there are another 100-times the words YAHWEH and ELOHYM are used 50-times each that expanse out from the second chapter of Genesis to the eleventh chapter. This pattern of 32 (5), 3 and 100 (1) is the transposition of the Vesica Piscis 153. The fact that the words Yahweh and Elohym are split into being used 50-times each point to the MATRIX OF WISDOM being in play; because, that is precisely how the MATRIX OF WISDOM is set up.

If the reader can envisage via meditational contemplative thought the synchronicity between the historical mythos of Chartres Cathedral built in the French Capetian dynasty period[1] with the mythos of the books of Genesis it may benefit those readers to also research the Gallo Roman Church c. 500AD[2] then continue to research and meditate contemplatively on the Merovingian Church[3] and then the Carolingian Church[4].

Each of the churches: Roman Gallo, Merovingian and the Carolingian burned down prior to Bishop Fulbert starting building the Romanesque Church in 1020AD and a brief history of their mythoi can be found on the internet[5]. What transpired before the Genesis Creation Account can only be hypothesized via the zodiacal cycle; whereas, more nuances can come out of due diligence on the reader's part. The mythoi of Chartres Cathedral prior to the fire of 1020AD may supply more nuances as to those prior spiritual psychic events of Gen. 1:1.

Here is an image of Bishop Fulbert's Chartres Cathedral. It is very interesting to see the Sun and the Moon towers at opposite ends of the cathedral. There are no transepts on the north and south sides of the cathedral, which points to mere secular mores and not the Initiatic Visionary experience. The nuances of where the Sun and Moon towers are points to the laity entering the cathedral from DARKNESS (Moon) side of the cathedral and going towards secular LIGHT. This is very thick stone that the Fulbert cathedral was built from, which let in very little sunlight from the numerous windows. Bishop Fulbert's cathedral is rectangular like Solomon's Temple and later would be transformed into an octagon (cross) shape cathedral. The tower towards the apse is the Sun tower and is dominates the cathedral thoughts indicating that it symbolizes ego-consciousness. Much of this about Bishop Fulbert's Chartres Cathedral makes little sense unless this data is contrasted with the Sun and Moon towers built into the Royal Portal/West Façade in 1134 when the west side of the cathedral went on fire. The new west façade symbolizes the Initiatic Visionary Experience. The five churches: Roman Gallo, Merovingian, Carolingian, Bishop Fulbert's Cathedral and the present Gothic Cathedral symbolizes the five coffins the Popes are buried in.

---

[1] https://en.wikipedia.org/wiki/Capetian_dynasty
[2] https://en.wikipedia.org/wiki/Gallo-Roman_culture
[3] http://merovingiandynasty.org/details.php?id=merovingian_origins
[4] http://www.medievaltimes.info/medieval-europe-9th-to-13th-c/carolingian-empire/
[5] http://frenchmoments.eu/chartres-cathedral/

In 1134AD (numbers 1, 1 [2], 3 and 4 symbolic of Christ entering the fray) there was another fire in Chartres Cathedral, which burnt down only the West Façade portion of the cathedral and the rest of the Romanesque Cathedral remained intact; however, this above image of Chartres Cathedral is very problematic seeing the sun tower would have had to be deliberately torn down (not burnt down) to replace the west façade with two towers. To give an answer to this mystery of the two towers burning down when the historical mythoi would indicate that only one could have burnt down. I would suggest that Bishop Fulbert built his rendition of Chartres Cathedral in the image and likeness, on a symbolic level, of the MATRIX OF WISDOM. Those that understand the MATRIX OF WISDOM symbolizes the two-part psyche: ego-consciousness (Sun Tower) and the unconscious mind (Moon Tower) would see them as diametrically opposite to one another and the MATRIX OF WISDOM literally shows that they are in opposition to each other. In chapter eighteen it will be shown how the MATRIX OF WISDOM transforms into the Temple of God, which has symbolically the two towers at opposite ends of the MATRIX OF WISDOM; however, each tower has mirror-image each other alchemically mystically marrying each other by embracing each other symbolized by Christ sitting on his throne in the center of the Vesica Piscis on the west façade. This is the reason that both towers in Fulbert's cathedral had to be replaced in order for the new west façade to symbolize the Initiatic Visionary Experience. This symbolism is great; for the reason that, it shows that neither of the two towers was used to create the new west façade. This goes to illustrate that when the initiate receives the Initiatic Visionary Experience from God nothing in the initiates psyche other than his or her basic raison d'etre is used to breathe new life into the initiate's soul. From this above image of Fulbert cathedral and the mythoi of the many fires it can be envisaged that the whole of the plan for Chartres Cathedral was plan back when the Roman Gallo Christian Church was built. That may sound inane but pure contemplative thought on the mythoi and historicity of Chartres Cathedral will validate it.

The West Façade was rebuilt to symbolize the Initiatic Visionary Experience, which each member of the laity should receive directly from God if he or she was worthy to receive it. It is my theory that all of the fires from 500AD to 1134AD: from the pagan Roman Church to the primitive Merovingian and Carolingian Churches and the West Façade burnt down so the mythoi of the cathedral would center on and give background mythoi to the rebuilding of the West Façade and this kind of symbolism is not unprecedented.

Michelangelo painted the fresco of the LAST JUDGMENT on the West Wall (Altar Wall) of the Sistine Chapel; for the reason that, it was planned before the first stone of the foundation of the building was put into place just as all those fires in Chartres Cathedral were planned mythologically to rebuild the West Façade and a later fire was planned mythologically for 1194AD to tear down old Romanesque Cathedral to build the Gothic Cathedral. It matters not how long the symbolic plan of the Catholic Church takes to complete as long as the alleged history sound reasonable and sensible for a back-story as long as the mythoi of the project authenticate it spiritual truths. No religion tells untruths by giving false mythological histories. The goal of any religion is to use the mythoi of history as swaddling clothes to cloth the WORD OF GOD. The history of humanity is not the Roman Catholic Church's forte or its raison d'être; though, outwardly it may appear to be that way.

In 1194AD there is yet another fire and this time the whole of Chartres Cathedral burnt down except the ROYAL PORTAL/WEST FAÇADE. What were the 'gambling odds' that the West Façade would remain intact while the rest of the Church was destroyed when the opposite happened sixty (60) years before? The sixty (60) year period between the last two fires brings to mind the interpretation of the first word of Genesis: BERESHITH "separated six". The distance in time from 1020AD to 1134 is 114-years is also reduced to six (6). This separation of six (6) is solely based upon the esotericism of the Zodiac/Calendar year as recorded in the first four chapters of Genesis. The first chapter of Genesis symbolizes the first six days of creation: i.e. they symbolize the first six months of the Calendar year (exotericism): i.e. the alleged historical data; whereas, the next six signs of the Zodiac (esoterically) are completely hidden from view. In addition the years 1020AD (3), 1134AD (9) and 1194AD (6) reduce down the Mutable Quadruplicities Signs of Astrology: number 3, 6 and 9; whereas the there are 174-years between 1020AD and 1194AD. The numbers 1, 7 and 4 symbolize the Cardinal Quadruplicities Signs of Astrology. The last known fire in Chartres Cathedral is allegedly an unexplained fire in the roof section of the cathedral in 1836AD, which was replaced with a metal roof. The number 1, 3, 6 and 8 are the four months with thirty-days in the Zodiac/Calendar year and they collectively initiate the STAR OF DAVID (tetrahedral forces in the psyche). This is similar to what Michelangelo did on the ceiling of the Sistine Chapel by frescoing the Zodiac/Calendar year. The Star of David is there; but, it is esoterically invisible. The numbers 1, 3, 6, and 8 transforms into the numerical value of "LORD JESUS CHRIST" and 31.68 North Latitude is right where Bethlehem of Judea is located. In addition the years between 1020AD and 1836AD are 816, which is a number that is the transposition of the Golden Ratio 0.618. Is anybody truly supposed to believe that any of these fires in these particular years are all just coincidental?

There is absolutely no doubt in my mind that the West Façade of Chartres Cathedral symbolizes the *Initiatic Visionary Experience* that God blesses the worthy initiate with. Here at Chartres Cathedral the Catholic Church has codified that *Initiatic Visionary Experience* outlined in the first word of Genesis: BERESHITH into the West Façade of Chartres Cathedral.

The mythoi of the fire in Chartres Cathedral in 1194 has a priest running out of the burning cathedral holding in his hands the veil of the Virgin Mary declaring it was not destroyed. He failed to tell the laity that the true veil of the Virgin Mary is the Royal Portal/West Façade.

The first thing to understand about the Royal Portal/West Façade is to realize that old heaven and earth (old West Facade) had burnt down in 1134AD and a new heaven and earth (new West Facade) was being built. I see the numerics of the year 1134AD as symbolic of the *Initiatic Visionary Experience* that took place when the word BERESHITH was being formatted. The number 1134 is a transposition of the last three letters of the Hebrew alphabet that entered into manifested creation first: **TAV** ת **(400 - 4)**, **SHIN** ש **(300 - 3)** and **RESH** ר **(200: 2 = 1, 1)**. This is saying that the Vesica Piscis had been properly installed into the psyche (internal temple) of the initiate at Chartres Cathedral.

The first thing to know about the Royal Portal/West Façade is that it is completely different than the old Romanesque Chartres Cathedral. The Royal Portal/West Façade was built as a mixture of the Romanesque (materialistic) and Gothic (spiritual) architectural styles, which is symbolic of the God/Man Christ coming and gifting the initiate with the *Initiatic Visionary Experience*; thus, right from the start of rebuilding the Royal Portal/West Façade the *Initiatic Visionary Experience* was going to be laid out as esoterically narrated in the first word of Genesis: BERESHITH. I am now sure that the old Romanesque Chartres Cathedral had no north and south transepts.

It is falsely assumed that the teachings of Roman Catholic Church are generic and permanently concretized (canonized) and in every sense they are; however, God speaks to the initiate via his or her character and personality, which is unique to all the initiates on the earth. What the outer world calls identifying fingerprints God would call the character and personality of the soul, which are the identifying traits of the psyche; thus, every initiate that has the *Initiatic Visionary Experience* will treat the WORD OF GOD according to his or her unique character and personality making his or her interpretation of the WORD OF GOD unique amongst all the commentaries on the WORD OF GOD published or unpublished worldwide.

When the reader studies the Royal Portal (West Facade) and realizes that those that enter Chartres Cathedral that in itself is symbolic of going from the material world into spiritual aeons of the **Trinity/Empyrean**. Everything has been perfectly and artistically setup from a symbolic point of view to teach the WORD OF GOD. The first thing the reader should notice as he or she walks towards the Royal Portal/West Façade is that the two towers flanking the central triptych symbolically representing the Jachin (Sun) and Boaz (Moon) the two columns standing outside the Jewish Temple. These symbols Jachin (Sun – ego-consciousness) and Jachin (Moon –

unconscious mind) are not allowed in the temple unless they are mystically (alchemically) married. These two towers at the height of their namesake 365-feet for Jachin and 354-feet for Boaz represent the material (clockwise) and spiritual (counterclockwise) respectively. These are the two opposite towers of Bishop Fulbert's cathedral brought into synch with each other so that they can be mystically married to create Christ consciousness.

There are many spiritual mythological themes laid out sculpturally on the central section of the Royal Portal/West Façade. The first part is of course the triptych, with the central door larger than the other two flanking doors put together. This is symbolic of the Vesica Piscis. Above the central door is Christ sitting on his throne (Kamea of Saturn) in the center of a Vesica Piscis. The entire central section from the door at ground level to Christ standing at the top of the cathedral symbolizes the Seven Light Chakras. A Hindu Priest visited Chartres Cathedral and notice and confirmed this pattern being equivalent mathematically and symbolically to the Seven Light Chakras, which the Kundalini rises on. There are of course many other biblical featured sculptured into the Royal Portal/West Façade, which I will not discuss here in this present thesis.

Remember this was all contrived and built back in 1134AD; however, through fires of faith are the teachings of the Roman Catholic Church laid out on the Royal Portal/West Façade on Chartres Cathedral they are the reason the total Gothic aspect of the Cathedral was built. To understand these fires the reader should read Dante Alighieri's (1265-1321) La Divina Commedia (The Divine Comedy): Purgatory (vol. 2 – chapters 27 - 29). I seriously recommend that the reader choose a translation that has the original Terza Rima: three verse rhyme and not the prose versions. The twenty-seventh (27th) canto/chapter of the Divine Comedy speaks of this fire of faith (my interpretation); for the reason that, the beginning of the book of Purgatory Dante has the Gates of Saint Peter's, which I believe he was symbolically referring to as the Roman Catholic Church. The Roman Catholic Church is symbolic of the Garden of Eden and when getting through the wall of flames Dante and Virgil entered the Garden of Eden. The burning down of the Romanesque Chartres Cathedral and rebuilding it solely of the Gothic Cathedral architectural style is symbolic of the burning flames that burn down the thick granite rock the Romanesque Chartres Cathedral was build upon. Don't get me wrong the entire Romanesque building may have burnt down but the entire Gothic Chartres Cathedral still sits upon the Romanesque foundation and that is a serious nuance; for the reason that, the teachings of the Roman Catholic Church are based upon the Judaeo Christian Scriptures, which is the foundation of the Christian religion. The Romanesque is symbolic of that basic scriptural foundation.

Going west out of Chartres Cathedral via the Royal Portal/West Façade another extremely important missive is sent to the soul. The Rose Window on the Royal Portal/West Façade is all about the LAST JUDGMENT. This is very interesting from the perspective of the Sistine Chapel. The true entrance door of the Sistine Chapel is on the east side of that long rectangular building. When entering the Sistine Chapel the Altar Wall/West Wall has the Last Judgment on it. There is no doubt that the Popes in Michelangelo's time were inspired by the symbolism of Chartres Cathedral.

The labyrinth on the floor of the Romanesque's foundation of Chartres Cathedral is the same sized dimensionally as that of the Rose Window on the Royal Portal/West Façade. This is another very interesting nuance coming out of the Roman Catholic Church for it tell us to follow its teaching unerringly. Another nuance is the fact that Chartres Cathedral is built upon the old Romanesque foundation, which infers that if the initiate is not iconographic then at any moment the whole Church could vanished and egocentrism (iconoclasm) will reign once again.

The labyrinth of Chartres Cathedral is literally a single path to the center; yes, it path goes every which way but loose; but, as long as the individual member of the laity follows the provided path he or she will get to the center. The count of stones that make up the labyrinth is the amount of days that it takes a child to gestate in the womb; thus, the labyrinth is saying that if the individual laity follows the WORD OF GOD he or she will be BORN AGAIN.

It is very interesting to know that the labyrinth in Chartres Cathedral is associated with the Rose Window on the Royal Portal/West Façade; for the reason that, the Last Judgment has nothing to do with end of days. The Last Judgment is all about how the initiate believes in God. Following the single path of labyrinth to the center without fail symbolizes the proper way of believing and worshipping God.

In the Sistine Chapel the Last Judgment was build after destroying the Altar Wall/West Wall, which obliterated two lunettes, four popes, two windows and two frescoes. The Last Judgment on the Sistine Chapel's Altar Wall/West Wall hints at its purpose. All those symbols were destroyed that are also situated on the other three walls; thus, the Last Judgment is a commentary on the other three walls after destroying one of the four walls.

Do you believe in the ancestral kings of Christ? The other lunettes display Christ's ancestry.

Do you believe in the word of the High Priests that the other pope frescoes symbolizes?

Do you believe in the Communion of Saints? This is what the ministry and the lives of Moses and Christ's frescoes are all about.

Do you believe in nature? This light comes into the chapel through the windows.

Do you believe in the Last Judgment? This is the laity coming into the Sistine Chapel, which the bottom of the Last Judgment fresco is align to the crowds of people that flood the Roman Catholic Church.

Do you believe in ghosts, spirits and demons? These are those people rising from the dead and the demons in the fresco ushering the sinners into hell.

The Last Judgment placed upon the Altar Wall/West Wall symbolizes the entrance into the material world; thus, the Last Judgment has nothing to do with the end times per se; rather it has to do with how the initiate deals with the world in regards to his or her knowledge of God.

The MAZE has nothing whatsoever to do with the LABYRINTH; though, these two words and concepts that are diametrically opposite to each other are, for the most part, spoken about via scholars and academics interchangeably. Walking the Labyrinth of Chartres Cathedral is walking with God in the Garden of Eden via Christ consciousness; whereas, traversing a Maze is all about ego-consciousness. When walking a Maze an individual could very well lose his or her mind and end up in an insane asylum; because, it has many false, separate and diverse paths to navigate to reach the end goal, which are forever, traversed without any idea of how to get out of the Maze.

This is why the Greek poet Ovid had King Minos of Crete built a maze (societal mores) for his son the Minotaur and placed him there. Of course the stubborn bull symbolizes ego-consciousness. The Minotaur Bull (BETH בּ) symbolizes the archetypal beastly nature (ego-consciousness: original sin) that the individual is born with and this is why the Minotaur Bull had to be destroyed at the end by the spiritual powers of creation: i.e. God. Theseus kills the Minotaur Bull[6]; but, escapes the maze by turning it into a labyrinth with thread attached to the entrance to the maze.

---

[6] http://www.greekmyths-greekmythology.com/myth-of-theseus-and-minotaur/

CHARTRES CATHEDRAL
ROYAL PORTAL: WEST FAÇADE

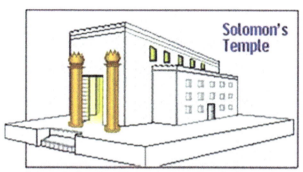

Solomon's Temple with two bronze pillars by its portico.

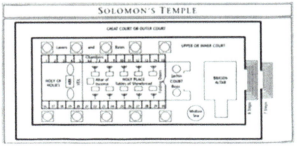

Chartres Cathedral
West Façade: Rose Window

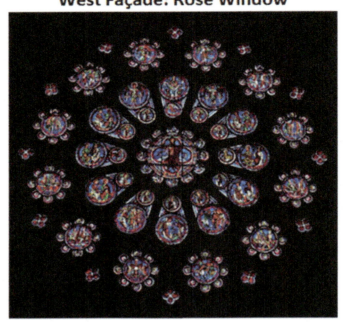

Chartres Cathedral
Labyrinth laid out on the floor

CHARTRES CATHEDRAL'S
LABYRINTH

MAZE

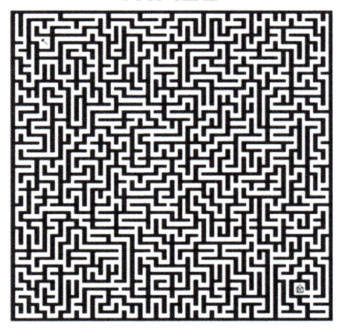

CHAPTER TEN

CYGNUS X-3, THE NORTHERN CROSS
AND THE CHILDREN OF THE SWAN

BERESHITH בראשיה shows RESH ר coming down from the north to cross BETH that lies prone horizontally just as Michelangelo frescoed God, on the Sistine Chapel ceiling, coming from on high to make Adam into his image; however, though the same texts can exudes many interpretations of different ideas here RESH ר does not actually cross BETH ב. RESH ר per se is the new PEI פ and BETH ב (new heaven and earth: raison d'être) as has been previously discussed. What RESH ר actually does is have its new heaven and earth (raison d'être) completely destroys and wipes out the old heaven and earth, which is symbolized by PEI פ and BETH ב and replaces it with itself. Analogously this is the horizontal completely wiped out and replaced by the star constellation: i.e. Cygnus X-3, which is known as the Northern Cross: i.e. Children of the Swan. This would be comparable to two countries at war and one country completely defeats the other and comes into that destroyed country and redefines its political raison d'être and at the same time is itself absorbed and amalgamated by the defeated.

The legends of the Swan (or other birds) are worldwide and Andrew Collin wrote THE CYGNUS MYSTERY[1] about these legends and the cosmic radiation that comes down to earth from this Northern Cross constellation.

The obelisk in Bernini's Square outside Saint Peter's Basilica in Vatican City and the obelisk: Washington Monument in Washington DC in alignment to both the Capitol Building and the White House symbolizes the cosmic rays from the constellation of Cygnus X-3.

As discussed previously RESH ר symbolizes the new PEI פ and BETH ב and from this respect in reading and interpreting the first word of Genesis: BERESHITH בראשיה it can be envisaged that it writes the first two verses of Genesis: *"In the beginning God created the heaven and the earth. And the earth was without form, and void; and darkness was upon the face of the deep. And the Spirit of God moved upon the face of the waters"*.

As it can be seen the last word of the first verse and the first word of the second verse of Genesis is the same: EARTH; hence, it is as if these two verses have been split into three sections. The second verse represents **SHIN (9-Sagittarius)**, THE center represents **ALEPH א** and the first verse symbolizes **RESH (8-Scorpio). ALEPH א** is in the center; for the reason that, its Gematria value is 318 (cross); thus, it represents the Northern Cross. Remember that RESH ר has a Gematria value of 501 – BETH ב 412 = 89 = 17 (PEI פ): i.e. the Vesica Piscis. RESH ר and BETH ב is the new spiritual raison d'être in addition it represents the **MATRIX OF WISDOM**: PEI פ and BETH ב combined.

Dr. Paul A. LaViolette realized that Scorpio and Sagittarius were the only signs in Astrology that had arrows in them, which crisscrossed each other not only creating its own esoteric (hidden) cross that overlaid the Northern Cross; but, that the center of those arrows crisscrossing pointed to the galactic core. Dr. Paul A. LaViolette wrote a book called EARTH UNDER FIRE: Humanity Survival of the Apocalypse[2] that discusses his theory and also put out a DVD with the same

---

[1] http://www.amazon.com/Cygnus-Mystery-Unlocking-Ancient-Origins/dp/1906787557/ref=sr_1_2?s=books&ie=UTF8&qid=1463695287&sr=1-2&keywords=the+cygnus+mystery

[2] http://www.amazon.com/Earth-Under-Fire-Humanitys-Survival/dp/1591430526/ref=sr_1_4?s=books&ie=UTF8&qid=1463697417&sr=1-4&keywords=paul+laviolette

name: EARTH UNDER FIRE: Humanity Survival of the Apocalypse[3]. Dr. LaViolette of course did not realized that his thesis about a galactic core explosion: i.e. Seyfert Galaxies was describing on a cosmic materialistic level what transpires spiritually in the psyche of the initiate when he or she has the *Initiatic Visionary Experience*.

The universe at large is a projection of the MATRIX OF WISDOM from out of the psyche and even if the outer world was to suffer another Galactic Core Explosion (psychically the Initiatic Visionary Experience) as depicted in the EARTH UNDER FIRE video just a small portion of humanity will survive sending all civilizations, if they survive, back to the stone age. This means few people would be able to replicate any of the technology that existed in the previous age prior to the Galactic Core Explosion. Societal mores per se, for the most part, of the previous age would be meaningless. Humanity would have to begin all over again from the most primitive depths living as cave dwellers becoming again hunters and gatherers.

What this means psychically is that the Initiatic Visionary Experience will wipe out the majority of those things that enamored and dominated the psyche leaving the initiate with the bare bones necessities of life. This means that the initiate will still have the memory of his or her life and knowledge of the societal mores; however, from that point forward the initiate has to reeducate him or herself religiously. It would be like going back to the antediluvian times to the Stone Age for the initiate will know absolutely nothing about religion. I can, personally, attest to this; for the reason that, I when through this experience from June 1978 up to the present time developing my own interpretations of the symbolism outlined in the sacred scriptures and the artworks, monuments and architecture of the world's religions. My only confidant is God.

If there was to be another Galactic Core Explosion in real time it will send that small percentage of survivors, on a materialistic and technological level, back to the Stone Age; however, the experience of each individual life psychically living in a primitive culture will still have the same spiritual experience of those living in so-called highly civilized civilizations. There is no ratio difference psychically between the pagan's spiritual vision continuing on with life from those experiencing it in what is considered highly civilized civilizations. For all intent and purpose, my experience, living in a so-called highly civilized civilization is basically the same as living amongst pagans; because, I lived these last 42-years amongst the pagan Protestant sects, including the Roman Catholic Church that has per se turned religiously Protestant: i.e. iconoclastic, that has no idea what religion is all about. I am still living in a world of iconoclasm and the world of iconoclasm literally cannot get any more primitive and pagan, on a psychic and intellectual level, than modernity.

Think of it this way. If the whole world was to regain an iconographic mindset it would be building pyramids worldwide not Greedy Corporate Headquarters towering over the poor and downtrodden.

---

[3] http://www.amazon.com/Earth-Under-Fire-Humanitys-Apocalypse/dp/B00014NEFS/ref=sr_1_2?s=movies-tv&ie=UTF8&qid=1463697886&sr=1-2&keywords=paul+laviolette

CYGNUS X-3, THE NORTHERN CROSS
CHRILDREN OF THE SWAN

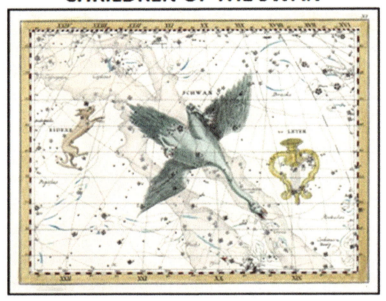

CYGNUS X-3

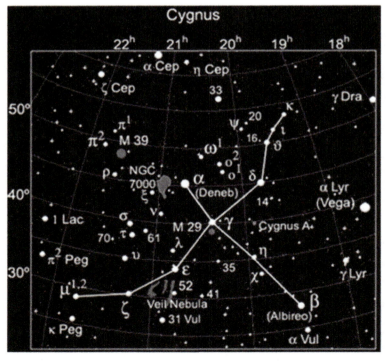

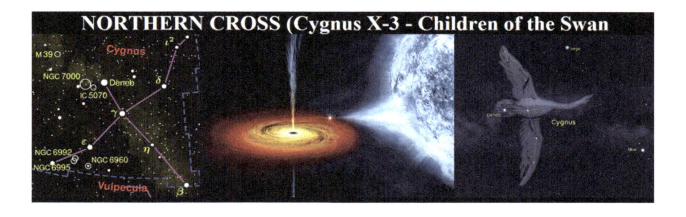

CHAPTER ELEVEN

MATRIX OF WISDOM (PART 1)
Development Stages

It is imperative for the reader to understand at least from a theoretically perspective how I came to conceptualize the inner dynamics of the **MATRIX OF WISDOM** and how I came to appreciate the matrix's significance not only on an individual level; but, on a universal level.

In December/January 1976/1977 I intuited a nine part cycle in the first chapter of Genesis. In October 1978 I envisaged the nine-part cycle as a twelve-part cycle; for the reason that, I had an Astrological thought, because, an astrologer, during one of his lectures, gave the audience a piece of paper with a one-line definition for each of the twelve signs of the Zodiac. The tenth sign of the Zodiac said, Capricorn (10) was *"the Goat that fed the gods"*, which immediately excited me. I knew at the time that Elohym meant angels or gods; however, Elohym was used in translation into English in the Old Testament as simply God. That immediate told me that the second verse of Genesis, which I saw as number nine (9): Sagittarius and the first day of creation could now be designated as the tenth sign of the Zodiac: Capricorn: i.e. *"the Goat that fed the gods"*, which makes the second day of creation designated as the eleventh sign of the Zodiac: Aquarius and the third day of creation designated as the twelfth sign of the Zodiac: Piscis.

These were only my fledgling thought on Astrology in the sacred scriptures conceptualized on that day in October 1978, which would greatly expand decades to come. Prior to that date I only saw the nine-part cycle as numbers in sequential order. Regardless of these initial thoughts on Astrology I immediately rejected Astrology; for the reason that, the Roman Catholic Church had forbidden the laity from looking into or dabbling into Astrology. So paradoxically for the next four and a half years I would search for an understanding of that cycle without so much as considering Astrology as being an answer to my queries about the cycle. Realistically, I search for answers to that cycle for a little over six years and in that period of time I went through scores of Protestants sects, philosophies and other religions and I basically had to summarily dismiss them all; because, I could not make head nor tails of them and of course I did not know anything about esotericism at the time.

Starting to research Dante Alighieri's La Divina Commedia's mathematics on April 15, 1983 took me away from book of Genesis; though, I did research much of the bible and the alleged histories surrounding the Dawn of Christianity at that time. Researching Dante's mathematics and correlating it to the dynamics of the **MATRIX OF WISDOM** enlightened me a great deal about what esotericism was all about (see Appendix).

First of all when I came to envisage the **MATRIX OF WISDOM** I did not previously know of its existence; though, it was known worldwide at the time. On April 15, 1983 I began my analysis on Dante Alighieri's La Divina Commedia and this came about; for the reason that, I had been searching endlessly, for over six years from December/January (1976/1977), in every library book I could think of to understand a nine-part cycle I intuited out of the first chapter of Genesis, which was developed into a 12-part cycle (Cycle of Darkness) in October 1978. Between April 11-15, 1983, I somewhat grasp the cycle's meaning (not all of it at the time) that had to do with Astrology, which was quite a psychological shock; because, the Roman Catholic Church banned Astrology. I almost immediately perceived these cycles as a system of 1584-cycles by calculating out the nuances in the first eleven cycles. I would discover years later these initial eleven cycles dealt with the first two chapters of Genesis, which I would researched and call them THE CYCLES OF DIVINE CREATION; however, on April 15, 1983 I realized that no one could possibly believe nor comprehend what I had discovered and initially developed on these cycles.

I reasoned at this time that if I was to continue my researches I would have to illustrate quite definitively that another literary work from out of antiquity would also have mathematics codified to it. Of course I had no idea if that was at all possible or could be achieved. These were my original thoughts on such a possibility. So I looked at the volumes in my personal and very scant library at the time, less than half a bookcase, and hesitantly thought that Dante Alighieri's work on La Divina Commedia could possibly have a mathematical science coded into it. My thoughts lean this way; for the reasons that, Dante's work was in three volumes and had exactly 100-cantos/chapters and thousands of verses; thus, 100 inferred percentages so I thought I would at least give it a cautious analysis. I thought this way about Dante's work because in reading some of La Divina Commedia I saw it had a three verse rhyme (Terza Rima) and it had at total of a hundred chapters. The reader can imagine my surprise that within about five minutes I had tentative evidence that Dante's work was mathematically structured.

In the next two years I worked on Dante's La Divina Commedia's mathematics and pretty well had it down pat; but, I was lisping literarily in trying to explain what I found in Dante's work; yet, in 1986 I would send in my request to the Library of Congress for my first copyright. I did not realize at that time that Dr. Gian-Roberto Sarolli had already achieved that level of Dante's mathematics in his paper _NUMERO_[1] published by Enciclopedia Dantesca (1970). I copyrighted my short paper in 1986. Almost immediately after sending my copyright request to the Library of Congress I had a) memory out of my teenage years (14-15) that took place around 1962-63, which aided me in explaining much of Dante's mathematics.

My father came home one day with a brainteaser, which is something he never did before or after. He asked my sister and brother and me to sit down and put into a tit-tac-box the first nine numbers, each number was to be used once, and all three rows, three columns and two diagonals had to add up to the same total, which he did not give us; because, it was part of the solution. In about ten (10) minutes I had the answer; however, it was not that mathematical problem that I was remembering. It was the tic-tac-toe box that would enable me to take Dante Alighieri's mathematics as I understood them at the time and place them in that tit tac toe box and align the volumes to the columns and sum-digits totals to the rows (see full analysis Dante Alighieri's mathematics in the Appendix); however, as the next ten years went by I was trying to understand the overall model that Dante used to structure, on the whole, his mathematical system. Something was intuitively telling me that there was an overall model that inherently governed Dante's entire mathematical system. In 1994 I was walking past a calendar and was looking at the date when it dawned on me that the columns (not rows) of numbers in the calendar month coincided, by casting out nines, the numbers in the Kamea of Saturn (tic-tac-toe box). This was a very strange and weird coincidence. Working on Dante Alighieri's mathematics for over a decade with this 3 x 3 square, which I later learned was named the Kamea of Saturn (Lo Shu in China) was known all over the world. What drew my attention to this apparent synchronicity between the Kamea of Saturn and the Calendar Month was the possibility that the entire numerical count could exude patterns out of the 3 x 3 matrix: Kamea of Saturn. I remember that in ancient times there were a different amount of days to the week and I wondered if these ancient customs had anything to do with the Kamea of Saturn. In my analysis of Dante's mathematics, as time went by, I realized that Dante did use this Kamea of Saturn as one of his essential tools in creating his mathematical system.

Those that follow the thesis of this book will realize that my observation of the numerics in the columns in the calendar month is analogous to Cygnus X-3 coming down from on high to cross the east-west corridor of time: i.e. seven day week to instigate this inspiration in my thought process. In other-words the columns come down vertically crossing the horizon. This very same process takes place in the Kamea of Saturn creating the Cross of Christ.

---

[1] http://www.treccani.it/enciclopedia/numero_%28Enciclopedia-Dantesca%29/

I came across a volume by Eviatar Zerubavel who wrote a book called THE SEVEN DAY CIRCLE: The History and Meaning of the Week[2]. It was this book that gave me the impetus as to how to continue my research into the Kamea of Saturn.

I decided to take each of the numbers, one through nine (1-9) and go out horizontally to the number's value and down vertically until repetition set (casting-out-nines) in (Origin of Numbers – Part 1). Then I took the last column of each number and placed them side-by-side (Origin of Numbers – Part 2). Then by studying what I had so far developed, I then color-coded the numbers according to the Quadruplicities of Astrology: however, the Mutable Quadruplicity numbers I colored somewhat differently: blue (3s, 6s) and black (9s); for the reason that, the 3s and 6s had creating the Kamea of Saturn 3 x 3 image. I realized that if I place a row of nines at the top of the columns and a column of nines alongside the rows on the left of the pattern (Origin of Numbers – Part 4) I developed it worked out serendipitously as a perfect matrix (Origin of Numbers – Part 5); however, when I completed this number doodling; because, that is all it was at the time, I put it aside in a desk draw and didn't think of it for a couple of months. When I did take it out again and studied it more seriously I began to color code it according to the patterns I saw in the matrix coinciding with the Kamea of Saturn (Origin of Numbers – Part 3). And I color-coded the matrix in accordance to its overall development (Origin of Numbers – Parts 1-4).

It was about this time that I came across a volume by Frederick van der Meer called the APOCALYPSE: Visions from the Book of Revelation in Western Art[3] and on page #25 I found the image of **Saint John and seven of his commentators** that came out of an eight century commentary on the Apocalypse of Saint John, which artistically depicted perfectly my understanding of the different columns in the 10 x 10 matrix. If you view the matrix in relationship to the way the opposites are positioned in reverse order of each other it can be seen that Saint John and his commentators' cloths are colored-code to pair-off the same way in addition to the way Saint John and his commentators hands are position also correlating to imitating each other. I would later give this matrix a number of names; however, finally giving it the nomenclature of the **MATRIX OF WISDOM**. This kind of discovery truly encouraged me in my researches.

My own spiritual awakening began around August 1974; however, I had deeper and more rewarding spiritual experience between December/January1976/1977 and June 1978. I can remember crossing certain barriers of thought that gave me conceptual access to deeper knowledge of what I now call the Esoteric Science. I could literally feel ethereal helping-hands so-to-speak guiding me through the labyrinth of knowledge I had to access to understand what the WORD OF GOD was all about. Today I fully understand that without those ethereal helping hands I would have been lost in a sea of chaos.

As I reread this manuscript I realized that even with this tsunami of images and commentary this work will still appear as a sea of chaos to the reader that does not have those ethereal helping hands guiding him or her through its labyrinth ways. I suggest to the reader to study the images in this work carefully before continuing onto to any other image or section of this book.

---

[2] http://www.amazon.com/SEVEN-DAY-CIRCLE-Zerubavel/dp/0029346800/ref=sr_1_1?ie=UTF8&qid=1463749139&sr=8-1&keywords=the+seven+day+circle

[3] http://www.amazon.com/Apocalypse-Visions-Book-Revelation-Western/dp/0500232946/ref=sr_1_2?ie=UTF8&qid=1463751316&sr=8-2&keywords=APOCALYPSE%3A+Visions+from+the+Book+of+Revelation+in+Western+Art

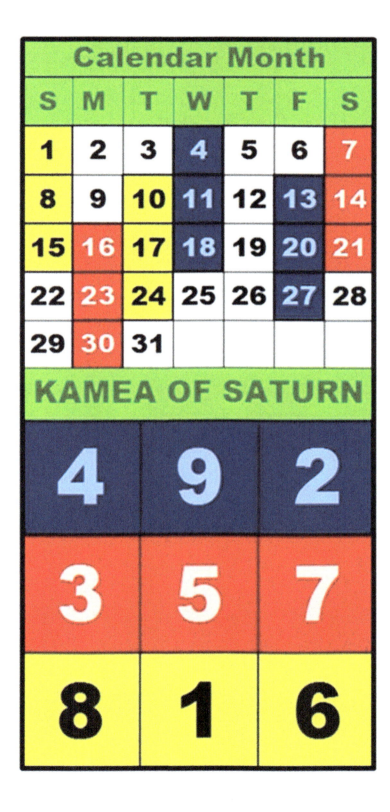

ORIGIN OF NUMBERS (Part 1)

ONE	TWO	THREE	FOUR
1	1 2	1 2 3	1 2 3 4
2	3 4	4 5 6	5 6 7 8
3	5 6	7 8 9	9 1 2 3
4	7 8		4 5 6 7
5	9 1		8 9 1 2
6	2 3		3 4 5 6
7	4 5		7 8 9 1
8	6 7		2 3 4 5
9	8 9		6 7 8 9

FIVE	SIX	SEVEN	EIGHT
1 2 3 4 5	1 2 3 4 5 6	1 2 3 4 5 6 7	1 2 3 4 5 6 7 8
6 7 8 9 1	7 8 9 1 2 3	8 9 1 2 3 4 5	9 1 2 3 4 5 6 7
2 3 4 5 6	4 5 6 7 8 9	6 7 8 9 1 2 3	8 9 1 2 3 4 5 6
7 8 9 1 2		4 5 6 7 8 9 1	7 8 9 1 2 3 4 5
3 4 5 6 7		2 3 4 5 6 7 8	6 7 8 9 1 2 3 4
8 9 1 2 3		9 1 2 3 4 5 6	5 6 7 8 9 1 2 3
4 5 6 7 8		7 8 9 1 2 3 4	4 5 6 7 8 9 1 2
9 1 2 3 4		5 6 7 8 9 1 2	3 4 5 6 7 8 9 1
5 6 7 8 9		3 4 5 6 7 8 9	2 3 4 5 6 7 8 9

SAINT JOHN and Seven of his Commentators

ORIGIN OF NUMBERS (Part 2)

1	2	3	4	5	6	7	8	9
2	4	6	8	1	3	5	7	9
3	6	9	3	6	9	3	6	9
4	8	3	7	2	6	1	5	9
5	1	6	2	7	3	8	4	9
6	3	9	6	3	9	6	3	9
7	5	3	1	8	6	4	2	9
8	7	6	5	4	3	2	1	9
9	9	9	9	9	9	9	9	9

ONE

1	2	3
4	5	6
7	8	9

TWO

4	9	2
3	5	7
8	1	6

KAMEA OF SATURN

4	9	2
3	5	7
8	1	6

THREE

1	4	7
2	5	8
3	6	9

FOUR

4	3	8
9	5	1
2	7	6

ORIGIN OF NUMBERS (Part 3)

1	2	3	4	5	6	7	8	9
2	4	6	8	1	3	5	7	9
3	6	9	3	6	9	3	6	9
4	8	3	7	2	6	1	5	9
5	1	6	2	7	3	8	4	9
6	3	9	6	3	9	6	3	9
7	5	3	1	8	6	4	2	9
8	7	6	5	4	3	2	1	9
9	9	9	9	9	9	9	9	9

ORIGIN OF NUMBERS (Part 4)

9	9	9	9	9	9	9	9	9	9
9									
9	1	2	3	4	5	6	7	8	9
9	2	4	6	8	1	3	5	7	9
9	3	6	9	3	6	9	3	6	9
9	4	8	3	7	2	6	1	5	9
9	5	1	6	2	7	3	8	4	9
9	6	3	9	6	3	9	6	3	9
9	7	5	3	1	8	6	4	2	9
9	8	7	6	5	4	3	2	1	9
	9	9	9	9	9	9	9	9	9

ORIGIN OF NUMBERS (Part 5 - Complete)

UNIVERSAL MATHEMATICAL MATRIX

9	9	9	9	9	9	9	9	9	9
9	1	2	3	4	5	6	7	8	9
9	2	4	6	8	1	3	5	7	9
9	3	6	9	3	6	9	3	6	9
9	4	8	3	7	2	6	1	5	9
9	5	1	6	2	7	3	8	4	9
9	6	3	9	6	3	9	6	3	9
9	7	5	3	1	8	6	4	2	9
9	8	7	6	5	4	3	2	1	9
9	9	9	9	9	9	9	9	9	9

The Multiplication Tables

1	2	3	4	5	6	7	8	9
2	4	6	8	10	12	14	16	18
3	6	9	12	15	18	21	24	27
4	8	12	16	20	24	28	32	36
5	10	15	20	25	30	35	40	45
6	12	18	24	30	36	42	48	54
7	14	21	28	35	42	49	56	63
8	16	24	32	40	48	56	64	72
9	18	27	36	45	54	63	72	81

CHAPTER TWELVE

MATRIX OF WISDOM (PART 2)
Internal Dynamics

Analyzing the MATRIX OF WISDOM should go a long way in convincing the uninitiated that the MATRIX OF WISDOM did write the sacred scriptures of the world. The sacred scriptures are not only the sacred literary libraries around the world that convey the WORD OF GOD. The WORD OF GOD is also spiritually codified into every thought, word and deed of each and every human being on the face of the earth whether they know it or not. The WORD OF GOD per se is universe; for the reason that, each human being lives his life symbolically between his or her ears. I say symbolically; for the reason that, *the world does not exist, it never did exist and it never will exist*. The world is merely a projection of the MATRIX OF WISDOM.

Anything that is thought to be the world is nothing more than the psyche's psychic projection unto a blank abyss: i.e. an ethereal cinematic screen that the psyche projects its psychic phantasmagoria against. Just as a person going to the movies cannot enter that cinematic screen and participate in that movie neither can the soul enter into that blank abyss that the individual psychic content is projected against; because, it does not exist. This idea of a blank abyss hails back to the above analysis on the Kabbalistic Tree of Life. The LIGHT per se culled out of the DARKNESS in the first day of creation does not exist. The instant LIGHT comes into manifested creation, against the blank abyss, is dissipates into the ethers. The movie screen in a theater is analogous to the blank abyss that the phantasmagoria of the psyche is projected against. The movie is analogous to the LIGHT culled out of the DARKNESS. The distance between the movie screen and the movie is symbolic of PI: 3.1415, which symbolizes God (Elohym) in the first chapter of Genesis.

Nothing whatsoever can take place individually, collectively or in the psychic universe unless it instantaneously conforms to the spiritual laws cosmically codified to the MATRIX OF WISDOM. It will be difficult to believe that every MATRIX OF WISDOM is individually programmed for the sovereignty and autonomy of the individual. This may sound strange when looking at the MATRIX OF WISDOM since it appears, for all intent and purpose, to be a generic mandate. The MATRIX OF WISDOM is a spiritually generic mandate; however, each soul has his or her own raison d'être codified symbiotically to his or her own generic MATRIX OF WISDOM that inherently obeys the universal cosmic laws of creation. Each individual lives in his or her own psychic universe via the MATRIX OF WISDOM and if he or she passes away other peoples psychic universes remain intact; for the reason that, each psyche universe: i.e. MATRIX OF WISDOM is not destroyed when an individual physically passes on.

The initiate must meditate thoughtfully about these psychic issues if he or she is to learn about the secrets of life. Knowing that *the world does not exist and never did exist and never will exist* should enlighten the initiate as to his or her actual spiritual essence. Since the world is the phantasmagoria of the psyche than even the human body does not exist outside of its own psychic projection. What does this say about the essence of the soul itself? To understand this aspect of the true nature of the soul the initiate should think about the concept of **TIME** and what it represents. Knowing that thought is literally faster than the speed of light should tell the initiate a great deal about him or herself. The psyche is obviously eternally young and never-ever ages. An initiate mind in his or her senior years is just as active as if he or she was still a teenager. The body may become decrepit as all material objects disintegrate; but, the psyche is eternally young. That alone should inform the initiate about his or her psyche true essence of being in creation.

Pyrotechnology should also be an intricate part of the initiate's psychic database of knowledge in relationship to its existence in the phantasmagoria of the psyche for that knowledge will explicitly inform him or her that everything in the phantasmagoria of the world is on fire; but, has been somewhat squelched by the chimera of the **TIME/SPACE CONTINUUM**. Everything has been slowed down to the lowest and furthest possibly extremes analogously from the speed of light down to the crawl of an ant or the speed of microorganisms. The only viable evidence humanity has individually and collectively concerning this issue, is that everything is on fire in the aging process of all organic life in the phantasmagoria of the world. If the **TIME/SPACE CONTINUUM** was not a product of the phantasmagoria of the psyche the entire manifested universe would be in flames or full of LIGHT and there would be no DARKNESS in the night sky. It is my contention that symbolically, not actually, each soul is liken to a star in the universe, which is one out of an infinite amount of stars. It would appear from an ethereal perspective, knowing that the phantasmagoria of the universe does not actuality exist, that each soul (star) existence is reduced down psychically to the finite realm of the *TIME/SPACE CONTINUUM*. I say symbolically the soul is similar to a star, which of course it is not; for the reason that, there is apparently no way of describing the ethereal nature of the individual life's ambiance in the realm of God. The soul's relationship to the spiritual forces in creation is just as unfathomable and indefinable as the nature of God. Because the **MATRIX OF WISDOM** is psychically discernible the initiate has at least ethereal evidence that the **TIME/SPACE CONTINUUM** is planned and well laid out by the spiritual forces of creation. If there was no TIME there would be no SPACE and if there is no SPACE there would be no TIME everything would collapses in upon itself, which would be a reverse BIG BANG phenomenon so-to-speak.

Olbers' paradox[1] talks about the phenomenon of the DARKNESS of the universe and further reading can be found in Edward Harrison wonderful work, DARKNESS AT NIGHT: A Riddle of the Universe[2]. This enigma about the DARKNESS of the universe has been ponder by humanity in all times and climes. From the construct of the **MATRIX OF WISDOM** it can be seen that the forty-nines (40 x 9) symbolize that DARKNESS demonstrates that the manifested and un-manifested universe is programmed to present itself in this manner.

What substantiate this interpretation of the **MATRIX OF WISDOM** is because Eve taken out of Adam is the **MATRIX OF WISDOM**. The words ADAM and EVE are automatically deemed as referring to the first human beings born on earth. And every time they are read and/or thought about this reasoning, this sleight of hand wording, immediately comes into play; however, the word EVE, which has a Gematria value of #19 symbolizes the **MATRIX OF WISDOM** via the auspices of the 19th letter of the Hebrew Coder: QOPH ק, which is a cosmic letter with a numerical value of 100 and a Gematria value of 186. Always remember that all words in the sacred scriptures multitask into numerous and varied mythological thought patterns. The word EVE takes on this mantle; of QOPH ק for the reason that, her Gematria value is 19, which is seemingly the supposed combination of BETH ב and PEI פ just as Joseph was considered the supposed father of Jesus. The Gematria value of QOPH ק 186 symbolizes both PHI 0.618 and PI; because, 168 is the diameter of the 32-Elohyms laid out in the first chapter of Genesis, which indicates that Eve also symbolizes the Kundalini Serpent. Eve symbolizes Christ coming into the world continuously every nanosecond of time. Eve (19) symbolizes the tetrahedral forces of the psyche; because, she is placed against PEI פ, which has the Gematria value of 81; however, this seem to be how it is done outwardly; however, it is not quite that way: i.e. Eve is not added to PEI פ; because, the old heaven and earth had been destroyed. Eve symbolizes QOPH with the numerical value of 100: 10 x 10 **MATRIX OF WISDOM**. This means that just prior to every thought, word or deed Eve symbolizes God; however, the moment that Eve is concretized into thought, word or deed she instantly loses her divinity. This is why it is mentioned above that everything that is projected onto the psychic cinematic blank abyss is the **MATRIX OF WISDOM**: the sum total of all knowledge; however, that infinity of thought is

---

[1] https://en.wikipedia.org/wiki/Olbers'_paradox
[2] http://www.amazon.com/Darkness-at-Night-Riddle-Universe/dp/0674192702?ie=UTF8&psc=1&redirect=true&ref_=oh_aui_detailpage_o00_s00

brought down to a finite thought, word or deed the moment it is manifested (projected psychically) onto the blank abyss and is comprehensively conceptualized and organized by ego-consciousness.

THE FIRST IMAGE below is the 1000-Pedal Lotus, which symbolizes the **MATRIX OF WISDOM**; for the reason, that this 10 x 10 matrix when cubed (10^3): i.e. is the 1000-Pedal Lotus.

THE SECOND IMAGE is the **MATRIX OF WISDOM** and it should be analyzed from all four directions and of course in numerous other manners.

THE THIRD IMAGE is the MATRIX OF WISDOM, which is a commentary on the MONAD, which is split into the two-part psyche: ego-consciousness and the unconscious mind. Ego-consciousness, symbolically the sun, has no concept that the unconscious mind, symbolically the moon, exists; despite the fact that, the unconscious mind does recognize ego-consciousness projecting itself, concretized knowledge, unto it. It is not the spiritual forces in creation (God: MONAD) per se that splits the soul into a two-part psyche it is the child enamored by the pleasures of the world in addition to the child's education into the family and societal mores, which causes the MATRIX OF WISDOM to split in half instead of remaining seamless Temple of God: Christ consciousness.

THE FOURTH IMAGE is an extraordinarily beautiful painting: THEOLOGUE, by Alex Grey[3]. This image perfectly exudes how the MATRIX OF WISDOM works in the psyche. If the man in the center of the image is interpreted as the pineal gland: MONAD: Soul, Christ consciousness it can be conceptually intuited how the phantasmagoria of the world is manifested onto the cinematic psychic screen. Much can be envisaged by meditating on this image.

THE FIFTH IMAGE was created to illustrate that the MATRIX OF WISDOM goes out infinitely. It is very much like going into a gigantic warehouse where the motion sensors turn off the lights as one move throughout the warehouse. The MATRIX OF WISDOM of wisdom cannot be psychically escaped from for it is eternally the soul's guiding hands: i.e. psyche.

THE SIXTH IMAGE is breaking down the MATRIX OF WISDOM knowing that the first eight numbers: 1 and 8, 2 and 7, 3 and 6 and 4 and 5 pair off in reverse of each other. When each of these sets is separated out from the others they create their own sacred and hidden geometry. These four sets of numbers collectively symbolize the LIGHT of the first four days of creation: Earth (1st Day), Air (2nd Day), Water (3rd Day) and Fire (4th Day). These four sets of numbers also fit perfectly to Pythagoras theorem on the Tetractys. Of course the MATRIX OF WISDOM is the multiplication tables casting-out-nines. Initially, the most incredible discovery concerning this MATRIX OF WISDOM was learning that it wrote the Judaeo Christian Scriptures and this was determined by the Kabbalistic Tree of Life and the Star of David being inherently geometrically patterned into the MATRIX OF WISDOM. This was much more convincing when the precision of codifying the Star of David into the first chapter of Genesis was so perfectly laid out in the texts of the first chapter of Genesis that it mirror image the pattern of the Star of David in the MATRIX OF WISDOM. The manner in which the Star of David can be envisaged as being codified to the first chapter of Genesis is to note the pattern of the fours and the fives that are not used to create the Star of David in the Matrix of Wisdom. Note the fours and five locations in the MATRIX OF WISDOM and then compare the four and five spaces between the six Elohyms in the Kabbalistic Tree of Life's Elemental category that represents the six points of the Star of David. It would also seem that the MATRIX OF WISDOM is even putting the TIME/SPACE CONTINUUM into play via the numbers 1 and 8.

---

[3] http://alexgrey.com/

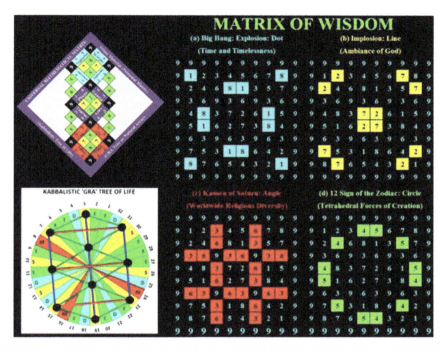

PATTERNS FOUND INHERENT IN THE MATRIX OF WISDOM are the

most important group of symbols in this entire theses, outside of the MATRIX OF WISDOM; for the reason that, they represent definitive evidence on a totally scientific basis that the Judaeo Christian Scriptures were written based upon the mystical mysteries inherent in the dynamics of the MATRIX OF WISDOM. These patterns found inherent in the MATRIX OF WISDOM literally explains how the initiate is to live in the phantasmagoria of the psyche. It is as if, and probably true, that the MATRIX OF WISDOM is a psychic database of knowledge downloaded into the soul as life's manual to guide him or her in the phantasmagoria of the psyche.

FIRST OF ALL one has to truly do a meditational study on the wording of the first chapter of Genesis; especially, the first word of Genesis BERESHITH בראשית in relationship to the MATRIX OF WISDOM Kabbalistic Tree of Life. This means a full study of all the Hebrew letters and in-depth study of the numerics of MATRIX OF WISDOM, Astrology, and Star of David; for the reason that, there is one extremely confusing factor that has to be conceptually hurdled is order to understand what the initial event was that took place in the Genesis Creation Account before the first day of creation. This generic paradigmatic event crystallizes the whole of spirituality and defines what religion is all about.

The word Christ (krst) is written in Greek in the first word of Genesis: BERESHITH בראשית and the last four letters of the Hebrew coder: קרשת, using Hebrew letters. This sudden appearance of Christ in the first word of Genesis brought about the harmonious consensus of the Trinity: Christ, Elohym (Aleph) and Yahweh (Yud) קראשית. Unless the reader understands how the Genesis Formula was created the next part will be difficult to understand.

God: i.e. spiritual forces of creation (soul) exist outside of the time/space continuum and this is illustrated in the Trinitarian aspects of the Genesis Formula. God cannot enter into the time/space continuum, which implies that prior to God sending his only begotten son (Christ: i.e. LIGHT) into the world the soul and God: i.e. spiritual forces of creation are one and the same.

However, the soul walking with God in the Garden of Eden can cull out the LIGHT (Christ) from the DARKNESS. In the BERESHITH בראשית aspects of the Genesis Formula the soul is not visible; for the reason that, the soul also cannot enter the blank abyss of the world; however, the soul phantasmagoria of the psyche can project the LIGHT (Christ) onto the cinematic screen (blank abyss) of the world; thus, psychically living in the Garden of Eden (Christ: God's

Ambiance) via the phantasmagoria of its own psyche. It is from this perspective that the first verse of Genesis can be read; because, the soul lives with God in the Garden of Eden (Vesica Piscis), which is called Heaven; whereas, that which is built upon the LIGHT is the Earth (mastaba). In every sense the Kabbalistic Tree of Life (natural array) three dimensionally is analogous to the Obelisk in Vatican City's Bernini's Square and the Washington Monument on the National Mall. If you look at Kabbalistic Tree of Life in the MATRIX OF WISDOM it can be seen that the first Sefirah sits motionless through the zodiacal signs of Sagittarius and Scorpio, which symbolizes TIMELESSNESS crossing the east-west corridor of TIME.

The only way to truly analyze these patterns in the MATRIX OF WISDOM is to do so with the Kabbalistic Tree of Life at hand in both the MATRIX OF WISDOM and the Kabbalistic Tree of Life codified to the first chapter of Genesis (see chapter four) and a study of the two hemispheres of the brain in relationship to the four cerebral lobes.

The second thing to understand is that all number 1-8 (1 & 8, 2 & 7, 3 & 6 and 4 & 5): i.e. LIGHT are culled out of the nines (DARKNESS). These four sets symbolize Earth, Air, Water and Fire respectively in the first four days of creation.

The third thing to point out is that number 1, 2, 4, 5, 7, 8 all have six cells in the MATRIX OF WISDOM and that number 3 and 6 each have twelve numbers, which is twice as much as the other six numbers.

The analysis of the Kabbalistic Tree of Life in the first chapter of Genesis (see end of chapter four) illustrates the contrast between the Vesica Piscis (spiritual) and the Fibonacci sequence (material).

1. **Numbers 1 and 8 (NORTH):** symbolize TIMELESSNESS and TIME respectively. These numbers symbolize the DARKNESS (1) and the LIGHT (8) in the first day of creation as they ethereally and conceptually epitomizes collectively numbers 2 and 7, 3 and 6 and 4 and 5; however, they also symbolize all four categories of the Kabbalistic Tree of Life just as the LIGHT in day one of creation symbolizes all four of the first four days of creation.
    a. The numbers one (1) and eight (8) also symbolizes the Sefirahs in the Kabbalistic Tree of Life, which are stationary symbolizing the BODHI TREE.
    b. Number 1 and 8 are used six times each and each number is evenly distributed on both sides of the MATRIX OF WISDOM
    c. And distributed on both sides of the Kabbalistic Tree of Life (see end of chapter four) as they are evenly distributed between LIGHT and DARKNESS exuding the Vesica Piscis.
        i. Number One (1) symbolizes the Vesica Piscis (153) and number (8) symbolizes the Fibonacci sequence.
        ii. Compare the number ones (1s) and the number eights (8s) in the MATRIX OF WISDOM with the 32-Elohyms in the first chapter of Genesis codified to the Kabbalistic Tree of Life: 5-sets of Sefirahs, 1-set of Mother Letters and 3-sets of Elemental Letters. Each group is place half in the LIGHT and half in the DARKNESS (see end of chapter four).
            1. This pattern of 5, 1, and 3 symbolizes the numbers ones (1s) and the number eights (8) in the Kabbalistic Tree of Life to contrast the Vesica Piscis (TIMELESSNESS in Time) and the Fibonacci sequence (TIME in Timelessness): i.e. Garden of Eden.
            2. This precise patterning codified to the Kabbalistic Tree of Life in the first chapter of Genesis demonstrably demonstrates that the MATRIX OF WISDOM was secretly veiled into the mythoi of the Judaeo Christian Scriptures.

2. **Numbers 2 and 7 (EAST):** Symbolizes the LIGHT: i.e. Christ consciousness: i.e. God's Ambiance culled out of the DARKENSS.
    a. The 2s and 7s symbolizes the Ambiance of God and this is seen in the three Mother Letters, which Freemasonry uses the Templar Cross to symbolize God's Ambiance.
    b. This Cross of Christ is coming from the east; because, when God's Ambiance permeates the soul it is symbolic of the Spiritualized Soul (sun) coming from the east.
    c. Number two (2) symbolizes the LIGHT as does the number seven (7): both pivots in the center of the cross, which is what I interpret as elongating the cross seeing the obelisk, in Washington DC, is on the east side of the transept. Notice that Christ's head (RESH ר) rest on the center of the cross (center of the MATRIX OF WISDOM): Sabbath culling the Kundalini Serpent out of the old raison d'etre.
        i. What is meant by this is that when numbers one (1) and eight (8) descend from the North they are baptized in the waters of the east- west corridor of TIME (Jordon River) then the Kundalini Serpent (New Testament) works its way out of that milieu by shedding the old serpent's skin (Old Testament).

3. **Numbers 3 and 6 (WEST):** There are twelve threes (3s) and twelve sixes (6s), which place six of each number: 3 and 6 is the DARKNESS and places six of each number 3 and 6 in the LIGHT.
    a. Because the WORD OF GOD is silent the astrological aspects of the constellations of the Zodiac cannot be visible.
    b. The 3s and 6s symbolize the spiritual mastaba (Garden of Eden): i.e. Dryland - Earth (3rd day of creation) that is created from out of the LIGHT.
        i. The 3s and 6s symbolize the ELEMENTAL LETTERS.
        ii. Notice that when the numbers 4s and 5s go on to one place (transept of the temple) the dryland (mastaba) appears.
    c. The numbers three (3) and six (6) symbolizes orderly civilized structure of the WORD OF GOD: literature, artworks, monuments and architecture. The materialistic aspect of the Trivium (grammatical arts) can be concretized and not the ethereal numerics that symbolize the Quadrivium that is analogous to the WORD OF GOD.
    d. In God's Ambiance these numbers three (3) and (6) symbolize the altar in God's Temple in the soul. This is why the east-west corridor of TIME is split in half by the LIGHT by God's Ambiance; because, the west takes the LIGHT of the east and transubstantiates it into the Body and Blood of Christ: i.e. Eucharist. What I mean by this is that everything in the west in the Garden of Eden is the Eucharist (spiritual food for the soul).

Numbers 2 and 7 and numbers 3 and 6 symbolize the numbers two (2) and three (3) gathering together in the Kabbalistic Tree of Life harmoniously, as Christ says in the New Testament, *"For where there are two or three gathered together in my name, there am I in the midst of them (Matthew 18:20)."*

4. **Numbers 4 and 5 (SOUTH):** symbolizes DOUBLE LETTERS and they symbolize the tetrahedral forces in creation: i.e. spherical geometry. The Star of David symbolized the constellations of the zodiacal cycle that symbolize the DARKNESS. For the other six signs would represent the month of the year that will symbolize the LIGHT (months - TIME) culled out of the DARKNESS.
    a. The DOUBLE LETTERS in the MATRIX OF WISDOM is symbolized in the Kabbalistic GRA Tree of Life (Natural Array) by numbers 2, 5 and 8: Fixed Quadruplicities of Astrology and these numbers total to eighty-two, which is analogous to the Hebrew letters PEI פ (numerical value = 80) and BETH ב (numerical value = 2) creating the Hebrew letter QOPH ק (Gematria value = 100) that formulates the MATRIX OF WISDOM. The obelisk in Vatican Square is 82-feet high.

      i. PEI פ (numerical value = 80) and BETH ב (numerical value = 2) are numerical in this sense because they represent Fixed Quadruplicities in TIME transubstantiating into QOPH ק (Gematria value = 100): Eucharist, which symbolized God outside TIME existing in TIMELESSNESS.

    b. The two great luminaries in the fourth day of creation are TIME (to rule the day) and TIMELESSNESS (to rule the night).

    c. The number four (4) and five (5) symbolizes the new manner of conceptualizing the universal generic spiritual paradigm into the new religious mythoi.

      i. In Washington DC the National Mall is flanked by Constitutional and Independence Avenues, which symbolizes the new east-west corridor of TIME.

      ii. Whereas, south of the National Mall is Jefferson Memorial, located on the transept, who wrote both the Declaration of Independence and the Constitution of the United States, which authenticates the validity of why these two avenues that flank the National Mall are so named.

Essentially, what is being conveyed is that the NORTH and the SOUTH (TIMELESSNESS) create the transept that crosses the EAST-WEST corridor of TIME.

It must be realized that these four images symbolizing the ethereal nature of the pairing of the numbers 1 and 8, 2 and 7, 3 and 6 and 4 and 5 are deliberate segues in the MATRIX OF WISDOM to piecemeal conceptually the Kabbalistic Tree of Life into diverse parts like different parts of a machine that are laid out before they are assembled. In this case the Kabbalistic Tree of Life can be said to be the portal to timelessness: i.e. Garden of Eden.

THE SEVENTH IMAGE shows how the average city street, river bank, ocean front, etc. symbolically in the phantasmagoria of the world represents the MATRIX OF WISDOM: i.e. the New Jerusalem comes down from heaven as Saint John narrates in Revelations of Jesus Christ. This image of the MATRIX OF WISDOM confronts the initiate every single time he or she walks out the door of his or her house. It goes a long way in illustrating how the MATRIX OF WISDOM goes out infinitely block by block, from city to city, from county to county from state to state and from country to country. Think of the oceans as symbolically large rivers to traverse.

THE EIGHT IMAGE is another way of looking at the MATRIX OF WISDOM via the Quadruplicities of Astrology, which will be discuss further as this thesis progresses.

THE NINTH IMAGE is again the multiplication tables and is placed sided by side with the tenth and eleventh images to contrast the MATRIX OF WISDOM with these different conceptual ideas relating to it.

THE TENTH IMAGE shows how these four sets of numbers in the MATRIX OF WISDOM also represent the inner planets of the Earth's solar system: i.e. Mars (1 and 8), Venus (2 and 7), Mercury (3 and 6) and the Moon (4) and Sun (5) around the Earth respectively via the Sun Signs of Astrology. Notice how Jupiter, Saturn, Uranus, Neptune and Plato are beyond the reach of the inner planets of the solar system. What these signs in relationship to the MATRIX OF WISDOM convey is that these other planets have similar ideas as the ancient Greek and Roman gods. Jupiter circular orbit around the sun symbolizes the spiritual forces of creation that defeated Cronus/Saturn: Father of Time. There is a great deal to think about here.

THE ELEVENTH IMAGE is about the Game of Chess and how it; basically, images the patterns of inner planets of the solar system. The Chess pieces are based upon the numerical pattern of these four sets of numbers and the manner in which the pieces move on the chessboard during the game is analogous to the four basic pattern of the DOT (Rook), LINE (Bishop), ANGLE (Knight) and the CIRCLE (Queen and King). The Game of Chess seems to be a spiritual device that illustrate how each initiate battles his unconscious mind every moment of everyday and the things that the individual will sacrifice to achieve his or her goals.

1000 PEDAL LOTUS

MATRIX OF WISDOM
UNIVERSAL MATHEMATICAL MATRIX:
Prima Materia (Perennial Matrix)

9	9	9	9	9	9	9	9	9	9	9
9	1	2	3	4	5	6	7	8		9
9	2	4	6	8	1	3	5	7		9
9	3	6	9	3	6	9	3	6		9
9	4	8	3	7	2	6	1	5		9
9	5	1	6	2	7	3	8	4		9
9	6	3	9	6	3	9	6	3		9
9	7	5	3	1	8	6	4	2		9
9	8	7	6	5	4	3	2	1	9
9	9	9	9	9	9	9	9	9	9	9

UNIVERSAL MATHEMATICAL MATRIX:

EGO-CONSCIOUSNESS   **UNCONSCIOUS MIND**

9	9	9	9	9	9	9	9	9
9	1	2	3	4	5	6	7	8	9
9	2	4	6	8	1	3	5	7	9
9	3	6	9	3	6	9	3	6	9
9	4	8	3	7	2	6	1	5	9
9	5	1	6	2	7	3	8	4	9
9	6	3	9	6	3	9	6	3	9
9	7	5	3	1	8	6	4	2	9
9	8	7	6	5	4	3	2	1	9
9	9	9	9	9	9	9	9	9

AN IMPLIED INFINITY OF UNIVERSAL MATHEMATICAL MATRICES

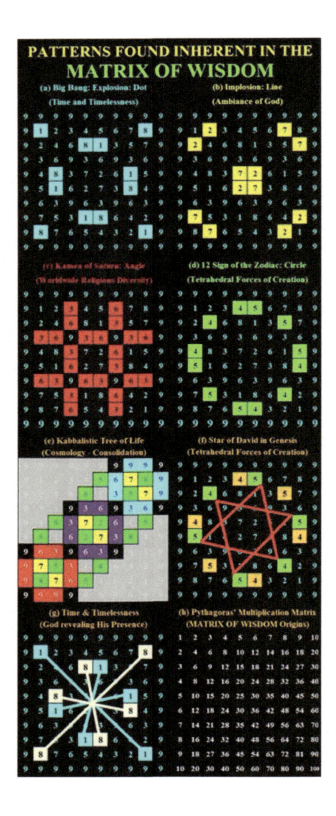

UNIVERSAL MATHEMATICAL MATRIX
AVERAGE CITY BLOCK

| | LIFE | EVEN NUMBERED HOUSES | Lawn and Telephone Wires | Traffic Going ↓ | Traffic Going ↑ | Lawn and Telephone Wires | ODD NUMBERED HOUSES | LIFE | |

UNIVERSAL MATHEMATICAL MATRIX

9	9	9	9	9	9	9	9	9	9
9	1	2	3	4	5	6	7	8	9
9	2	4	6	8	1	3	5	7	9
9	3	6	9	3	6	9	3	6	9
9	4	8	3	7	2	6	1	5	9
9	5	1	6	2	7	3	8	4	9
9	6	3	9	6	3	9	6	3	9
9	7	5	3	1	8	6	4	2	9
9	8	7	6	5	4	3	2	1	9
9	9	9	9	9	9	9	9	9	9

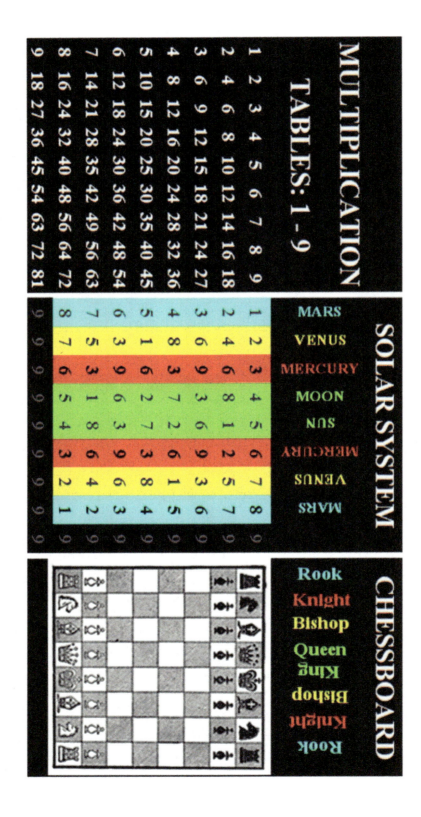

CHAPTER THIRTEEN

MATRIX OF WISDOM (PART 3)
Generating the Genesis Formula

A ll spiritual and legitimate ideas and concepts that exude interpretively from the sacred scriptures were initially derived from the MATRIX OF WISDOM (Fibonacci sequence): **IMAGE #1**.

Studying the MATRIX OF WISDOM via **IMAGE #2** it will be envisaged that the two-part matrix that splits into ego-consciousness and the unconscious mind are mathematically in reverse of each other. What this mathematical pattern is conveying is that the two parts of the psyche are diametrically opposite to one another (see chapter nine: i.e. how Bishop Fulbert built the Romanesque Chartres Cathedral). Ego-consciousness speaks the vernacular in thoughts, words and deeds; whereas, the unconscious mind communicates its message via sacred geometry and images and it is through the harmonious interrelationship between WORDS and IMAGES that the sacred scriptures of the world are written. Ego-consciousness; however, is masculine and summarily dismisses sacred geometry and abstract images via iconoclasm just as in the real world of the patriarchal cultures treats the feminine gender of the species as second class citizens. These masculine personality traits are inherent to the masculine ego-centric psyche; for the reason that, it is the law of the material, not the spiritual, creation.

Studying the MATRIX OF WISDOM via the **IMAGE #2** it can be seen that the first eight numbers are laid out in the second row sequentially: 1, 2, 3, 4, 5, 6, 7, and 8 and this kind of mathematical symmetry is what is expected in the real world on a scientific basis. It is deemed reasonable and logical; whereas, what is expected by the status quo in the real world is not necessarily a spiritual harmonious relationship. From a spiritual point of view these first eight numbers: i.e. two-part psyche, which are laid out in a materialistic sequential order are actually, unintentionally, in an eternal conflict diametrically opposed to each other, 1, 2, 3, 4 vs. 5, 6, 7, 8 (India's churning of the Milky Ocean) and there is no ego-centric way out of that predicament; thus, from this perspective the MATRIX OF WISDOM is conveying the idea that the individual on his own volition cannot get out of that quagmire. To the average person living in the world, not knowing about the MATRIX OF WISDOM, this would sound totally irrational that he or she was living life satanically: via ego-centrism; because, reason and logic tell him or her that he or she is going about life's trials and tribulation sensibly in pursuit of a decent life.

I have been somewhat blessed in life to see why the world is being governed ridiculously by those elites that are allegedly in power. On a materialistic level government officials are going with the flow of the Fibonacci sequence, which ethereally allows the laws of the land to change continuously and endlessly relative to the next swing of the Golden Ratio; however, politicians have no way of knowing intellectually that they have drunk the cool-aid of the masses via Democracy: "mob rules": see CRAZY KING: Individuality versus Conformity[1]. Examples of this is found in Constitutional Law prohibiting the sale of alcohol[2]; whereas, that law vanished as are the laws prohibiting marijuana drugs[3] vanishing, which million of people have been arrested and jailed for; however, drugs have been legalized via prescription drugs, which are endlessly abused by the very system that created it. Such prescription drug abuse is only sensationalized in the news media when celebrities like Elvis Presley, Jimi Hendrix, Michael Jackson, Whitney Houston, etc., etc. die of overdoses of legalized drugs. There is no oversight to such blatant and in-your-face corruption regarding prescription drugs. Too much money is involved. If there was

---

[1] https://danfabrizio.com/2011/09/02/the-crazy-king-a-parable-about-individuality-vs-conformity/
[2] https://en.wikipedia.org/wiki/Prohibition_in_the_United_States
[3] http://www.safeaccessnow.org/federal_marijuana_law

such an oversight organization independent to the American Medical Association, relating to prescription drugs with social security numbers instantly archived in a national database by doctors, nurses, hospitals and pharmacy legalized drug overdoses would be curtailed. There are of course the age old laws prohibiting homosexuality[4], which have basically vanished in countries that have Democratic governments. Women are allowed to prance around in men suits taking on masculine jobs and/or women are taking over the rolls of ministers by getting on pulpits in Protestant Churches, which is essentially blaspheme. I, personally, have no opinions on any of these materialistic antics today in my life; because, they don't concern me on a materialistic level; however, they all are inherently destroying the symbolism in the outer world that reflects the true nature of spirituality. Most young people do not know that these laws ever existed and those people in their middle or old age years are so comfortable in their lifestyles they have become so enamored too they do not question such changes in how the nation is being governed.

Knowing what I know about the GENESIS FORMULA'S ten-digit numerical layout and the numerical aspects of the MATRIX OF WISDOM'S two-part psychic's pattern I decided to see if I could envisage how the GENESIS FORMULA was derived from the MATRIX OF WISDOM.

The central 64-cells of the MATRIX OF WISDOM via **IMAGE #1** is made up of the first eight multiplication tables (casting-out-nines) and it is seen that from all four directions of the matrix these eight multiplication tables were mystically laid out perfectly in the same format. This MATRIX OF WISDOM from its normal perspective is perfectly and scientifically laid out; however, its basic message from this perspective is that this is the human psyche that has lost its spiritual sheen in its adolescence years; because, it is laid out via ego-consciousness. Ego-consciousness wants everything laid out perfectly in ORDER in accordance with it egocentric ways and what it deems as CHAOS is not its forte.

The **IMAGE #3** "Ego-conscious in sync with the Unconscious mind" shows that the 5, 6, 7 and 8 Multiplication Tables seen in **MATRIX #2** have been reversed to 4, 3, 2 and 1 syncing the two-part psyche. This syncing of the two part psyche has the appearance that only the Unconscious mind capitulated and reversed it pattern. I would beg to differ and believe that this pattern symbolizes that both aspects of the psyche sacrificed what they thought was their sovereignty and instinctual archetypal birthright of self-preservation: i.e. ego-consciousness and the unconscious mind both deflated themselves and now they face each other on an equal footing.

The **IMAGE #4** depicting all the multiplication tables moving towards each other simultaneously is crucial for the reader to meditate upon to understand the process of scriptural writing. For here the appearance is that the Unconscious Mind's numbers are going from east to west and Ego-consciousness numbers are going from west to east. This is the same concept initially read in the Prologue of the Zohar and seen worked out in the first word of Genesis: BERESHITH via the Genesis Formula; however, this is not actually, on a spiritual level, what is actually taking place here.

When studying the numbers from north to south the numbers sequences are the same as seen in the third image and this indicates as the study of the Hebrew letters BETH and RESH demonstrated the raison d'être (new heaven and earth) given to the initiate is completely different from the raison d'être (old heaven and earth) that has passed away images one and two. The first four images are all about **IMAGE #1** and **IMAGE #4**. **IMAGE #1** is how the MATRIX OF WISDOM is the psyche from a materialistic ego-centric perspective, which completely blocks out unconsciously the knowledge that the unconscious mind offers to the overall psyche. **IMAGE #2** show without the color and fanfare so-to-speak what **IMAGE #1** looks like from a realistic point of view. **IMAGE #4** is a completely different raison d'être than what **IMAGE #1** depicts and **IMAGE #3** illustrate the deflation of both ego-consciousness and the unconscious mind, which is the passing away of the old raison d'être (old heaven and old earth). **IMAGE #6** below is **IMAGE #4**, without the color and fanfare. The Genesis Formula is actually conceptually

---

[4] http://www.religioustolerance.org/hom_laws.htm

IMAGE #6; for the reason that, there is no male or female in the Kingdom of God. The Genesis Formula depicted by the Hebrew word BERESHITH is highlighted here only to illustrate it out of the ten rows. Another nuance out of this is that the number nines: i.e. DARKNESS, which symbolizes the Kingdom of God that the LIGHT is culled out of has transmogrified into LIGHT illustrating that the Initiatic Visionary Experience is the Garden of Eden or Atlantis or Shangri La, etc.

One of the nuances in understanding what has taking place in the MATRIX OF WISDOM: **IMAGE #1** transmogrifying into **IMAGE #4** is that all the rows from their own perspectives are simultaneously rewriting numerically the GENESIS FORMULA. It is a fundamental principle of the sacred scriptures that there are thousands of vignettes explaining the same Initiatic Visionary Experience using different mythological storylines to convey that primary theme relating to the WORD OF GOD. Life in the TIME/SPACE CONTINUUM is eternally redundant ad nauseam using difficult motifs to traverse life's experiences. Life is all about experiencing the WORD OF GOD.

This rhetorical redundant genre of thought using different mythological motifs throughout life to express one's own raison d'être is thought of as addiction and/or obsession. The reason obsession is allocated to the Garden of Eden, Atlantic, Shangri La, etc. is because **IMAGE #1** is eternally redundant in-so-far as egocentrism takes over and completely negates the unconscious mind. Just as the story in the second chapter of Genesis describes God as taking a rib out of Adam to make woman (Eve), which symbolizes that inherent redundancy in the psyche that is built into a new raison d'être.

Looking at this theme about the WORD OF GOD somewhat differently realize that the MONAD is the core principle (big bang: i.e. commentary) that creates the MATRIX OF WISDOM: i.e. **IMAGE #1**. Each of the numbers after the number one (1) 2, 3, 4, 5, 6, 7, 8 and 9 (all numbers beyond are superfluous) is a variance on the MONAD mythologically creating the MATRIX OF WISDOM in its (2, 3, 4, 5, 6, 7, 8 or 9) own image and likeness in relationship to the systemic system of the nine multiplication tables (casting-out-nines). The number two is the first two in the second multiplication table, four is the second two and six is the third two, etc. and this is the primary theme of the entire Old and New Testament to continuously repeat the same initial spiritual idea relating to the WORD OF GOD ad nauseam. Life eternal is all about experiencing the spiritual laws of creation: i.e. God. From this perspective even the other numbers in the first multiplication tables would be redundant from a mythological point of view; thus, this makes the entire MATRIX OF WISDOM symbolically the Hebrew letter QOPH that has the cosmic numerical value of 100.

IMAGE #5 is going over the process of ego-centrism transforming into the Initiatic Visionary Experience. Letter-A represents **IMAGE #1**, Letter-B represents **IMAGE #3**, and Letter-C represents **IMAGE #4**.

Letters-D, E, and F numerically and Gematrically codes the numerical sequence in the Genesis Formula: **IMAGE #4** according to the Hebrew Coder's Archetypal, Existential and Cosmic letters. The Archetypal letters formulates the MATRIX OF WISDOM: two part psyche; the Existential letters chooses the means that life is lived in the phantasmagoria of the psyche and the Cosmic letters symbolizes the Initiatic Visionary Experience. The Archetypal, Existential and Cosmic letters are generic theme, which are individually culled out of the worthy initiate receiving the Initiatic Visionary Experience.

The MATRIX OF WISDOM will be illustrated below to have been developed by the Fibonacci sequence, which would indicate that everything material and mental in the life of the initiate would conform to the mathematical equation of the Golden Ratio.

The MATRIX OF WISDOM exudes many patterns and if one is not careful these patterns can be suggesting something from an egocentric perspective when it means something totally different from a spiritual perspective and this is why the initiate has to be eternally vigilant in his or her studies.

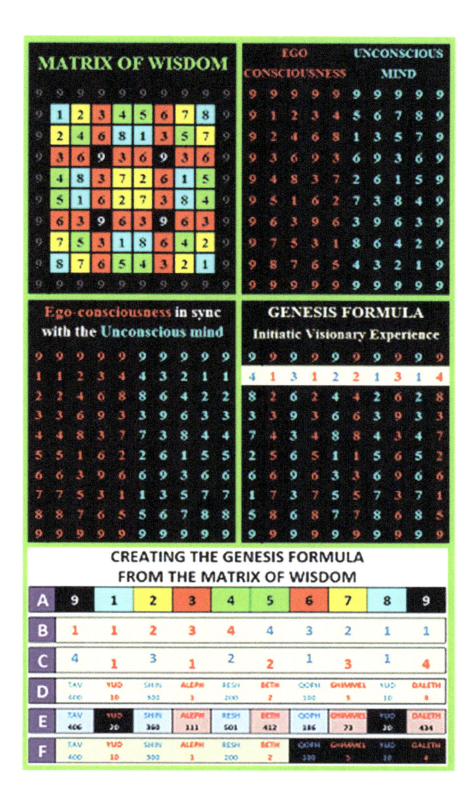

GENESIS FORMULA
Initiatic Visionary Experience

9	9	9	9	9	9	9	9	9	9
4	1	3	1	2	2	1	3	1	4
8	2	6	2	4	4	2	6	2	8
3	3	9	3	6	6	3	9	3	3
7	4	3	4	8	8	4	3	4	7
2	5	6	5	1	1	5	6	5	2
6	6	9	6	3	3	6	9	6	6
1	7	3	7	5	5	7	3	7	1
5	8	6	8	7	7	8	6	8	5
9	9	9	9	9	9	9	9	9	9

CHAPTER FOURTEEN

MATRIX OF WISDOM (Part 4)
Astrology

THE CEREBRAL LOBES AND THE ZODIACAL CYCLE RELATING TO SCRIPTURAL WRITING

Ego-consciousness symbolizes the Sun in the Earth's solar system, Yahweh (Kamea of the Sun) is a deity in the Old Testament, the zodiacal sign of Leo the Lion in Astrology and the right Frontal Lobe of the brain; whereas, the Unconscious mind is symbolized as the Moon in the Earth's solar system: Elohym (Kamea of the Moon) is a deity in the Old Testament and the zodiacal sign of Cancer the Crab in Astrology and the left Frontal lobe of the brain.

Each of these symbols for Ego-consciousness and the Unconscious mind has their own interior nuances that provide an additional database of information about each partition of the two parts of the psyche's overall internal makeup. Julius Caesar and Augustine Caesar harmoniously creating the Julian (Cancer/July) and Augustus (Leo/August) Caesars' calendars is a beautiful mythology symbolically relating to the alchemical mystical marriage of the Unconscious mind to Ego-consciousness inaugurating the Christian mythoi[1]. Furthermore, the so-called history (mythoi) of Christianity such as Emperor Constantine's mythological battle with Maxentius on the Milvian Bridge perfectly lays out the mythoi of the first word of Genesis: BERESHITH in relationship to ego-consciousness and the unconscious mind.

If the brain is looked at astrologically in relationship to the cerebral lobes it will be seen that the cerebral lobes mirror image the function of the Sun Signs of Astrology and the major pieces of the game of Chess. It is as if every soul goes into confrontation, via the Game of Chess, with every other soul it comes into contact with while living out life in the material world; thus, it can be envisaged that the brain's cerebral lobes mirror images the construct of the MATRIX OF WISDOM as has already been demonstrated with the Sun Signs of Astrology and the Game of Chess. There can be no doubt civilizations in antiquity and those vanished empires in all times and climes were by-products of the MATRIX OF WISDOM.

The King (ego-consciousness) and the Queen (unconscious mind) goes a long way in understanding exactly how the Judaeo Christian Scriptures were developed and why.

In the next image the zodiacal cycle is laid out in the exact same format as the first chapter of Genesis and the Kabbalistic Tree of Life is outlined in the MATRIX OF WISDOM in the precise format as the Zodiacal/Calendar Year is laid out in the first four chapters of Genesis; though, the Kabbalistic Tree of Life per se is graphically depicted in the first chapter of Genesis.

In a study of the second, third and fourth chapters of Genesis it is easily envisaged that these three chapter were deliberately written to give the appearance of being inserted into the scriptural texts between the first and fifth chapters. That scribal appearance of the second, third and fourth chapter of Genesis being inserted into the texts invoked the Documentary Hypothesis[2] that has enamored academic and religious scholars throughout academia and Christianity continuously from the eighteenth century up into the twenty-first century. The real reason the second, third and fourth chapters of Genesis gives the appearance of being brought in from outside of the original scribal texts is; for the reason that, they collectively along with the first two verses of Genesis represent DARKNESS as opposed to the first six days of creation. This pattern is extremely similar to the LIGHT and DARKNESS circle seen in the first chapter of Genesis. The first two

---

[1] See my paper on the Birth of Christ that goes into this concept in great detail
http://www.slideshare.net/williamjohnmeegan/the-birth-of-christ-and-the-initiatic-visionary-experience
[2] https://en.wikipedia.org/wiki/Documentary_hypothesis#The_Wellhausen_.28or_Graf.E2.80.93Wellhausen.29_hypothesis

verses of Genesis represent the 21-spiritual forces in creation relating to the 21-Major Arcana Tarot Cards and the fifth day relates to the discussion on the 56-Minor Arcana Tarot Cards. In addition the fifth and sixth days of creation's 206-words discusses the skeleton structure of the human body mythologically informing how the LIGHT was imbued into the first four days of creation. The Axial Skeleton is analogous to the unconscious mind, which feeds and energizes the Appendicular Skeleton: i.e. ego-consciousness. It is that feed (birds - angels) from the Axial Skeleton (dormant) from the fifth day of creation that reinvigorates the soul into the tug-of-war that symbolizes the churning of the Milky-Ocean. Yahweh (iconoclastic - words) and Elohym (iconography - images) are continuously proselytizing each other converts to their way of thinking making and creating these neophytes into their images and likeness, which, for all intent and purpose, is the churning of the Milky-Ocean. Ego-consciousness is the Minotaur Bull, which will attack anything that even appears to be opposed to the status quo and this is why true religious thought has no place in iconoclastic thought. An image (iconography - Elohym) tells the whole truth at a glance; whereas, words (iconoclasm - Yahweh) have to be laboriously culled out of the psyche in an attempt to explain the inexplicable (image); the vernacular's vocabulary is extremely limited via one word definitions, which forces the writer into endless rhetorical literary schemas trying to explain to the reader what he or she is trying to convey. The image per se does not reveal the WORD OF GOD; however, the image say at a glance what authors write entire books about. Images if contemplatively studied actually say infinitely more than what an author is trying to convey in his or her writings. Only God can reveal his ambiance in WORD and/or IMAGE.

The discussion previously about PEI פ (numerically 80 = iconoclasm and its Gematria value 81 = iconography) symbolizing the Kamea of the Moon goes to illustrating as the seventeenth (17th) alphanumeric Hebrew letter, which is an Existential number 80 PEI פ is merely iconoclastically living life in the material world via the auspices of the Fibonacci sequence, which would reduce PEI פ 80 = 8 down to a set in the Fibonacci sequence 3/5. This is precisely what the first 35-verses of Genesis symbolize. The first chapter of Genesis' 32-Elohyms illustrates 32 = to 3/2. Jesus said, ***"When two or three are gathered together in my name there am I in the midst of them."*** Those 32-Elohym also symbolize the number five (5), which symbolizes the Sun, which governs the astrological sign of Leo. These 32-Elohyms collectively symbolizes the word PEI פ: Mouth of God: i.e. 32-teeth (RESH ר) gnawing[3] on the LIGHT (Eucharist); whereas, the invisible divide between the first and second chapter of Genesis symbolizes the number one (1): i.e. Aleph (silent) and the three Elohyms mentioned in the first three verses of the second chapter of Genesis symbolizes SHIN ש (Mastaba: i.e. creation mound = dryland: i.e. Earth in the third day of creation).

These first 35-Elohyms in the first two verses of Genesis is precisely why Dante wrote, ***"Midway this journey of our lives"***[4]; for the reason that, the second, third and fourth chapters of genesis contain another 35-times that Elohym's Trinitarian names are used in different formats; however, when all the names of God in the first four chapters of Genesis are categorized: Elohym 40-Times, Yahweh 10-times and Yahweh Elohym 20-times, which totals to seventy (70): i.e. birth of consciousness and the 40, 10 and 20 reduces down to 412, which is the Gematria value of BETH ב: i.e. first written letter of the sacred scriptures. Can this hidden pattern of 412 be coincidental when the same number transposed as 142 was found in the 69-groups of words held together by 80-hyphens in the first chapter of Genesis?

---

[3] I use this word 'gnawing'; for the reason that, that is how the New Testament words it in relationship to partaking of the Eucharist. I interpret the word 'gnawing' to symbolize meditational contemplative thought.

[4] *This first verse of the Inferno in Dante's La Divina Commedia should be translated, "Midway this journey of my life"; because, the whole of the poem and his life in the world is based upon two swings of the Golden Ratio and Dante is not talking about anybody other than himself.*

I believe the reason that this second and larger example of LIGHT and DARKNESS (Zodiac/Calendar) is thrust upon the initiate it to present the fact that the TIME/SPACE CONTINUUM is symbolized by Capricorn and Aquarius governed by Saturn/Cronus (Father of Time) in the first two days of creation. I believe that Saturn, which governs Capricorn and Aquarius, is called the Father of Time because the tenth and eleventh letters of the Hebrew Coder are Existential letters, which infers living in the outer world. The LIGHT culled out of the DARKNESS can be said to symbolize the Archetypal letters, which morph into the Existential letters when they enter into manifested creation. Capricorn and Aquarius in the first two days of creation are also seen as the LIGHT; thus, it is neither just the first four days of creation nor just the four Zodiacal signs: Gemini, Taurus, Aries and Pisces that represents the LIGHT. The TIME/SPACE CONTINUUM is created by the activities of the tetrahedral forces of the psyche. Without that psychic activity of the tetrahedral forces of the psyche projected unto the cinematic screen of the blank abyss call the manifested universe the TIME/SPACE CONTINUUM would not exist in the phantasmagoria of the psyche and this creates a symbiotic relationship between ego-consciousness (word = Trivium) and the unconscious mind (image = Quadrivium) and in turn is the foundation of how the sacred scriptures are written alphanumerically. It is literally mind-boggling to see an iconoclastic individual literally living in the midst of the phantasmagoria of his own psyche not realizing the world is images out of his own psyche symbolizing his thoughts. This would euphemistically be analogous to drowning in the ocean not knowing you are surrounded by water. It is living on the planet Earth not consciously aware that galaxies of stars surround the planet or it is analogous to walking down the streets of modernity not consciously attentive to the fact that surveillance cameras are constantly recording and archiving the activities of the masses: humanity collectively has Attention Deficit Disorder.

If the initiate meditate contemplatively on the reason why the mythoi of Jupiter have him defeating Saturn/Cronus it becomes quite obvious; for the reason that, Sagittarius ruled by Jupiter is symbolically outside the TIME/SPACE CONTINUUM and when it comes down and passes through the east-west corridor of TIME it merges with the raison d'etre of Pisces becoming the God/Man Christ/Jupiter that conquers Time.

> *Jesus said, "I have told you these things, so that in me you may have peace. In this world you will have trouble. But take heart! I have overcome the world (John 16:33)."* **This is Christ consciousness (God's Ambiance): i.e. contented life.**

Consider that Aquarius and Capricorn represent the occipital lobes of the brain; for the reason that, they provide sight when focusing on the blank cinematic abyss representing the outer world. Why would the occipital lobes be designated as Aquarius and Capricorn, govern by Cronus/Saturn the FATHER OF TIME? It is because only through the auspices of the TIME/SPACE CONTINUUM does the soul has the ability to experience and envision its own thoughts.

Consider the second chapter of Genesis: seventh's day of creation governed by the Cancer and Leo to be the only day of creation, verse or chapter in the first four chapters of Genesis to have two signs of the zodiac associated to it and that is; for the reason that, the second chapter of Genesis portraits symbolically the total eclipse of the sun. Notice how Cancer and Leo in the seventh day of creation are one hundred and eight degrees (180°) opposite Aquarius and Capricorn in the first and second days of creation and this is not to omit the fact that the signs numbers' are also 180° from each other.

In the latter part of this chapter indisputable evidence will be presented to illustrate that the MATRIX OF WISDOM illustrates quite definitively that the Ambiance of God is outside the TIME/SPACE CONTINUE. The MATRIX OF WISDOM will further illustrate that the manifested creation (Calendar Months) and the Zodiacal Signs are two diametrically different modes of thought and literally have to be recognized symbolically in that manner.

The six months of the Calendar Year as outlined in the first chapter of Genesis is codified onto the ceiling of the Sistine Chapel, which is symbolized as the first six days of creation: i.e. January round to June hence, the days of creation numbered one to six, which is known as the LIGHT culled out of the DARKNESS is depicted as Capricorn (Zachariah) round to Gemini (Libyan Sibyl) and is a direct commentary on the six frescoes beneath the popes symbolizing the life of Moses frescoed on the South Wall. This has to be seen as an extraordinary revelation about the Sistine Chapel relating to the first chapter of Genesis (augmenting the fifth chapter).

Above the last chapter in the book of Zachariah was discussed about the Mount of Olives splitting in two halves creating a valley and one half went north and other half went south. The valley between the north and south symbolically represents the east-west corridor of Time. If you envisage the Sistine Chapel's nave as the valley created by the splitting of the Mount of Olive as the east-west corridor of Time then the north wall should be seen as the Northern Cross (the heavens), which is symbolized by Scorpio (fresco: i.e. Gift of the Keys to Peter) and Sagittarius (fresco: i.e. Last Supper).

This means that the zodiacal signs in the first two verses of Genesis: Scorpio and Sagittarius and the signs representing the second, third and fourth chapters of Genesis: Cancer, Leo, Virgo and Libra represent the life of Christ frescoed on the North Wall of the Sistine Chapel symbolizing the DARKNESS.

What initially confused me about the bible was that I was theorizing that the first two verses of Genesis were literarily out of place or at least an overlooked clerical error; because, these first two verses of the sacred scriptures did not appear initially to synch with the biblical Genesis Creation Account. The first two verses of Genesis appear to me in my fledgling years of studying the bible to have been inserted into the texts. They appear to be rehashing the creation account before the six days of creation were created (as insane as that sounds).

One thing the reader has to realize is that Christ: i.e. the spiritual forces (God) in creation (soul) cannot cross over the barrier: east-west corridor of Time that symbolizes the SPACE/TIME CONTINUUM. In the Sistine Chapel the corridor of Time is symbolized by the east-west passage down the nave of the church to the altar wall. When the LIGHT of Christ comes into the world it is morphed instantaneously into the consciousness of the worthy initiate. In the case of the Sistine Chapel that individual was Moses; thus, the light of Christ transmogrifies into the Life of Moses, which is artistically illustrated in six frescos on the south wall. This is why the Roman Catholic Church considers every member of the laity to be Christ. Every member of the Roman Catholic Church's laity is a priest after the Order of Melchiezidek, which of course is not a secular ordained priest.

The first two verses of Genesis plus the second, third and fourth chapter of Genesis appear to be inserted into the sacred scriptures and they are written deliberately to appear as if different writers wrote the texts of the first four chapters of Genesis. The first two verses of Genesis and the second, third and fourth chapters of Genesis symbolically represent the zodiacal signs from Cancer round to Sagittarius, which in the Sistine Chapel are symbolized by the frescos depicting the Life of Christ.

If the reader can comprehend that the Zodiac Constellations and Calendar year are being used symbolically to illustrate that when the divine LIGHT: Christ comes into the world it is manifested by its earthly counterpart: thus, the zodiacal signs from Capricorn round to Gemini cannot enter into the manifested creation per se; but, they can be represented by their counterparts January round to June. Of course this is a paradigmatic thought; whereas, symbolically any six signs of the Zodiac and their six counterparts in the Calendar Year can symbolically represent this generic spiritual paradigm.

What makes the second, third and fourth chapters of Genesis, from a grammatical perspective, appear to be inserted between the first and fifth chapters of Genesis is found in the sixth day of creation when it says:

"God created man in his *own* image, in the image of God created he him; <mark>male and female created he them</mark> (Gen. 1:27)".

"This is the book of the generations of Adam. In the day that God created man, in the likeness of God made he him; <mark>Male and female created he them</mark>; and blessed them, and called their name Adam, in the day when they were created (Gen. 5: 1-2)".

The point I am getting at here is that between the first and fifth chapters of Genesis the words *male and female* are not mentioned again; however, the words man and woman are used instead. When reading the six days of creation in the first chapter of Genesis and then continue immediately into reading the texts of the fifth chapter of Genesis no interruption whatsoever in the textual plot seems to interfere with the transition. It is as if the second, third and fourth chapters of Genesis never existed; thus, it can be envisaged how the first two verses of Genesis and the second, third and fourth chapters of Genesis symbolize the DARKNESS in which the LIGHT was culled from. When it is recognized that the first letter of the Hebrew Coder: Aleph א is SILENT it is not a great leap of logic to understand that that SILENCE is what is being conveyed by these six zodiacal signs.

This LIGHT and DARKNESS outlined in the first chapters of Genesis goes to illustrating how the six calendar months symbolize the LIGHT and the six Zodiacal Signs symbolize the DARKNESS; however, notice that from Sagittarius round to Cancer literally in silence represent the diameter of the circle just as [Earth's Terminator](#)[5] illustrates the same point.

There is a very good reason for this and it is because from Gen. 2:4; to Gen. 11:32; (end of the antediluvian times: Matriarchal period) the words YAHWEH (Sun) and ELOHYM (Moon) are used precisely 100-times (see chart): 50-times for Yahweh and 50-times for Elohym; however, Yahweh Elohym merge into one phrase as if they symbiotically united as [Boaz (Sun) and Jachin (Moon)](#)[6] [columns outside the Masonic Temple](#)[7] mystically alchemically marrying before entering the sacred space of the Masonic Lodge or a Christian church like Chartres Cathedral. It is the mythical alchemical marriage that symbolizes Christ consciousness.

The second to the eleventh chapters of Genesis does illustrate the harmoniously interrelation of the MATRIX OF WISDOM morphing into the Genesis Formula (see chapter eighteen); but, additionally the first eleven chapters of Genesis: i.e. 1 + 10 symbolizes Virgo holding the Scales of Libra (Anubis). This MATRIX OF WISDOM pattern in how the names of the Trinity are displayed goes to symbolizing the CYCLES OF DIVINE CREATION that I discovered in the first two chapter of Genesis (see chapter nineteen). Of course the question that Scales of Libra is asking is, are you iconoclastic or iconographic. What this symbolizes is that the Patriarchal society (iconoclasm) has to morph its ideology into the Matriarchal society (iconography).

I want to segue for a moment out of this discussion and explain what I think inspired the texts of the first eleven chapters of Genesis and why they were written. Humanity traditionally classifies those unrecorded periods of time in antiquity as the antediluvian times or the period of the Matriarchal society governed by the Mother Goddess of nature; however, I believe it goes deeper than that; for the reason that, the sacred scriptures speaks to the Initiatic Visionary Experience that the initiate receives directly from God; thus, the sacred scriptures are not talking about history; rather, they are discussing the dynamics of the soul that has come into the world.

The sacred scriptures commences with the use of the feminine word for deity: i.e. Elohym. This infers the Mother Goddess that takes care of the raw archetypal beast that comes into the world just as a child that comes into the world is protected and

---

[5] https://en.wikipedia.org/wiki/Terminator_%28solar%29
[6] http://www.freemasons-freemasonry.com/larsonwilliam.html
[7] [https://images.search.yahoo.com/yhs/search?p=boaz+and+jachin+images&fr=yhs-iry-fullyhosted_003&hspart=iry&hsimp=yhs-fullyhosted_003&imgurl=http%3A%2F%2Fwww.centrosangiorgio.com%2Foccultismo%2Fmondialismo%2Fimmagini%2Fboaz_jachin.jpg#id=328&iurl=http%3A%2F%2F3.bp.blogspot.com%2F-zMRp0e6KYMM%2FUF_zxNY7_7I%2FAAAAAAAAQ2A%2Fw9Y0UqE80l0%2Fs1600%2FDSC05217.jpg&action=close](#)

taken care of by its mother whom is symbolically the Mother Goddess. The adolescent years are symbolically equivalent to the whole of life in the antediluvian times not only because they are hard to remember; but, even our court system does not record the misbehavior and criminal antics of children.

The text of the eleven chapters of Genesis discusses the deluge that Noah and his family built an ark to protect themselves against. The deluge is obviously the tsunami of belief systems in the outer world: i.e. family and societal mores. The family of Noah symbolizes the Kamea of Saturn, which has four males and four females. Michelangelo frescoed a panel on the ceiling of the Sistine Chapel showing Noah's family circling a cubed altar of fire: Agni: Hindu God of Fire.

Then the building of the Tower of Babel is discussed, which is basically condensing the totality of humanity's endeavors, to know God, down to this one pyramidal structure, which is again a temple, like Noah's Ark built to protect against the belief systems of the outer world.

Both the Deluge and the building of the Tower of Babel are obviously a retelling of the mythoi of the fifth and sixth days of creation (Taurus and Gemini) and the evidence of the second, third and fourth chapters of Genesis confirms that interpretation with the 21-Yahweh Elohym, which symbolizes the 21-Hebrew Letters (symbolizing the 21-words in the first chapter of Genesis) that have come into creation to educate the initiate about the WORD OF GOD.

In the first chapter of Genesis the Kabbalistic Tree of Life is analyze, and more fully gone into (see chapter sixteen) and it is shown to symbolize the Vesica Piscis that denotes the LIGHT culled out of the DARKNESS. Mythologically it has been shown that the first chapter of Genesis in its entirety symbolizes the LIGHT. The first chapter of Genesis, with it 434-words (Daleth ד), also symbolizes the DOOR: i.e. Christ, that is knock on to obtain that LIGHT; whereas, the next ten chapters of Genesis; chapters two to eleven (2-11) is a retelling of the first two verses of Genesis and the fifth and six days of creation: i.e. DARKNESS in a far more comprehensive manner.

The first chapter of Genesis symbolizes the spiritual teachings in its entirety epitomizing the generic paradigm of creation codified into the book of Genesis. The first chapter of Genesis should be envisages as COSMIC teachings: i.e. the spiritual Initiatic Visionary Experience ; this COSMIC classification is further broken down into three basic classifications: the first four days of creation symbolize the ARCHETYPAL; whereas, the fifth and sixth days of creation symbolize the EXISTENTIAL and the first two verses of Genesis represents the COSMIC; hence, the breakdown and classifications of the Hebrew Coder in the first chapter of Genesis.

Genesis chapters' two to eleven (2-11) have just been discussed above and they collectively represent the ARCHETYPAL, which are broken down and classified: chapter two symbolizes the COSMIC; for the reason that, the 21-Yahweh Elohym mimic the 21-words of the first two verses of Genesis. The third and forth chapters of Genesis symbolize the Archetypal. Noah and the deluge (learning to rise above the din and clamor of the world to build one's own eternal temple to God – remember the incident of Peter learning to walk on water (Matthew 14:22-33)) and the Tower of Babel symbolize the EXISTENTIAL (living in a world surrounded by iconoclasm, which in contrast to iconography is confusion: i.e. the din and clamor of the world).

The reader should always remember that in reading the sacred scriptures the symbolic patterns per se throughout are autonomous; however, once a pattern is entirely envisaged via being classified, diversified and individualized via psychic assimilation by the initiate, such patterns can also be envisaged as merging into other iconographic materials creating a much larger pattern emphasizing a previous pattern and/or elucidating another spiritual concept via another pattern. This can create a great deal of psychic confusion in the minds of the readers. The MATRIX OF WISDOM is the platform that the Tower of Babel (Temple within) is built upon. The Tower of Babel was incomplete like the Great Pyramid of Egypt; for the reason that God is unfathomable. This is why the second to the eleventh chapters of Genesis shows the two part psyche coming together harmoniously in Christ consciousness.

The story of the Tower of Babel (Genesis 11:1-9) is told with the sleight of hand maneuver. The one language is the Esoteric Science via the alphanumeric structure (Quadrivium) of all religious languages around the world. Building the Tower of Babel is basically building religious and secret societies temples and creating religious literature and arts, which is symbolically Adam and Eve sewing aprons for their religious organizations. All religions and secret societies have their own mythoi: i.e. allege confusion in the Trivium (grammatical arts). Putting the slime (Trivium) to bricks and mortar (Quadrivium) to build the Tower of Babel is the manner in which the alleged confusion was created. In addition; though, all religions have mythologies in the vernacular each and every member of the laity in those religions also have their own understanding of their religion that is different than every other member of the laity. Always remember, remember, that surface texts of the sacred scriptures is speaking about the Existential and not about the Archetypal; though, it may infer the Archetypal and the surface texts never discusses the Hidden.

Now you ask why the Tower of Babel was never finished. Well of course God can never be understood. Once a neophyte becomes the master he no longer needs his religion. Like a 33° Mason has risen above the frozen milieu of the other members of Freemasonry that are 32° or below. There are many pictures of the Masonic Order's Aprons that show the temple complete and the Masonic Order's tools carelessly scattered on the floor as if they were never to be used again. The inference is that once the inner temple is built you do not need the outer worldly organization.

There is the story of the Buddhist neophyte that asks his master, *"The monk that arrived on yonder shores has gone inland and has left the Little Ferry Boat (Buddhism) behind"* and the master said, *"Once you get to the land of Nirvana (Buddha Consciousness) you no longer need the Little Ferry Boat (Buddhism)."*

Genesis chapters 12-50 symbolize the EXISTENTIAL, which is also broken down into the three basic classifications. The equinoctial ages of Taurus (Bull – ego-consciousness - Yahweh) symbolizes the EXISTENTIAL and Aries (Ram) symbolize the hidden COSMIC forces and the life of Abraham and his descendents live out their lives on the 1234-verses (Gemini) symbolizing the ARCHETYPAL. The 1234-verses are tantamount symbolically to the first four Hebrew letters into creation symbolizing CHRIST; however, as a Mastaba the LIGHT that was Christ concretized and therefore is no longer the LIGHT; but, now is the unconscious mind (Elohym). Remember that the tetrahedral forces of creation in the first eleven chapters of Genesis represent 0.195% (299) of 1533-verses. These numbers 1, 2, 3 and 4 also symbolize Pythagoras' Tetractys. The numbers 1, 2, 3 and 4 (MATRIX OF WISDOM) used in the context of 1234-verses symbolizing the ARCHETYPAL does point to the spirituality of the Pyramids of Egypt, which the Israelites fled from; however, leaving Goshen does not mean that the Israelites actually escaped from the inevitable; for the reason that, the entire sacred scriptures are built upon the pyramidal structure of the MATRIX OF WISDOM.

The 1234-verses as the platform for the 12-50 chapters of Genesis appears to symbolize the platform: i.e. MATRIX OF WISDOM that represents the mastaba: mound of creation (limits and boundaries. The numbers 3, 6 and 9 formulates the Kamea of Saturn in the MATRIX OF WISDOM).

It is interesting that chapters 12-39 in the book of Genesis clarifies why the roles of Yahweh and Elohym. Yahweh is ego-consciousness (Fixed) and Elohym is the unconscious mind (Mutable) in the MATRIX OF WISDOM. Aries (Ram) symbolizes the

Cardinal (initiating creation); remember that it was an angel that advises Abraham during the binding of Isaac (Akedah[8]) and the ram was sacrificed instead.

It is interesting to see that Abraham is sent into the desert from the land of his father, which was a Babylonian city called Ur, which had in its midst the Tower of Babel, then his descendent leave Egypt, which has the Giza Plateau's Pyramid Complex in its midst and the entire texts from the 12th to the 50th chapter of Genesis is dominated by a calculation (1234-verse) that symbolizes the pyramid's platform.

Also consider that the second to the eleventh chapter of Genesis symbolizes the opposites harmoniously becoming equal to each other. This process will be further evaluated in the eighteenth chapter below. Think of Abraham and Sarah who only became equal to each other when Abram/Abraham became 99 (18 reverse of 81: 9 x 9 Kamea of the Moon) and Sarai/Sarah was 89 (17: PEI פ, which is known to be the Kamea of the Moon). Prior to her name being Sarah (princess) it was Sarai (contentious); thus, this illustrates that equality has to be achieved before spirituality can be gifted by God.

Breaking down the book of Genesis into nine parts symbolizes envisaging it as the Kamea of Saturn (see chapter seventeen), which has nine parts: 1, 2 and 3 Cosmic, 4, 5, and 6 Archetypal and 7, 8 and 9 are Existential or 1, 4 and 7 (Cardinal - Cosmic), 2, 5 and 8 (Fixed - Archetypal) and 3, 6, and 9 (Mutable - Existential): Quadruplicities of Astrology. This is Solomon's Temple in the octagon shape: i.e. Mastaba: mound of creation. It symbolizes the Holy of Holies. It had to be the Kamea of Saturn that structured the book of Genesis into its nine parts; for the reason that it symbolizes TIME.

The book of Genesis nine parts remind me of the very first discovery I made in the bible about a nine part cycle and then twenty-months later morphing it into a twelve part cycle. This nine part cycle as the book of Genesis implies is missing the 10th, 11th and 12th signs of the Zodiac, which symbolizes Saturn (TIME) and Jupiter (TIMELESSNESS) would infer the New Testament: i.e. Pisces. These last three signs of the zodiac that are mystically invisible are inferring the battle between TIME and TIMELESSNESS, which will be discuss further as discuss the mystical nature of the Cross, when discussing Freemasonry symbolism on the National Mall in Washington DC. The Capitol Building grounds in Washington DC are deliberately set up to symbolize the skull and the brain denoting TIMELESSNESS (see chapter sixteen).

Capricorn (10) and Aquarius (11) total to twenty-one (21) as does Pisces (12) and Sagittarius (9) totals twenty-one (21). Aries and Scorpio total to nine (9) as does Cancer (4) and Leo (5) total to nine (9); thus, Capricorn, Aquarius, Cancer and Leo total to thirty (30) as does Pisces, Sagittarius, Aries and Scorpio total to 30. Put a pathway from Capricorn and Aquarius (occipital lobes) down to Cancer and Leo (Frontal Lobes) and the upright post of the Cross is formed. This is called the east-west corridor of time. Then put a transept going from Sagittarius and Scorpio (Parietal lobes – left hemisphere of the brain) across to Pisces and Aries (Parietal lobes – right hemisphere of the brain) and the Cross of Christ if finished (see zodiacal image below). It is obvious that the two parts of the cross each total to thirty (30), which reduces down to number three (3). Both parts of the cross would symbolize thirty-three as in thirty-three (33) as in thirty-three degrees (33°) in Masonic symbolism. It can now be envisaged why Jesus started his ministry at the age of thirty (30) and died at the age of thirty-three (33). Until I understood this about Astrology I did not understand the Gematria value of the word "MAN (311)" in the narrative discussing the creation of Eve (19) in the second chapter of Genesis. When the MAN and EVE merge the total is

---

[8] https://en.wikipedia.org/wiki/Binding_of_Isaac

330 or reduced to 33. The number nineteen (19) is QOPH ק, which symbolizes the highest spirituality. And the MAN and EVE became one flesh.

I have discussed all this now to illustrate why the first eleven chapters have to be seen as the Mother Goddess' age before the patriarchal period of Abraham begins. These first eleven chapters of Genesis symbolically represent the mother training her child to live in the outer world and these eleven chapters symbolize what the initiate has to be educated into before he ventures out into the din and clamor of the world.

Before the first use of the phrase Yahweh Elohym in the second chapter of Genesis there are three mentions of Elohym; thus, that would make a total of 35-uses of the word Elohym before Elohym united symbiotically as Christ consciousness with Yahweh. Dante Alighieri used that nuance of thirty-five (35) to write the first canto (chapter) of his work La Divina Commedia for his work is a commentary on the first chapter of Genesis: *"Midway along the journey of our lives"* inferring the 70-years mentioned in Psalms 90:10. For right after his 35th year of life Dante Alighieri writes La Divina Commedia with 100-canto/chapters, which represents the MATRIX OF WISDOM. That is a total of 135-uses of the words for deity in the first eleven chapters of Genesis (antediluvian times): i.e. either Elohym (85-times) or Yahweh (50-times). This is important to note; for the reason that, 135 is the transposition of the number 153: i.e. Vesica Piscis: i.e. 32 (5)-Elohyms in the first chapter of Genesis, 3-uses of the word Elohym in the first three verses of second chapter of Genesis and 100 (1): 50-Elohyms and 50-Yahweh between Gen. 2:4 – Gen. 11:32. This partitioning the different sections of Elohyms and Yahweh into three sections to deliberately place the pattern of 5, 3 and 1: i.e. 153 in reverse is just a bit too obvious.

It has already been discussed above how Elohym is interpreted as symbolically representing PI: 3.1415 and that Elohym additionally symbolizes any portion of the Trinity: Aleph 1, Yahweh 10 and Qoph 100. When it is seen that the Elohym and Yahweh individually are mentioned 29-times between Gen. 2:5 – Gen. 11:32 this number twenty-nine (29) would have to symbolize the Father of Time: i.e. Cronus/Saturn it is, apparently, besides the point symbolically that it takes Saturn[9] about 29.6 – 29.7 years to orbit the sun it is still symbolized as the number twenty-nine (29).

The 21-Yahweh Elohyms added to the 29-Elohyms and 29-Yahwehs creates the MATRIX OF WISDOM (58 + 42 = 10 x 10), via the Genesis Formula (see chapter eighteen discussing the Fibonacci Sequence), which has 50-cells on each side of the divide; but, here I would not think the Yahwehs and the Elohyms would separate; rather, they would symbiotically come together merging into Christ consciousness, which creates the Genesis Formula. I would interpret these 21-Yahweh Elohyms that are inserted into the second chapter of Genesis as the 21-spiritual forces of creation (God) that symbolize the Hebrew alphabet going through the conduit of BETH ב. It is known that the second chapter of Genesis has 328-words symbolizing DARKNESS Kamea of the Moon totally eclipsing the Kamea of the Sun. The mathematics of the texts is substantiating the mythoi of the textual storyline.

It also has to be remembered that the first eleven chapters of Genesis (antediluvian times) that contains these 135-uses of the word deity as Yahweh and Elohym has already been envisaged as symbolizing the Tetrahedral Forces of Creation: i.e. 0.195 x 1533 (amount of verses in Genesis); however, the Tetrahedral Forces in a planetary orb is on both axis poles of the spherical orb in the outer universe: i.e. 0.195 x 2 = 39, which would symbolize the mathematical formula of the Golden Ratio. I believe what the sacred scriptures are saying via these mathematical patterns in the book of Genesis is that; though, the initiate has Christ consciousness that does not dismiss the dynamics of the outer world symbolizing the phantasmagoria of the psyche that creates the cinematic screen called the outer world.

---

[9] https://simple.wikipedia.org/wiki/Saturn

It should also be pointed out that the amount of verses in the book of Genesis being 1533 is too analogous to the Vesica Piscis: i.e. 153.3 not to take notice of. Remember that it was only because of the mathematics of the volume of the sphere that the word BERESHITH that created the quotient 33.51..., which indicates that, the additional three verses (Gen. 2:1-3???) in the book of Genesis was to accommodate that calculation; however, it also gave the nuance of 1234-verses in the 12th-50th chapters of Genesis. Consider these calculations culled out of the book of Genesis as the spiritual reason that Moses left Egypt. I would suggest that the tetrahedral forces mythoi codified into the book of Genesis forced the lackadaisical Israelites in the Goshen mythology to leave Egypt. It is written that Abraham was forced out of the city of Ur into the desert due to these tetrahedral forces and now it is known why his descendents were also forced into the desert at the end of the book of Genesis.

This spiritually forced relocation of the Israelites out of Goshen was to accommodate the spiritual Initiatic Visionary Experience that was about to descend upon the Israelites in the desert. Having come to this conclusion about the book of Genesis having a direct influence on the activities outlined in the book of Exodus I would suggest very strongly that every book of the Bible is influence by the book that preceded it.

Finally, on this topic relating to the Vesica Piscis (153) symbolizing the 135-uses of Elohym and Yahweh narrated into the texts of the antediluvian times inferred by the first eleven chapters of Genesis I connect these 135-uses of Elohym and Yahweh to the 135-Arago Medallions laid out along the Paris Meridian in 1994[10] ostensibly by Freemasonry (see image of the map of Paris). I attached an image of a globe to the image of the Paris Meridian showing the longitudinal line illustrating the prime meridian, which demonstrably demonstrate the diameter of the Earth and it is known that Elohym symbolizes the formula for pi and therefore to create the Prime Meridian in Paris for this purpose alone indicates that Freemasonry knew what they were doing. Of course I know that the Greenwich Meridian[11] is the official meridian recognized around the world so that is not an issue.

What the zodiacal cycle implies in the cerebral lobes, the Sistine Chapel and the first four chapters of Genesis is that the DIVINE-LIGHT culled out of Christ consciousness: i.e. DARKNESS comes from outside of the TIME/SPACE CONTINUUM and this is why Zeus/Jupiter is seen as defeating his father Cronus/Saturn in Greek mythology.

Early on in this thesis I showed how the 32-popes were allocated to the odd or even numbers, which divided the Sistine Chapel in half with the even numbers on the North Wall and the odd numbers on the South Wall. There was one-set: numbers three and four that were in reverse symbolizing the clasp on the mantle, which symbolizes taking on the mantle of the papacy. The beheading of the pope on a symbolic level (cutting off the cowl: West Wall) illustrates the deflation of ego-consciousness.

What I believe the life of Christ on the North Wall symbolizes is that when spirituality inaugurates the Initiatic Visionary Experience in the psyche of the initiate the clasp symbolized the union of both hemispheres of the brain. Ego-consciousness and the unconscious mind from this perspective are having a harmonious interrelationship. This infers that the life of Moses is divine; because, he is not living on the horizon going East to West; but, he ascends and descends vertically upon Mount Sinai (obelisk) to speak directly to God. This vanishing of BETH (East going West) illustrates how the Genesis Formula was generated (see chapter eighteen).

The clasps on the mantle of the pope could, and probably does, symbolically represent ego-consciousness and the unconscious mind psychically switching sides of the brain's hemispheres. Leo ego-consciousness is in the right Frontal Lobe and it governs the left side of the brain and Cancer is in the left Frontal Lobe allowing it to govern the right side of the brain. Only ego-consciousness has the power to discriminate and to concretize thought. This is why Gemini

---

[10] http://chrismolloy.com/page.php?u=p152#s00579

[11] http://www.thegreenwichmeridian.org/tgm/articles.php?article=0

(Pyramids), Taurus (Bull), Aries (Ram) and Piscis (Fishes) represent the central portion of the Kabbalistic Tree of Life outlined in the MATRIX OF WISDOM.

Those that have been carefully observing this cerebral lobe and zodiacal concept can see how Christ was never born into the material world per se. The Initiatic Visionary Experience: Christ consciousness cannot be manifested (concretized) into the world on any basis whatsoever. The Sistine Chapel literally illustrates iconographically that the teachings of the Roman Catholic Church is, for all intent and purpose, the Garden of Eden, Atlantis, Shangri La, etc.

PINEAL GLAND

The Northern Cross (Cygnus X-3, Swan) can only be seen through the gateway between Scorpio and Sagittarius; however, that is extremely problematic when it is realized that the zodiacal constellation have already been shown to symbolize the cerebral lobes; thus, the implications are that one has to look between the rare parietal and temporal lobes in the right hemisphere of the brain to view the Pineal Gland, which would symbolize the galactic core since the zodiacal signs make up the Milky Way Galaxy. The old ancient saying: KNOW THYSELF is applicable here by going deep within one's self to know the deep mysteries of God. The initiate is so use to seeking answers about his or her religion outwardly in the blank abyss of the world; rather, then honing his or her cognitive abilities towards one's own psyche.

Below there is a montage of images that symbolize the Pineal Gland. Of course there are many more symbols; but, each symbol has a host of nuances that further augments one understanding of its concept. Having these many symbols here will allow the reader to realize comprehensively that the Pineal Gland like all words of the sacred scriptures cannot be defined by a one word definition. These images are not just different concepts per se; but, they are all symbolizing the same spiritual concept.

1. **OBELISK:** symbolizes the cosmic rays that come from Cygnus X-3
2. **THIRD EYE:** is an Egyptian symbol symbolizing the Pineal Gland
3. **PINECONE:** symbolizes the Pineal Gland; because, it symbolizes the tetrahedral forces of the psyche similar to the Star of David. The pinecone is also mathematically attuned to the Golden Means. There is a PINECONE sculptures in the Vatican City courtyard.
4. **CAGED BIRD:** symbolizes the inaccessible Pineal Gland; because, ego-centrism has closed off contact with it. Satan imprisons the soul in the milieu of materialism.
5. **CROSS:** symbolizes RESH ר coming vertical down on BETH ב, which lies horizontally in the first word of Genesis: BERESHITH. The center of the cross: QOPH ק symbolizes the Pineal Gland.
6. **VESICAL PISCIS:** like the Pinecone and the Star of David it symbolizes the tetrahedral forces of the psyche.
7. **STAR OF DAVID:** symbolizes the tetrahedral forces of the psyche.
8. **SWAN:** symbolizes the mythological image of the Northern Cross.
9. **HOLY SPIRIT:** symbolized by the Dove represents the initiation rite of Baptism that Christ partook of and it symbolizes the Pentecostal fire that spiritually ignited the psyches of the disciples (twelve signs of the Zodiac) and the only way that could have happen is through the Pineal Gland.

THE ZODIACAL CYCLE AND
THE EGYPTIAN TEMPLE OF ESNEH

One of the most rewarding meditational contemplative exercises I had ever done on Astrology was to research the Egyptian zodiacal cycle on the ceiling of the Temple of Khnum at Esneh. I would never have been able to accomplish this feat if it wasn't for the commentary Jim A. Cornwell[12] rendered on the zodiacal cycle on the ceiling of the Temple of Khnum. I was initially enamored and stunned by the beauty of the artwork that laid out Astrology in a manner that I was only beginning to understand about all twelve signs. With Jim A. Cornwell commentary I also found a colorized version of the ceiling's artwork (see the two zodiacal images below). I wrote a paper on these researches: ASTROLOGY'S UNIVERSAL PARADIGM: The Egyptian Temple of Khnum at Esneh: A Commentary on the ceiling's Zodiacal Cycle[13]. It is in the process of doing research like this that knowledge is imbued into one's being. It is in these private hours of meditational contemplative thought that the initiate will find he or she learns the most about the deep mysteries of religion. I found that there were universal laws that govern the rules and regulation of how Astrology as a symbolic, numeric and linguistic tool is to be used.

Researching how other religions understand Astrology and in envisaging the numerous similarities between cultures firmly instills into one's psyche that all cultures are studying the same religious teachings using different mythoi to express the WORD OF GOD.

This confirming that all religions uses the same source material and are worshiping the same God goes a long way in eradicating psychically bias, prejudices and preconceived notions.

---

[12] http://www.mazzaroth.com/Biography.htm
[13] http://www.slideshare.net/williamjohnmeegan/egyptian-temple-of-khnum-at-esneh

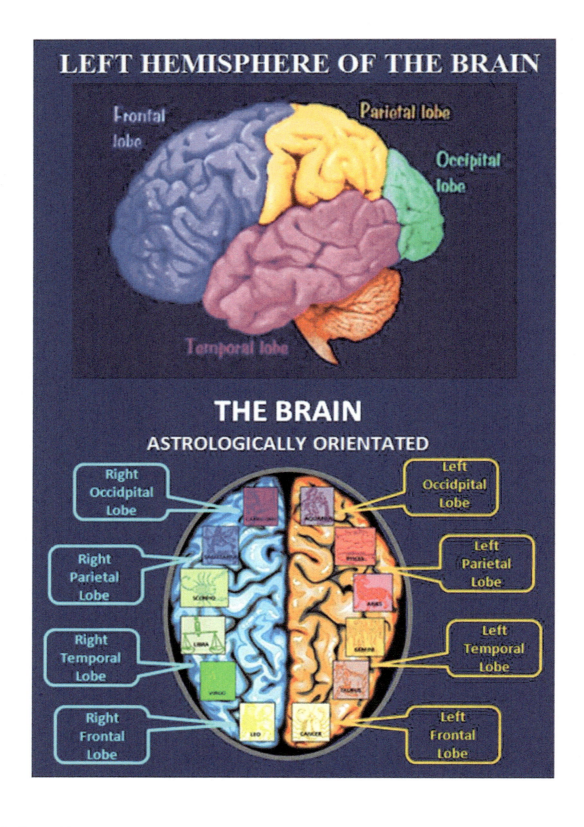

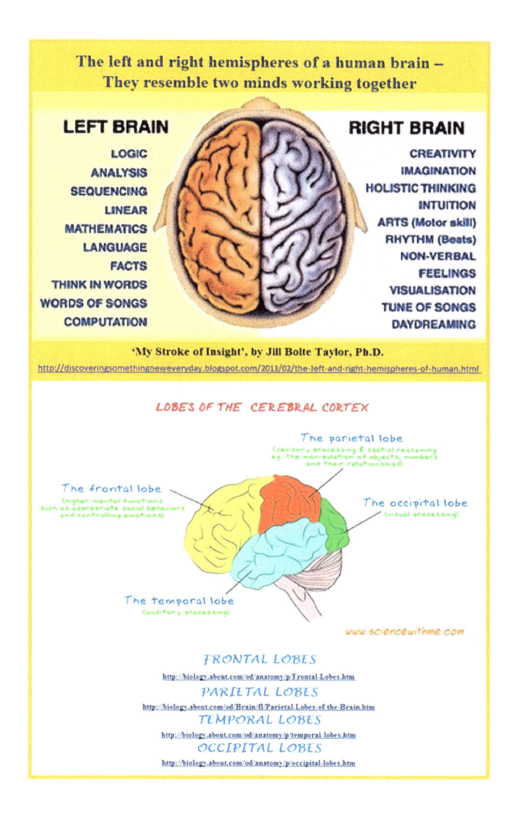

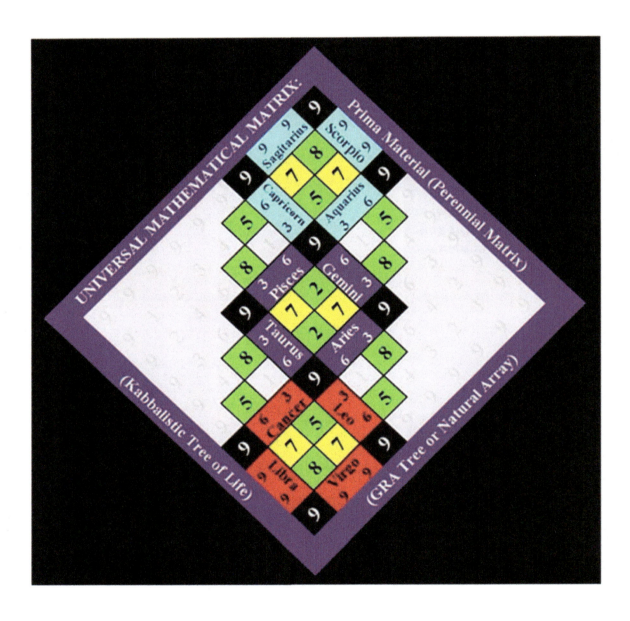

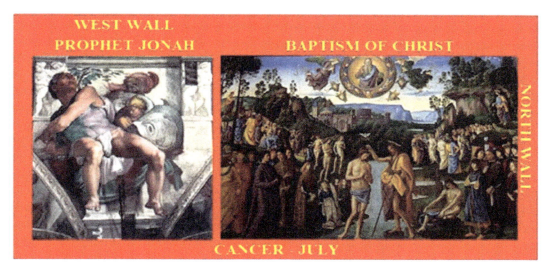

	Yahweh Elohym	Yahweh	Elohym
Gen. 2:4 - 25;	11	0	0
Gen. 3:1 - 24;	9	0	4
Gen. 4:1 - 26;	0	10	1
Gen. 5:1 - 32;	0	1	5
Gen. 6:1 - 22;	0	5	7
Gen. 7:1 - 24;	0	3	2
Gen. 8:1 - 22;	0	3	3
Gen. 9:1 - 29;	1	0	7
Gen. 10:1 - 32;	0	2	0
Gen. 11:1 - 32;	0	5	0
Totals	21	29	29

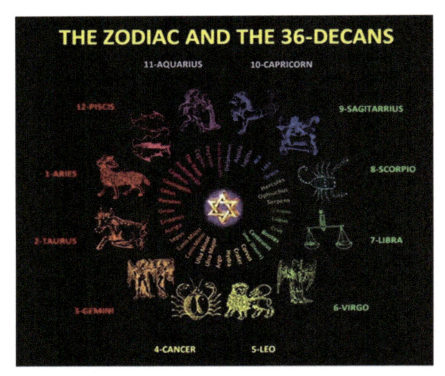

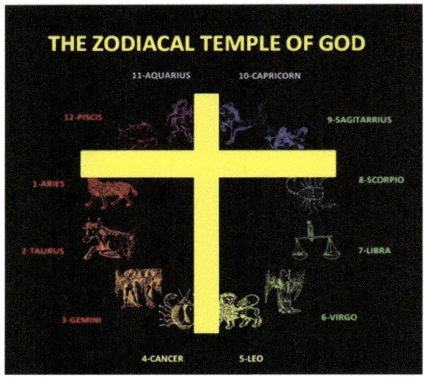

PARIS MERIDIAN - ARAGO MEDALLIONS

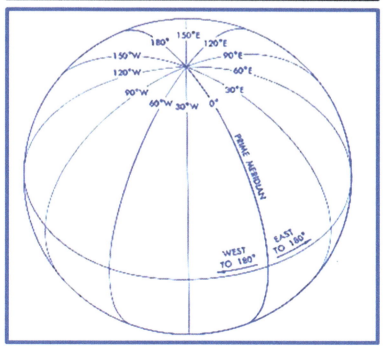

IMAGES SYMBOLIZING THE PINEAL GLAND

OBELISK

THIRD EYE

PINECONE

CAGED BIRD

CROSS

VESICA PISCIS
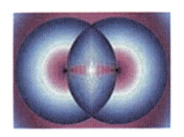

STAR OF DAVID

SWAN

HOLY SPIRIT

A detail commentary on the Egyptian Temple of Esneh

Two lion-headed deities holding hands, with two small lions following them. On ESNE pl. 87 a similar image is located before Sagittarius.

Boötes, not Virgo, but a male figure with a club or bone in right hand and a knife in his raised left hand. On ESNE pl. 87 a similar figure is between Leo and Cancer.

Bird-like figure with a crocodile head and two extra pair of wings in flight. On ESNE pl. 87 above Orion.

Amset, son of Horus is seen as a mummified man, but this could also be Ptah.

Auriga, seen also on ESNE pl. 87 upper section.

Seb (Seb, Sobek), the crocodile-god worshipped at the city Arsinoe (Crocodilopolis).

Sitting and Standing Deities at the end of the cycle.

Anubis

Sitting and Standing Deities moving toward the beginning of a new cycle.

Crocodile headed figures connected to each other at the torso. On ESNE pl. 87 upper section is a similar figure above Orion except it has ram heads.

Coma

Leo   **Cancer**   Lepus

Virgo   **Libra**   **Scorpius**

Saturn

Gemini   **Taurus**   **Aries**   **Pisces**

Osiris-like

Aquarius

Mars

Shu, has an ostrich feather for a head.

Sagittarius   **Capricornus**

Male figure with a sun disi head. Seen on the Grand Temple Decan 17, and Denderah Zodiac Decan 4.

Sphinx, body of a lion, head of a man with a Cobra and sun disi crown, as seen on the Grand Temple Decan 8.

Figure with serpent humps and a winged figure at each end with a beetle between the wings. ESNE pl. 87 has similar figure, but upside down.

A. Vol. I ESNE (LATOPOLIS) Pl. 79.
ZODIAQUE SCULPTE AU PLAFOND DE PORTIQUE
Zodiac sculpture on the porch of the Temple of Esneh

COLORIZED VERSION OF THE EGYPTIAN TEMPLE OF ESNEH

THE AMBIANCE OF GOD

How were the Judaeo Christian Scriptures conceived? This is a rhetorical question; for the reason that, I know that neither a prophet of the Old Testament nor a disciple of the New Testament wrote so much as a word of the Judaeo Christian scripture for these are merely mythological characters. Those spiritual mystical scribes that did write the sacred scriptures of the world could not have written anything without the full consent of the overall steering committees that oversaw the sacred scriptures' development. Yes, I fully understand that God guided the steering committee and the mystical scribe; however, for such a large project such as the bible to have been conceived and canonized would have taken a spiritual think tank of sought to work it all out esoterically perfectly.

The initiate should get out of his head the false histories of religions. Religions have no histories per se and its mythological storylines whether it is alleged history or whatever the written sacred scriptures have to be sacrosanct is contrast to the societal mores. The whole bible are vignettes: i.e. parables, folklore, myths or whatever was needed to allegorize the WORD OF GOD into a sustainable order so that the worthy initiate could cull out the WORD OF GOD via God's guidance. The WORD OF GOD cannot be allegorized per se the scribes of antiquity could only write what they envisaged out of the MATRIX OF WISDOM and the Fibonacci sequence.

The first thing that should be noticed about the sacred scriptures; though, it is normally the last thing, is that the MATRIX OF WISDOM is based solely upon the two-part psyche: ego-consciousness and the unconscious mind; thus, the sacred scriptures are based upon the two-part psyche. The study of Astrology as a symbolic, numeric and linguistic tool is indispensable for the initiate to obtain an understanding of the dynamics of explaining the process of why the sacred scriptures are codified, for the most part, on only four equinoctial signs out of the Zodiac: Gemini, Taurus, Aries and Piscis; though, all twelve signs of Astrology are recognized throughout the bible. Those that read the surface texts of the Judaeo Christian Scriptures will notice that the history of the bible goes back mythologically over six thousand years before Christ and I take my authority for this from Saint Augustine who declared it was 6000BC and not from Bishop Ussher, who went back to only 4004BC. Saint Augustine was not referring to the dawn of mankind he was referring to the age of the surface narrative of the bible. About 6000BC it was the beginning of the equinoctial age of Gemini, which infers the pyramids: Tower of Babel. The Old Testament speaks of Bull (Taurus) worship while Moses was on Mount Sinai. The Akedah speaks of Abraham sacrificing the Ram instead of his son Isaac. Of course the New Testament is all about Pisces the Fish.

Astrology is not based upon the fantasy and nonsense of fortune telling. Astrology may have predictive tools; however, that is based upon the fact that it is symbolically and alphanumerically structured and its predictions are generically based upon how the sacred scriptures are structured mathematically; though, there may well be a generic classification of character and personality types based upon the month/sign that the individual is born in; however, I don't myself get into that aspect of Astrology; for the reason that, I am attuned to the left hemisphere of the brain and not the right hemisphere.

One of the most profound discoveries I, personally, made out of the MATRIX OF WISDOM was to take that 10 x 10 square and contemplatively cube it: 10^3 (like a rubric cube), which totals to a 1000-cells, which in the Hebrew alphabet is a large ALEPH א. It dawned on me that if I was to take the MATRIX OF WISDOM and surround it with another twenty-six (26) like rubric cubes the mathematics would be 28^3 cubed, which totals to 21,952-cells and that is extremely close to Astrology's Equinoctial Year of 25,920 years. The fact that it is now known that the sacred scriptures were written directly out of the MATRIX OF WISDOM and that the texts of the bible are dominated by the four equinoctial signs: Gemini, Taurus, Aries and Piscis this alone provide the researcher with the authority to study the bible from an astrological perspective. Once that is done the entire bible will be seen to be astrologically structured.

The difference between 25,920 and 21,952 was 3968. Dividing 3968 by 25,920 the quotient came to 0.153..., which is the mathematical equation of the Vesica Piscis symbolizing Christ (Tao, Buddha, Krishna, Horus, etc.). What I believe the MATRIX OF WISDOM is saying here is that the 3968 symbolizes Christ coming from outside of the TIME/SPACE CONTINUUM to present the initiate with a new raison d'être: new heaven and earth. This speaks to the TIMELESSNESS of the psyche.

Therefore, it is no stretch of the imagination to envisage the MATRIX OF WISDOM per se symbolizing the TIME/SPACE CONTINUUM. In every sense these calculations on the MATRIX OF WISDOM is saying that the initiate walked out of the Garden of Eden (Christ consciousness) and walked into the TIME/SPACE CONTINUUM: i.e. MATRIX OF WISDOM.

Yes, the number 153, and in this case 0.153...% symbolizes Christ and the religious have to wrap their minds around the 15% symbolizing the Trinitarian whole; whereas, 0.8469...symbolizes 85%: MATRIX OF WISDOM or a set 5/8 in the Fibonacci sequence illustrating that it symbolizes the oscillation of the Golden Ratio. These numbers #8 and #5 symbolize the Gematria value of Yahweh (26 - 8) and Elohym (86 - 5).

I believe that this Vesica Piscis that symbolizes 15% represents the Holy of Holies and the reason why the Holy of Holies is structured 15' x 15' in Solomon Temple, which would make the Holy of Holies analogous to the Kamea of Saturn.

What I see also as intriguing is that the number 3968 could also represent 3168; for the reason that, in the creation of the Genesis Formula it was seen that the nines: ninth multiplication table was transformed into the first multiplication table; thus, the nine in 3968 was also transformed into number one (Monad): 3168, which is Gematria value of the name "Lord Jesus Christ" and on 31.68 North Latitude is where Bethlehem of Judea is located. Also the 3168 are the four months with 30-days: 1, 3, 6 and 8, which creates the butterfly pattern that the other eight signs imitate by creating two more butterfly patterns creating the Star of David: i.e. tetrahedral forces in creation. Transforming the nines into LIGHT spiritualizes the entire manifested creation into spiritual LIGHT when Christ consciousness is given to the initiate via the Initiatic Visionary Experience. This may well be the answer to the mystery as to why there is Darkness at Night.

In the next image, which all this discussion is about, I color coded the numbers in the central MATRIX OF WISDOM cubed 10^3 to denote the soul culling out the LIGHT from the DARKNESS: i.e. Christ consciousness (LIGHT). All the numbers in WHITE symbolized the stars in the galaxy: manifested creation and all the nines symbolize 0.409...% of 28^3; whereas, the manifested universe calculates out to half of the equinoctial zodiacal year: 12,960: 27 x (60 x 8) [the MATRIX OF WISDOM has 60-cells with numbers 1-8 and 40-cells with 9s]; whereas 12,960 divide 28^3 = 0.590...%. The nines cannot be calculated out in a condense rubric cube 28^3 unless they are subtracted from the whole: $21,952 - 12,960 = 8992 / 21,952 = 0.409...\%$.

The fact that the manifested universe calculates out to half the equinoctial year totaling 25,920 years mandates that the entire bible be studied astrologically.

Here it is clearly seen that the first word of Genesis: BERESHITH (one of its traditional translation is "separated six") is derived from this matrix cubed 28^3; for the reason that, the manifested universe (the white and colored numbers) totals to half the equinoctial year (12,960), which represent six of the twelve zodiacal signs. The other six zodiacal signs are in the number nines (9s) and the 0.153...% that is not of the universe per se; but, comes from outside of the TIME/SPACE CONTINUUM. This is the answer as to why the Sistine Chapel has six zodiacal signs on the North Wall covering the Life of Christ frescos and six calendar months on the South Wall covering the Life of Moses frescos. This same scenario with the zodiacal signs and the calendar months are worked out in the first four chapters of Genesis; whereas, the first six days of creation (manifested creation) symbolizes the calendar months.

Adding the 15.3% to LIGHT (numbers 1-8) and the DARKNESS (9s) representing 0.590...% and the 0.41...% (symbolically the Golden Ratio) disrupts and destroys the oscillation of the Fibonacci sequence mystically and psychically transcending TIME to TIMELESSNESS. This is the same manner that the Kabbalistic Tree of Life was analyzed via the 153 symbolizing the Vesica Piscis.

- LIGHT: $12,960 + 3968 = 16928 / 29,888 = 0.566...$
- DARKNESS: $8992 + 3968 = 12,960 / 29,888 = 0.433...$

Thus, it is clearly shown here how the calculations of the Fibonacci sequence are completely skewed transforming the material minded to the Christ consciousness.

Notice that the calculation of the 0.153... was not suppose to be incorporated into the 0.590...% and the 0.41...% calculations for the Genesis Formula; though, above, I just presented those calculations. I did this to illustrate what would be normally expected from a materialistic viewpoint. This is exceedingly important to understand; for the reason that, the Initiative Visionary Experience is symbolized by the 0.153...: i.e. Vesica Piscis, which does not negotiate with the Fibonacci sequence. This is the Christ Child spiritually imbued and saturated into the deflated psyche of the Born Again initiate. This is the Christ Child that is discussed throughout the New Testament.

The fact that the 0.153...% calculation, which literally symbolizes nothing: ex nihilo (out of nothing) can be mathematically intuited out of this MATRIX OF WISDOM is inexplicable evidence directly from God revealing his ambiance.

This calculation that exudes 0.153... fills all the requirements of what humanity presently knows about God. The name of God cannot be known and to name God is to concretize that particular concept of God and the initiate would have to begin again to attempt to know God. That concept 0.153...% (Vesica Piscis) cannot be called LIGHT or DARKNESS; for the reason that the 0.590...% and the 0.41...% calculation for the Genesis Formula symbolizes LIGHT and DARKNESS. This calculation 0.153... (Vesica Piscis) can be said to be the Unknown God that Saint Paul talks about in the New Testament book: Acts of the Apostles, *"For as I passed by, and beheld your devotions, I found an altar with this inscription, TO THE UNKNOWN GOD. Whom therefore ye ignorantly worship, him declare I unto you. Acts: 17:23"*.

I suggest that the reader consider that the calculation 0.153… can also be interpreted as symbolizing Holy of Holy, which is said to be cubed: i.e. 15^3 in Solomon's Temple.

Another calculation is in order here in relationship to the overall cube of space 28^3 and the Vesica Piscis. The central cube, that represent earth (soul) out of the twenty-seven (27) cubes have 480 cells that represent LIGHT; whereas, the total out of the 27-cubes that represents LIGHT is 12,960 that symbolizes half the equinoctial year, which makes the central cube only a mere 0.037…% of the LIGHT. It has already been illustrated that the missing portion of the equinoctial year is 0.153…%, which symbolizes the Vesica Piscis. When 0.153 is added to 0.037 the quotient is 0.19…%, which is extraordinary. It has already been shown that nineteen (19 – QOPH ק) is added to eighty-one (9^2 - PEI פ) to make the Kamea of the Moon into the 10 x 10 MATRIX OF WISDOM. When Eve was created her Gematria value became nineteen (19 – QOPH ק) and this Hebrew letter QOPH ק completes the spelling of the word Christ in the first word of Genesis: Bereshith. Man was the only thing left after Eve was created for Adam died as portrayed by Michelangelo on the ceiling of the Sistine Chapel in the panel depicting the Birth of Eve. I interpret these calculations to mean that the spiritual force of creation cleanse the entire psyche of the soul creating a whole new heaven and a whole new earth and then enters into the life of the initiate making the initiate into the image of Christ by formulating him or her into the third aspect of the Trinity: QOPH ק.

I fully understand that there is an innumeracy problem *(unfamiliar with mathematical concepts and methods; unable to use mathematics; not numerate)* in the world. To tell the reader the truth, that is not my problem. As you can see I have used basic forms of arithmetical calculations (addition, subtraction, multiplication and division) throughout this volume, which are mathematical concepts that were well known and permeated the public school system in my youth; whereas, in so-called modern times instructing students in the use of calculators rather than the mathematical principles permeates our public school system. These simple mathematical concepts have served me well throughout my lifetime of spiritually researching the esoteric sciences.

In my youth a calculator was not allowed during a math test or a zero was the mandated grade for cheating students, now in the dumb-down America's Public School System, the course curriculum in regards to a math test cannot be conducted without the student having a calculator in hand to aid him or her in what I, personally, considered the simplest of all school test in my adolescence years. In fact; now, here in the twenty-first century, 50-60-years later, the teacher conducting the test will lend the student a calculator to aid him or her during the test: is this not nationwide mental dyslexia?

I know that it will be difficult for the average person to get his or her mind wrapped around the idea that mathematical calculations can conceptualizes God's Ambiance and I fully understand that the calculations themselves do not prove God's Ambiance per se; though, calculations may conceptualize that concept of the Vesica Piscis they can tell nothing about that TIMELESSNESS.

I have already in this volume revealed enough evidence that explicitly proves that the sacred scriptures and all religious teachings and buildings around the world are by-products of the MATRIX OF WISDOM, which has been illustrated as a commentary on the MONAD. It is quite apparent, to me, that God has revealed His ambiance not that anybody has to prove His existence. The spiritual inference from these calculations' nuances is that God exist outside of the TIME/SPACE CONTINUUM.

MATRIX OF WISDOM
UNIVERSAL MATHEMATICAL MATRIX
PRIMA MATERIA (Perennial Matrix)
Days two and three in the Genesis Creation Account

```
1 2 3 4 5 6 7 8     1 2 3 4 5 6 7 8     1 2 3 4 5 6 7 8
2 4 6 8 1 3 5 7     2 4 6 8 1 3 5 7     2 4 6 8 1 3 5 7
3 6   3 6   3 6     3 6   3 6   3 6     3 6   3 6   3 6
4 8 3 7 2 6 1 5     4 8 3 7 2 6 1 5     4 8 3 7 2 6 1 5
5 1 6 2 7 3 8 4     5 1 6 2 7 3 8 4     5 1 6 2 7 3 8 4
6 3   6 3   6 3     6 3   6 3   6 3     6 3   6 3   6 3
7 5 3 1 8 6 4 2     7 5 3 1 8 6 4 2     7 5 3 1 8 6 4 2
8 7 6 5 4 3 2 1     8 7 6 5 4 3 2 1     8 7 6 5 4 3 2 1

1 2 3 4 5 6 7 8     1 2 3 4 5 6 7 8     1 2 3 4 5 6 7 8
2 4 6 8 1 3 5 7     2 4 6 8 1 3 5 7     2 4 6 8 1 3 5 7
3 6   3 6   3 6     3 6   3 6   3 6     3 6   3 6   3 6
4 8 3 7 2 6 1 5     4 8 3 7 2 6 1 5     4 8 3 7 2 6 1 5
5 1 6 2 7 3 8 4     5 1 6 2 7 3 8 4     5 1 6 2 7 3 8 4
6 3   6 3   6 3     6 3   6 3   6 3     6 3   6 3   6 3
7 5 3 1 8 6 4 2     7 5 3 1 8 6 4 2     7 5 3 1 8 6 4 2
8 7 6 5 4 3 2 1     8 7 6 5 4 3 2 1     8 7 6 5 4 3 2 1

1 2 3 4 5 6 7 8     1 2 3 4 5 6 7 8     1 2 3 4 5 6 7 8
2 4 6 8 1 3 5 7     2 4 6 8 1 3 5 7     2 4 6 8 1 3 5 7
3 6   3 6   3 6     3 6   3 6   3 6     3 6   3 6   3 6
4 8 3 7 2 6 1 5     4 8 3 7 2 6 1 5     4 8 3 7 2 6 1 5
5 1 6 2 7 3 8 4     5 1 6 2 7 3 8 4     5 1 6 2 7 3 8 4
6 3   6 3   6 3     6 3   6 3   6 3     6 3   6 3   6 3
7 5 3 1 8 6 4 2     7 5 3 1 8 6 4 2     7 5 3 1 8 6 4 2
8 7 6 5 4 3 2 1     8 7 6 5 4 3 2 1     8 7 6 5 4 3 2 1
```

Do not forget to conceptually cube this square: i.e. 28^3

The central colored rubric cube symbolizes the Earth (LIGHT) that is culled out of the un-manifested LIGHT of creation: i.e. DARKNESS

The other twenty-six rubric cubes symbolizes the un-manifested LIGHT of creation: i.e. DARKNESS

The MATRIX OF WISDOM is per se the world in a numerical format. It is what is projected out of the two-part psyche: ego-consciousness and the unconscious mind as the real world. Remember that the MATRIX OF WISDOM per se does not exist it is a commentary on the MONAD: i.e. God. The MATRIX OF WISDOM being a commentary on the MONAD: i.e. God illustrates that the MONAD: i.e. God per se cannot come into the real world just as the soul cannot come into the real world. The soul is basically carved up into pieces via the MATRIX OF WISDOM. The soul: i.e. MONAD: i.e. God is divided into ego-consciousness and the unconscious mind. Since both God and the soul cannot enter the blank abyss of the world it is obvious that they are one and the same being. The calculation of the Vesica Piscis (0.153...) outside of the TIME/SPACE continuum illustrates that. If it was not for that sole calculation it could not be said that the soul was God.

It has to be stated very clearly that the psyche does not exist per se outside of the illusion that it does exist. If it wasn't for the illusion of the TIME/SPACE continuum ego-consciousness and the unconscious mind would not be a factor in the discussion concerning the soul; because, without the turtle-crawl of TIME the birth of consciousness would not come about.

It is the task of each initiate to stabilize his or her psyche to the point of permanently living psychically in the state of Christ consciousness. Living nanosecond by nanosecond in the state of ego-consciousness battling the unconscious mind is like living paycheck to paycheck. It is the initiate mission (task) to stabilize the flow of Christ consciousness to the point of permanency.

Ego-consciousness and the unconscious mind is the phantasmagoria of the psyche. That 0.153... quotient outside of the TIME/SPACE continuum is liken to the soul sitting in a theater looking at the blank abyss of the cinematic screen; however, the soul participates in the activities of the psychic activity projected onto the cinematic screen of the blank abyss.

That mathematical calculation 0.153... outside of the MATRIX OF WISDOM literally illustrates that the Vesica Piscis symbolizes the God-Man Christ existing outside of the TIME/SPACE continuum. Since the soul is Christ then it has to be understood and conceptualized that the soul is God that exist outside of the TIME/SPACE continuum. This cannot be argued; because, Catholicism fears not to tell every member of the laity that individually they are the Christos. If; therefore, the soul is the Christos then the soul is God.

This would mean that the MATRIX OF WISDOM (the real world) is created by the soul: i.e. God-man Christ nanosecond by nanosecond creating the TIME/SPACE continuum.

This is going to be difficult to grasp; because, there are billions of people on the face of the earth and it is difficult to grasp that each soul exist in its own universe.

As humans we give the SPIRITUAL FORCES OF CREATION the nomenclature of GOD and then anthropomorphize that materialistic concept into human characteristics. Humans have to get their vocabularies on the same page. Just call God what he is: i.e. the Spiritual Forces of Creation, which all humans have psychically as their birthright. We as humans becoming in the real world God: i.e. the Christos only allows the worthy initiate to live life contentedly in the Garden of Eden so-to-speak via Christ consciousness. The Christ consciousness is what prevents the initiate from trying to dominate over another. The moment that one tries to exude authority over another the Christos leaves the psyche. The Christos will have no other god (ego-consciousness) before it. That is why Christ in the New Testament tells Satan to get behind Him.

That 0.153... calculation outside the TIME/SPACE continuum inferring the Vesica Piscis symbolizes the Holy of Holies: i.e. Christ consciousness: Temple of God in the psyche, which is lived in the soul outside the TIME/SPACE continuum. Living psychically inside of the TIME/SPACE continuum is per se conjuring up ego-consciousness and the unconscious mind.

CHAPTER FIFTEEN

MATRIX OF WISDOM (Part 5)
Religious Architectural Creativity

The MATRIX OF WISDOM is the primordial ethereal spiritual inspiration for all religious creative activity in antiquity and in all times and climes. It is only when the MATRIX OF WISDOM is transformed into the spiritual mindset of the Garden of Eden, Atlantis, Shangri La, etc. that the sacred scriptures can we written otherwise the soul spends eternity in Hell governed by the frozen mind-set of Satan: i.e. ego-consciousness' status quo.

In this MATRIX OF WISDOM (Part 5) I again return to the first word of Genesis: BERESHITH and the Genesis Formula; for the reason that, the whole of religious thought around the world is based solely upon the MATRIX OF WISDOM, which is symbolized by the Northern Cross (Children of the Swan, Cygnus X-3), the first word of Genesis: BERESHITH symbolizes the Northern Cross: BETH ב goes horizontally and RESH ר comes down vertically smashing ego-consciousness to pieces. The entire aspect of BETH ב is not destroyed; however, the YUD and TAV aspect of the spelling of BETH ב is wiped out completely symbolizing the annihilation the old sun-god and the old heaven and earth. The YUD י and TAV ת aspect of BETH ב spells out the Hebrew word of 'SIGN' as in the sign of the Zodiac. It is not that manifested creation is created in RESH ר per se; rather, it is creation created in the initiate via the FIRST SIGN, which for any soul could symbolize anyone of the twelve zodiacal sign plus Christ consciousness. The old sign past away via YUD י and TAV ת; however, from biblical parlance it is Christ being born. This would mean that every single child is Christ born into the world or every initiate receiving the Initiatic Visionary Experience is given a new raison d'être. Now the spiritual powers in creation cannot on their own volition merge a new raison d'être to the psyche of the initiate without a foundation to base it upon. Chartres Cathedral gives a very good example of this. The Romanesque Chartres Cathedral is build and then the West Façade burns down and a new West Façade is build. The old West Façade was liken to the head of John the Baptist being cut off so that a new spiritual one can replace it; however, notice that the rest of Chartres Cathedral burns down and the Chartres's Gothic Cathedral is built to replace it; yet, what is not discussed is that the foundation of Chartres Cathedral remains. It is that foundation of the old Romanesque Cathedral that the entire Christian mythoi are built upon. This is why when RESH comes down to smash ego-consciousness and only the letter BETH ב in the word BETH ב remains as the foundation of the new heaven and earth that is willing to follow the lone path of the labyrinth.

In my detailed analysis on the first word of Genesis: BERESHITH I envisaged aspects of it structure that made me realize that the Egyptian culture, particularly the Sphinx and Pyramid Complex on the Giza Plateau (Rostau and/or Zep Tepi: First Times), influenced those that wrote the Judaeo Christian Scriptures.

The MATRIX OF WISDOM has the Kamea of Saturn embossed into it generic structure. The Kamea of Saturn per se has the Northern Cross embossed into its structure as does the MATRIX OF WISDOM. That cross structured with odd numbers in the Kamea of Saturn is what inspired the ancient mystics to write the word BERESHITH to memorialize that cross. In studying both the Kamea of Saturn and the Matrix of Wisdom it becomes quite obvious that the cross is fixed and solid: i.e. ego-consciousness surrounded by even numbers, which symbolizes female: unconscious mind. What this suggests is that the cross is the mastaba: i.e. mound of creation, which emerged from the depths of the oceans in Egyptian mythology. This mastaba: the primeval mound of creation is symbolic of the birth of consciousness: Christ (Horus) consciousness. In ancient times this mastaba was called Zep Tepi: First Times. Pyramids are symbolic structures symbolizing the mastaba.

The six letters of BERESHITH בראשית the first word of Genesis appear to map out the landscape of the Giza Plateau; for the reason that their alphabetic categories: Archetypal, Existential and Cosmic letters appear to correlate with the basic structure of Giza Plateau pyramids designs.

Breaking down the Archetypal, Existential and Cosmic letters that makes up the word BERESITH into their individual categories it becomes easier to envisage that all six of the letters can be separated into two groups. The six letters of Bereshith symbolize the six queen pyramids that flank both Khufu's and Menkaure's pyramids. The six queen pyramids symbolize the shattering of ego-consciousness. The six small pyramids symbolize the spiritual forces in creation that are the raw material that build the three great pyramids before they are manifested into the world similar to how the Christian churches are completely build before they are manifested into the world. The two Archetypal letters [Beth ב and Aleph א] and one Existential letter [Yud י] symbolically builds Menkaure's pyramid the smallest of the three big pyramids. From out of the Bereshith the three Hebrew Cosmic letters symbolically build Khafre's [Tav ת, Shin ש and Resh ר] and Khufu's pyramid is built from all four Hebrew Cosmic letters [Tav ת, Shin ש, Resh; whereas, Qoph ק is invisible liken to the third eye] (see images below).

It has already been discussed how the first word of Genesis: BERESHITH transforms into the Trinity by PEI פ and BETH ב transmogrify into QOPH ק and it was also discussed how the last four letters of the Hebrew Coder spell out the word Christ (krst) in Greek using Hebrew letters: Tav ת-Shin ש-Resh ר-Qoph ק. There is no need to go into all that again.

However, in my analysis on the first word of Genesis: BERESHITH it was exceedingly interesting that the four Hebrew Cosmic letters literally and graphically exuded the head of the Sphinx that is said to guard the Giza Plateau's pyramid complex. TAV ת = Mark on the Forehead, SHIN ש = Tooth, RESH ר = head and QOPH ק = back of Head.

When I saw John Anthony West's presentation on the Magical Egypt series he showed a statue of Pharaoh with Horus Falcon resting on the back of the head symbolizing Horus Consciousness. This image of the Pharaoh with the falcon on the back of the head perfectly illustrated how I intuited what the Genesis Formula was conveying. In addition without the falcon on the back of the head QOPH ק would simply be BETH ב, which would make it the Sphinx's head protruding from the sands of the desert. The first word of Genesis: BERESHITH was conveying the idea that all the Hebrew and Greek letters of the Judaeo Christian Scriptures symbolized the sands of the deserts hiding the body of the Sphinx. The Sphinx as the lion symbolizes ego-consciousness. The fact that it is known the granite rock that originally surrounded the body of the Sphinx was removed and used to build a temple in front of it. I would suggest that most of Giza Plateau landscape was used as a quarry to harvest the granite rocks that build the pyramid complex. There may well be many tunnels and buildings beneath the Giza Plateau's Pyramid Complex a great deal more than has thus far been found and/or theorized about. This would not be difficult to wrap one's mind around seeing the sands of the deserts and the sediments of the Nile's yearly floods would eventually have fill in the used quarry.

What Graham Hancock, Robert Bauval, Adrian Gilbert and Andrew Collins did not comprehend, whatsoever, in their researches, published in three separate volumes: THE MESSAGE OF THE SPHINX[1] and THE ORION MYSTERY[2] and THE CYGNUS MYSTERY[3]

---

[1] http://www.amazon.com/Message-Sphinx-Hidden-Legacy-Mankind/dp/0517888521?ie=UTF8&keywords=message%20of%20the%20sphinx&qid=1464521850&ref_=sr_1_1&sr=8-1

[2] http://www.amazon.com/Orion-Mystery-Unlocking-Secrets-Pyramids/dp/0517884542/ref=pd_sim_sbs_14_1?ie=UTF8&dpID=51sbBpIi6iL&dpSrc=sims&preST=_AC_UL160_SR107%2C160_&refRID=0YH2ZVQWYMM6G1142YB6

was the results of a dual mythologies that governed the Giza Plateau Pyramid Complex. Robert Bauval and Andrew Collins appeared to be in an eternal warfare as to what inspired the creation of the Giza Plateau's Pyramid Complex: i.e. the Orion Constellation or the Cygnus Constellation? All four of these authors did not realize that they were looking at two disparate mythologies intertwined into the Giza Plateau: i.e. Rostau and/or Zep Tepi: First Times.

These authors of course did not know there were two mythologies interlaced; rather they thought the mythos of the Giza Plateaus was one unified mythological systemic system of thought. These researchers of the Egyptian culture did not know the rudimentary principles behind the Initiatic Visionary Experience, which the entire Giza Plateau Pyramid Complex is, build upon.

Robert Bauval and Andrew Collins are two modern day researchers that unwittingly got caught up in an ethereal systemic system of symbolism based solely upon their individual characters. Everybody that has ever lived is caught up in that ethereal systemic system of symbolism; however, most people are not noticed in this manner; for the reason that, they have not tossed themselves into the fray of public opinion. With Bauval and Collins it is more noticeable because they published themselves into the mainstream thought. Bauval symbolizes ego-consciousness and Collins symbolizes the unconscious mind neither recognizing the other; whereas, I see them as a unified system. Notice how Bauval is more popular in modernity; because, his symbolizes ego-consciousness.

This same phenomenon took place between the two great psychiatrists Sigmund Freud (ego-consciousness) and Carl G. Jung (unconscious mind). Freud's work was geared more towards the first part of life and Jung's work was geared towards the latter part of life. Freud is more recognized; though, all his theories have been proven wrong over Jung work; because, Freud deals with the secular atheistic world; whereas, Jung deals more with the religious, mythological and symbolic aspects of life.

Mary Baker Eddy the discoverer and founder of Christian Science also ran into her adversaries; because, of the numerous mind and spirit cults of her time; yet, she alone emerge amongst that fray to build a worldwide organization.

Another interesting example is Albert Einstein theory: E=MC2[4], by David Bodanis, which discuss how Einstein united the researches and theories of a number of other scientists that published before his unification of their works.

The two most important questions to ask about the pyramids on the Giza Plateau are, why was not any pharaoh buried in one of the three pyramids on the Giza Plateau? And why was not there any hieroglyphics carvings place on the walls of the interior of those pyramids? When looking at all the other pyramids in Egypt there are found the remains of pharaohs and pyramids texts. It is this that contrasts the Giza Plateau Pyramid Complex from the rest of the pyramids of Egypt

To obtain a better understanding of how both Robert Bauval's and Andrew Collins' theories are attuned to one another the reader should look that map images I provide below of the Giza Plateau (Andrew Collin's image) and my overlaying that map with the Kamea of Saturn. I am not saying that Bauval's and Collins' theories amalgamate, which they of course do not.

The Great Pyramid (Khufu); though, it is facing North it is the pyramid that is the furthest East of the three main pyramids. The Bird Caves, which are also in the North are West of the Great Pyramid. This can get confusing to some people. When looking at the Menkaure's pyramid it is found to be the furthest pyramid West of the Great pyramid; though, it gives the appearance

---

[3] http://www.amazon.com/Cygnus-Mystery-Unlocking-Ancient-Origins/dp/1906787557/ref=sr_1_2?s=books&ie=UTF8&qid=1464522030&sr=1-2&keywords=the+cygnus+mystery
[4] http://www.amazon.com/mc2-Biography-Worlds-Famous-Equation/dp/0425181642?ie=UTF8&psc=1&redirect=true&ref_=oh_aui_detailpage_o04_s00

of being South of the Great Pyramid. Yes, Menkaure's pyramid is in the South; but, not in the contact of the Kamea of Saturn. Khafre's pyramid is in the center of the three pyramids. Gebel Ghibli is further South of all five positions in the Kamea of Saturn. Ghibli is a cemetery or land of the dead. All five positions on the Giza Plateau sit perfectly into the Kamea of Saturn's odd numbers. It is extraordinarily interesting that the 9, 5 and 1: Fire Triplicities signs of Astrology go from North to South and that 3, 5 and 7 are numbers that can transpose into 753, which is the years 753BC that the Roman Empire began; thus, interpreting itself as the FIRST TIMES. The odd numbers symbolizes the cross or mastaba that rises out of the primordial creation. The 7, 5, 3; though, symbolizing the horizon also symbolizes the second and seventh multiplication tables that symbolizes the LIGHT culled out of the DARKNESS.

There can be no doubt that the three great pyramids represent Rostau imitating the Duat in the heavenly constellation of the Orion Constellation; however, this symbolizes ego-consciousness and what exemplifies that are the four star shafts located in the King and Queen Chambers (see image of the star constellation aligned to the pyramid's star shafts).

Notice that both the King and Queen's chambers have two star shaft one point to the Northern Sky and other towards the Southern Sky. I do not believe that this is a choice nor liken to the scales of Anubis. Rather I see these two shafts in both the Queen and the King's chambers as illustrating what takes place when the initiate is gifted with the Initiatic Visionary Experience.

I think it is more than coincidental that the King (masculine) chamber's star shaft point to Taurus (Orion Constellation – Osiris) and the Queen (feminine) chamber's star chapter points to the Canis Major (Sirius - Isis). The fact that the King chamber's star shaft is pointing to Taurus: Orion: Osiris in the southern sky inferring a patriarchal culture, which was directly influenced by it north star-shaft pointing to Sagittarius: Draco in the northern sky.

Let me also point out that the Dog Star Sirius is chasing the Orion Constellation (see image below) very similar to the dog that yip at the heel of the FOOL in the Tarot Cards. I, interpret, Taurus the Bull (hubris) as ego-consciousness unfettered. This is the Minotaur Bull that a maze (societal mores) was constructed to keep it caged.

Whereas, the Queen chamber's star shaft in pointing to Gemini: Sirius: Isis the Goddess in the southern sky inferring a matriarchal culture, which was directly influenced by it north star-shaft pointing to Cancer: Ursa Minor in the northern sky. It also has to be realized that the Queen star shafts were block off from external vision. It is interesting that it was a member of Freemasonry that tap on the walls of the Queen's chamber and the discovered the star-shafts. And Cancer symbolizes the unconscious mind. Gemini is in the antediluvian times when the Great Goddess reign.

I interpret the King and Queen's chambers to be influenced by egocentrism; because, the King and the Queen had separate chambers and they were both influenced by different stars constellations. It is as if the Great Pyramid is saying it is following what it believe is the spiritual mandate of creation; because, it is following the northern skies mandates by implementing them in the south. The Great Pyramid is illustrating the error of splitting ego-consciousness from the unconscious mind and this latter fits perfectly with Robert Bauval's theory.

When it is realized that the cosmic radiation that come down from the Northern Cross: i.e. Cygnus X-3 permeating the granite rock of the pyramids as they do Shamanic Caves all over the world it reveals the spiritual ambiance of creation. It is my assumption that the pyramids were created so that they would be pitch dark chambers that the initiates being trained into the Egyptian priesthood would go and mediate on in that darkness to see the radiation sparks as other Shamanic initiates do around the world in their underground caves.

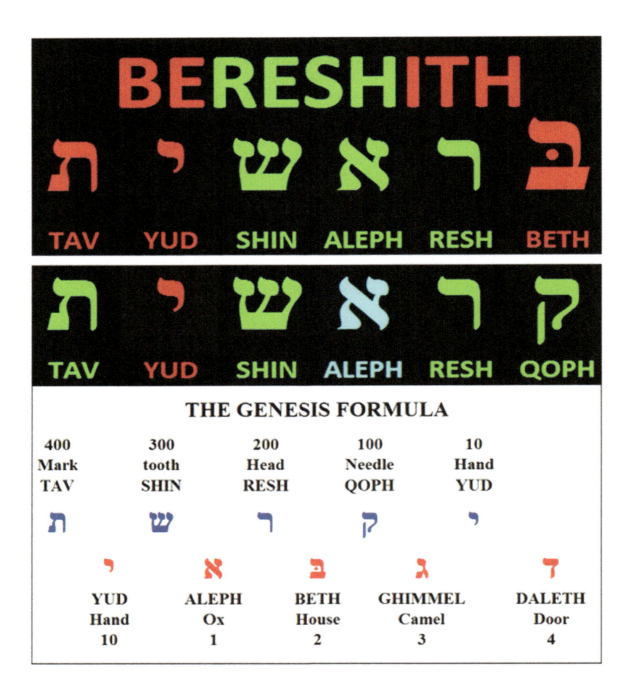

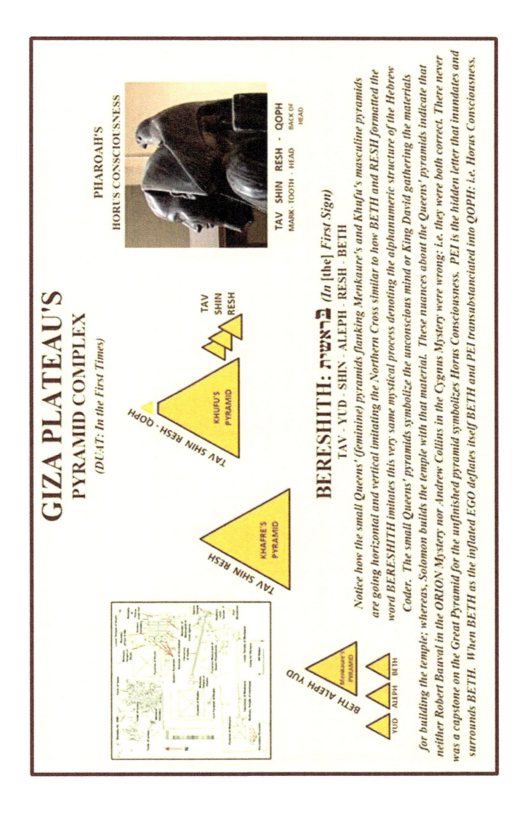

GIZA PLATEAU'S
PYRAMID COMPLEX
(DUAT: In the First Times)

PHAROAH'S

HORUS CONSCIOUSNESS

TAV SHIN RESH - QOPH
MARK - TOOTH - HEAD   BACK OF
                       HEAD

TAV
SHIN
RESH

KHUFU'S
PYRAMID

TAV SHIN RESH - QOPH

KHAFRE'S
PYRAMID

TAV SHIN RESH

MENKAURE'S
PYRAMID

BETH   ALIPH   YUD

BETH ALEPH YUD

BERESHITH: בראשית *(In [the] First Sign)*
TAV - YUD - SHIN - ALEPH - RESH - BETH

Notice how the small Queens' (feminine) pyramids flanking Menkaure's and Khufu's masculine pyramids are going horizontal and vertical imitating the Northern Cross similar to how BETH and RESH formatted the word BERESHITH imitates this very same mystical process denoting the alphanumeric structure of the Hebrew Coder. The small Queens' pyramids symbolize the unconscious mind or King David gathering the materials for building the temple; whereas, Solomon builds the temple with that material. These nuances about the Queens' pyramids indicate that neither Robert Bauval in the ORION Mystery nor Andrew Collins in the Cygnus Mystery were wrong: i.e. they were both correct. There never was a capstone on the Great Pyramid for the unfinished pyramid symbolizes Horus Consciousness. PEI is the hidden letter that inundates and surrounds BETH. When BETH as the inflated EGO deflates itself BETH and PEI transubstanciated into QOPH: i.e. Horus Consciousness.

THE EGYPTIAN GIZA PLATEAU'S PYRAMID COMPLEX

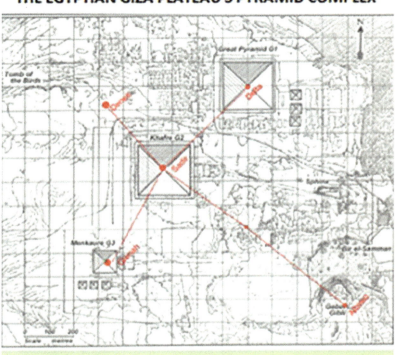

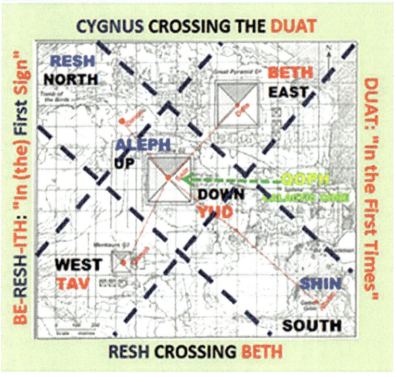

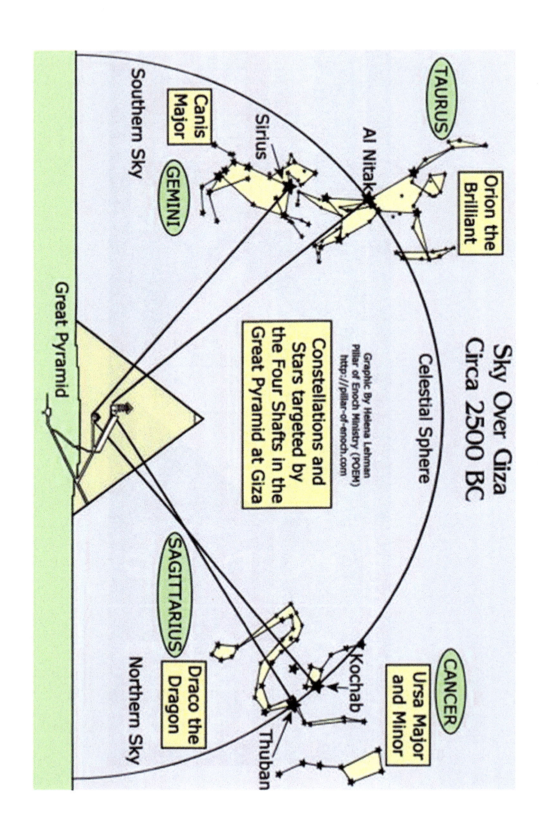

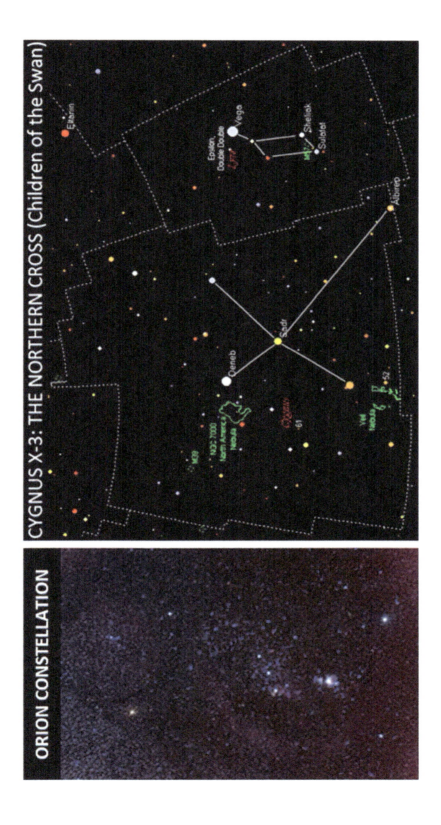

CHAPTER SIXTEEN

MATRIX OF WISDOM (Part 6)

WASHINGTON DC

Washington DC should not even be in this volume's discussion of religious symbolism according to what the United States' Citizens think their Constitution is all about; however, my research finds that Thomas Jefferson wrote to the Governor of Virginia in 1778, just two years after the Revolutionary War, and asked him to secede land for the seat of government: Washington DC., which is actually provided for in the *United States Constitution Article 1, Section 8[1]*,

*"To exercise exclusive Legislation in all Cases whatsoever, over such District (**not exceeding ten Miles square**) as may, by Cession of particular States, and the Acceptance of Congress, become the Seat of the Government of the United States, and to exercise like Authority over all Places purchased by the Consent of the Legislature of the State in which the Same shall be, for the Erection of Forts, Magazines, Arsenals, dock-Yards and other needful Buildings;-And".*

The ten Miles square is of course the MATRIX OF WISDOM and I have provided two maps of Washington DC that can be access on the Internet. Apparently Freemasonry is secretly dressing up the streets and buildings of Washington DC with symbolism that reflects the universal spiritual beliefs of all cultures around the world.

I want to point out right away that Washington DC sit on the edge of the Atlantic Ocean, which I believe Freemasonry symbolically has representing the Hebrew letter PEI פ similar to how the meteor impact crater inundates and surrounds Serpent Mound that symbolizes the Hebrew letter BETH ב. Of course Washington DC 10 x 10 matrix landscape would symbolize the DARKNESS; whereas, the rest of the United States would symbolize LIGHT culled out of the DARKNESS; however, as with the bible symbolism Freemasonry redundantly repeat this symbolic motif several more times within the precincts of the MATRIX OF WISDOM. Redundancies of symbolic motifs are put into place to illustrate that this is not a coincidence or accidental presentation of symbolism.

The House of the Temple, Masonic Temple, was built in 1911 and is located at 1733 16th St NW, Washington DC, which is a little distance on the same street that goes towards the center of the White House. I point this out; for the reason that, the House of the Temple can be seen to have been designed based upon the MATRIX OF WISDOM. The Masons do not hide their symbolism per se; because, most people neither understand symbolism nor what they are looking at when they are in Masonic a Lodge nor what they see on the streets and buildings of Washington DC. For the most part the United States citizenry knows nothing of symbolism being basically a Protestant nation. It is very much like the laity in the Roman Catholic Church not knowing that Catholicism has anything to do with symbolism no less being spiritually attuned 100% to iconography.

The history of Washington DC is somewhat skewed. Above I mention Thomas Jefferson writing the Governor of Virginia in 1778 to secede land for the city of Washington DC; yet, Pierre Charles L'Enfant writes George Washington in 1789 for permission to plan the city's outline. Congress doesn't pass the Residence Act until 1790.

In addition Maryland used to be called Terra Aqua: "land by the sea" and it was later change to Maryland, which is also a proper interpretation of that previous name. The word MARY means WATER and TERRA means LAND. Maryland today has a different back-story as to why the state is named Maryland; for the reason that Freemasonry will not allow explicit knowledge of symbolism to be divulged.

---

[1] http://constitutioncenter.org/interactive-constitution/articles/article-i

Freemasonry and the Founding Fathers wanted to give Washington DC a secret name: i.e. VIRGIN MARY, which is derived from the names of the two states that seceded land for the ten Miles square: **VIRGIN**IA and **MARY**LAND. Pierre L'Enfant was French, American born, gave the added nuance that all cathedrals of France are dedicated to Notre Dame (Our Lady). As an architect he would have studied the cathedral blueprints of Europe especially since America was in its infant stages at the time. Is the American People supposed to believe this is all coincidence?

There is more to Washington DC[2] than that. The land that Virginia seceded was returned. As if euphemistically saying the Virginity had gone out of Democracy. The planning stages of laying out that ten Miles square, with the Potomac running through it, before Virginia's land was return to it, was to calculate out the land (61.05 miles) to mirror the calculations of the Golden Ratio: 0.618..

The Potomac River symbolizes MARY and the LAND (present Washington DC). VIRGINIA and the POTOMAC that sits between the two-part-city of Washington DC symbolize VIRGIN MARY.

The most extraordinary calculation to come out of these three sections of the ten Miles square is the Potomac's 7.29 miles. Remember that 729 figure is the cube of nine (9) and; for the reason that, the Potomac is an everlastingly flowing river it would seem to symbolize the tetrahedral forces of creation.

Virginia seceded land is 31.66 miles of the MATRIX OF WISDOM, which is extremely close to the cube of Pi and it has already been determined that Elohym (God) symbolizes Pi. In this case Virginia would symbolize VIRGIN knowledge, which would be symbolically outside the time/space continuum.

The amount of land mass that Virginia and the Potomac River total to is 38.95 miles, which very close to the 60/40 ratio of the Genesis Formula that is shown to be created by the MATRIX OF WISDOM. If it wasn't for Washington DC sitting upon the MATRIX OF WISDOM these calculations would have no meaning other than the fact that they have been shown previously relating to the MATRIX OF WISDOM.

Another nuance to consider out of the 31.66 miles that Virginia seceded to the Federal Government and then having it return to them makes no sense. Did the Federal Government have the right to constitutionally return the land to Virginia after it was gifted by cession to the people of the United States? When did anybody ever hear of the United States Government ever giving anything to anybody? The 31.66 miles of land that Virginia ceded to the Federal Government is only 34% of the land mass seceded by both States. Maryland gives up 66% inferring the number of the beast 666. In addition the number 7.29 (729) is symbolic of 9³ and the figure 31.66 is also extremely close to the figure 31.68 North Latitude of the equator where Bethlehem of Judaeo sits. Notice that the land Maryland seceded could have been reduce to 61.03 miles and Virginia could have given the whole of 31.68 miles; however, the number 61.03 is the amount of laws: i.e. 613 in the Old Testament that are culled out of the ten commandments. It very well may have been too explicit and upfront to lay out accurately in the landscape of Washington DC; the number 613 would have been recognized by many especially in those days and ages. In fact there is little doubt that that is precisely what, I believe, the figure 61.05 figure symbolizes; for the reason that, Washington DC is the seat of government that legislates the laws.

I have previously written a paper, which I published on the Internet, called THE GREAT SEAL OF THE UNITED STATES: Freemasonry's Influence on the American Pathos[3].

What Freemasonry has additionally symbolically worked into the landscape of Washington DC was to have the vertical streets named numerically and the horizontal streets alphabetized and the diagonal streets are named after the first thirteen colonies. This is the same spiritual theme that the Northern Cross has in symbolically representing the Initiatic Visionary Experience descending upon the worthy initiate. The dynamic forces of creation symbolized by abstract mathematics (Quadrivium: four mathematical sciences) descend upon the materialistically mundane (Trivium: three grammatical arts).

The next image shown is a picture taken from the Capitol Building overlooking Washington Mall towards the Washington Monument's obelisk and beside this image is another picture taken from Saint

---

[2] https://en.wikipedia.org/wiki/Washington,_D.C.
[3] http://www.slideshare.net/williamjohnmeegan/the-great-seal-of-the-united-states-freemasorys-influence-on-the-american-pathos

Peter's Basilica overlooking Bernini's Square at Vatican City, Rome. Both pictures practically mirror-image each other. The two diagonal streets going towards the White House and the Jefferson Memorial symbolizes the two colonnade arms in Bernini's Square and the Washington Mall mirror images the street that continues on pass Vatican City; however, both Washington Mall and the straight line (street) going from Vatican City has the obelisk on both sites following the same patterns; however, each of their patterns go in the opposite direction. The National Mall in Washington DC goes from East to West similar to the layout of the Sistine Chapel and Saint Peter's Basilica; whereas, Bernini Square at the Vatican goes from West to East. As has been previously shown the Vesica Piscis is laid out in the landscape at the foot of the Washington Monument. Similarly the Vesica Piscis can be envisaged around the obelisk in the center of Bernini's Square.

The next image is an aerial photograph of the White House, Washington Monument, Lincoln Memorial and the Washington Mall. There is a red line going north to south from the White House down to Jefferson Memorial and another red line going horizontally east to west from the Capitol Building to the Lincoln Memorial. There is a large wording "ALIGNMENT FAIL". This photograph was used by someone that did not know what he or she was looking at. The person that set up this photograph expected a perfect alignment of Washington Monument aligning to the White House and Jefferson Monument vertically and he or she further expected simultaneously a perfect alignment aligning the Capitol Building, Washington Monument and the Lincoln Memorial. This person failed in his or her observations; for the reason that, he or she did not know what they were looking at.

Looking at a map of Washington DC with those particular five sites in play it is easily seen that the CROSS laid out in the landscape aligning the White House, the Washington Monument and Jefferson Memorial vertically crossing the Washington Mall between 15th Street NW and 17th Street NW; whereas, the Capitol Building, Washington Monument and Lincoln Memorial along the length of the Washington Mall rest on the landscape between Constitutional Avenue NW and Independence Avenue SW.

When considering the planning of the streets surrounding these five locations isn't in intriguing that the Washington Mall is seemingly the demarcation zone that separates the North from the South? All streets south of the Washington Mall change to South West when crossing the Mall; however, what is very intriguing is that it is the Capitol building not the Washington Mall that is the primary demarcation zone that planned the layout of the streets of Washington DC insofar that it is the Capitol Building that separate the east from the west and the north from the south.

For what purpose would the Capitol Building have been given that kind of religious authority on a symbolic level unless it had further abstract meanings? There is a great deal to be considered here since Freemasonry's complete and utter focus is on what is West, North West and South West of the Capitol Building. Apparently, the fact that the East is not involved directly with these five sites under consideration the East has to symbolically represent what comes toward BETH ב as the first letter of the Torah for nothing happens politically in the United States unless it comes through the Capitol Building.

The Apotheosis of Washington[4] on the ceiling of the Capitol Building is what the Washington Mall and the obelisk: Washington Monument is all about. Consider that George Washington was the first president; thus, he is the United States' first raison d'être (reason for existence). Like all Catholic popes take on the mantle of Peter so to all presidents of the United States takes on the mantle of George Washington. It is very interesting that there are 72-stars circling the Apotheosis of George Washington symbolizing the 72-names of God. George Washington was a Freemason and there is no hiding that fact. The symbolism of the Washington Mall having the cosmic rays of Cygnus X-3 (Northern Cross) descending upon it symbolized by the obelisk: Washington Monument illustrates that spiritual raison d'être. The obelisk is clearly suggesting that the president of the United States is spiritually selected by the higher powers of creation; however, it has to be understood by the reader that George Washington (like the Catholic pope) symbolizes the lone initiate seeking to take control of his life, as the Freemasons say going from a Good Man to a Better Man.

---

[4] https://en.wikipedia.org/wiki/The_Apotheosis_of_Washington

The arithmetical data relating to the creation of the Apotheosis of Washington is symbolic of the spiritual process being discussed in this book. The Dome of the Capitol was finished in 1863, which is the year that President Abraham Lincoln signed the Emancipation Proclamation on January 1st, which freed the slaves. The numerical digits of 1863 (1, 3, 6 and 8) has everything to do with Christ and the Star of David in the Zodiac/Calendar Year that symbolizes the tetrahedral forces in creation (psyche). An in 1865 the war is over and the union is reunited; hence, Washington Mall separating or is that uniting the North and South.

Constantino Brumidi painted the Apotheosis of Washington in 1865. Out of all the painters in the entire world this one has to be named Constantino (CONSTANT) who also worked for the Vatican? Coincidence? Really? The word CONSTANT symbolizes ORDER out of CHAOS. This is analogous to Emperor Constantine defeating Maximinus on the Milvian Bridge: i.e. bringing ORDER out of CHAOS. Also think of the 72-Cherubs that circle the ceiling of the Sistine Chapel symbolizing the 72-names of God and Constantino Brumidi came right out of that spiritual artistic milieu. Michelangelo frescoed the Shemhamphorasch: i.e. 72-names of God on the ceiling of the Sistine Chapel.

Actually, this kind of symbolism defines Democracy in a more explicit and definitive light. For the masses symbolizes CHAOS. That is what Democracy means: i.e. MOB RULES, which illustrates what the people psychically elect to their ruling government. This is what symbolically comes through the front door, which I believe is symbolically on the east side of the Capitol Building. All events in Washington take place on the west side of the Capitol Building as if it poured in from the east via the public and goes out the rear west door via Congressional legislation. Looking at the Capitol Building's east and west images for they present a more precise understanding of what Freemasonry accomplished. It would be, at this time, extremely difficult to believe that the Roman Catholic Church was/is not directly involved in this artistic endeavor of spiritually and symbolically structuring the United States Capitol. From that perspective it would mean that there are many people that belong to the hidden hierarchy of Freemasonry and the hidden inner hierarchy of the Roman Catholic Church that is secretly conspiring (as they should) to keep this knowledge hidden from the profane public (infidel).

Yes, it can be seen by those that have ears to hear and eyes to see that Freemasonry and Catholicism is creating this spiritual genre of thought in Washington DC; however, remember that when spirituality is written into the manifested world simultaneously the material façade (sleight of hand) has to be incorporated into the artistic mix.

The entire Washington Mall going from east to west from the rear entrance of the Capitol Building to Lincoln's Memorial is all about war monuments; whereas, from the White House down to Jefferson Memorial implies that all coming from the Capitol building should be totally Constitutional as if to infer that the United States Constitution was ordain by the spiritual forces of creation. This is why I believe that the diagonal streets of Pennsylvania Avenue going from the White House to the Capitol Building and Maryland Avenue going from Jefferson Memorial to the Capitol Building is in a pyramid tetrahedron design: thus there is no failed alignment. It is not of course a four-sided pyramid; nonetheless, the symbolism of the tetrahedron appears to imitate the Great Pyramid initially without a capstone. The Dome of the Capitol building appeared in 1863 and the Apotheosis of George Washington frescos the ceiling inferring a cap-less pyramid. In addition there is that Statue of Peace on top of the Capitol Dome symbolizing the capstone of the pyramid. It would seem that Peace and War are two symbolical themes in Freemasonry's overall plan; for the reason that Peace is another word for living life contentedly. I will get to this Pease and War theme later.

Furthermore, I hypothesize that there is a second tetrahedron that is esoterically implied that is generated by Congress' constituency (the electorate) via the tetrahedral forces that are generated by the two tetrahedrons creating the Star of David or what the Hindus would call Churching of the Milky Ocean.

This is not projecting something that is not there. Remember the layout of the Sistine Chapel where the popes are divided between the odd (Moses' life cycle) and even (Christ's life cycle) numbers. The even numbers are on the North Wall and the odd numbers are on the South Wall symbolically separated by the valley going east to west created by splitting Mount Olive (last chapter of Zachariah) in twain where one half went north and other half went south. Via the twelve zodiacal signs outlined on the Sistine

Chapel ceiling the invisible Star of David is also envisaged. It has been discuss how the Sistine Chapel morphs into an octagon shape: Kamea of Saturn. This same phenomenon was seen at the Giza Plateau when Cygnus X-3 is considered as the source material for designing the pyramid complex. I provide an image that does a comparative analysis of Washington DC and the Giza Plateau. Washington DC in every way seems to have been designed to symbolically abstractly symbolize Solomon's Temple morphing into a Christian octagon shape Church. Remember the Sistine Chapel has the measurements of Solomon's Temple. The entrance door in the east seems to be the pivotal point that determines the directions on both sides of it entrance/exit door just as the Capitol Building is the pivotal point that determined the designs in the streets of Washington DC.

Abraham Lincoln's Memorial sits perfectly at the end of the stretch from the Capitol building; however, it seems to symbolize the smallest of the three pyramids on the Giza Plateau: i.e. the sun: ego-consciousness setting in the west. The sun setting symbolizes acquiescence to spirituality. Remember Abraham Lincoln in signing the Emancipation Proclamation freeing the slaves on January 1st 1863 has a great deal more to do with freeing the human psyche of slavery then freeing the Negro slaves in the secular world. Most people living in the world have no idea that that is the major battle they are confronting in life. That is why the whole Capitol Mall symbolizes a war zone: i.e. the White House symbolizes the divine edict and Washington Monument (Cygnus X-3, Northern Cross) separating Church and State (Jefferson Memorial). Abraham Lincoln symbolizes reuniting this psychic divide. It is alright to live in society via a separation of Church and State; however, the spiritual laws of God should govern the initiate's Christ consciousness not some secular government. This is basically what I see the city of Washington DC symbolizing. Abraham Lincoln symbolizes the Last Judgment in the Sistine Chapel. Sitting there in his memorial monument he is asking the individual citizen the question, "Have you united Church and State? Most people live their lives thinking they are slaves to materialism; rather than being CONTENT with what they have. That is the difference between slavery and a freeman.

There is a great deal of precedence for Abraham Lincoln freeing the slaves. In the Old Testament when Abraham sent Hagar into the wilderness with Ishmael and Abraham did that he had his friendly angels help her.

Then there is the story of Joseph and his brothers going into Egypt. Studying the story of Joseph becoming the overlord of Egypt creating what would appear to be a brutal government by taking the people's money, animals, land and then taxing them 20% (ego-consciousness) of their gross income; whereas, Joseph relatives were not so willing to go along with that agenda thinking that kind of life was slavery; yet, the Egyptian people abhorred the Jews for their domestication of animals, which symbolizes archetypal instincts, which is basically the psyche being guided by ego-consciousness and not Horus consciousness. The Jews fled Egypt; because, they weren't going to be allowed to live in paradise without acquiescing to spirituality. Think of the story of the Prodigal Son's brother who felt that he was a slave on his father's property; whereas, the Prodigal Son returned to be a slave rather than live in the outer world.

Then there is the legend of how many Federal troops died (365,000 – nice round figure) during the Civil War and how many Confederate troops died (258,000 – nice round figure); however, this numbers have everything to do with the Ten Commandments. Out of the Ten Commandment come 613-laws: 365-Thou Shalt Nots and 248-Thou Shalts. It is extremely interesting that these figures numerically mirror-image the calculation of how the MATRIX OF WISDOM was divided up between Maryland, Potomac and Virginia. The 365-Thou Shalt Nots is symbolic circle of DARKNESS found in the first chapter of Genesis. The split between 365 and 248 is a 60/40 or 3/2 ratio (Genesis Formula) with the Ten Commandments symbolizes Pi: 3.14159 that divides the Thou Shalts (248) from the Thou Shalt Nots (365) the 3-1-2 (Elohym separating the Heavens and the Earth) in the numerical sequence of the Gematria value of RESH ר. Essentially the Ten Commandments are saying that the Thou Shalt are derived from the Thou Shalt Nots. Thus, the symbolism of Washington DC is declaring that it is BERESHITH: *"In the beginning"*.

The White House symbolizes the Apotheosis of Washington; because, in symbolizing the presidency (POTUS) represents the highest political achievement in the secular world, which symbolizes here the ascension into heaven; however, on the Giza Plateau it would symbolize the Bird Caves (Cygnus X-3,

Northern Cross and Children of the Swan). The Jefferson Memorial would symbolize Gebel Ghibli a hill south of the second large pyramid that overlooks the Giza Plateau and is a perfect place to oversee its construction. Tomas Jefferson wrote the Declaration of Independence and the Constitution of the United States and his memorial symbolizes that and this is why it most likely is placed where it is representing Gebel Ghibli symbolically overseeing the dynamics of the seat of government in Washington DC.

The designs in the diagonal streets of Washington DC give off very unique patterns mirror imaging the Kamea of Saturn (Octagonal shape). Pierre Charles L'Enfant's architectural design in the streets of Washington DC centers mainly on Pennsylvania and Massachusetts Avenues. I happen to be an ardent reader of the works of Carl G. Jung in his psychic-autobiography not a historical autobiography: MEMORIES, DREAMS, REFLECTIONS[5] and he talks about a dream he had in 1927. He drew a rough draft of the dream images and then worked it into a more beautiful mandala image. As I was doing my analysis on the Pierre Charles L'Enfant's design I was surprised to see the same pattern locked into the Capitol Building connected to the White House and Seward Square. I don't think that CG Jung dream had anything to do with Washington DC; though, the patterns worked out in Washington DC and others cities throughout the world are best seen as psychic patterns.

I want the reader to reflect contemplatively upon the Founding Fathers of the United States, whom obviously had a Freemasonry agenda. I find it most curious that symbolically SLAVERY, which included White Man's Indenture Slavery, was their overall focus. I believe I have shown that that slavery issue did not spiritually have anything do with Negro Slavery per se; though, the Negro Slaves were used symbolically to outline Freemasonry's overall spiritual teachings. Nonetheless, this analysis of Washington DC illustrates that slavery both spiritually and materialistically were on the minds of the Founding Fathers and their raison d'être was to work towards freeing the slaves in both the North and the South in both the spiritual and materialistic realms. There is no way that any 'initiate': the Founding Fathers, could solve all his or her issues at once. Simply because the War of Independence was over did not mean that slavery on both sides of the divide would be immediately eradicated. If Washington insisted upon such a thing the Civil War at that time would have weakened the colonies to such a state that the British Army would have come in and taken over the new found fledgling government of the United States as they tried in 1812.

Having gone through both Catholicism's and Freemasonry's esoteric symbolism laid out on the landscape of Washington DC I have to warn those iconoclastic literal minded readers that are not yet fully conversant with iconography not to take symbolism literally or else they will feel the backlash of terror. This will cause the diehard fundamentalists to inappropriately protest against what they don't understand and what they idiotically and foolishly conjured up in their paranoia minds.

The world stop being a Garden of Eden the moment that ego-consciousness reared its ugly head in the psyche of the individual, which was about a few years after birth. Egocentrism is all about being self-centered and having an uncontrollable hubris. Envisage that definition of ego-consciousness exponentially worldwide into the psyche of every human being especially more so into the iconoclastic religious and political fields: behold modernity is at your doorstep.

There is not an esoterist, mystic or any individual in the world that does not have ego-consciousness guiding it spiritually or materialistically otherwise the psyche would be completely caught up in the tsunami of the unconscious mind. In fact the iconoclastic realm of modernity is in fact caught up in the tsunami of the unconscious mind: psychiatric ward (The Crazy King parable[6]); but, that mental condition is not as severe as many of those in the more restrictive wards of the insane asylums. Ego-consciousness is held fast to when it believe erroneously that it is above the fray of the world.

I give this warning; for the reason that, many may see the United States' Founding Fathers as deliberately maintaining slavery when in fact before Abraham Lincoln was the sixteenth president most of

[5] http://www.amazon.com/Memories-Dreams-Reflections-C-G-Jung/dp/0679723951/ref=sr_1_1?ie=UTF8&qid=1465005224&sr=8-1&keywords=MEMORY+DREAMS+AND+REFLECTIONS%2C+CARL+JUNG
[6] https://danfabrizio.com/2011/09/02/the-crazy-king-a-parable-about-individuality-vs-conformity/

the country had laws forbidding slavery, including as far west as California, except for fifteen southern states, which eleven were Confederate states.. In fact I, personally, saw indentured slavery (servitude – call it what you want) well established in the northern states that was worse than the Negro slaves in the south; yet, paradoxically indentured slavery[7] was considered legal; though, many white children were kidnapped in their native lands and sold into indentured servitude. It is difficult to believe that the United States Constitution was written in the midst of that milieu.

Also Abraham Lincoln having the name ABRAHAM is too coincidental to the Abraham of the bible. Abraham (Abram) of the bible also had two families: Hagar and Ishmael and Sarah (Sarai) and Isaac and when the Gematria value of these two family are conducted they all total to 1863, which coincidentally happens to coincide with the years that Abraham Lincoln signs the Emancipation Proclamation (see accompanied image of calculation of the two families)?

This two tier classification system of slavery: indenture slaves in the north and Negro slaves in the south cannot be a coincidence when considering the layout of Freemasonry's symbolism in Washington DC. Presently in modernity slavery is still well established throughout the United States only it is now called semantically minimum (not a living) wages or college students graduating with a camel's weight of debt upon their backs. If this latter is not indentured slavery I don't know what is. Remember that student when he or she graduates still has to go further into debt just to live decently in society. This kind of treatment that is thrust upon America's children is, for all intent and purpose, slavery. This treatment of American children has become so common place in the United States the graduate students are willing to take the blame for their financial burdens saying they agreed to accept the debt when in actuality they had no choice other than to go out and earn a minimum wage salary and be in poverty for the remainder of their lives.

The point that I am trying to drive home here is that all peoples of the world are, for the most part, in slavery. The real task in life is to turn that awesome burden of slavery into being a free person by becoming *CONTENT* with what one's has.

The initiate's due diligence, if he or she is to validate this esoteric argument concerning the construct of Washington DC, is to cull libraries, bookstores and the internet concerning the different sites under discussion: White House (finished 1800), Capitol Building (finished 1800), Washington Monument (began 1848 finished 1884), Lincoln Memorial (dedicated 1922), Jefferson Memorial (1943), Pennsylvania Avenue (first mention in Jefferson's letter in 1791) and much more. By establishing when these five sites were created it is a great deal easier to understand what was going through Freemasonry's mind during those different stages of development. For example the planning stages of Washington DC via the MATRIX OF WISDOM were already in the planning stages via Thomas Jefferson's writing it into the US Constitution: Article 1, Section 8 and via Jefferson's letter to the Virginia's governor 1778 and the US Constitution wasn't signed until 1789. Washington Monument (1848) was a foregone conclusion that it would not line up with the White House; however, it does perfectly line up with the Capitol Building at this point along the Washington Mall. Washington Monument symbolizes the cosmic rays coming from Cygnus X-3 (Northern Cross: Children of the Swan): i.e. Initiatic Visionary Experience. The White House in line up with Pennsylvania Avenue (a diagonal street) in line to the Capitol Building illustrates that concept of symbolically outlining the Initiatic Visionary Experience was complete before the Constitution of the United States was written.

People will wonder why it is taking so long for this project to be completed by Freemasonry. All esoteric projects take centuries to complete otherwise it would be too overtly exposed. Such spiritual progress does not happen overnight. This latter may be the actually reason that such project take so long to symbolically represent the initiate task of unraveling the spiritual mysteries of creation. Chartres Cathedral, which began in 1020, was literally finished in 1836. It is no surprise to me that Washington DC is taking so long to finish. Another example is Saint Peter's Basilica is still being worked on. Pope Paul II mythoi, since his death, have been worked into the mosaic of the floor of Saint Peter's Basilica.

---

[7] https://en.wikipedia.org/wiki/Indentured_servant

The longest esoteric project that I envisaged in the history of Catholicism took place between 27AD to 1560 (1533 years) from the death of Jesus Christ to the expulsion of Catholicism from Great Britain by Queen Elizabeth I (7 September 1533 – 24 March 1603). Notice that Queen Elizabeth is born in the year 1533 and she was 27-years old when she expelled Catholicism from England. Coincidence? Hardly. The 1533-years symbolize the EXODUS, which began right after the book of Genesis was complete. The book of Genesis has 1533-verses.

The mythoi of Mary Queen of Scots and her illegitimate sister is another historical theatrical skit that is reworked into a biblical narrative. Remember that New Testament lore has Elizabeth as John the Baptist's mother and Mary her cousin was the mother of Jesus Christ. Mary Queen of Scots (Catholic) was the legitimate Queen of England before Queen Elizabeth 1 (Protestant). I will not go into all that mythology surrounding these events. My purpose for mentioning them is that Mary Queen of Scotts is imprisoned by her sister Elizabeth and executed (beheaded) eighteen years later.

Here in this mythological history it can be seen how biblical stories can be reversed from male to female and the beheading of Mary Queen of Scots by a Queen rather than a King is clearly referencing John the Baptist's beheading by King Herod. The EXODUS of Catholicism from England is clearly a reverse narrative of the Israelites fleeing the land of Egypt. Catholicism is diametrically opposite to the Jews that were cast into the wilderness in the EXODUS story and in every sense Elizabeth 1 Queen of England (Protestant) cast Catholicism into their own Diaspora.

I, personally, see all of history as mythology. After September 11, 2001 the USA citizenry have seen numerous times the US Government manipulating history: ad nauseam the government claimed that Iraq had WMDs (Weapons of Mass Destruction), which was the United States Governments primary reason for invading Iraq and destroying that country killing hundreds of thousands of Iraqis (innocent men, women and children) and then the America People learned there were no WMDs. Yet, in the 2016 Republican debates Republicans Politicians were denying that President George W. Bush ever said there was WMDs. Almost on a daily basis the government is deleting news article off the Internet as if those news events never took place. I use this example of current history being mythologized; because, it is current news being deleted and it is so blatant and in your face and the government doesn't care that the people see history being wiped clean. Most people have the attention span of a gnat and books, cds, DVDs, and all kinds of archives will not survive the ravages of time. Even if they did survive when the government gets their hands on it, it all seems to disintegrate because it old technology. Who has not witness the eighteen minutes of the Nixon Tapes or the 30-thousands email erased by criminal-Hillary? Oops, is the only answer the government has for not having what it should have and never wants anybody to know; because, it does fit the mythoi of what Freemasonry is trying to accomplish on a spiritual level.

Another important fact to look at is the indisputable fact that the American People are drowning in the tsunamic of repetitive violent news cycles continuously arguing political mayhem into the faces and ears of the America People. I find it comical that the government and news cycles claim that violence on TV causes violence in the world. I found that not watching the news bring peace and solace to the psyche; thus, I see news cycles creating violence throughout the world. Not watching the news cycles takes away the aggravation and anger, which news cycles are, geared to stirs the psyche into utter turmoil.

Each new generation of voters in the United State of America neither knows its history nor the history before and/or after their generation. The Public School System only teaches alleged history going back a century. The average generation of Americans is essentially ignorant of at least three generations of histories. When the youth of America is told by their elders why news cycles are false the younger generation does not believe their own family's memories of past events; for the reason that, truth often sounds ridiculous to those with attention deficit disorder. And with those kinds of repetitive cycles of inattentiveness the government literally can do whatever it pleases. Most people basically have the memory and attention span of a gnat simply because the news cycles are not only deliberately repetitive; but, they are deliberately violent and viciously argumentatively presented to the people so they don't want to watch the news. The news talk-show channels have guests that viciously argue with each other deliberately not giving each other time to speak a sentence making the entire news cycle chaotic. Watching news programs like that creates anger in the hearts and minds of the viewer and it more pleasant not to watch the news then to listen to the ramblings of news commentators and their guest that neither respects themselves, each other or their viewers. Remember those news-anchors and commentator get pay enormous amounts of money to stage all their nonsense.

Another grand mythological pattern I want to discuss, which I have dealt with somewhat already is again the pattern seen in the Ten Commandment creating 613: 365 + 248 and the Ten Commandment is the divide. This same pattern was seen with the Potomac separating the Maryland and Virginia sections of the 10 x 10 MATRIX OF WISDOM, which is the landscape of Washington DC. This same divide is seen the bible split between the Old and New Testaments where Malachi is the divide between them. In the Appendix it will be seen in my analysis of Dante Alighieri's La Divina Commedia Mathematic System that his use of the MATRIX OF WISDOM is entirely design to separate out the chapters that contain the Garden of Eden in the Purgatory volume and the 33-chapters that contain Paradise from the chapters that contain Hell and Purgatory, which solely based upon the formula for the Golden Ratio and I have colorized Dante's matrix to illustrate this pattern. The last pattern that I discovered along these lines is the map of the Civil War between 1861 (digits of the Golden Ratio: 1.618) to 1865 showing the Federal States in contrast to the Confederate States. It is as if starting the war in 1861 is a deliberate taunt because the Golden Ratio symbolizes the tetrahedral forces in creation; which symbolizes *"In the beginning"*. In the image I present notice the divide between the Federal and Confederate States being called the Border States (slave states align to the Federal States). The Border States and the Confederate States all seceded from the Union; though, the Border States allied themselves with the Federal States

Readers that comprehend this material should consider him or herself, outside of Washington DC, in the vast open space of the United States they could write back to Congress, not saying "Houston"; rather, they should say, *"CONGRESS WE HAVE A PROBLEM";* though, I put this last here as a pun I think the reader will get my drift. It is difficult for me, personally, to believe that every member of Congress is not a member of Freemasonry; for the reason that, too much is happening on Washington DC National Mall and the US taxpayer is footing the bill for all this. Most important is that the US Congress: i.e. House of Representatives and the Senate basically make sure nothing is actually done to help the people per se; rather, it appears blatantly as if the government agenda is to deliberately keep the citizenry angry and frustrated. Things like that sounds ridiculous; but, look at all the problems in America that can easily be solved by the use of reason and logic by men and women using common sense; yet, everything that the US Congress does negate reason and logic especially negating the use of common sense.

I take everything the US Congress is doing day to day as the sleight of hand as if they are completely oblivious of the esotericism that is symbolically being codified into the streets of Washington DC. For example: there are 535-members of Congress, which is analogous to the MATRIX OF WISDOM'S 100-cells (Senate) and the amount of words 434 words in the first chapter Genesis and the first word of Genesis: BERESHITH is two words: i.e. "separated six" (House of Representative). The number 535 is the Gematria values of LIGHT (207) DARKNESS (328). Freemasonry is always instituting esotericism into the US Constitution. Look at the Electoral College[8], which requires a presidential candidate to obtain at least 270-votes. The MATRIX OF WISDOM has a total count of 630, which 270-represent the LIGHT: i.e. 1s, 2s, 3s, 4s, 5s, 6s, 7s and 8s. Freemasonry developed everything in the US Federal Government, which is of any genuine importance, on the numerics of the MATRIX OF WISDOM. Three votes were added to the Electoral College in 1960: 535 + 3 = 538 / 2 = 269; thus, 270-votes represent the majority.

The next image in this series is to show other ways that the MATRIX OF WISDOM was used to create artistic designs; though, I did mention them previously: the Egyptian pyramid, the Buddhist Stupa, the Hindu Temple, the Chinese I Ching, the Christian Cathedral and the Mayan Pyramid.

I want to illustrate the Interactive Floor Plan of Saint Peter's Basilica in Vatican City. What I found most interesting about this basilica is that it has over a hundred shrines throughout the structure. The Vatican has a website that links every one of those 100-sites. The basilica has many patterns throughout its structure that most visitors will completely overlook. Though the building is over five hundred years old it is still upgrading and putting the finishing touches to its overall design.

---

[8] https://en.wikipedia.org/wiki/Electoral_College_(United_States)

MASONIC ORDER: HOUSE OF THE TEMPLE

View from the Dome of the Capitol Building

View from Saint Peter's Basilica

WASHINGTON DC

THE APOTHEOSIS OF GEORGE WASHINGTON

CAPITOL BUILDING OVERLOOKING WASHINGTON DC

Washington DC - Capitol Building Rear Entrance (West)   **Washington DC - Capitol Building Front Entrance (East)**

Clear arial view of the main streets going horizontally: Independence and Constitutional Avenues flanking the Washington Mall with a clear view of the Washington Mounument and Lincoln's Memorial and a clear view of Pennsylvania and Maryland Avenues going diagonally to the White House and Jefferson's Memorial

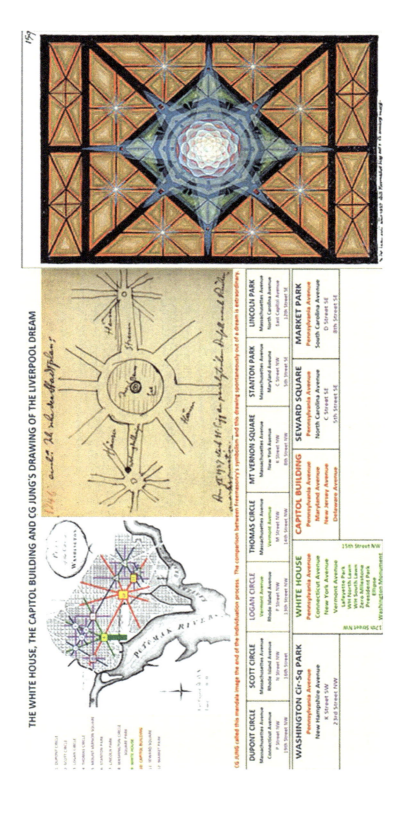

THE WHITE HOUSE, THE CAPITOL BUILDING AND CG JUNG'S DRAWING OF THE LIVERPOOL DREAM

- 243 = Abram [אברם][1] before his name was changed to Abraham
- 208 = Hagar [הגר]
- 451 = Ishmael [ישמעאל]
  902 = Total

- 248 = Abraham [אברהם] previously Abram [אברם 243]
- 505 = Sarah [שרה] (Princess) previous Sarai [שרי = 510] (Contentious)
- 208 = Isaac [יצחק]
  961 = Total

Grand Total = 902 + 961 = 1863; a transposition of the numbers 1-3-6-8.

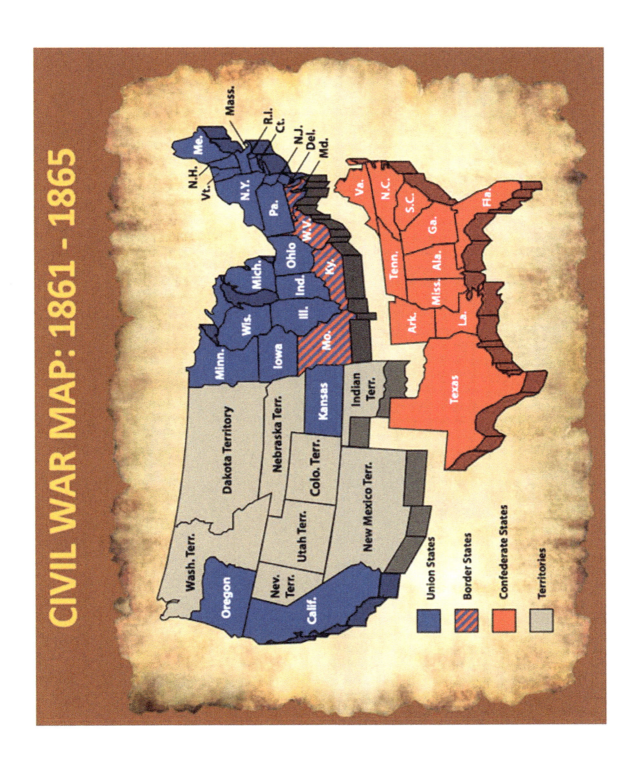

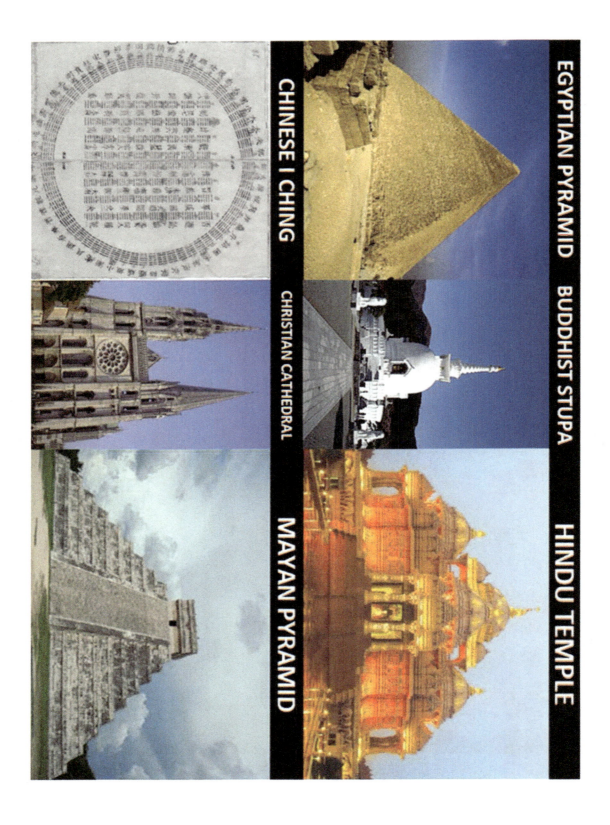

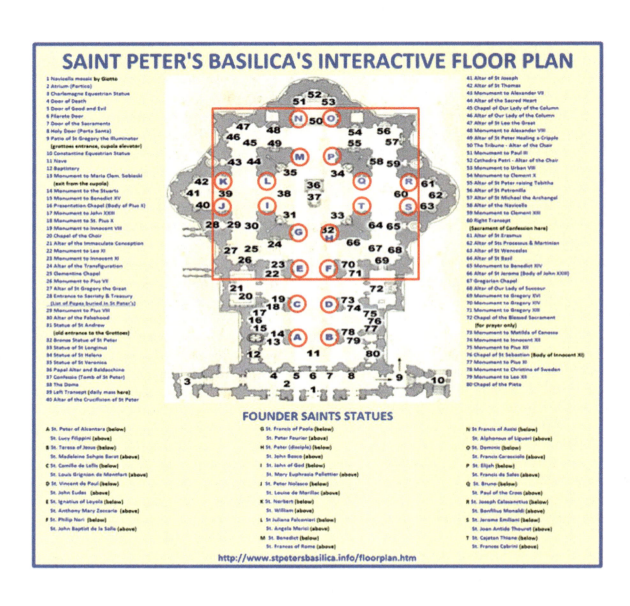

WASHINGTON DC's NATIONAL MALL
AND THE MYSTICAL NATURE OF THE CROSS

Whatever most people do not consider is what the CROSS symbolizes; though, they think they do. Washington DC's National Mall depicts an elongated cross: i.e. Catholic. I call it 'catholic' because it is not equilateral as is the Cross in the Kamea of Saturn or the MATRIX OF WISDOM that is universal[9], which is also widely used by the Roman Catholic Church. The elongated cross I believe is a symbolic misnomer meaning that it is used to simultaneously illuminate and to mislead. All symbolism is mystically exhibited in that manner. This is the main reason that iconoclasm takes symbolism exoterically and iconography takes it esoterically. Iconoclasm is linear thought and this is why the National Mall is laid out the way it is: i.e. from the Capitol Building in the East going toward the Lincoln Memorial in the West. This is analogous to the hubris: egocentrism facing forward going West; though, it is mostly thought that humans symbolically face North. I would agree with that latter assessment if the individual was an initiate guided by God; because, the HEAD (RESH ר) faces North. Religious symbolism denotes these esoteric nuances in writing the sacred scriptures.

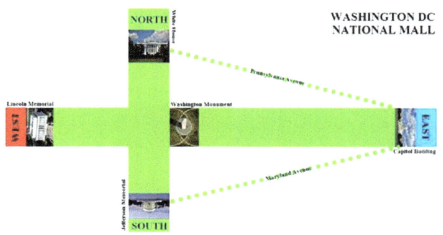

The National Mall like the MATRIX OF WISDOM (illustrated above) is symbolic of every single street in the United States of America[10]. This is very well depicted on the streets of Washington DC where the vertical North/South bound streets are named numerically and designated as North or South; whereas, the horizontal East/West bound streets are named alphabetically, which are designated as East or West; thus, each street numerically named intersects with an alphabetic street similar to how every Hebrew and Greek letter in the Judaeo Christian Scriptures is alphanumerically structured. The Capitol Building is the center of the city and all four directions designating the streets numerically and alphabetically centered on that one lone building. The mystical ramification of that symbolic nuance hails back to the letter BETH ב where religious nuance exudes from it as does all legislation of the United States radiates out from the Capitol Building. Just as the spiritual powers: i.e. twenty-one additional letters of the Hebrew alphabet come through BETH ב via the East so do the laws of the United States come from the East going toward the West. In setting up the mythoi of the National Mall it was very advantageous in those times during the Revolutionary War that the United States of America was being instituted on a new continent to explore a vast new wilderness where people like Horace Greeley[11] said, *"Go west young man"*,[12] which is symbolic

---

[9] The word UNIVERSAL is interpreted as catholic not necessarily representing the Roman Catholic Church.

[10] Actually this mystical concept is played out on every street throughout the world; but, here we are dealing with the American mythoi.

[11] https://en.wikipedia.org/wiki/Horace_Greeley

of living out life in the material world. This westward bound movement in the early years of the United States of America was most likely the core fundamental reason why Washington DC's landscape was positioned so close and center to the country's east coast at the dawn of its inception. Maryland and the Potomac is perfectly located to symbolize the Hebrew letter BETH ב surrounded by the letter PEI פ.

In no way am I promoting the idea that Freemasonry was advocating Judaism and/or Catholicism per se; rather, Freemasonry in using the esotericism codified to the Judaeo Christian Scripture in imitating the scriptural literary techniques of the early biblical scribes in covertly, via landscaping and architecture, promoting esotericism. Freemasonry like John the Baptist cannot characterize both John the Baptist's Old Testament's esotericism and Jesus Christ's New Testament genre's of though promoting the WORD OF GOD less chaos reigns. Freemasonry symbolizes the teachings of John the Baptist, whose mission it was to point to the teachings of Jesus Christ. Notice that Freemasonry takes on the task of promoting esotericism in the selfsame manner (iconography) as the biblical scribes in silence without much fanfare; whereas, Catholicism does the selfsame spiritual task in the din of silence esoterically for its laity via its artwork (iconography). If the initiate take these abstract nuances of the surreptitious iconoclastic activities of Freemasonry and the din of artistic silence that Catholicism present its iconography artworks than the mystical nature of what Judaism and Christianity is all about will present itself in that contemplative meditational state.

Remember the bible is totally symbolic and it is not discussing in the narrative of the surface area of the storyline the activities of the common man, which is not considered, a *"Good Man: i.e. religious and law abiding"*.

The initiate is ordered by Yahweh Elohym (Christ) to symbolically name the organizational groups of the bible such as the ROMANS, JEWS and CHRISTIANS and all other symbolic terms throughout the bible just as Adam was ordered to name the animals (zodiacal signs) of the universe. All iconographic (symbolic) throughout the bible are archenemies of iconoclasm; thus, symbols are vicious and animalistic similar to when Jacob wrestled with the angel wanting to name it. There is no way to diversify, classify and individualized (name) the teachings of Christ. In other words Adam was told to learn the language of symbolism and the reason why he received the Initiatic Visionary Experience is; for the reason that, he put his *whole heart, mind, soul, time, finances and resources* into that endeavor. He was still without a mate; however, that is the whole point *'man can do nothing of his own volition'*. Adam's endeavors to name the symbols (animals) of the bible were his sincere prayers DESIRING to know God.

❖ **ROMANS**[13]: barbarians (Babylonians, Egyptians, Greeks, etc.) that ostensibly knew nothing of Judaism's esotericism continuously destroyed Solomon's Temple.
   o The Egypt and Babylon clearly had a great deal to do with writing the Old Testament not only being part of the narrative; but, also in its esoteric structure; for the reason that, they were Gentile religions.
      ▪ Babylon's destruction of Solomon's Temple is clear evidence of it Gentile (Christian) minded mentality. Who else other than Christian minded people could destroy Solomon Temple?
   o My analysis on the nativities of Jesus Christ and John the Baptist in the New Testament[14] illustrates how the Roman Empire and other cultures had a great deal to do with the birth of the Christian Religion originating out of Judaism.
   o The Greeks proved their knowledge of esotericism by writing the New Testament in the proper esoteric alphanumeric format.
      ▪ All of the above cultures were deemed pagan by Judaism and I believe that is because Jews (iconoclastic thinkers from all religious cultures around the world) symbolically are too culturally isolated: meaning they are too much into their culture's religious

---

[12] https://en.wikipedia.org/wiki/Go_West,_young_man

[13] In no way am I suggesting that other Mystery Schools in other cultures did not know esotericism, which of course they did; however, in the mythoi of the sacred scriptures it is falsely assumed they didn't know symbolism.

[14] http://www.slideshare.net/williamjohnmeegan/the-birth-of-christ-and-the-initiatic-visionary-experience

histories, traditions, dogmas and theology to intellectually and egocentrically expand beyond those religious orthodoxy.

- Every materialistic culture in the world is caught up in this iconoclastic heritage; however, it is only in the spiritual initiate's ability to intuit that there are numerous disparate iconoclastic cultures that use the same Esoteric Science esoterically to write the WORD OF GOD symbolically in their own vernaculars that will convince a diehard members of another religious cult[15] to reconsider the manner in which he or she conduct his or her spiritual contemplative meditation.

o The birth of a Christian from the hordes of Judaism is also a reason that Solomon Temple is symbolically destroyed psychically on an individual level morphing it into an octagon (Kamea of Saturn: i.e. Matrix of Wisdom) Christian (Gentile) Temple.

❖ **JEWS:** members of secret societies that know the teachings of esotericism iconoclastically, via the Hebrew letters' meanings of the literal and historical scriptural texts and not the spirit of the WORD OF GOD and via this fanaticism they endeavor spiritually to obtain an invitation into the Holy of Holies, which like purgatorial inmates is out of their mental acuity to envisage. The Jews of the bible knew that symbolism per se; however, they did not know of their own volition how to traverse the chasm and/or even know that there was a great abyss to negotiate between iconoclastic thought and iconography that would enable them to receive the Eucharist of Christ: Christ consciousness. Jewish Gnostics often coming across contemplative meditational thought akin to the teachings of Christ found them to be too intellectually difficult via hubris to grasp, which prohibited them from understanding the teachings of Christ; for the reason that, the true WORD OF GOD became psychically and spiritually out of bounds. This is prolifically illustrated in Jesus Christ's discussions between the scribes and the Pharisees in the annals of the New Testament.

The Jewish Gnostics of the bible had no idea that they had to egocentrically genuflect (deflation of ego consciousness) when entering the internal Temple of Solomon, which every Protestant-Catholic does by rote in modernity in their materialistic concretized churches without knowing why they do it. They think that genuflection is merely giving respect to God. They do not know what that respect entails (ego immolation not play acting or lip-service).

❖ **CHRISTIANS (Babylonians, Egyptians, Greeks, Romans, etc.):** those Jews that genuflects their ego (no longer Jews) are taught by Christ the WORD OF GOD; for the reason that, they have reached psychically the state of existing in the Holy of Holies: i.e. Garden of Eden.

Like the Judaeo Christian Scriptures, which were written to perfection, so too is the National Mall depicted as imitating the concepts of BETH ב and RESH פ in creating the first word of Genesis: BERESHITH (In the beginning).

1. BETH ב: Capitol Building (East)
2. YUD י: Obelisk – Washington Monument (Center)
3. TAV ת: Lincoln Memorial (West)
   And then the transepts
4. RESH ר: White House (North)
5. ALEPH א: Obelisk - Washington Monument (Center)
6. SHIN ש: Jefferson Memorial (South)
7. QOPH ק: Obelisk - Washington Monument symbolizes the central spherical position of the Trinity: i.e. Yahweh (YUD י), Elohym (ALEPH א) and Christ (QOPH ק)

The image of the National Mall going from the Capitol Building to the Lincoln Memorial is depicted as a stake or pole (tunnel vision) only symbolizes that which is going towards the west analogous to ego-consciousness. This is; for the reason that, the sun is in an eternal orbit around the Earth. Anything east of the Capitol Building should be considered colored totally blue coming out of the Atlantic Ocean symbolic of the unconscious mind: i.e. tsunami of the populace of the American Culture. If it wasn't for

---

[15] The word 'CULT' refers to any organization or any religion: i.e. Jewish or Gentile. The word 'cult' does solely have to do with the so-called New Age terminology. Occult

the North/South transepts crossing the National Mall I would have colored the entire National Mall west of the Capitol Building red to symbolize ego-consciousness; however, because of the transepts only that which is west of the Lincoln Memorial is color red symbolizing the vast untamed and uncivilized wilderness of the blank abyss that is the material world. Every child born into the material world is educated by societal mores to go west and carve out an existence. Two hundred years of State and Congressional legislation has not in any way shape or form tamed or civilized what the 'WEST' esoterically and psychically symbolizes.

Remember that the Capitol Building is the East/West divide as it is also the North/South divide; however, it only becomes symbolically the North/South divide under the auspices of the Initiatic Visionary Experience otherwise it is merely the East/West corridor of time, which is colored red. The North/South divide (transepts) on a spiritual level (not materialistically), via the obelisk, is wiping out the corridor of time (colored red: i.e. west) and creating a Bodhi Tree for the initiate.

Churches are normally built along the West/East divide where the altar is normally in the east; however, I believe the more spiritually inclined Churches built in Catholicism are going East to West. I believe the difference is that the Altar on the East Wall would imply that the Ordained Priests are in charge analogous to Congressional Representatives; whereas, the Altar on the West Wall puts the individual in the NAVE of the Church, which is east of the transepts and the priest in the APSE inferring the initiate is in charge of his own soul, which is not spiritually governed by a materialistic hierarchy; though, that is mainly thought to be the case. The soul is symbolic of the Pope and the Pope in turn would be analogous to the President (POTUS), which is the ultimate authority of the country: i.e. meaning the soul with the guidance of the spiritual forces of creation (God) is the sole authority of his own life.

The North/South transepts, which is similar to how Christian Churches are built does not have the an altar in its wake, which is west of the transepts in the APSE and not in the center of the transepts for that would infer that the soul should live in heaven via the Garden of Eden as oppose to living in the material world. Because the (obelisk) is off center to the transepts positioned in the NAVE that nuance illustrates that the soul is meant to live in the Garden of Eden. It is not possible to live in heaven; for the reason that, there is no male (ego-consciousness) or female (unconscious mind) in heaven (no opposites) that would allow for thought, word or deed. Remember, that all symbolism refers to the soul and not to some materialistic nonsense. The reader should make that nuance a primary focus in his or her contemplative meditational states of prayer. Prayer is not for '*give-me*': God already knows what the soul needs. Prayer is the search for God and that alone is all that God require of the soul: i.e. to continuously focus on learning about its spiritual origins.

In ancient times crucifixions were conducted on a stake or single poles symbolically going from east to west and only on special occasion were people crucified on crosses. The crucifixion on a stake or pole is symbolic of living in the materialistic world iconoclastically governed by ego-consciousness, which is the primal cause of all pain in life. The crucifixion on a pole is analogous to being sentenced to hell: the land of the dead where egocentric people are cast as iconoclastic thought illustrates; though, those in hell living in the material world will negate the fact that they are in hell; because, they know nothing more than iconoclastic thought[16]. Those in ancient times as in modern times (contemplatively) that were crucified to a cross were additionally punished by making them journey to the crucifixion site with the cross beam of the cross strapped to his or her shoulders that would be set on the crucifixion site's central pole. In this manner Christ traveling to Golgotha (Place of the Skull) is analogous to Christ symbolizing the Cygnus Swan coming from the Cygnus X-3 (Northern Cross: i.e. obelisk). Christ symbolizes the pineal gland, which is in the center of the skull; thus, Golgotha is, exactly right, where Christ is suppose to be and this is why the veil of the temple split in twain. The Temple of God is in the Soul. The Temple of God is not in some materialistic architectural structure. The Veil of the Temple is obviously the east-west corridor of time that was split when Christ came down from the north to be crucified.

---

[16] Jehovah Witness are at least right about one thing, people were crucified on one stake pole in ancient Rome; however, anything else they have to say I would not bet the farm on.

The splitting of the veil in Solomon Temple (rectangular, three squared, building) into two part is analogous to the National Mall being split by the transepts with the White House in the North and the Jefferson Memorial in the South. The National Mall east/west corridor of Time is symbolic of being Solomon's Temple. This is what the MATRIX OF WISDOM is spiritually conveying and it is the reason why every single Roman Catholic Church in the world is built with the transepts splitting the APSE (Lincoln Memorial) from the NAVE (Capitol Building): i.e. separating the Heavens and the Earth. This is exactly what Carl G. Jung[17] was talking about when he said that Protestants do not have symbolism to stay off the tsunami of the unconscious mind in matters of religion and that is why Protestants are more often in the psychiatrist's office than Catholics are. The seamless veil (garment) of the psyche: Solomon's Temple denotes ego-consciousness unfettered access to the unconscious mind. It is symbolism outlined in the Gentile religions (labyrinths – one way paths), which Christian-Protestantism iconoclasm is no part of, that prepares and protects the psyche against the onslaught of the mystical teachings of God. Venturing into the mystical realms of God without a spiritual guide (labyrinth: i.e. Guru), which I interpret as symbolism left behind by the ancients scribes via the sacred scriptures, artworks, monuments and architecture is a very dangerous undertaking; for the reason that, there is no way out of that maze (incalculable choices) and the Minotaur Bull (ego-consciousness)[18] will destroy anyone that dares to violate that sacred space without a guide. Who is the Minotaur Bull? The Minotaur Bull is none other than one own ego-consciousness. Remember that the Minotaur Ball is also symbolic of the religious and academic scholars in the midst of their status quo representing modernity's mainstream thought. In every sense ego-centrism is the vicious satanic viper and that is why the central pole of the cross symbolizes the 'horizon (east to west)'; because, it eternally controls the life of the individual until physical death; though, the good citizens will think he is a pious religious person never realizing he or she is in the clutches of satanic thought; because, decency and societal mores are not considered satanic.

Most Jew and/or Christians and/or Muslims do not know that the first letter of the Torah: BETH ב open space is not facing west; symbolically, the open space symbolizes the North, which firmly illustrates that BETH ב in this respect symbolizes Christ consciousness, and the east and west are barricaded by the North/South transepts to allow RESH ר the new heaven and earth into creation. When thinking about the open space in the Hebrew letter BETH ב facing northward and then facing what would be considered westward would in effect be ego-consciousness genuflecting.

BETH

Ego-consciousness
Genuflecting

There is not many in the Catholic laity that will study the procedures of the Roman Catholic Mass to understand what it is truly conveying; however, the architectural construct of the Church building also should go into interpreting the Mass Services.

1. **APSE:** The area where the altar is located is called the APSE. The APSE is where the ordained priest conducts the daily Mass. It is symbolically from the NAVE, where the laity is located, that the ordained priest via his chosen parishioners culls out the three readings from the sacred scriptures (LIGHT) and from where the priest culls out his sermon (LIGHT) from the DARKNESS.
   a. The Ordained Priest symbolizes Christ consciousness walking with God in the Garden of Eden. The Priest in giving the Eucharistic Host to the laity is symbolically feeding back Christ consciousness from where he received it. It is as if the MASS is an eternal self-sustaining life-cycle (eternal life – Ouroboros) in the Garden of Eden.
   b. The APSE is the Garden of Eden: LIGHT of Christ consciousness.
2. **TRANSCEPTS:** what takes place before the Eucharistic Reeling amongst the laity in the pews? For it barricades the APSE from the NAVE. The transepts would symbolize the dawn of a new consciousness: i.e. Christ consciousness; for the reason that, it is at the Eucharistic Reeling, that the laity kneels (genuflecting), in the midst of the transept, receiving the Eucharistic Host. The kneeling

---

[17] https://en.wikipedia.org/wiki/Carl_Jung
[18] https://en.wikipedia.org/wiki/Minotaur

to receive the Eucharistic Host placing one head across the reeling to receive the Eucharist is symbolically being beheaded like John the Baptist. The laity receiving the Eucharist is like that ancient picture of the mystic sticking his head out into the spiritual realm.

3. **NAVE:** is where the laity is located. The laity symbolizes DARKNESS: i.e. tsunami of the unconscious mind from where all spirituality is culled from.

The Catholic Mass and the architectural structure of the Church Building (Noah's Ark: Matrix of Wisdom); though, the stage is design and choreographed as a theatrical skit symbolizes the APSE as the sacred scriptures (Leo, Gemini, Taurus, Aries, Pisces and Aquarius), the TRANSCEPTS as the pineal gland, which incorporates the NAVE symbolizing the Garden of Eden. Everything east of the Capitol building symbolizes the second hemisphere of the brain (Cancer, Virgo, Libra, Scorpio, Sagittarius and Capricorn).

I am mixing all these diverse symbols interchangeably so the reader can see that it is his or her task to see all this symbolism as being interchangeable; thus, it can be envisaged from this process of blending symbols that the psyche is the Garden of Eden: Christ Consciousness.

Everything outside of the Capitol Building on the National Mall is symbolic of the phantasmagoria of the psyche projected outwardly on the psyche's cinematic screen signify as the blank abyss, which will be discussed further below; however, this outward projection is structured on a perfect spiritual state of Christ consciousness just as the Hebrew and Greek indigenous languages that writes the sacred scriptures written on a spiritual precision level as are the artworks of Catholicism created esoterically on a perfect level.

The National Mall can be envisaged as having been designed similar to a Church structure. What the transepts in any Roman Catholic Church and at the National Mall esoterically conveys is that TIME has literally been put to a screeching halt of TIMELESSNESS and this is illustrated by the transepts creating a divide in the center of the east/west corridor of TIME: i.e. National Mall. Materialistically there is no way of amalgamating opposites or negotiating via compromises the nature of opposites. It is seen in every single marriage and in every political party the strongest personality rules the roost; yes, every marriage begins with absolute equality; however, it is not long after marriage vows that mystical ambiance of equality disappears. I point this out about the opposites; for the reason that, there is no way from a materialistic standpoint of negotiating the different natures that are inherent in the existential opposites.

The Capitol Building is the exact center of Washington DC not only on a physical level; but, also the Capitol Building is centrally located esoterically for it symbolizes the third eye at the top of a mystical pyramid created when the transepts (White House, Obelisk and Jefferson Memorial) crossed the east/west corridor of TIME (National Mall). This mystical pyramid is symbolically illustrated via Pennsylvania and Maryland Avenues that go diagonally to the White House and Jefferson Memorial respectively from the Capitol Building. There is no doubt in my mind that these two avenues symbolize a mystical peripheral vision that every initiate obtains when he or she receives the Initiatic Visionary Experience. The reason that I say 'mystical peripheral vision' is because the National Mall itself symbolizes the tunnel vision that all mortals possess along with earthly peripheral vision. The earthly peripheral vision has nothing whatsoever to do with 'mystical peripheral vision', which would be more clearly understood as Christ consciousness. The mystical peripheral vision is received when symbolically the cosmic rays from Cygnus X-3 smashes through the east/west corridor of Time; however, this mystical Christ consciousness peripheral vision is spherical in all directions not just from east to west. These cosmic rays are symbolized by the Washington Monument with the Vesica Piscis at its base. In fact below I show the Capitol Building surrounded by this mystical Christ consciousness peripheral vision similar to how the Great Pyramid of Egypt is an eight sided pyramid **(see images below)**[19]. This is the reason that I believe the Pyramid with the third eye above it is symbolized on the back of the one dollar bill[20].

The Vesica Piscis symbolizes the merging of the spiritual and the material just as the transepts crossing the National Mall created a cross analogous to the Vesica Piscis. In real time I had worked all

---

[19] http://www.catchpenny.org/concave.html
[20] http://www.thetp.com/ypyramid.htm

this out contemplatively via the diagonal avenues going from the Capitol Building to the White House and the Jefferson Memorial. This esoteric interpretation was quite obvious to me; however, when I started researching the Capitol Building I was somewhat surprised that its grounds' landscape back up that interpretation 100% from a number of perspectives. First there are no streets numerically or alphabetically coming directly towards the Capitol Building. There are four streets coming east, north and south to or from the Capitol Building; however, they are all Capitol Streets, which creates a cross dead center to the Capitol Building. There is no Capitol West Street; though, I believe the National Mall takes its place and is per se symbolic of Capitol West Street. Considering that the cross radiating out from the Capitol Building it can be understood why the Apotheosis of George Washington was frescoed on the ceiling of the Capitol's Dome. The Statue of Freedom on the top of the Capitol Dome makes no sense unless the Initiatic Visionary Experience is understood to be the primal cause of that freedom. Winning a war or edicts from a Congressional Legislation does not free a slave from the burdens of the world. Only God can do that.

The confined space of the Capitol Building's grounds mystically places that piece of landscape outside of the time/space continuum. As it has been pointed out there are neither numerical vertical streets nor alphabetic horizontal streets coming toward or away from the Capitol Building; though, there are diagonal streets creating a gigantic Templar's Cross surrounding the Capitol Building. And it is the Capitol streets that are the divides that denotes the beginning and ends of the four cardinal directions in Washington DC. The Capitol Building is being symbolized as the Bodhi Tree: Axis Mundi: i.e. center of creation.

What I found quite interesting is that there are twenty-two streets going west of the Capitol Building to the Lincoln Memorial. In fact the twenty-third (23rd) street goes down the center of the Lincoln Memorial. I mention this to point out that there are only twenty-two letters in the Hebrew Coder. As I pointed out previously every single Hebrew letter is alphanumerically coded. This cannot be a coincidence by any stretch of the imagination; for the reason that, the mythoi in the Prologue of the Zohar discusses the twenty-two letters of the Hebrew Coder from the last to the first coming into creation through BETH ב and the Capitol Building symbolizes BETH ב. In that limited space across the National Mall having only twenty-two streets is just amazing if the common citizen is suppose to believe it was unintentional.

If I am interpreting the twenty-two (22) streets, intersecting the National Mall, as symbolizing the twenty-two (22) letters of the Hebrew Coder then they would collectively symbolize twenty-two (22) transepts crossing the National Mall: i.e. the corridor of Time. This pattern is seen in the first word of Genesis: BERESHITH בראשית, which the cosmic letters give a skip-pattern-sequence in spelling out the word BERESHITH בראשית.

In Chapter Eight I discuss Raphael Santi fresco THE SCHOOL OF ATHENS, which illustrates three transepts crossing the corridor of Time.

In Chapter Eighteen below I illustrate how the how the Genesis Formula is created not by compromise; rather, by the spiritual forces in creation descending upon the initiate to gift him with an entirely new raison d'être. Out of the spelling of the word BETH ב: Beth ב – Yud י – Tav ת only BETH ב remains because the old heaven and earth have passed away. It is that letter BETH ב that gives the spiritual forces in creation the ability to revitalize the soul of the initiate with the Initiatic Visionary Experience; for the reason that, all the spiritual forces come through BETH ב, which I believe symbolizes the initiate raison d'être.

Notice that all twenty-two (22) numerical streets cross the entire array of alphabetic streets before and after crossing the National Mall, which I believe symbolizes that every single Hebrew letter symbolizes collectively all the letters and this of course would create symbolically twenty-two (22) transepts across the National Mall. Of course that could not happen on a symbolic level; for the reason that, the symbolism would not be notice under a tsunami of the same symbolism.

The transept that has the White House connected to the Jefferson Memorial is inaugurated by sixteenth (16th) street. The fact that the sixteenth letter of the Hebrew alphabet corresponds to the eye and the Capitol Building's landscape is made in the image and likeness of the eyes the correlation between the spiritual powers of creation synching with the Capitol Building indicates that any letter of the Hebrew Coder could have been used to represent the National Mall transept. That would mean that the Capitol Building's landscape would have to take on the symbolism of the chosen Hebrew letter that would represent the transept.

Curious enough when viewing the two maps below of the Capitol Building's grounds and the two images of the vision of sight in the brain, it is interesting to see that they practically mirror image each other. The secret to symbolic images of this nature is that once they are discovered and recognized for what they are merely mentioning blandly what they are affiliated to on a materialistic secular level is literally unbelievable to the uninitiated; thus, the only viable option in discussing such inexplicable symbols that seemingly come out of nowhere is to research those symbols to understand why they are used to express a mystical nuance. In this case the eyes' vision developed in the brain is not symbolizing normal earthly egocentric vision; rather, these eyes on the Capitol ground are meant to symbolize a mystical peripheral vision. Notice how the eyes sit right on the periphery of the 1st Street SW, which is symbolically just on the borderline of the time/space continuum. The Capitol Building sitting between two first streets is symbolic of being in the embrace of God. The number one symbolizes the letter ALEPH, which in the sacred scriptures symbolize the Trinity and it symbolizes the Cross. ALEPH also symbolizes ELOHYM, which has been shown to symbolize God and the formula for PI: 3.1415. When it is realized that it is these two 1st Streets that divide the west from the east: i.e. the heavens from the earth (Genesis 1:1), from each other then the Capitol Building is more apt to be envisaged as being symbolized as the Bodhi Tree.

The east is where the sun comes from and the sun is always in the east trying to vanquish the west. If the initiate was to locate the numerical streets that intersect the National Mall and number them off up to twelfth (12) street, which would symbolize the twelve zodiacal signs it will be found that the 2nd, 5th, 8th and 11th streets are not part of the mystical peripheral vision between Pennsylvania and Maryland Avenues. These four streets: 2nd, 5th, 8th and 11th represent the Fixed Quadruplicity Signs of the Zodiac. If I am reading the absence of these four streets not being within the mystical peripheral vision then the Fixed Quadruplicities would give the impression of representing the LIGHT culled out of the DARKNESS. The Cardinal Quadruplicity Signs 1st, 4th, 7th and 10th streets and the Mutable Quadruplicity Signs 3rd, 6th, 9th and 12th appear to symbolize the number of the beast, which is two-thirds percentage of twelve, which would symbolize the never-ending search for God. Such dynamic in the psyche would not allow for fixated thought. The mystical peripheral vision symbolized the tetrahedral forces in the psyche. I found on the Internet a diagram that literally illustrates this premise.

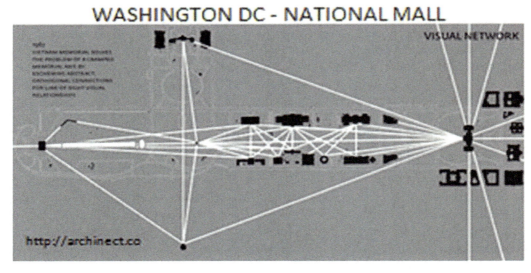

The diagram that I presented early on in this book that looks somewhat like this was done months before I ever found this illustration of the National Mall on the Internet; thus, I would say these people at

Archinect are obviously not part of the Freemasonry Think-Tank that is putting these designs into the streets of Washington DC. This image I do not believe is correct in bringing the Vietnam Veterans Memorial into the fray. The tetrahedral forces conducted from the government buildings along the National Mall implements the laws of Congress indicating they are alive and doing that. The Vietnam Veterans Memorial symbolized death and the whole National Mall is laid out with war monuments and none of them are use to illustrate the tetrahedral forces of the psyche.

In addition it is not possible to direct the mystical peripheral vision out into the world as this diagram illustrates beyond the Lincoln Memorial. Nor is it possible for Congress to influence on a spiritual and mystically level anything that is not positioned within the boundaries of the mystical peripheral vision symbolized by the North, East, South and West diagonal streets radiating out from the Capitol Building. The diagonal streets emanating out from the Capitol Building: North, East, South and West are:

1. **NORTH: New Jersey Avenue NW**
2. **NORTH: Delaware Avenue NE**
3. **EAST: Maryland Avenue NE**
4. **EAST: Pennsylvania Avenue SE**
5. **SOUTH: New Jersey Avenue SE**
6. **SOUTH: Delaware Avenue SW**
7. **WEST: Maryland Avenue SW**
8. **WEST: Pennsylvania Avenue NW**

In looking at the map of the UNITED STATES these four states, centrally located between the thirteen original colonies, are positioned in the exact same positions geographically on the map as the four named diagonal streets surrounding the Capitol Building. In the milieu of these four states, Pennsylvania is to the Northwest and Maryland is to the Southwest; whereas, New Jersey is to the North East and Delaware is to the Southeast.

I believe that the true purpose that these four states were chosen to name the streets surrounding the Capitol Building grounds is not only because they are centrally located between the thirteen original colonies; but, because they symbolically represent the four equinoctial signs of the Zodiac that the sacred scriptures are mythologically structured on based upon the guidance of the MATRIX OF WISDOM. These four signs of the Zodiac symbolize Gemini, Taurus, Aries and Pisces that represents the LIGHT that is culled out of the DARKNESS.

The Moon Calendar Year has thirteen signs and that is what, I believe, Freemasonry had to be symbolizing with the original thirteen colonies. It is too much of a coincidence that the twelve signs of the Zodiac are positioned diagonally along the Kabbalistic Tree of Life, Elemental Letter, and on the Washington Mall the 13-colonies are positioned on the diagonal streets.

Everything in between the streets going west of the Capitol Building towards Lincoln Memorial and between the diagonal lines going North, East and South of the Capitol Building symbolizes the Garden of Eden (see diagram below), which mystically has nothing to do with the outer world, which is symbolized outside the boundaries of the Templar Cross emanating from the Capitol Building. Yes, the outer world does receive Congressional Legislative Laws; however, the outer world will not have the inherent mystical way in which to deal with those legislative laws; whereas, the material minded individual will perceived and react to those same laws as tyrannical legislation. The initiate living in the Ambiance of God; i.e. the Garden of Eden would not find those legislative laws burdensome at all; for the reason that, a mystic wants nothing to do with the material aspects of world. The Templar Cross emanating out from the Capitol Building symbolizes Christ consciousness existing upon the MATRIX OF WISDOM. Anywhere the psyche goes spiritually on the MATRIX OF WISDOM it would be within the boundaries of the Garden of Eden.

The Good Man as vetted by Freemasonry is clearly an individual that obeys society mores. The two avenues going down to the White House (Pennsylvania Avenue) and Jefferson Memorial (Maryland Avenue) infers that he or she that lives within the confines of the Declaration of Independence and the Constitution of the United States: i.e. symbolized by the two horizon streets flanking the Capitol Building and the National Mall: i.e. Constitutional Avenue NW and Independence Avenue SW, is an initiate that will become a BETTER MAN obtaining Christ consciousness. This is reasoned out because it is Thomas Jefferson that wrote both the Declaration of Independence and the Constitution of the United States. This Washington DC and National Mall project has been going on, I would imagine, long before 1776 possibly when Freemasonry instituted the Masonic Order on June 24, 1717 (the mythoi of John the Baptist's birthday).

Freemasonry laying out the KNIGHT TEMPLAR'S CROSS on the National Mall in Washington DC reveals, I believe, what the foundation of the mythoi of the Knight Templar[21] were all about. Personally, I do not believe that the Knight Templars per se actually ever existed outside of the mythology and artwork that was developed to convey their spiritual alphanumeric message as a commentary on the sacred scriptures.

Another extremely important nuance that can be extrapolated out from the Templar Cross surrounding the Capitol Building is that the western portion of the cross that shows the main architectural work of Freemasonry is showing only that LIGHT that is manifested into the world. It does not negate the other three branches of the cross. I point to John's gospel as extremely mystical in comparison to the other three gospels as an example of the Templar's Cross on the National Mall. The four gospels represent the Fixed Quadruplicities and John's gospel signifies the Water Triplicity, which would point west. Another example of this is the New Testament as a whole symbolizes the Water Triplicity going west; however, it does not negate the other three equinoctial signs: Gemini, Taurus and Aries that represent the other three Triplicity signs.

The very next chapter of this book deals with the Kamea of Saturn, which is exactly what the Knight Templar Cross is all about. The central column and the central row of the Kamea of Saturn have odd numbers creating a cross; whereas, the four corners of the Kamea of Saturn have only even numbers. The Even numbers symbolize the unconscious mind (DARKNESS); while, the odd numbers symbolize the odd number discriminating the LIGHT from the DARKNESS. The central column's numbers are 9, 5 and 1, which are the Triplicity signs of Astrology symbolizing the Fire elements symbolizing the cosmic rays of Cygnus X-3 (Northern Cross); whereas, the Kamea of Saturn's central row's numbers are 3, 5 and 7 or what Christ says in the New Testament, *"when two or three are gathered together in my name there am I in the midst of them"*. The 3, 5, 7 going horizontally symbolize the 7, 14 and 21 in the seventh multiplication table or 1, 2, 3, which is the Gold Ratio (see Chapter Eighteen) going from TIME to TIMELESSNES. The number 753 is also the year that the Roman Empire began, which symbolizes *"in the beginning": i.e. BERESHITH, the first word of Genesis.* Also in the next chapter I placed the image of a Masonic Apron illustrating the Masonic Temple with the Holy of Holies in the center of an octagon gazebo. What the Knight Templar Cross symbol is conveying is that when Christ consciousness comes down upon ego-consciousness the entire spiritual/material soul of the individual (vertical and horizontal) symbolically creates a cross (Temple of God: i.e. Garden of Eden) in the soul.

A little more so-called history (mythoi) of the Knight Templars is appropriate in order for the reader to get a good sense of what the Knight Templars symbolized. Ostensibly there were nine crusaders that when to the Dome of the Rock[22] that is in the shape of the Kamea of Saturn (octagon shape), which I believe starts the mythoi of the Knight Templar per se symbolizing the first nine numbers that are placed in the Kamea of Saturn to obtain the quotient of fifteen (15) in all directions: vertical, horizontal and diagonal. This is precisely how Washington DC was constructed: i.e. the numeric streets crossing the alphabetic streets creating the alphanumeric KNIGHT TEMPLAR'S CROSS. The Knight Templar Cross inundating and surrounding the Capitol Building is not only epitomizing; but, also strongly emphasizing the alphanumeric structure of Washington DC streets.

As the mythoi of Knight Templars continue the pope gives them supreme power, which he could, do nothing less than that because the Knight Templar Cross symbolizes Christ consciousness: i.e. the

---

[21] http://www.co-masonry.org/History/KnightsTemplar.aspx This material cannot be understood outside of esotericism.
[22] https://en.wikipedia.org/wiki/Dome_of_the_Rock#Crusaders

Ambiance of God. Then allegedly on October 13, 1307 another pope gives the kings of Europe the powers to arrest and destroy the Knight Templars. Very few were arrested and no Knight Templar treasure was found. An iconoclastic king cannot comprehend numbers; for the reason that, that entails understanding iconography (abstract symbolism).

In the first sixteen hundred years of the Roman Catholic Church the hierarchy literally created artwork that mystically and artistically rewrote the mythoi of the bible iconographically; yet, at the end of that sixteen hundred years the Church seemingly stop and went Protestant via iconoclasm.

The White House sits between the 15th and 17th streets and 16th street is not within that space; though, 16th Street is coming towards the White House from the rear: North as if symbolically coming from Cygnus X-3 (Northern Cross) dividing the 15th + 17th = 32 into two halves separating LIGHT and DARKNESS creating a Vesica Piscis via the Washington Monument. This is precisely what happens in the first chapter of Genesis when the 32-Elohyms are sequentially placed in a circle. As in the bible the transepts crossing the National Mall has the Washington Monument with the Vesica Piscis at it base. The sixteenth letter of the Hebrew Coder is AYIN ע[23], which symbolizes the EYE. AYIN ע has the numerical value of seventy (70), which makes it an existential alphanumeric letter in the Hebrew Coder. The bible says:

> *"The days of our years are threescore years and ten; and if by reason of strength they be fourscore years, yet is their strength labor and sorrow; for it is soon cut off, and we fly away (Psalms 90:10)."*

I believe that it is AYIN ע that points to what this verse in Psalms is saying about the seventy (70) years; for the reason that, life cannot really be lived in the material world without spirituality. Remember that *'Adam only became a 'living soul' after Yahweh Elohym breathed the breath of divine inspiration of life into him'*. Living in the material world via egocentrism is living in the land of the dead. The eighty (80) years referred to in this above verse is via the seventeenth Hebrew letter PEI פ, which symbolizes the Vesica Piscis. It has already been discussed how the twenty-two streets from the Capitol Building to the Lincoln Memorial signifies the twenty-two letters of the Hebrew Coder. I suggest that the reader make it a point to study up on the Hebrew Coder; for they mystically explain the reason that the National Mall is set up in the manner it is. Look at the fifteenth Hebrew letter symbolized by 15th Street, which it along with 17th Street flank the White House grounds. The fifteenth Hebrew letter is SAMECH ס, which means 'beginning and end' more widely known as the Ouroboros. SAMECH symbolizes the whole of the twenty-two letters of the Hebrew Coder; for the reason that, they represent the spiritual powers of creation. Even the four numbered streets: 2nd, 5th, 8th and 11th absent from the mystical peripheral vision of the National Mall have overall knowledge to convey concerning the spiritual import of the Hebrew alphabet. I recommend Rabbi Yitzchak Ginsburgh work: THE HEBREW LETTERS: Channels of Creative Consciousness when studying the Hebrew Coder[24]. The point I am trying to put into words here is that without the transepts smashing through the east/west corridor of Time (National Mall) the mystical peripheral vision could never have taken place in the psyche of the individual.

The most important point concerning the mystical peripheral vision is that anything beyond 1st Street SW is a projection from the Capitol Building concerning the phantasmagoria of the psyche. Symbolically, anything beyond 1st Street SW is a blank abyss. Even 1st Street SW is ethereally part of that blank abyss. This is analogous to each person living in the material world, which is nothing more than a blank abyss. Life is lived between the ears not outside the skin enveloped.

The four streets surrounding the Capitol Building symbolizes the skull of Golgotha. Golgotha is not where the Washington Monument is located; rather, that entire Cross on the National Mall symbolically aligns to the Capitol Building. This has been the legend of Calvary for thousands of years that the

---

[23] https://thehebrewclub.wordpress.com/2013/01/02/ayin-the-16th-hebrew-letter/ I recommend those that visit this internet site to view the 5.4 minute YOUTUBE video that discusses the letter AYIN ע.

[24] https://www.amazon.com/Hebrew-Letters-Channels-Consciousness-Teachings/dp/9657146070/ref=sr_1_1?ie=UTF8&qid=1467345512&sr=8-1&keywords=the+hebrew+letters+channels+of+creative+consciousness

crucifixion of Christ was on the site of Golgotha. Golgotha symbolizes HEAD, which is represented by the twentieth letter of the Hebrew Coder: RESH ר, which means 'beginning'. The entire National Mall, which includes all the space within the range of the mystical peripheral vision, symbolizes the eternal spiritual Temple of God. The mystical peripheral vision mythologically narrates and illustrates the internal Temple of God every initiate should be creating in his or her own psyche. I see the National Mall, which includes the White House and the Jefferson Memorial as mirror imaging the Temple of the Sphinx in Egypt build out of the granite rock that was surrounding its head.

Another very interesting part of the Capitol Building is that from 2000 to 2007 a very large extension was added to it structure on the east side of the building called Emancipation Hall – Capitol Visitor Center[25]. Ostensibly the Great Hall was renamed Emancipation Hall in January 2008. I do not see how Emancipation Hall could ever have been called the Great Hall when it was never in use with that name. Actually, Emancipation Hall – Capitol Visitor Center was not opened until December 2, 2008 to coincide with the 145th anniversary that the Statue of Freedom that was placed on the dome of the building in 1863. This is again a sleigh of hand having the visitor view one idea as oppose to the more important idea. On January 1st 1863 Abraham Lincoln signed the Emancipation Proclamation and George W. Bush ostensibly signed the renaming of the Great Hall as Emancipation Hall in January 2008. It sounds a bit too ridiculous that a bill has to be put through Congress and the president has to sign it just to rename a hall in a building. Is the American People suppose to believe that it is merely coincidental that Barack Obama a Black/White American citizen becomes POTUS (President of the United States) within a year of President George W. Bush signing that bill naming the Great Hall the Emancipation Hall? I am suggesting that Obama per se was chosen; rather, I am suggesting the a black man was chosen before the year 2000AD and Barack Obama merely happen to be in office at the time a black man per se was needed to be president.

I also want to point out that the two circles representing the eyes on the Westside of the Capitol Building are name Peace Monument[26] and Garfield Statue[27] this I believe is important to point out; for the reason that, in relating them to the Emancipation Hall go to the end of the National Mall and there sits Lincoln Memorial, which has been pointed out symbolized Abraham Lincoln who signed the Emancipation Proclamation and that is on the eastside of the Lincoln Memorial; whereas, on the Westside of the Lincoln Memorial there are two other monument called the Arts of Peace and the Arts of War[28]. This kind of synchronization of the Capitol Building projects with the Abraham Lincoln Memorial illustrates that the entire mystical peripheral vision, as is normal vision, is a projection of the psyche onto the screen of the blank abyss.

Notice how a lot of these projects on the National Mall have just been started and completed from 2000 to the present date illustrating that it takes years to complete the Cathedral of Democracy as it took 816 years to complete Chartres Cathedral. Spirituality is a never-ending journey so I hope that the initiate never-ever gets to a destination or may God have mercy on his or her soul.

Finally, this Freemasonry issue concerning the symbolism constructed in Washington DC, I have to ask a very inexplicable question that will make no sense to the uninitiated. Were all the religions in the entire world created covertly, via secret societies, in the midst of the **rabble-rousing public never-ever knowing what was going on in their midst?** Initially I did not for decades believe this latter. It was too ridiculous to believe. How could great religions, not civilizations, be created covertly? However, knowing the ignorance of the Catholic laity and knowing that Freemasonry is not revealing to the people of the United States what is going on in Washington DC, I cannot help but believe that, yes, all religions were created covertly; because, the truth is only for those that are worthy to envisage it.

Thus it is not difficult to imagine why Freemasonry puts the word FREE in their nomenclature for it symbolizes that they are not constricted to societal mores, religious orthodoxy or the status quo.

---

[25] https://en.wikipedia.org/wiki/United_States_Capitol_Visitor_Center#Emancipation_Hall
[26] http://www.aoc.gov/capitol-grounds/peace-monument
[27] http://www.aoc.gov/capitol-grounds/garfield-monument
[28] https://en.wikipedia.org/wiki/The_Arts_of_War_and_The_Arts_of_Peace

THE CAPITOL BUILDING
and the KNIGHT TEMPLAR'S CROSS

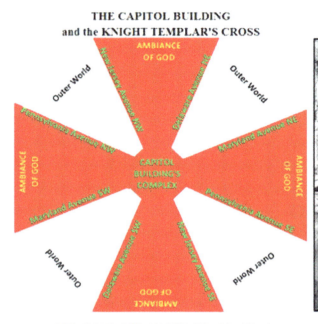

GREAT PYRAMID ON THE GIZA PLATEAU
CONCAVED INTO AN EIGHT SIDED PYRAMID

GREAT PYRAMID ON THE GIZA PLATEAU
CONCAVED INTO AN EIGHT SIDED PYRAMID

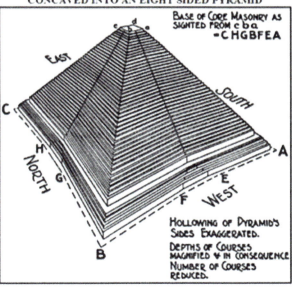

MAP OF THE GIZA PLATEAU

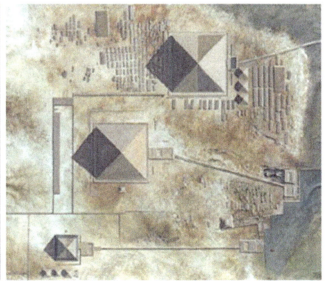

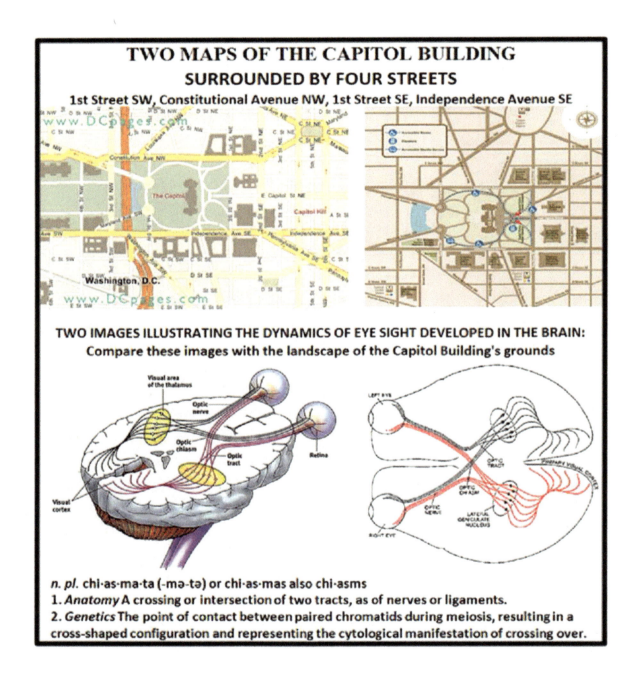

CHAPTER SEVENTEEN

MATRIX OF WISDOM (Part 7)
KAMEA OF SATURN

The Kamea of Saturn (3 x 3 Magic Square) is one of the most important images that are culled out of the MATRIX OF WISOM as if it the 3 x 3 square was the 10 x 10 square's mini-version. An analysis of the patterns of the numbers in the Kamea of Saturn exudes the same pattern that the multiplication tables worked into the MATRIX OF WISDOM. The Kamea of Saturn's obverse and reverse numerical patterns pair off the first eight numbers into the Sun Signs of Astrology just as the MATRIX OF WISDOM does: four mystic elements: Fire, Earth, Air and Water.

Of course one can see the Cross of Christ in the odd numbers of the Kamea of Saturn, which is all about Christianity. It represents the Initiatic Visionary Experience.

This Kamea of Saturn is known worldwide and it's called the Lo Shu in China. All kinds of images in religious artworks are based upon this 3 x 3 design. Being that magic squares are associated to Talismanic Magic seven different talismans images are based upon the seven basic magic squares (seven Sun Signs), which of course the Kamea of Saturn is one of them.

Then there is the image of Christ giving the keys to Peter, which shows the octagon shape chapel in the background of the fresco image. If the reader was to contemplate that image with what has been discussed about the Sistine Chapel in this book he or she will realize that Christ is in the north and the other side of the gazebo chapel is in the south. Remember the even numbers are on the north wall, which houses the frescoes depicting the Life of Christ. Behind Christ is east and in front of him is west. The congregant enters the Sistine Chapel in that manner. Peter is in the center in alignment with the north entrance. Looking to the east and west of the gazebo chapel it can be envisaged that the area to the east is a bit barren and to the west the vegetation is plentiful. The message of this fresco seems to be saying that one has to deflate his or her ego (be beheaded) before entering the Garden of Eden, which would be in the west and the wilderness would be in the east. It can be envisaged why Abraham Lincoln sits at the western gate to America for didn't Horace Greeley say, *"Go west young man"*. Abraham Lincoln sitting between the north and south divide on the Washington Mall seems to be holding the Scales of Anubis or Libra.

The keys to the Kingdom of Heaven symbolize the harmonious relationship between ego-consciousness and the unconscious mind via Christ consciousness and that only can take place in the dynamic maelstrom generated via the tetrahedral forces in creation (psyche).

The next image is the Masonic Apron, which has a great deal of symbolism. Its message is of course universal. The Boaz and Jachin columns symbolizing the Moon and the Sun are outside of the octagon gazebo, which symbolizing the Holy of Holies. The fact that the image show both Boaz and Jachin has a pinecone on each column shows that they have united in unanimity. This apron image clearly illustrates that the Christian Church symbolizes the Holy of Holies, which is a sacred sanctuary in Solomon's Temple. The image of the sun emanate eighteen rays with four point (further rays) at the end calculating out to 72-rays, which is precisely how many rays come out of the sculptured image in Saint Peter's Basilica call Saint Peter's Chair. These 72-rays symbolize the 72-names of God, which has already been discussed in this volume with other material. The Moon is symbolized as a cloud without form. The Compass superimposes itself over the octagon gazebo implying that the circle that symbolizes the whole of infinity rules the basic concept of the apron. The checkerboard floor is obvious meant to image the MATRIX OF WISDOM, which is the foundation of all religion. The seven stairs symbolizes the Seven Liberal Arts: Quadrivium and Trivium. The eight columns holding up the roof symbolize the eight basic numbers that symbolizes the LIGHT culled out of the DARKNESS. The scales on top of the Holy of Holies symbolize the Scales of Anubis or Libra. In the fold of the apron at the top of the image the Pentagram, roses and the G images symbolizes what I believe to be the concept the Golden Ratio. The Golden Ration symbolizes the tetrahedral forces of creation (psyche), which is the primal cause for the creation of this octagon Holy of Holies.

Finally, there are tools laid out on the floor as if they were discarded as trash. Nobody treat his or her tools like that in any given profession. Notice that even the square is in the midst of that fray of garbage. Remember that the tools of the world: literature, artwork and monuments are only means of obtaining access to one's goal.

There is a story that comes out of a Buddhist monastery told by Joseph Campbell in his mythology lectures. *'The Little Ferry Both is the symbolic name for Buddhism. Buddhism teaches neophytes how to navigate life and each neophyte is giving daily chores to accomplish that goal. One day a neophyte went up to his master and asked him what another Buddhist monk did when he got to yonder shores leaving the Little Ferry Boat behind and his master answered that when one gets to the land of Nirvana the Little Ferry Boat is no longer needed'*.

This is the way of the Initiatic Visionary Experience. No organized or orthodox religion is needed once one is face to face with God. A 33° Mason should not consider himself a Freemason simply because he has outgrown the teachings of Freemasonry. The symbolism of the 33rd degree Mason is that he has risen above the ice glacier known as the STATUS QUO he was entombed in. Symbolically Masonic Order members not 33rd degree Masons is frozen in the same ice glacier that Satan is portrait in Dante's INFERNO. The tools on the floor of the temple courtyard symbolize the casting away of the permanency of orthodoxy's STATUS QUO; however, an initiate cannot simply toss the tools of the trade aside until he is completely apprised of the knowledge they have to convey. The tools of the world are what aid the initiate into building his inner temple and woe to him or her that does not complete his or her mission in this lifetime.

The Kamea of Saturn is what develops the multi-religious cultures around the world. A perfect illustration of this is by learning the Swastika can only be developed in a three by three (3 x 3) square called the Kamea of Saturn; for the reason that there are three different Swastikas: Male, Female and Neutral and when these patterns are aligned to their individual circle the individual swastika literally draw the Fish Symbol of Christianity, the Scarab of Egypt or the Clothing and Architecture of the Chinese culture (see images below).

Additionally, the Kamea of Saturn developed the Templar Cross, via the neutral swastika. The neutral swastika negates the male and female swastikas, which denote God's Ambiance; for the reason that, there is no male or female in heaven; thus, I believe that this is why the Templar's Cross is designed around the Capitol Building in Washington DC. The reader would be wise to research the mythoi of the Knight Templar's alleged history. The story goes that nine knights went to Jerusalem and were allowed access to the Temple of the Rock, which is an Islamic mosque, which totally eradicated Solomon's Temple similar to what takes place via meditational contemplative thought in the Sistine Chapel. The Temple of the Rock is Solomon's Temple in the round: i.e. octagon shape (Kamea of Saturn). The great treasure that the mythoi of the Knight Templars infers is that the nine knights are symbolically the first nine numbers (1-9) that fit perfectly into the nine cells of the Kamea of Saturn creating the Holy of Holies.

The next two sets of images (2 x 2) deals with the assume development of the Chinese I Ching and Freemasonry symbol of the Square, Compass and G cull out of the Kamea of Saturn. The Masonic Order is a worldwide organization; though, it was originally organized in modern times on June 24, 1717 (John the Baptist birthday) in England. Yes, I do believe that Freemasonry goes back to early antiquity under different nomenclatures: that is a given. This idea comes to me solely from the present argument under discussion that the Square, Compass and G come from the Kamea of Saturn, which like the I Ching goes back to the dawn of time. I use the phrase 'dawn of time' to point out that the sum total of all knowledge is embedded in the Kamea of Saturn: i.e. mini-version of the MATRIX OF WISDOM. Whatever can be culled out of the MATRIX OF WISDOM can be culled out of any of the SEVEN MAGIC SQUARES.

The Kamea of Saturn illustrates clearly that the I Ching and the Square, Compass and G were culled out of the Kamea of Saturn simultaneously. I see this link between the Chinese and Freemasonry as a contrast between the East and the West. Also I envisage the symbolism of the I Ching as going East to West; whereas, the Square, Compass and G goes from West to East. Symbolically, the I Ching symbolizes the new Sun continuously and everlastingly going from East to West: this is similar to Catholicism contrasting Judaism. Judaism is what John the Baptist symbolized and that is what Freemasonry is all about. It has only been the last decade or so that I have become aware of the extreme importance of Judaism for the Christian laity. The symbolism of the Square, Compass and G symbolizes the Sun dying; however, it continues to circle the earth and in that roundabout away goes from West to East and returns as a new Sun. Do not misunderstand me here. Both religious methods of the East and the West are necessary for the individual initiate to contemplate with all intentions of amalgamating; though, amalgamation is not possible unless God gifts the initiate with the Initiatic Visionary Experience. It is only when this latter happens to the initiate psychically he or she stops going from West to East and begins to go from East to West. It is like going making a U-turn in Hell. Worshipping towards the East is paradoxically worshipping the STATUS QUO; whereas, going from East to West is, for all intent and purpose, going into new frontiers and that is what Paradise is all about.

These two sets are linked in this discussion; for the reason that the Chinese seem to have used the Lo Shu nine basic models culled out of the Kamea of Saturn; however, the Chinese only applied the Fixed Signs of Astrology digits: 2, 5 and 8 in the process of developing the I Ching. I am fully aware of the mythoi that surround the Yarrow Sticks, which are said to have developed the I Ching; nonetheless, I am more interested in how I Ching was contemplatively culled out of the MATRIX OF WISDOM not how it was mythologized.

In looking at the three (2, 5 and 8) out of nine kameas models culled of the Lo Shu (Kamea of Saturn) that the Chinese used to develop the I Ching it can be seen that only the odd numbers are considered as the primal tools to create the eight trigrams. Six out of the eight trigrams are developed from the Fixed Quadruplicities and the other two are brought into play through the means using simple reason and logic. The fact that the I Ching has sixty-four (64) hexagrams points to the central portion of the MATRIX OF WISDOM that is known as the LIGHT culled out of the DARKNESS. The New Testament, as it has already been discussed above, uses also only the Fixed Quadruplicities of Astrology to write the four gospels that have their own Triplicities: Fire, Earth, Air and Water, which the Chinese I Ching breaks down into the 64-hexagrams using family members like Noah, his wife, three sons and three daughter-in-laws. The 64-hexagrams are in incomprehensible unanimity.

The odd numbers symbolizes the male or that which ego-consciousness discriminated out of the DARKNESS. The unconscious mind symbolizes the even numbers and the female, which cannot discriminate. The unconscious mind spiritually impels (suggest) and from a materialistic perspective compels (mandates); however, the unconscious mind, in and of itself by itself, cannot discriminate it needs ego-consciousness to carry out its suggestions or mandates otherwise it is nothing more than a vacuum. Here I am discussing the symbolism of the psyche not men or women in the real world. Yes, the unconscious mind can force dreams upon the psyche; however, that is merely the unconscious mind having a captive audience; whereas, ego-consciousness is conscious of itself and its surrounding.

When the initiate obtains the Initiatic Visionary Experience personally from God ego-consciousness and the unconscious mind are in unanimity, which means that there is neither ego-consciousness (male) nor an unconscious mind (female) *[There is neither Jew nor Greek, there is neither bond nor free, there is neither male nor female: for ye are all one in Christ Jesus (Galatians 3:28)][1]*, which means that Christ consciousness is the spiritual Sun and the Holy Spirit

---

[1] It is interesting that Saint Paul used the third chapter twenty-eight verses (328) in structuring this sentence: 328 is symbolically the Gematria value of DARKNESS, which the LIGHT is culled from. Also

is the spiritual Moon conveying the WORD OF GOD. How this works is essentially what I am doing now. I am writing about the MATRIX OF WISDOM; however, as much as I know I do not know the intricate details that goes along with it and even upon learning those nuances I am still infinitely ignorance of the vast spiritual laws that are inherent in the MATRIX OF WISDOM; thus, in my writing about the MATRIX OF WISDOM impelling suggestions come to mind via the Holy Spirit (mystical guiding hands) as to what to write; therefore, it is not me writing this per se otherwise where would I have gotten all these ideas throughout the last four decades? I am, personally, no more important to God than anybody else on earth. It is just that I am more attuned to the spiritual laws of the MATRIX OF WISDOM, which has given me the eyes to see and the ears to hear the WORD OF GOD.

The reader should study these two sets of images that develop the I Ching and the Square Compass and G until he or she fully grasp the concepts being conveyed here so that he or she will understand these extremely subtle nuances in the Esoteric Science.

The Square, Compass and G symbol is developed somewhat differently from the I Ching because unlike the Fix Signs of Astrology: i.e. Lo Shu's (Kamea of Saturn) models (2, 5 and 8) Freemasonry uses Astrology's Cardinal (1, 4 and 7) and Mutable (3, 6 and 9) Quadruplicities' models of the Kamea of Saturn (Lo Shu). Essentially, the Square, Compass and G is conveying the old occult maxim *"as above so below"*. Even culling the Square, Compass and G out of the Kamea of Saturn conveys the concept of *"as above so below"*. This is not me repeating myself it is the symbolism itself that is redundant.

Looking at the Cardinal (1, 4 and 7) and Mutable (3, 6 and 9) models culled out of the Kamea of Saturn by adding the columns and rows it can be seen that the columns and rows have different quotients. I took the large quotient twenty-one (21) in the Cardinal Quadruplicity to design the pattern of the Square, Compass and G and then I took the low quotient in the Mutable Quadruplicity to cull out the Square, Compass and G; thus it can be easily seen how the two symbols literally are mirror images of each other.

Let me segue here for a minute and mention that Robert Bauval, as much as I respect his research and writings, misinterpreted the Egyptian mirror imaging the Orion Constellation by setting up the Pyramid Complex on the Giza Plateau. Robert Bauval's hubris forced him into applying the concept of the Precession of the Equinoxes into his intuitive discovery; therefore, misinterpreting the true message that was being conveyed by the pyramids on the Giza Plateau. Here in the Kamea of Saturn (Lo Shu) it clearly illustrates what mirror imaging the heavens is all about. Robert Bauval serendipitously by applying the concept of the Precession of the Equinoxes stumbled upon the idea of megalithic works created by the ancients, in antiquity, around 10,500BC and before. Robert Bauval, himself, did not make the discoveries of any megalithic site created in antiquity; however, when these ancient megalithic sites were discovered by other researchers Robert Bauval hooked his thesis to their wagons of discoveries assuming he was correct. Actually, what Robert Bauval has blatantly shown the world is that REASON AND LOGIC are not the end all and be all of contemplative meditation, in fact REASON AND LOGIC can be very destructive if not applied correctly to Christ consciousness. The question that should always remain in the forefront of thought is, *'is it hubris or Christ developing this idea'*?

To continue on, when contemplating the message that the Square, Compass and G standing alone outside of the Kamea of Saturn (Lo Shu) conveys it become obvious that the Compass symbolizes Heaven and the Square symbolizes the Earth and the G in the center does symbolize God (Golden Means, Cygnus X-3, Holy Spirit, geometry, Northern Cross). Throughout this book I have mainly discuss this theme symbolizing the first verse of Genesis: *"Elohym (God) separated the Heavens and the Earth"*.

---

328 are the digits denoting a set in the Fibonacci sequence: 5/8, which symbolizes the tetrahedral forces of the psyche.

The next image deals with the SEVEN MAGIC SQUARES; however, I added the number one and two to fill in the obvious gaps. These two sections of the Kamea of the Moon inside the MATRIX OF WISDOM are Magic Square per se; however, they are part of the whole; therefore, they cannot be summarily dismissed. I colored the diagonal line going down the MATRIX OF WISDOM to point out the numerical value of each of the Magic Square's quotient brought down to their lowest common denominators. What I am actually illustrating here is the Kundalini Serpent. When looking at the combined Magic Squares totals the add up to 285, which are the digits in the Fixed Quadruplicities of Astrology that is because they have been culled out of the Kamea of the Moon inherent in the MATRIX OF WISDOM. When the quotient 285: sum total of all nine numbers is divided by the eighty-one (81) cells they were culled out of the quotient is, 3.5… symbolizing the dormant Kundalini Serpent. When considering there are nine-base numbers then when 285 is divided by nine (9) the quotient is 31.66... This last hails back to the calculations performed on the different sections that made up the ten Miles square that the city of Washington DC rest on. Virginia seceded 31.66 miles of land to the city of Washington DC. The Potomac is calculated out as 7.29 miles, which also is a calculation relating to the Kamea of the Moon: i.e. 9^3 equals 729.

The Magic Squares even numbers squared totals: 120 / 285 = 0.42… in contrast to the odd numbers squared totaled: 165 / 285 = 0.57…, which is equivalent symbolically to 60/40% seen in the Genesis Formula and this is further worked out in the cube section of the Magic Squares. The even numbers cubed out to 800 / 2025 = 0.39… and the odd numbers cube out as 1225 / 2025 = 0.60…

The final point about the Magic Squares concerns the forbidden sin of Adam and Eve. The reader should study each of the Magic Square; for the reason that, the odd number squares symbolize the Labyrinth that is seen in Chartres Cathedral. What I mean by this is that if the initiate take each of the odd number Magic Squares and follow the numbers 1/+ sequentially he or she will see that any odd number magic square whether it is one of the original Magic Square or any odd number Magic Square beyond the original will be structured sequentially using the same technique. Any odd number Magic Square can be created offhandedly without much thought; for the reason that, the technique is that simple. For example if the initiate wanted to do up a Magic Square of 11, 13, 15, 17, etc. it would not take much time. It should be mentioned that, yes, the odd number Magic Squares can have multiple ways of creating a perfect Magic Square except the Kamea of Saturn, which is lock into place. It cannot be manipulated out of its raison d'être.

Whereas, trying to figure out how the even number Magic Square is done up is like going through a maze. It not only will take a great deal of time to do it; but, even number Magic Squares has multiple ways of creating that Magic Square and the one that is sought most likely will most likely not be obtained. It is literally ego-consciousness not Christ consciousness that invokes the psyche into things it has no business in. It is mere hubris that has been activated.

The initiate should reread the argument that Eve has with the serpent in the third chapter of Genesis while studying this argument about the odd (labyrinth) and even (maze) Magic Squares. Yes, I will agree wholeheartedly with the assessment of anybody that say he or she can acclimate themselves to the even number Magic Square no matter how far beyond the original Magic Squares they are ask to create; however, no matter the argument that knowledge can only come through hubris.

The even number Magic Squares symbolizes nothing more than ego-consciousness not having anything to with Christ consciousness. It is the individual's will not to have Christ guide him or her.

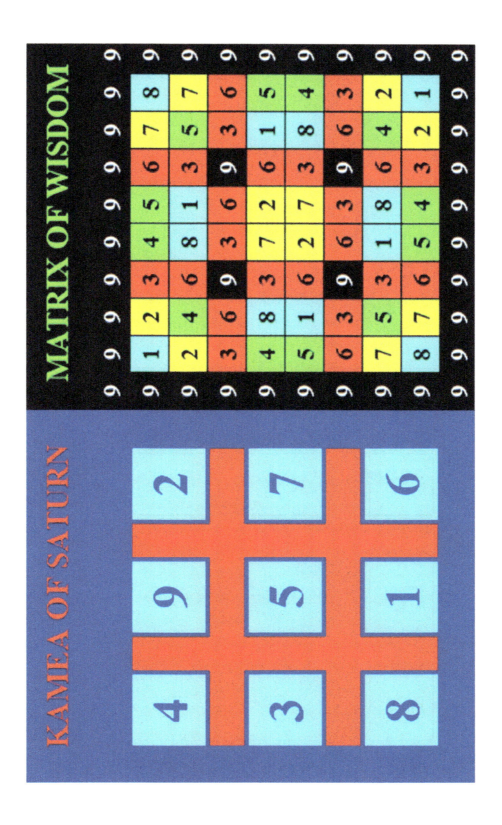

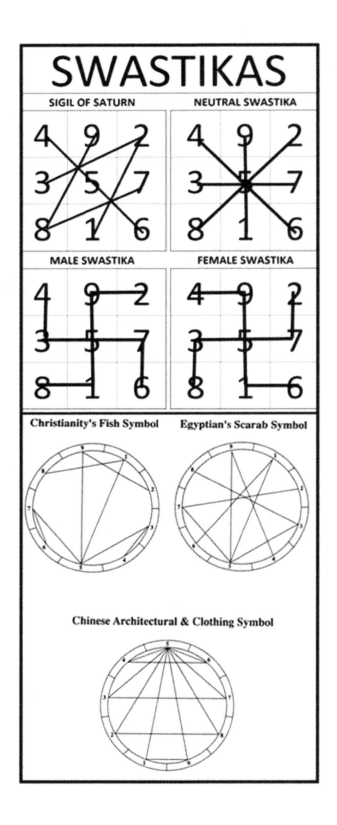

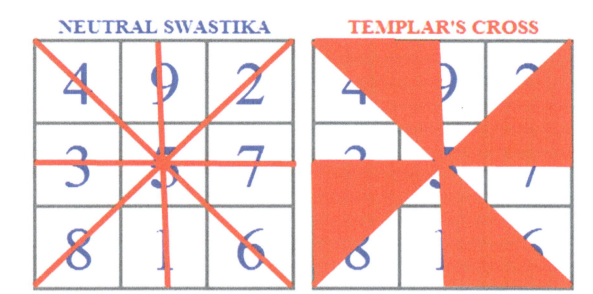

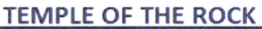

TEMPLE OF THE ROCK

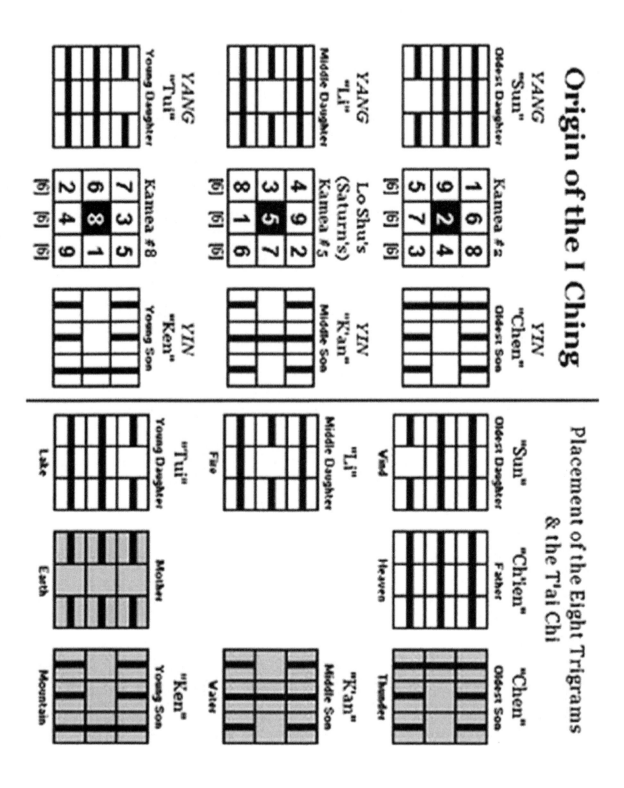

Origin of the I Ching

Placement of the Eight Trigrams & the T'ai Chi

Chinese I Ching - 64 Hexagrams

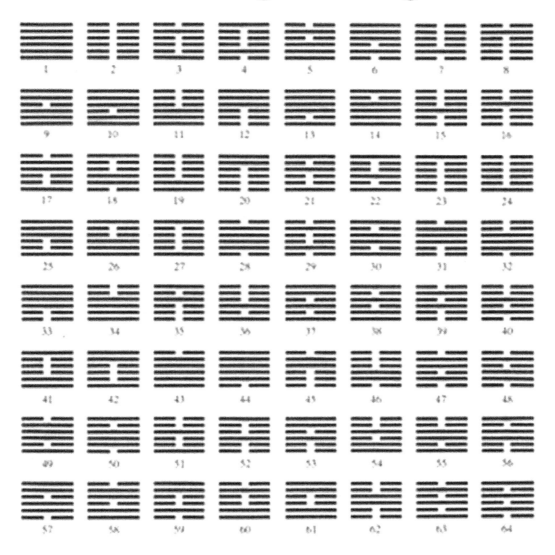

The Nine Basic Kameas

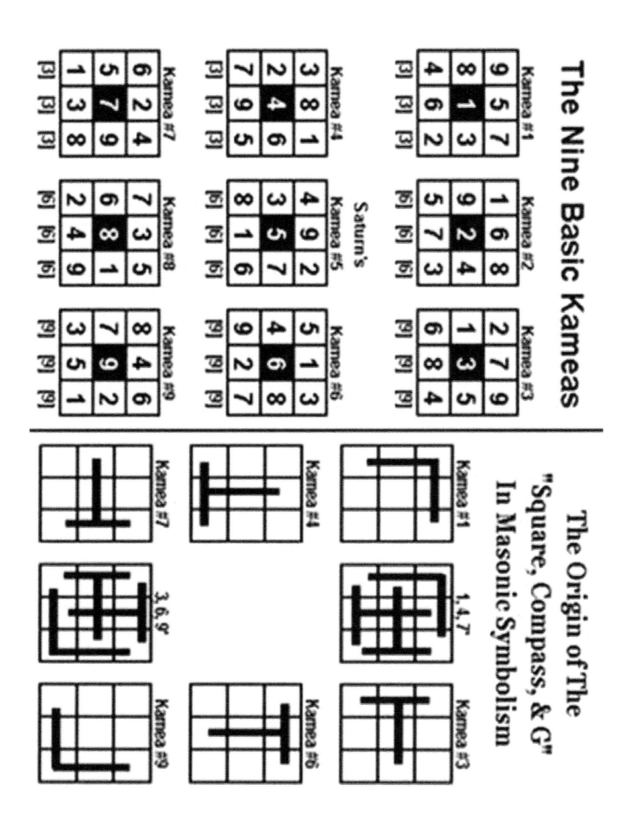

Saturn's

The Origin of The
"Square, Compass, & G"
In Masonic Symbolism

MAGIC SQUARES

KAMEA OF SATURN

4	9	2
3	5	7
8	1	6

KAMEA OF JUPITER

4	14	15	1
9	7	6	12
5	11	10	8
16	2	3	13

KAMEA OF MARS

11	24	7	20	3
4	12	25	8	16
17	5	13	21	9
10	18	1	14	22
23	6	19	2	15

KAMEA OF THE SUN

6	32	3	34	35	1
7	11	27	28	8	30
19	14	16	15	23	24
18	20	22	21	17	13
25	29	10	9	26	12
36	5	33	4	2	31

KAMEA OF VENUS

22	47	16	41	10	35	4
5	23	48	17	42	11	29
30	6	24	49	18	36	12
13	31	7	25	43	19	37
38	14	32	1	26	44	20
21	39	8	33	2	27	45
46	15	40	9	34	3	28

KAMEA OF MERCURY

8	58	59	5	4	62	63	1
49	15	14	52	53	11	10	56
41	23	22	44	45	19	18	48
32	34	35	29	28	38	39	25
40	26	27	37	36	30	31	33
17	47	46	20	21	43	42	24
9	55	54	12	13	51	50	16
64	2	3	61	60	6	7	57

KAMEA OF THE MOON

37	78	29	70	21	62	13	54	5
6	38	79	30	71	22	63	14	46
47	7	39	80	31	72	23	55	15
16	48	8	40	81	32	64	24	56
57	17	49	9	41	73	33	65	25
26	58	18	50	1	42	74	34	66
67	27	59	10	51	2	43	75	35
36	68	19	60	11	52	3	44	76
77	28	69	20	61	12	53	4	45

MATRIX OF WISDOM

9	9	9	9	9	9	9	9	9	9	9
9	1	2	3	4	5	6	7	8	9	
9	2	4	6	8	1	3	5	7	9	
9	3	6	9	3	6	9	3	6	9	
9	4	8	3	7	2	6	1	5	9	
9	5	1	6	2	7	3	8	4	9	
9	6	3	9	6	3	9	6	3	9	
9	7	5	3	1	8	6	4	2	9	
9	8	7	6	5	4	3	2	1	9	
9	9	9	9	9	9	9	9	9	9	

SUN SIGNS	MAGIC SQUARE	EVEN SQUARED	ODD SQUARED	TOTALS SQUARED	EVEN CUBED	ODD CUBED	TOTALS CUBED
	1		1	1		1	1
	2	4		4	8		8
SATURN	3		9	9		27	27
JUPITER	4	16		16	64		64
MARS	5		25	25		125	125
SUN	6	36		36	216		216
VENUS	7		49	49		343	343
MERCURY	8	64		64	512		512
MOON	9		81	81		729	729
		120	165	285	800	1225	2025

CHAPTER EIGHTEEN

THE MATRIX OF WISDOM (Part 8)
THE FIBONACCI SEQUENCE

On November 7, 2012 I happen to be watching a film on the Fibonacci sequence on the Esoteric Online Social Network for Sacred Science and the commentator was demonstrating that all organic life on Earth owes its existence to this mathematical formula. Now I have known of the Golden Ratio for most of my adult life. I even found it used in the mythoi of Dante Alighieri's life in relationship to when he began writing La Divina Commedia and when he finished it on the day of his death. Dante additionally uses the Golden Ratio in the manner he lays out the plot of his La Divina Commedia. The structuring of the first chapter of Genesis uses the Fibonacci sequence in many ways especially in how it is used in the Gematria values of the two names of God: Yahweh (26 = 8) and Elohym (86 = 5), which is a set in the Fibonacci sequence. This has everything to do with what Christ said, *'when two or three are gathered together, in my name, there am I in the midst of them'*. When Christ is in the midst of Yahweh and Elohym the Trinity emerges in a harmonious consensus. Every set of the Fibonacci sequence breaks down into a 2/3 ratio.

Having said the above I personally could not see how all of these infinite forms of life on earth that owe their existence to this equation did not have some kind of basic patterns to its overall formatting process. PHI did not present itself like the formula for PI: 3.14159… merely calculating the diameter of a circle, which is a universal and infinite law. Pi has been illustrated to symbolize God. This is not saying that God is Pi per se; rather, it is saying that God is not DARKNESS; rather, He is the LIGHT. In Saint John's gospel it say, *"God is LIGHT and in Him there is no DARKNESS"* and in that respect God separates the LIGHT from the DARKNESS. I saw in the Fibonacci sequence a whole new set of rules.

Pi is basically a constant; whereas, PHI is also a constant as is Pi; however, PHI continuously culls out the LIGHT from the DARKNESS. This is what I believe generates the dynamics of TIME; whereas, the previous cells generated deteriorate at a minute cadence as new cells begin to replace them; hence, physical old age and death is a given; however, in order to keep this constant cadence pace forward (replacement) and backward (deterioration) there had to be a limitation to the Fibonacci sequence otherwise its reproduction cycle would replicate out like a tsunami like in the rare cases of Progeria. I was also envisaging that this PHI formula does not stop at the physiological aspects of life and that it also seem to play on the mental aspects of life in relationship to the educational pace of a new born baby to adulthood and the cadence pace of physical and mental illness, which includes the cadence pace relating to the onset of addictions. I include addictions into this discussion; for the reason that, when a person is forcibly removed from his addiction; because, of illness or imprisonment it does not curtail the addictive cadence on a mental level. When the physical aspects of the addicted habit commences once again the cadence pace of the addiction process from the perspective of PHI never seems to have diminished in anyway whatsoever during the abstinence period; rather, the addiction process seems to have continued its psychic growth even though there was a temporary abstinence of one's physical addictive habit.

I began to see the importance and the reason for the Quadruplicities of Astrology in relationship to PHI. I understood the Triplicities of Astrology are basically of the spiritual realm and that the Quadruplicities belonged to the physical and it domination on ego-consciousness' aspects of life; however, I did not know how Quadruplicities applied to the materialistic realm other than that they did. I also visualized that PHI has everything to do with spiritual growth once one receives the Initiatic Visionary Experience. Eventually, I began to realize that PHI has everything to do with all aspect of life: Physical, Mental and Spiritual.

CARDINAL QUADRUPLICITIES OF ASTROLOGY: SPIRITUAL

Infinite spiritual growth, after the Initiatic Visionary Experience, is also proportional to the initiate contemplative meditational concentration on the spiritual aspects of life. All aspects of life are spiritual for without the physical and the mental the spiritual life cannot be experienced.

The idea came into my head to test the Fibonacci sequence by breaking down each calculation to its lowest common denominator just to see if some kind of a visual pattern would reveal itself. Performing this minor calculation, casting-out-nines, initially on the multiplication tables allowed me to envisaged patterns I would never have otherwise envisaged in their materialistic format; thus, I questioned, why would not the Fibonacci sequence also produce patterns not normally visible to sight or the human intellect.

About the thirty-second (32nd) calculation I began to realize that pattern replication was settling into the array of calculations I set up. It would appear that after the twenty-fourth (24th) calculation [Pattern 1], all quotients reduced to their lowest common denominators, were redundantly repeating the prototype that was the first pattern. When I finished the forty-eighth (48th) calculation [Pattern 2] I had a complete second pattern that was redundant of the first set of calculations. I realized that a third set of calculations [Pattern 3] spanning out another twenty-four (24) calculation, to the seventy-second (72nd) calculation, would be needed to convince any scholar and/or academic that I was on to something.

MUTABLE QUADRUPLICITES OF ASTROLOGY: MENTAL

Education generates unlimited possibilities proportional to an adult own attentive meditational motivations to that which enamors its psyche; however, I believe this has everything to do with physical maturity coinciding with mental growth activity. Governments forcing stringent mental activity on children prior to physical parity will create psychic aberrations for a certainty. Knowledge should not be thrust upon children; rather, knowledge should be acclimated to according to the cadence of the individual's physical growth and mindset.

Addictions and/or obsessions are generated psychically experienced proportional to the use of, on a physical level, whatever enamors the psyche. This is not just abuse of drugs or alcohol. It would also be inclusive of anything psychic or materialistic: money, skills, professions, reading, gambling, sex, fishing, hunting, traveling, swimming, running, walking, socializing and/or whatever even after physically discontinuing use of them in the mental or physical aspects of the addictions and/or obsessions. Psychically addictions and/or obsession will continue to increase infinitely, without conscious knowledge of and/or ignorance of those aspects of one's life that have enamored the psyche until physical death.

FIXED QUADRUPLICITIES OF ASTROLOGY: PHYISCAL

Fixed Quadruplicities are limitations; for the reason that, thoughts, words and deeds are seemingly fixed; though, they are transient; because, of the physical aspects of the creation of objects and/or addictions and/or obsessions. The Fixed Quadruplicities instantly concretizes the Triplicities: Fire, Earth, Air and Water, which collectively represent the LIGHT culled out of the DARKNESS.

The best example of this is the New Testament culled out of the esoteric nature of the Old Testament in such a perfected form via mystical spiritual insight that nothing more needs to be added or taken away from it. These are canonized texts. This does not of course mean that the mystic cannot learn anymore from what he or she has written from such inspiration.

From a secular iconoclastic level the same process of culling LIGHT from the DARKNESS is essentially in play; however, unlike the New Testament, which is perfection via its indigenous language when a modernist cull and idea out of his or her head it is basically in it rawest adolescence format no matter how ingenious he or she may think it is; nonetheless, its primal pattern (raison d'être) is encapsulated in that idea, which is developed to a greater extent from that point forward: i.e. the Model T-Ford automobile compared to what modernity has today in the world.

This is precisely how the sacred scriptures should be read and its teachings developed over time in the heart and mind of the initiate.

ANALYZING THE PATTERN IN THE FIBONACCI SEQUENCE

I remember in my teenage years (half a century ago) that there were about twenty-three (23) sets of chromosomes in every cell and here I was coming up with a sequence of twenty-four (24) calculations in the Fibonacci sequence. It was not too far of an intellectual reach equate the Fibonacci sequence to the 46-chromosones of each cell; for the reason that, the Golden Means has everything to do with organic life. If this pattern is a constant, as I believe it is, it may well give the biologists an easier way of mapping out Human, Animal and Vegetable DNA structure. I did not realize as I wrote this last sentence that this pattern of twenty-four (24) calculations would inform me a great deal as to how the Judaeo Christian Scriptures were written; thus, informing all mankind about the minute detail about life not just giving information to biologists.

I have found that by studying the lowest common denominators in the sequential pattern of twenty-four (24) calculations the numbers one (1) and eight (8) each takes on five of the 24-calculations: five (5) sets of 1 and 8, which can be envisaged as being pulled out of the number nine (9). This left fourteen (14) calculations for the other numbers: 2, 3, 4, 5, 6, 7 and 9; however, nine (9) is not in the same classification with the other six numbers: 2, 3, 4, 5, 6 and 7 for each had two of the remaining fourteen calculations in the pattern that, in and of themselves, have also been culled out of the number nine; for the reason that, each of these numbers pair off into set with the numerical sun signs of Astrology: 2 – 7 (Venus), 3 – 6 (Mercury), 4 – 5 (Sun and Moon) just 1 – 8 symbolized Mars.

I hypothesize that the second pattern of 23+1-chromosones mirror image the Fibonacci sequence for the mental aspects of the psyche. If the sizes of the chromosomes have anything to do with the Fibonacci sequence (see image of U.S. National Library of Medicine) these 24-calculations in the Fibonacci sequence should be seen as 23 x 9 = 207, which is the Gematria value of the word LIGHT in the first and fourth days of creation. If I am reading this arithmetical data properly this pattern of twenty-three (23) calculations would symbolize the LIGHT culled out of the DARKNESS; for the reason that, it is a concise and repetitive pattern that oscillate out infinitely; yes, the pattern is twenty-four (24) calculation; however, each (9) in the sequential pattern of twenty-four (24) begins the second half of the cell's pattern. It is as if each organic cell goes out infinitely; thought, each cell is categorized with 46-chromosones. It is as if the number nine separating each group of eleven sets of chromosomes is a strict limitation barrier: "***Hitherto shalt thou come, but no further*** (Job 38:11)."

The reader should realize that reading the numerical data of the Golden Ratio reduced down to their lowest common denominators is no different than a computer programming expert reading the zeros (0s) and one (1s) in the binary system nor is that different than the Jews reading and/or speaking the Hebrew language or any other culture reading and/or speaking their language. It is just that the Golden Ratio is symbolic as are all languages' letters and words symbolic of thoughts going on in the psyche. Language merely brings psychic content into a condensed compact form of physical manifestation. The moment that mental and/or spiritual thoughts are brought into physical manifestation they concretize and new ideas have to be culled out of the DARKNESS. The DARKNESS is what was previously considered LIGHT before it was condensed and concretized (crucified) into physical form. This is analogous to crucifying Christ. Christ has to be continuously and everlastingly crucified nanosecond by nanosecond in order to understand what spirituality is all about.

This concretizing thought goes to illustrating why an atom is so compact that when it is split open it creates a tsunami of explosive light destroying all materialism around it

ANALYZING THE FIBONOCCI SEQUENCE

I am about to discuss the data I envisaged out of the arithmetical diagrams below. I advise the reader to study these diagrams meticulously in relationship to what I am discussing.

Rows-A and F: is the arithmetical numerical sequential count from 1 – 24.

Rows-B and E: is the Fibonacci sequence up to the 24-calculations; however, I, firmly, believe that the sequential count is only up to eleven (11); for the reason that, the first eleven (11) out of the twelve (12) calculations sequences, symbolizes masculine (ego-consciousness), whereas, the second eleven (11) calculations would symbolize the feminine (unconscious mind). Viewing this oscillation process between the two 11+1 calculation sequences totaling 24-calculations illustrate the rationale for the Golden Ratio spiral to function as it does.

Rows-C and D: is reducing the Fibonacci sequence **Rows-B and E** down to their lowest common denominators via casting-out-nine (9). The number nine (9) can be divided into four sets of numbers (the first eight numbers): 1 and 8, 2 and 7, 3 and 6, and 4 and 5; nevertheless, **Rows-C and D** clearly illustrates that the number nine (9) represents the gender barrier: i.e. the X or Y chromosomes; therefore, the array is actually 23+1 meaning that the number nine (9) separates the two patterns of eleven calculations flanking it. Each nine (9) in the array of 24-calculation begins the sequence of chromosomes for the opposite gender; thus, the next nine (9) and every other subsequent nine (9) will have the masculine (red) and feminine (blue) chromosomes flanking it: 11 + 1 + 11 = 23-sets of chromosomes. This pattern below merely is set up to illustrate the first 72-calculations and the patterns they exude.

1123584371898876415628191123584371898876415628191123584371898876415628191123584371898876415628191123584371898876415628191 9

There is another pattern envisaged in each of the eleven arrays of calculations flanking the nines (9s). The pairing of the first eight numbers 1 and 8, 2 and 7, 3 and 6 and 4 and 5 clearly illustrates how the MATRIX OF WISDOM is created through the tetrahedral forces of creation (psyche).

Looking at **Rows C and D** they are color coded blue (feminine) and red (masculine); because, the blue (feminine) holds the numbers one (1) and eight (8) and the red (masculine) area denotes numbers two, three, four, five, six and seven (2, 3, 4, 5, 6, 7). I named these calculations groups masculine and feminine; for the reason that, in my research on the Genesis creation account Eve has the Gematria value of nineteen (19) as does the Hebrew letter QOPH ק and Yahweh has the Gematria value of twenty-six (26). When the blue areas in **Row C** are added they total to nineteen (19) and the blue area in **Row D** total to twenty-six (26). Both **Rows C and D** total the blue areas to forty-five (45), which is the Gematria value of Adam. This obvious sync between the Genesis Creation Account and the numerics of the Fibonacci sequence cannot be coincidental especially when it is known that the 46-chromosones deals with the gender aspect. There can be no doubt that this is precisely where the scribes of the bible obtained their information to codify into the words ADAM and EVE.

What convinces me that the Fibonacci sequence has everything to do with the 46-chromosones, inherent in each cell, is how its limited pattern of 24-calculations when pair into two sets of twelve (12) calculation they lineup against each other perfectly as if creating in each cell the physical and the mental aspects of the MATRIX OF WISDOM. This 24-calculation pattern infers a hidden set of 24-calculations, which is not hidden in the cell per se; because, it denotes the actual 46-chromosones illustrating how they are to complement each other: i.e. how ego-consciousness and the unconscious mind should harmonize and how the grammatical texts of the sacred scriptures should harmonize with the mathematical data codified to each of the letters of the sacred scriptures. What this is conveying is that there are hidden forces all around the initiate that are there to aid the initiate in his or her endeavors.

This image directly below does not symbolize the 46-chromosones; rather, it merely shows how the two disparate set in the first twenty-three (23) out of twenty-four calculations complement each other.

There is no doubt that the Fibonacci sequence second set of 24-calculation and onward infinitely is merely a repetition of the first 24-calculations simply to hold in place the cell's raison d'être: i.e. this pattern sequence is the foundation of all diseases and addictions and/or obsessions whatever they may be, which would include the stability of the initiate's place in the Garden of Eden if he or she is so grace to enter into the realm of God's abode.

Rows G and H slightly revises **Rows C and D** by twisting its rows into alignment (calculations 5, 6, 9 and 11, 17, 18, 21 and 23) similar to what the double helix implies. The Fibonacci sequence does precisely what my analysis on the MATRIX OF WISDOM does in reversing the multiplication tables in the unconscious mind to sync with ego-consciousness before the Genesis Formula is developed; however, the Fibonacci sequence is conveying the very same schema that the synching process between the opposites can be from either side of the equation: i.e. from ego-consciousness and/or the unconscious mind. For all intent and purpose this is a universal cosmic mandate coming directly from the Fibonacci sequence, which symbolizes the 46-chromosones of every cell of the human body. In other words; for the reason that, there are 46-chromosones to every single cell there are no exceptions to this universal law whatsoever. The initiate must become attune to this cosmic law spiritually, mentally and physically.

There is another amazing factor implied by the Fibonacci sequence and that is that every calculation casting-out-nine infers it exudes it own complete multiplication table casting-out-nines. The Fibonacci sequence, which is a variance on the Golden Ratio, is a fixed calculation: 0.618034…; thus, making every calculation equal to the last. As each of the first eight basic multiplication tables is studied it is easily seen that all multiplication tables beyond the first is developed in the image and likeness of the first multiplication table. Just as the Golden Ratio is redundant the systemic system of multiplication tables rhetorically expresses the same idea that everything in an individual's life is redundant.

The mathematics in the Fibonacci sequence and the interpretations thereof would imply that that is not the message being conveyed; for the reason that, the mathematics used in the esoteric science is generic and the implication of this is that fractional ratio mathematics can be expressed via any fractional ratio. This would be a false interpretation of the mathematics outlined in the Fibonacci sequence; for the reason that, the MATRIX OF WISDOM illustrates a divine presence, which no other fractional ratio can possibly exude on its own volition.

Continuing the analysis on the Fibonacci sequence **Rows G and H** and **Rows I and J** conveys a great deal of information as to how the bible was written. **Rows B, C, D and E** shows the first eleven number are separated by blue and red via the ones (1s) and the eights (8), which, I believe, symbolizes the divine presence. **Rows G and H** illustrate how **Rows B, C, D and E** come into sync with each other; thus, creating the MATRIX OF WISDOM.

I see **Rows G and H** red and blue sections separated by the black area denoting one (1) and eight (8). This reminded me of the CYCLES OF DIVINE CREATION where there are eleven cycles in the first two chapters of Genesis: Virgo holding the Scales of Libra. I had pondered for years as to where the precedent for these cycles were imbues in the Genesis Creation Account and now the answer is, the MATRIX OF WISDOM.

Rows G and H I take as human reasoning as to the most logical way of expressing how humanity tends to believe ***"God separates the heavens and the earth"***; however, I see this pattern as symbolizing the bare minimum requirement of ego-consciousness and the unconscious mind deflating itself trying to sync together realizing that the psyche is not the end all and be all and that only a higher spiritual power can be of any assistance to life's endeavors. I do believe that Anubis' scales and/or Libra's scales symbolize the state of the psyche: ego-consciousness and the unconscious mind at materialistic death: i.e. ego-deflation not physical death. The initiate's genuflection of his or her psyche in total submission to God is in effect requesting that God enter his or her life. Human reason and logic says, **Rows G and H** should move forward toward each other intermingling with each other forming the Genesis Formula; however, from the perspective of Psychotherapy ego-consciousness having intercourse with the unconscious mind is called the Transcendent Function[1], which aids the patient along the Individuation process, becoming oneself as a human being, and it may lead the initiate into an Initiatic Visionary Experience; however, the Transcendent Function per se is not a spiritual function.

Whereas, **Rows I and J** may appear to be in sync with the Transcendent Function concept; however, it is diametrically opposite to **Rows G and H** thought process. Think of **Rows G and H** as going west to east (red) and east to west (blue) to intertwine with each other: this is iconoclastic thought because it only believes in what it sees on the horizon: ***"if I don't see it I don't believe it"***.

---

[1] https://www.amazon.com/Transcendent-Function-Psychological-Dialogue-Unconscious/dp/0791459780/ref=sr_1_1?s=books&ie=UTF8&qid=1466782461&sr=1-1&keywords=transcendent+function

"Then Jesus said to Thomas "Put your finger here and look at My hands. Reach out your hand and put it into My side. Stop doubting and believe." Thomas replied, "My Lord and my God!" Jesus said to him, "Because you have seen Me, you have believed; blessed are those who have not seen, and yet have believed (John 20: 27-29)."

Now think of **Rows I and J** smashing into **Rows G and H** from the north going south; thus, creating a whole new paradigmatic way of life: raison d'être. That is the Initiatic Visionary Experience. This entire book is based upon that concept alone.

This north/south paradigm (Holy Spirit - Cygnus X-3) crossing the east/west horizon is similar in every way to the chaotic laws of Washington DC (north) going through the Potomac River (east/west horizon) into Virginia (south) where the initiate has to turn those tyrannical THOU SHALT NOT laws into fit for human habitation THOU SHALT laws. The Potomac River (horizon) symbolizes the same old same old; for the reason that, the tyrannical laws coming out of Washington DC or any government do not seem impeachable unless of course politicians are bribed to dilute the laws into being superfluous. This latter is satanic and ego-driven and not spiritual. To live life in any part of the world one has to be guided by the spiritual laws of the universe and not through hubris.

The first verse of Genesis reads *"In the beginning God 'separated' the beginning and ends of the heaven and the beginning and ends of the earth".* What does it mean by saying *"the beginning and ends",* which is an interpretation of the Hebrew word את, which are the first (Aleph) and last (Tav) letters of the Hebrew coder (alphabet). This word את is used twenty-six (26) times, which symbolizes Yahweh in the first chapter of Genesis and it is never-ever translated into the vernacular of other languages. I interpret this word to mean "beginning and ends"; for the reason that, the two letters that make up the word are the first and last letters of the Hebrew alphabet, which implies that there is a complete Hebrew alphabets being inferred every time ALEPH א and TAV ת are use together to form the Hebrew word את. One is spiritual: i.e. Quadrivium (heaven) and one is materialistic: i.e. Trivium (Earth). And this is precisely why every single letter in the Hebrew and Greek alphabets in the Judaeo Christian Scriptures has a numerical digit assigned to it. This, essentially, makes every single letter of the bible a Vesica Piscis: i.e. the God/Man paradigm. **Rows I and J** illustrate this beginning and end paradigm via numerical digits (Quadrivium); whereas, the first chapter of Genesis denotes that very same concept via the Trivium (Hebrew alphabet).

Finally, I want to point out and emphasize the obvious that arithmetical and grammatical data, colors, literature, paintings, monuments, diagrams and charts are merely tools that allow each initiate to express his or her understanding of the WORD OF GOD. These tools per se are superfluous and meaningless unless what they express is understood.

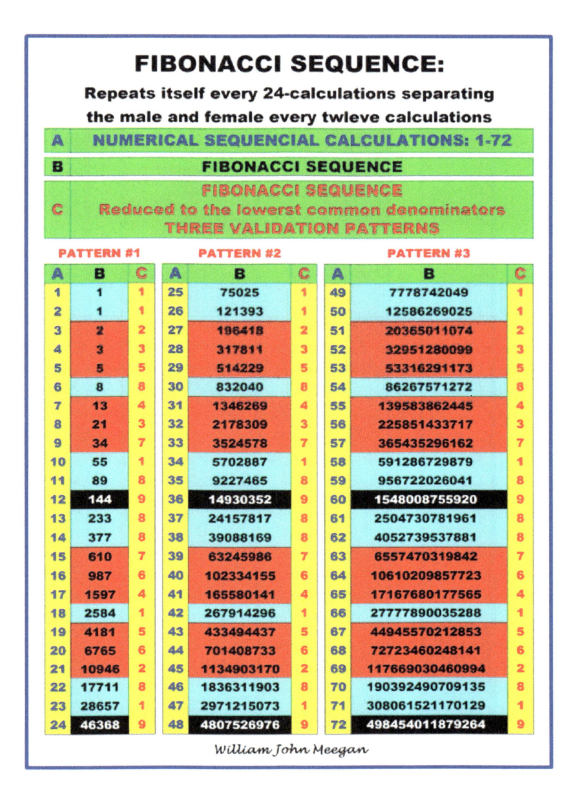

FIBONACCI SEQUENCE:

Repeats itself every 24-calculations separating
the male and female every twleve calculations

A	NUMERICAL SEQUENCIAL CALCULATIONS: 1-72
B	FIBONACCI SEQUENCE
C	FIBONACCI SEQUENCE Reduced to the lowerst common denominators THREE VALIDATION PATTERNS

PATTERN #1

A	B	C
1	1	1
2	1	1
3	2	2
4	3	3
5	5	5
6	8	8
7	13	4
8	21	3
9	34	7
10	55	1
11	89	8
12	144	9
13	233	8
14	377	8
15	610	7
16	987	6
17	1597	4
18	2584	1
19	4181	5
20	6765	6
21	10946	2
22	17711	8
23	28657	1
24	46368	9

PATTERN #2

A	B	C
25	75025	1
26	121393	1
27	196418	2
28	317811	3
29	514229	5
30	832040	8
31	1346269	4
32	2178309	3
33	3524578	7
34	5702887	1
35	9227465	8
36	14930352	9
37	24157817	8
38	39088169	8
39	63245986	7
40	102334155	6
41	165580141	4
42	267914296	1
43	433494437	5
44	701408733	6
45	1134903170	2
46	1836311903	8
47	2971215073	1
48	4807526976	9

PATTERN #3

A	B	C
49	7778742049	1
50	12586269025	1
51	20365011074	2
52	32951280099	3
53	53316291173	5
54	86267571272	8
55	139583862445	4
56	225851433717	3
57	365435296162	7
58	591286729879	1
59	956722026041	8
60	1548008755920	9
61	2504730781961	8
62	4052739537881	8
63	6557470319842	7
64	10610209857723	6
65	17167680177565	4
66	27777890035288	1
67	44945570212853	5
68	72723460248141	6
69	117669030460994	2
70	190392490709135	8
71	308061521170129	1
72	498454011879264	9

William John Meegan

THE FIBONACCI SEQUENCE SEPARATES THE MALE AND THE FEMALE

A	1 2 3 4 5 6 7 8 9 10 11 12
B	1 2 3 5 8 13 21 34 55 89 144
C	1 1 2 3 5 8 4 3 7 1 8
D	8 8 7 6 4 1 5 6 2 8 1 9
E	233 377 610 987 1597 2584 4181 6765 10946 17711 28657 46368
F	13 14 15 16 17 18 19 20 21 22 23 24

MASCULINE (ego-consciousness)

G	1 1 2 3 4 5 1 4 5 6 7 8 1 9
H	8 8 7 6 5 8 5 6 7 8 8 9

FEMININE (unconscious mind)

GENESIS FORMULA

I	4 1 3 1 2 1 2 1 3 1 4 1 9
J	5 8 6 8 7 7 8 6 8 5 1 9

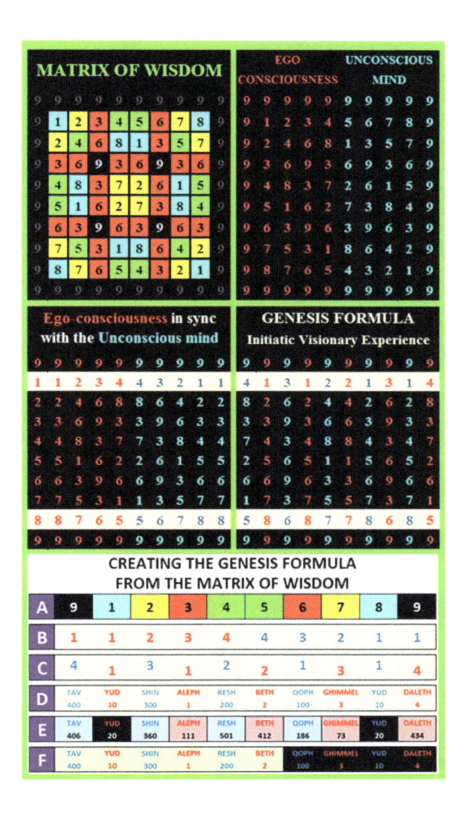

HOW MANY CHROMOSOMES DO PEOPLE HAVE?

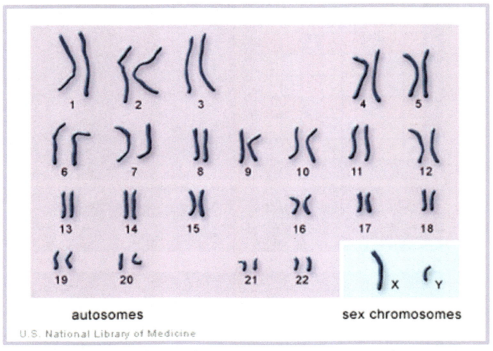

"In humans, each cell normally contains 23 pairs of chromosomes, for a total of 46. Twenty-two of these pairs, called autosomes, look the same in both males and females. The 23rd pair, the sex chromosomes, differs between males and females. Females have two copies of the X chromosome, while males have one X and one Y chromosome."

"The 22 autosomes are numbered by size. The other two chromosomes, X and Y, are the sex chromosomes. This picture of the human chromosomes lined up in pairs is called a karyotype."

https://ghr.nlm.nih.gov/primer/basics/howmanychromosomes

THE TEMPLE OF GOD

Apparently, the whole purpose of religion is to build the Eternal Temple of God in the Soul and the only way that can possibly be done is for the initiate to be Born Again and to have God as his only confidant.

A comparative analysis between these two patterns in the MATRIX OF WISDOM will bring forth what the initiate is commissioned to do with the four mystical elements: Fire (Dot), Earth (line), Air (angle) and Water (circle) that are inherent in his or her psyche (see chapter twelve: Patterns in the Matrix of Wisdom).

Going from the Fibonacci sequence (Time) to the Genesis Formula (Timelessness) is taking LIGHT creation and building The Eternal Temple of God. Here in the above image it can be envisaged how Chartres Cathedral was built (see chapter nine).

1. The 1s and 8s (Fire) symbolized the spiritual light of creation: i.e. God that comes through the windows and dome of the sacred building.
   a. This would be symbolic of light coming in through the stain glass windows to spiritually interpret the biblical stories painted on them, which would be analogous to the stone statues telling biblical stories that surround the building.
2. The 2s and 7s (Earth) symbolized the concretized statues displaying biblical story that surround the cathedral.
3. The 3s and 6s (Air) is the generic pattern of the churches, cathedrals, temples and other sacred spaces that are created for religious purposes.
4. The 4s and 5s (Water) symbolizes all the elements of creation coming together in unanimity.

There is more to analyzing these two images in the MATRIX OF WISDOM than I have discussed here. I want to leave something for the reader to find.

CHAPTER NINETEEN

THE CYCLES OF DIVINE CREATION AND THE FIRST TWO CHAPTERS OF GENESIS

My first discovery in the bible was a nine part cycle I intuited out of the first chapter of Genesis around December 1976/January 1977. I was at this time about two and half years into my biblical studies when I came across the writings of Mary Baker Eddy: SCIENCE and HEALTH: with Key to the Scriptures[1]. Mrs. Eddy's works is based upon Christian metaphysics and her writings educated me into an excellent understanding of God, which my birth religion, Catholicism, failed to provide me with up to that point in my life. Mrs. Eddy talked mainly about the falsehoods that mortal mind believes and is prone to. I reasoned out that if Mrs. Eddy is right and I believe she is, there is no doubt in my mind that somehow her teachings were already mythologically codified in the bible. Since I was born a Roman Catholic and Catholicism is basically symbolism and Mrs. Eddy metaphysics were devoid of symbolism I was working against a paradox of opposites that I knew needed to be somehow psychically integrated as one unified system of thought.

December 1976/January 1977 was extremely important to me because I finally found someone teaching Christianity that made rational sense; however, I still found it tremendously difficult to understand anything about the bible. I had read the bible twice from Genesis to Revelations since August 1974 and I was literally horrified by what I read. The wars and various criminal activities in the Old Testament were incredible considering I was taught from adolescent years that it was very spiritual library of books. I knew after a few years of studying the bible that something was out of synch as to how the bible was interpreted. I could not fathom why human history was permeated with religious war over the content of the bible. My 26th-30th-years were excruciatingly mind-boggling for me to wrap my mind around this difficult and inexplicable issues relating to questioning the bible and understanding its biblical teachings.

As the years went by this Gordian Knot so-to-speak was being untied for me psychically for I realized there were two types of people on earth that read the sacred scriptures around the world iconoclastically: i.e. with absolutely no knowledge of symbolism: they read the bible literally from a fundamental perspective and the other type of bible reader read the sacred scriptures via symbolism: i.e. iconographically and/or metaphysically.

In the early stages of my studying the bible, not knowing what else to do, I decided to read just the first chapter of Genesis over and over again on a daily basis to see if something would emerge from it over time. Within a matter of a few weeks I notice that the there was no feasible reason, that I could reason with, for the first two verse of Genesis to be the prologue of the bible. It initially appeared to be a rehashing of creation before creation even began.

Another problematic issue I was having with the bible at this time is that many Christian and Jewish Scholars were making comments about the bible that literally made no sense whatsoever. For example, Saint Augustine in his work, CONFESSIONS[2] says, '*I will not say what one author says, that God was creating hell before he created the heavens and the earth.*' When I went to the first verse of Genesis trying to figure out what Saint Augustine was talking about I

---

[1] http://www.amazon.com/Science-Health-Key-Scriptures-Authorized/dp/0879520000/ref=sr_1_1?s=books&ie=UTF8&qid=1464396255&sr=1-1&keywords=science+and+health+with+key+to+the+scriptures
[2] http://www.amazon.com/Confessions-Saint-Augustine-Image-Classics/dp/0385029551/ref=sr_1_6?ie=UTF8&qid=1464478516&sr=8-6&keywords=st+augustine+confessions

was totally perplexed. It would take me almost twenty-years to figure out what he was talking about.

By chance I learned one day that the word **"BARA"** in Hebrew was interpreted not only as **"created"**; but, also as **"choose, select and separated"**. This got me thinking that the first verse of Genesis could read, *"in the beginning God 'separated' the heavens and the earth'*. This idea is similar to Atlas hold up the world separating the Earth from the Sky. The second verse of Genesis has *"the spirit of Elohym moved (pouted, brooded) over the face of the waters and darkness was on the face of the deep"*.

Now I knew about the circumcision rite performed on every male child on the eight day after being born, *"And when eight days were accomplished for the circumcising of the child, his name was called JESUS, which was so named by the angel before he was conceived in the womb (Luke 2:21)."* Circumcision was a separating process.

Then I looked at the bleakness of the second verse of Genesis in contrast to the crucifixion of Christ, who died on the ninth hour:*"Now it was about the sixth hour, and there was darkness over all the earth until the ninth hour. Then the sun was darkened, and the veil of the temple was torn in two. And when Jesus had cried out with a loud voice, He said, "Father, 'into your hands I commit My spirit.'" Having said this, He breathed His last (Luke 23:44-46)"*.

I reasoned of course that with the first six days of creation and the first two verses of Genesis as eight (8) and (9) that somehow the seventh (7) day of creation: chapter two of Genesis had to be involved in this cycle. It took another twenty months to October 1978 to develop the nine part cycle into a twelve part cycle.

Serendipitously, I went to a social gathering where a man by the name of Dennis Cole (Astrologer) gave a lecture on Astrology and he handed out a single sheet of paper with a one-line definition for each sign of the Zodiac. I was immediately captivated by the tenth sign of the Zodiac Capricorn having the line, *"the goat the fed the gods"*. I already knew that the Hebrew word for God: ELOHYM was interpreted as "gods, angels". In the first day of creation *'Elohym desired that there be light and there was light'*. If Darkness was the *"the goat that fed the gods"* then it would represent Capricorn the Goat. This was not difficult to accept; because, Capricorn was the DARKEST month of the year.

I felt that the first nine cycles were the first nine Zodiac signs, which would make DARKNESS as the tenth house in the first day of creation. In the eleventh house HEAVEN symbolized number two and the FIRMAMENT symbolized number eleventh in Aquarius and in the third day of creation EARTH symbolized the number three and ELOHYM represented number twelve in the house of Pisces.

The curious thing about that sheet of paper on the twelve Zodiacal signs that Dennis Cole gave me that day, I immediately rejected Astrology after it inspired my thought to developed the nine part cycle into a twelve part cycle; because, Catholicism prohibited studying Astrology.

These were my fledgling thoughts and though I was somewhat wrong I was unknowingly right about many aspects of it. Now I had a twelve part cycle: **10-1, 11-2, 12-3, 4, 5, 6, 7, 8 and 9** that I correctly manipulated into **10-1, 11-2, 12-3, 7-4, 8-5 and 9-6**. I knew absolutely nothing about Astrology outside of what was on that sheet of paper. I called this intuited cycle the CYCLE OF GENESIS, which I would rename four and a half years later on April 11-15, 1983 the CYCLE OF DARKNESS when I finally discovered what the CYCLE OF GENESIS was about.

During that twenty-month period between December/January 1976/1977 and October 1978 I was continuously studying Christian Science metaphysics and one day I was instantly cured of a very addictive smoking habit on December 30th 1977. On that day my mind went into a spiritual state of upheaval that Christian Science calls **Mental Chemicalization.** What caused the upheaval of forces to be activated in my psyche that day was the realization that the sacred scriptures were totally symbolic. At the moment of the healing I was actually studying three separate accounts of the scriptures for hours over the similarities between the stories of Noah's Ark raised above the waters and Moses serpent in the wilderness was raised to heal the people and Jesus Christ was raised up on the Cross. I was flipping back and forth between the three accounts trying to synchronize them into a comprehensive understanding of symbolism. Previous to that moment I only read the bible symbolically from a theoretical perspective.

Mrs. Eddy described the mind in this state of **Mental Chemicalization** as the stirring of the muddy river bed where the sediments had to settle back down again so the waters would be cleansed; however, at a later date I related my cure of being addicted to cigarettes as analogous to the New Testament account of the Pool of Bethesda where an angel periodically came down and cured the first man into the pool (John 1:1-15). I believe that this spiritual healing took place; for the reason that, it was a spiritual prerequisite to what was to spiritually transpire in June 1978. The story in John's gospel about the Pool of Bethesda and the cripple man being healed by Jesus is; for the reason that, the man understood that he could not get down into the pool on his own volition.

In June 1978 I had my Initiatic Visionary Experience gifted to me by God. I saw the sum-total of all knowledge; I had a glimpse of eternity. Of course the psyche cannot possibly retain that nanosecond of time; but, I knew instantly there was no such thing as death and I understood that a billion years of time was as if it was nothing more than a nanosecond of time. It took me many decades of research to understand what that vision was all about.

On April 11th 1983 I came across a volume on the [12 Sons and 12 Signs: Astrology in the Bible](http://www.amazon.com)[3], by David A. Womack, I purchased it from a book warehouse for $0.44 now on the internet it is worth comparatively a fortune. Synchronistically Mr. Womack wrote that book in 1978.

On April 11th 1983 David A. Womack book taught me the basics of Astrology. What initially enamored me into purchasing it was the fact that it had to do with the twelve sons of Jacob, which was a basic part of the Genesis storyline. I never did understand, nor did I try to understand, David A. Womack thesis; though, I am grateful for his 101-thesis on Astrology teaching me about the four Triplicities: Earth, Air, Fire and Water of Astrology in contrast to the three Quadruplicities: Cardinal, Fixed and Mutable signs of Astrology. Some readers may see the Triplicities and the Quadruplicities as the rudimentary alphabet of Astrology and so they are; however, to me at the time it was a great revelation for I knew nothing about Astrology and I was about to violate one of the Roman Catholic Church great edicts: not to inquire into Astrology. I was frustrated not to have had any success whatsoever in finding something, in the libraries of the world, about the cycle I discovered in the first chapter of Genesis. Purchasing that book was a moment of frustration lashing out at the edict of Catholicism against researching Astrology and the Tarot Cards. Some years before in the beginning of 1976 I was introduced to the Tarot Cards, which I summarily dismissed after six months; however, years later I would research them again in greater detail.

Over the decades that followed I would learned that; though, Catholicism explicitly provides the laity with the secret mysteries of the bible, hidden esoterically in plain sight, via the Roman Catholic Church's literature, artworks and monuments Catholicism hierarchy prevent the unworthy initiates, that practically includes 99.9...% of its one billion members, from discovering the secret mysteries of the sacred scriptures and the secret teachings of the Roman Catholic Church's by publishing edicts that would literally prevent the laity from discovering the truth about the mysteries of the bible. This is all about how the WORD OF GOD is supposed to be taught mystically to the laity by God's chosen mystics covertly

---

[3] http://www.amazon.com/12-signs-sons-Astrology-Bible/dp/B0006CT73I?ie=UTF8&keywords=12%20sons%20and%2012%20signs&qid=1464464048&ref_=sr_1_1&sr=8-1

via the Esoteric Science rather than overtly exoterically as societal mores are taught to the citizenry. The laity has absolutely no idea that they are imprisoned in eternal hellfire and damnation and/or purgatory in this lifetime via their own ignorance of iconography (esotericism). The average member of the laity has no idea that he or she has to venture out on his or her own volition into the forest, serendipitously, in search of the Holy Grail. There is no physical grail; for the reason that, the search itself is the grail; however, it is nigh unto an impossibility to get a lackadaisical individual out of his or her lounging on the oceanic beach in the phantasmagoria of the tsunami-paradise they each have psychically conceived and created for themselves. Joseph Campbell the great mythologist called it, *"the twinkle-twinkle principle"*. You heard the old saying, *"life is what happens to you while making plans"*. Daydreaming and making plans is, basically, doing nothing while the world spins around you.

What happened on those four days between April 11th and April 15th sent my mind into another psychic upheaval, which would not allow me to sleep for 96-hours and I had to seek help from doctors to get sleeping pills to force sleep. The same month that Dennis Cole gave me that sheet of paper, September 1978, a Jungian student showed a film to the same social group of Carl G. Jung[4] in his old age being interviewed. He made a remarkable statement, *"I don't believe there is a God, I know there is a God"*. I knew instantly; because, of my vision in June 1978, what he was talking about.

I read a number of Carl G. Jung's works; thus, I was somewhat prepared for what happened to me between April 11th to 15th, 1983. I realized that what was happening to me was my unconscious mind was trying to come forward to dominate my conscious life. After sleeping for a number of days I looked back over what I had accomplished with numerous circular diagrams spread all over the place.

What happened during that four day period was that I took the CYCLE OF GENESIS and compared it to the CYCLE OF LIGHT: Astrological Cycle numbered sequentially 1-12 and by doing a comparative analysis after learning about both the differences and the symbiotic interrelationship between the Triplicities and the Quadruplicities in Astrology it was quite apparent that the CYCLE OF GENESIS obviously was dealing with these two diverse concepts of Astrology. This forced me to analytically compare continuously ad nauseam how the CYCLE OF GENESIS was possibly derived from the CYCLE OF LIGHT. By using the number seven (7), as in the seventh day of creation in the second chapter of Genesis, as an anchor I completed the first sector (11-cycles) of the seventh sign of the Zodiac out of Astrology's twelve signs, which totaled to 1584-cycles. Each sign of the Zodiac would have a 132-cycles (and this is based upon the premise that each sign of the Zodiac allowed each of the twelve numbers to be anchored in its primary house. Those 132-cycles of each sign of the Zodiac would later relate to the letter RESH ר; because, 132 is a transposition of the number 213, which the letters of RESH ר breaks down to. This infers that the rib taken out of Adam was the sign of the Zodiac he was born into. This latter would not be discovered until years later.

The next thing I did with the cycles was to try to astrologically orientate each word of the sacred scriptures to each of the eleven cycles. This is where I reflected back to October 1978 when I created the CYCLE OF GENESIS by originally designating certain words to different signs of the zodiac, which showed me that I initially had the right idea back then.

Neither the months between December 1976/1977 and October 1978 nor the years between October 1978 and April 1983 were wasted. There was much I did not know about religion and during that almost seven years period I went through many sects of Protestantism to learn if there was any truth to them and basically what I learn about Protestantism boiled down to the intellect of the charismatic leader of the group. Years later I would learn that I had instinctively done what Parzival[5] did in his quest for the Holy Grail and what Siddhartha[6] did in his quest for a spiritual leader to educate him.

---

[4] https://en.wikipedia.org/wiki/Carl_Jung
[5] http://www.amazon.com/Parzival-Penguin-Classics-Wolfram-Eschenbach/dp/0140443614/ref=sr_1_1?s=books&ie=UTF8&qid=1464472482&sr=1-1&keywords=parzival
[6] http://www.amazon.com/Siddhartha-Hermann-Hesse/dp/8129102048/ref=tmm_hrd_swatch_0?_encoding=UTF8&qid=1464472378&sr=1-1

A very remarkable thing happened after going over those charts and papers, I practically stopped studying the bible per se for almost twelve years not completely but almost and it came about because of the following.

'Who was going to believe my report'? My work on the bible just brought me incontrovertible evidence that the bible was symbolically and mathematically structured. I was living in a world where everybody around me would not believe a word of it. So I looked around my library, which was one bookcase at the time and found that only Dante Alighieri's La Divina Commedia (The Divine Comedy)[7] was the only possible book I could immediately test for such a possibility. My thoughts along these lines about Dante work was that there were a hundred chapters and thousands of verses, which could possibly generate percentages in the compositional structure of his work. In less than five minutes I would see that it was obvious that Dante did codify some kind of a mathematical system to his work (see Appendix).

It took me twelve years from April 1983 to almost the end of 1994 to figure out Dante Alighieri mathematical system and that is; for the reason that, to finish my mathematical analysis on his work I needed to envisage the MATRIX OF WISDOM, which I did not know existed at the time of my discovery of it.

The reason that I have gone into these trials and tribulations so-to-speak concerning my first twenty-years in biblical studies was to warn the reader via the evidence of my own experience about the dangers of going into this research unprepared as I was. The reader has to understand that he or she has to give his or her *whole heart, mind, soul, time, finances and resources* to search for knowledge of the WORD OF GOD. If the initiate does enter into the quest for the knowledge of God with his or her *whole heart, mind, soul, time, finances* and resources God with protect the worthy initiate. If the individual goes into the quest halfheartedly or for fame and fortune, may God have mercy on his or her soul.

I got into numerous other subjects in my researches over the next twenty some odd years after I finished my mathematical research on Dante's La Divina Commedia and I returned to my studies on the Cycles of Divine Creation[8], which I wrote an independent Academic paper on. Below I provide an image denoting the names I gave each of the CYCLES OF DIVINE CREATION after I culled them out of the first two chapters of Genesis. By studying this image of eleven cycles it can be easily envisaged that they symbolically create the Scales of Libra held aloft by Virgo. The reader can imagine my surprise when I finally figured out what Saint Augustine was talking about. I discovered, for myself, that God was creating hell before he created the heavens and the earth. The reason that Virgo holds the Scales of Libra is; because, there is an ancient astrological law that the zodiacal cycle cannot move unless Virgo moves first. The secret is that the first decan of Virgo is Coma, which in Hebrew means **DESIRE**.

These eleven cycles could very well represent the oscillation process of the Fibonacci sequence relating to the 23-sets of chromosomes. In fact I do believe that his is what the Scales of Libra are all about spirituality or materiality. And this judging process goes on nanosecond by nanosecond infinitely.

There can literally be no doubt that these are symbolically the scales of Anubis. Notice how the eleven cycles are split between the Triplicities (LIGHT) and the Quadruplicities (DARKNESS). These eleven cycles are analogous to the Labyrinth of Chartres Cathedral in contrast to the Maze that ego-consciousness creates for itself in the depths of its own egocentrism.

The months of the year and the signs of the zodiac are unaware of each other as are the Triplicities and the Quadruplicities as are the Trivium and the Quadrivium in writing the scriptures. Ego-consciousness is equally unaware of the unconscious mind.

Looking at the Fibonacci sequence, as outline n the last chapter, it can be envisaged that the oscillation of the Golden Ratio is also a symbol of the Scales of Libra, which the CYCLES OF DIVINE creation symbolizes. The question that the Scales of Libra (Anubis) ask is, *"do you live life iconoclastically or iconographically?"* This is the secret of life and the most important issue every soul has to face in life on an extremely mystical level.

---

[7] http://www.amazon.com/Divine-Comedy-3-Set/dp/B000J15V2C/ref=sr_1_4?s=books&ie=UTF8&qid=1464474486&sr=1-4&keywords=louis+biancolli
[8] http://www.slideshare.net/williamjohnmeegan/the-cycles-of-divine-creation-the-universal-mathematical-matrix

As I look back over the span of years to December/January 1976/1977 I see that nine part-cycle as a kernel of thought that extrapolated out over the years to all my research since; though, I am a Roman Catholic I credit the metaphysical writing of Mary Baker Eddy for that intuitive mystical insight.

THE CYCLES OF DIVINE CREATION

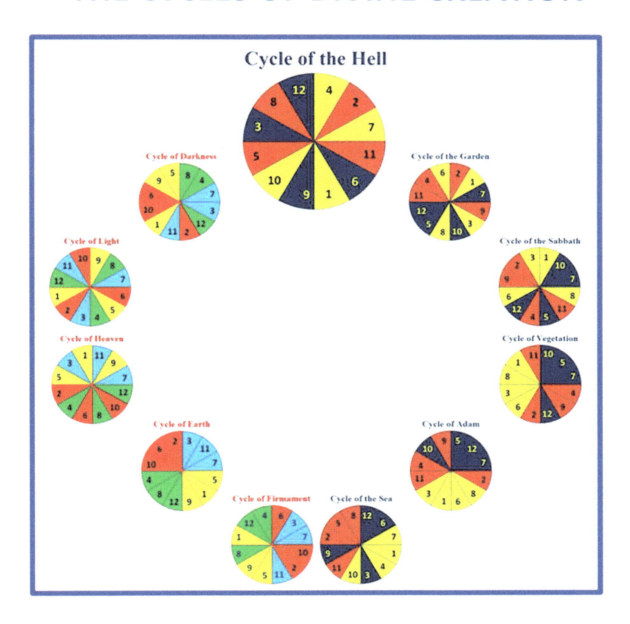

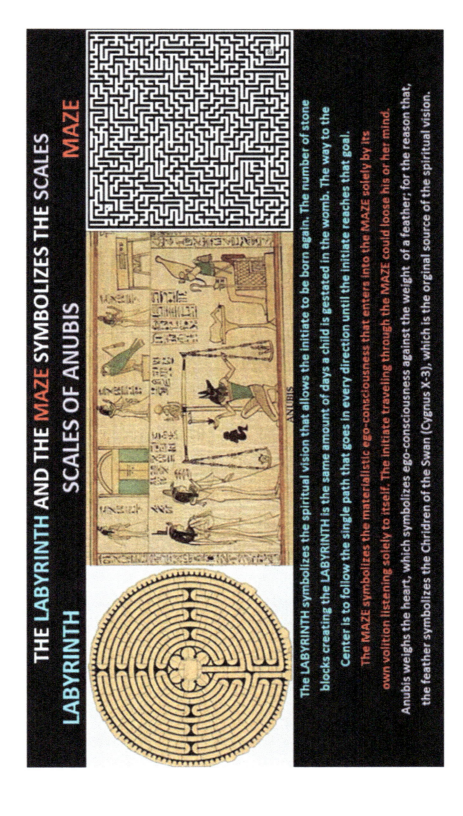

THE LABYRINTH AND THE MAZE SYMBOLIZES THE SCALES

LABYRINTH

MAZE

SCALES OF ANUBIS

The LABYRINTH symbolizes the spiritual vision that allows the initiate to be born again. The number of stone blocks creating the LABYRINTH is the same amount of days a child is gestated in the womb. The way to the Center is to follow the single path that goes in every direction until the initiate reaches that goal.

The MAZE symbolizes the materialistic ego-consciousness that enters into the MAZE solely by its own volition listening solely to itself. The initiate traveling through the MAZE could loose his or her mind. Anubis weighs the heart, which symbolizes ego-consciousness against the weight of a feather; for the reason that, the feather symbolizes the Chrildren of the Swan (Cygnus X-3), which is the orginal source of the spiritual vision.

APPENDIX

DANTE ALIGHIERI'S LA DIVINA COMMEDIA'S MATHEMATICAL SYSTEM

DANTE ALIGHIERI'S LA DIVINA COMMEDIA'S MATHEMATICAL SYSTEM

ABSTRACT

Esotericism is codified to normal everyday innocuous materials: literature, artworks and monuments. If scholars are to learn how to write esoteric documents in the future they will have to do it in a like manner in which La Divina Commedia's compositional structure was developed and formatted. The average person relaxed reading a book or nonchalantly walking around a cathedral would not expect there to be hidden meanings on every page or throughout the structure. These are featureless things that are seen every single day of our lives and we pay absolutely no attention to them. Who counts words and verses in a book and/or does an endless amount of mathematical calculations on that kind of material? It is said that psychiatrists see this kind of behavior as mental illness; thus, through peer pressure and societal mores the average person, if he or she ever heard of such behavior, discounts such means of obtaining knowledge in fear of being socially ostracized.

'Esotericism,' as I have come to understand the definition of that word means *'hidden knowledge'*. Esotericism is a precision mathematical and grammatical science: the SEVEN LIBERAL ARTS: Arithmetic, Music/Harmony, Geometry, Astronomy/Astrology, Grammar, Rhetoric and Logic/Dialectic integrated as one unify system of thought. It is the same Esoteric Science revered by the ancient Mystery Schools no matter where they are located around the world. It is the same universal mathematical and grammatical science utilized by all cultures in all times and climes. In using the word 'esoteric' or derivatives thereof I am not speaking as modernity does when using that word 'esoteric' in referring to nuances in a profession. I am speaking of God's Ambiance deliberately programming (codified esoterically) mathematical and grammatical sciences into the literature, artworks and monuments of different religions to teach the science of the psyche/soul.

In this paper I am going to present a clear and unambiguous example of esotericism from out of the mundane materials relating solely to the compositional structure of a trilogy: La Divina Commedia by Dante Alighieri (1265-1321). This means that just by knowing the amount of books (3) in the series, the amount of chapters in those books (100) and the amount of verses in those 100-chapters (14,233) a very sophisticated and esoteric mathematical system can be culled from them just by contemplatively analyzing that material.

This analysis demonstrates that from just one hundred three digit numbers (small amount of data) an enormous amount of knowledge was esoterically stored. From this analysis in can be envisaged that the ancient authors had a system of thought that allowed them to create by imitation (commentary on the MONAD) an extremely advance data storage and retrieval system.

This paper will discuss only the compositional structure of La Divina Commedia from a totally mathematical perspective and not from the allegorical mythology that the trilogy is written in: i.e. Dante mystic journey through the three realms of spirit: Inferno, Purgatorio and Paradiso. What I am expecting to demonstrate in doing this is that if the reader can grasp that the so-called innocuous materials in the compositional structure of the trilogy is codified esoterically then so too is the entire storyline (Dante's Mystic Journey) of La Divina Commedia structured esoterically within its fold.

INTRODUCTION

The mathematical system esoterically codified to La Divina Commedia by Dante Alighieri is the first ancient work that I was able to envisage a complete and undistorted esoteric system of thought. It took twelve years to completely cull this esoteric system from out of Dante's trilogy. The reason it took so long is because I unrealistically intuited that Dante used a model to mathematically structure and contain his overall system and I stubbornly refused to give up the idea of envisaging it. When I first independently visualize and developed the Universal Mathematical Matrix: Prima Materia (Perennial Matrix), which I now call the MATRIX OF WISDOM, by doodling with the first nine numbers, I did not think much of it; however, unpredictably it turned out to be the model I was seeking. After making the connection between Dante's La Divina Commedia and the one MATRIX OF WISDOM it took some time to analyze it in relationship to the trilogy's system of mathematics, which of course brought a great deal more material to the fore. In addition it took twelve years to analyze and develop this system because I was, for the lack of a better word, a pioneer, in this heretofore unknown discipline, at least from modernity perspective.

In December/January 1976/1977 I discovered a nine part cyclic pattern in the first chapter of Genesis (see chapter nineteen). It took me over six more years to figure out what that cycle was; however, that cycle inspired me to search for another work in literature that was mathematically structured. When I first embarked upon analyzing Dante Alighieri's La Divina Commedia, on April 15, 1983, from a mathematical perspective I had neither a college education[1] nor any serious mathematical training whatsoever and my knowledge of the world's disciplines in religion, mythology, symbolism, philosophies, etc., etc. was pitifully lacking. Like Parzival I entered the forest alone completely ignorant of my surroundings.

There is no precedence in modernity for the existence of the Esoteric Science, that I am aware of, that I am about to introduce in this paper. There are neither books[2] nor papers nor articles that can be reference concerning this very ancient and extremely simple; yet, sophisticated mathematical discipline being laid out here. I am probably, though I may be wrong, the first person in modernity, since the days of the alchemists in the wake of the Renaissance and Baroque periods, to envisage, develop and elucidate this mathematical and grammatical science in any meaningful way: i.e. explicitly. Though others claim to know what esotericism is I have yet to find one book, one paper, one article or any school of thought that is within light years of what I am about to lay out in this paper. Though I do not want to be critical of anybody it must be understood that modernity's present understanding of esotericism is preposterous when considering the content of this chapter and the forty years of my researches, which actually hails back to 1974[3]. In fact this chapter has been considerably shortened to accommodate modernity lack of knowledge concerning this Esoteric Science.

It also behooves me to point out the obvious. I entered into this research not knowing anything about esotericism or even of its existence. I was merely a fledgling student serendipitously working my way through years of research not really having a game plan as to how to gear my studies.

❖ I had no idea *if there was mathematics codified to ancient literature* outside of what I envisaged in the first chapter of Genesis.
❖ I had no idea, *if there was mathematics codified to ancient literature*, if it was sporadic or system-wide that encompassed every single word of the texts.
❖ I had no idea, *if there was mathematics codified to ancient literature*, if it would be laid out in simple or advanced mathematics.
❖ I had no idea, if I would in a few minutes, after picking up Dante Alighieri's trilogy; put it back on the bookshelf.
❖ Most importantly, I had no idea *if there was mathematics codified to ancient literature*, if it would be the same mathematical system as that laid out in the Judeao Christian scriptures or whether it would be an entirely different mathematical or numeric system altogether.

As time went by I would discover that the mathematical system codified to Dante Alighieri's La Divina Commedia was known worldwide and codified esoterically into all religions and mythologies in all times and climes.

So when the reader of this chapter sees how extremely simple this mathematical and esoteric system of thought is now *'neatly packaged and laid out as it is'* I want that person to realize that this is merely Dante Alighieri method of codifying the Esoteric Science to his creative work. There is not a work of literature, artwork or monument anywhere in antiquity and/or modernity that have the Esoteric Science codified to it that has been duplicated by other esoterists[4]. In antiquity that would be an anathema, *"thou shalt not steal (plagiarize)"*. Every single work of literature, artwork and/or monument from out of antiquity is a variation on this theme of esotericism. If the reader of this paper believes the mathematics outlined in this paper is so simple (child's play) I challenge that individual to explain how Dante Alighieri did it. Even as I outline and illustrate Dante's mathematical system that he esoterically codified to his work I cannot explain how he did it. There are so many incredibly difficult variants within his mathematical system that simultaneously he was creating multiple magic squares within each other with multiple graphic images within those mathematical variants. If by chance a reader is capable of grasping how Dante Alighieri did codify esotericism to his work that does not mean that the reader can simply go to the next esoteric work and understand how that artist did it. Yes, all esoterists use the one and only Esoteric Science to codify to their literary works, artworks and/or monuments. Artworks are the simplest to understand esoterically; however, literature entails different languages[5] and different mythologies (storylines). Translations[6] are an anathema for obvious reasons. Monuments are more difficult because schematics are necessary to obtain every mathematical nuance throughout the structure in order to appreciate its overall esotericism. That would be somewhat difficult without the blueprints at hand.

La Inferno, La Purgatorio and La Paradiso by Allen Mandelbaum[7] is recommended because it is a bilingual text Italian/English and is translated in the tradition of the Terza Rima (3-verse rhyme) in which Dante Alighieri originally wrote *La Divina Commedia*. There are also prose[8] translations that are not recommended because they distort the original intent of the author mathematically and are without knowledge of the hermetic (esoteric) science codified to the compositional structure of the Terza Rima. The Internet has many bilingual texts (translated and published in the original format of the Terza Rima). This work by Allen Mandelbaum and translations like it have the raw materials that the academic can study to confirm the validity of the esoteric science proffered and outlined here in this paper

The following materials in this paper are proffered to give a sense of the mathematical system codified to Dante Alighieri's *La Divina Commedia's compositional structure*. Below is but a small fraction of the esoteric system discerned from out of *La Divina Commedia;* though, it is comprehensive. This is given here to expound on Dante's use of the MATRIX OF WISDOM, which is a commentary on the MONAD.

I was looking for an ancient work that could possibly have a mathematical system codified to its textual structure. I had just made a remarkable discovery in the first chapter of Genesis relating to a numerical cycle I found there, which I will not discuss here in this article; however, those cycles can be read via the link THE CYCLES OF DIVINE CREATION & THE UNIVERSAL MATHEMATICAL MATRIX[9]. This discovery was so remarkable to my thought process at the time that it was overwhelming considering my world-view at the time. Such a discovery sent me looking for another ancient work that could possibly verify that this finding a mathematical structure in ancient literature was not a rare occurrence. In my library at the time there was but a few dozen volumes and Dante Alighieri La Divina Commedia was the only work that I could think of that could possible demonstrate a mathematical structure. It had three volumes, one hundred chapters and thousands of verses. *"One hundred chapters, possibly a hundred percent of something, may infer percentages"* or at least that was my initial thought process in thinking of Dante Alighieri's La Divina Commedia as a prospective candidate in my search for the possibility of mathematics codify to ancient literature. This idea led me to reach for Dante's trilogy to see if the possibility was there.

1. VOLUMES

The first thing that catches the reader's attention is the nature of the trilogy's compositional structure. Here Dante Alighieri delegates an exact amount of chapters/cantos, almost evenly throughout, to each one of the volumes in his trilogy. The very idea that Dante structured his La Divina Commedia (his personal narrative of his mystic journey) with such uniformity encouraged me at the outset to continue my initial probe into the trilogy's mathematical structure. The following pattern is revealed from out of the three volumes from a vertical perspective. Notice the verse-totals of the three VOLUMES. These totals would become crucial in the *finale* of this research.

❖ The first volume, *La Inferno* has 34 chapters/cantos (4720-verses).
❖ The second volume, *La Purgatorio* has 33 chapters/cantos (4755-verses).
❖ And the third volume, *La Paradiso* has 33 chapters/cantos (4758-verses).

2. SUM-DIGITS

La Divina Commedia has 100 (chapters), which hold a range of verses from 115-160, which has only 13-base numbers. Each chapter/canto is written in the tradition of the three-verse rhyme (Terza Rima) with the last verse ending singularly. This forces a pattern of each chapter/canto ending with a Sum Digit of 1, 4, or 7 *(take the first canto in La Inferno, which has 136 verses and reduce it to its lowest common denominator: 136 = 10 = 1 + 0 = 1, the second chapter of the La Inferno has 142 verses: 142 = 7, etc.)*; thus, across the expanse of 100 chapters/cantos of the La Divina Commedia, from a horizontal perspective, the following pattern reveals itself in the Sum Digits. Notice once again how the verses total per SUM DIGIT.

❖ There are 33 Sum Digit '1s' (4731-verses).
❖ And 34 Sum Digit '4s' (4825-verses).
❖ And 33 Sum Digit '7s' (4677-verses).

This vertical and horizontal pattern goes directly to symbolizing the worldwide indigenous religious paradigm; for the reason that the volumes symbolize fiery chaos: i.e. the Fire element coming down upon the fixed solid number symbolizing the Earth element symbolizing the east-west corridor of time..

3. CHART ILLUSTRATING THE VOLUMES AND SUM-DIGITS

Just from this above material from the Volumes and Sum Digits it can be envisage by a thoughtful individual knowing some "so-called" occult[10] materials that the Volumes represents chaos: a random disorder of numerical data scattered throughout the one hundred chapters. It was obvious to me that the Volumes represented **FIRE**: one of the four mystic elements in Astrology[11]: each of the Volumes produced a sum total of verses collectively all three volumes produced three totals totaling 14,233 verses. This idea that La Divina Commedia has mystic elements associated to it structure is because the Sum Digits displayed attributes of firmness such as the **EARTH** element seeing each Sum Digit is singular in nature and produces a sum total of verses: collectively all three Sum-Digits produced a total of 14,233 verses. Both the <mark>FIRE (Volumes)</mark> and <mark>EARTH (Sum Digits)</mark> elements each took on the entire content of the La Divina Commedia; therefore, it can be envisaged by the reader where my reasoning was leading me. There had to be two additional elements: <mark>AIR</mark> and <mark>WATER</mark> in La Divina Commedia mathematical system for my hypothesis to make any sense at all. This is based solely upon the cursory examination of the numerical structure of La Divina Commedia thus far. It doesn't take a rocket scientist to intuit that possibility. Here is where the idea that Astrology can be a predictive tool probably got its reputation seeing that mathematics itself is a predictive tool; however, that is about as far as I, personally, will venture into the realm of prognosticating future events.

Dante Alighieri's La Divina Commedia's Mathematics

Volumes

Inferno	Purgatorio	Paridiso
1) 136-1	1) 136-1	1) 142-7
2) 142-7	2) 133-7	2) 148-4
3) 136-1	3) 145-1	3) 130-4
4) 151-7	4) 139-4	4) 142-7
5) 142-7	5) 136-1	5) 139-4
6) 115-7	6) 151-7	6) 142-7
7) 130-4	7) 136-1	7) 148-4
8) 130-4	8) 139-4	8) 148-4
9) 133-7	9) 145-1	9) 142-7
10) 136-1	10) 139-4	10) 148-4
11) 115-7	11) 142-7	11) 139-4
12) 139-4	12) 136-1	12) 145-1
13) 151-7	13) 154-1	13) 142-7
14) 142-7	14) 151-7	14) 139-4
15) 124-7	15) 145-1	15) 148-4
16) 136-1	16) 145-1	16) 154-1
17) 136-1	17) 139-4	17) 142-7
18) 136-1	18) 145-1	18) 136-1
19) 133-7	19) 145-1	19) 148-4
20) 130-4	20) 151-7	20) 148-4
21) 139-4	21) 136-1	21) 142-7
22) 151-7	22) 154-1	22) 154-1
23) 148-4	23) 133-7	23) 139-4
24) 151-7	24) 154-1	24) 154-1
25) 151-7	25) 139-4	25) 139-4
26) 142-7	26) 148-4	26) 142-7
27) 136-1	27) 142-7	27) 148-4
28) 142-7	28) 148-4	28) 139-4
29) 139-4	29) 154-1	29) 145-1
30) 148-4	30) 145-1	30) 148-4
31) 145-1	31) 145-1	31) 142-7
32) 139-4	32) 160-7	32) 151-7
33) 157-4	33) 145-1	33) 145-1
34) 139-4		

Sum-Digits

7	1	4
Inferno	**Inferno**	**Inferno**
2) 142	1) 136	7) 130
4) 151	3) 136	8) 130
5) 142	10) 136	12) 139
6) 115	16) 136	20) 130
9) 133	17) 136	21) 139
11) 115	18) 136	23) 148
13) 151	27) 136	29) 139
14) 142	31) 145	30) 148
15) 124		32) 139
19) 133	**Purgatorio**	33) 157
22) 151	1) 136	34) 139
24) 151	3) 145	
25) 151	5) 136	**Purgatorio**
26) 142	7) 136	4) 139
28) 142	9) 145	8) 139
	12) 136	10) 139
Purgatorio	13) 154	17) 139
2) 133	15) 145	25) 139
6) 151	16) 145	26) 148
11) 142	18) 145	28) 148
14) 151	19) 145	
20) 151	21) 136	**Paradiso**
23) 133	22) 154	2) 148
27) 142	24) 154	3) 130
32) 160	29) 154	5) 139
	30) 145	7) 148
Paradiso	31) 145	8) 148
1) 142	33) 145	10) 148
4) 142		11) 139
6) 142	**Paradiso**	14) 139
9) 142	12) 145	15) 148
13) 142	16) 154	19) 148
17) 142	18) 136	20) 148
21) 142	22) 154	23) 139
26) 142	24) 154	25) 139
31) 142	29) 145	27) 148
32) 151	33) 145	28) 139
		30) 148

The four mystic elements are said to represent creation. Here it is seen that one hundred three digit number simulating chaos (<mark>FIRE</mark>) very much like the unconscious mind; whereas, ego-consciousness is needed to discriminate (<mark>EARTH</mark>) by classifying, diversifying and individualizing the one hundred three digit numbers into Sum Digit categories. CG Jung[12] tells us that ego-consciousness needs a discourse with the unconscious mind in order for there to be a Transcendent Function[13] (Third Option). This would not be what Catholicism calls the Eucharist[14]. The Transcendent Function as the third option is obtained by ego-consciousness cooperating via discourse with the unconscious mind, which is basically a Purgatorio state of mind and through this mythology in meditational contemplative thought the spiritual powers of creation: i.e. God could gift the initiate with the Initiatic Visionary Experience; thus, a Paradiso or cosmology (Garden of Eden) can eventually be achieved. The four mystic elements symbolizing the LIGHT, which represents the dawn of creation allows for that. These four mystic elements FIRE, EARTH, AIR and WATER are what Pythagoras[15] called the Tetractys[16]. All of this has to do with the creation process that goes on in the psyche of the individual not the race as a whole. Every single individual has a different creation process to deal with than every other individual in the world.

Furthermore, the 1s, 4s and 7s patterns representing the Sum Digits also inferred both the Zodiac and the Calendar year: there is 1-month with 28/29-days, 4-months with 30-days and 7-months with 31-days from the calendar perspective; whereas, the 1, 4, 7 also infers the Cardinal Quadruplicities, which denotes the 1, 4, 7 and 10 signs of Astrology. I will not discuss all the nuances coming from just these ideas.

There had to be a scenario that would point to the AIR element, which would also take up the entire count of verses in La Divina Commedia producing three totals for Sum-Digit 1. In fact I was able to envision that by obtaining these next three totals I could average each of the three sets of three totals from the Volumes, Sum-Digits and the Air element producing yet another set of three totals, which would produce the WATER element; thus, I could actually envisage, in this early stage of my research, the Zodiac/Calendar mathematically codified to La Divina Commedia by having a count of twelve totals; however, that was easily thought out than actually accomplishing the deed as quickly as I would have liked. It is reasoning such as this that allowed me to envisage as to where the science was going and thus discoveries can be made by persistently going after the envisaged goal.

4. LA DIVINA COMMEDIA'S KAMEA OF SATURN

The mathematical pattern thus far revealed in the Volumes and Sum-Digits is quite a remarkable feat to accomplish in a literary text. In fact just this small amount of data reveals a great deal of information if it is analyzed properly. For example: the best manner in which to analyze this initial material of Volumes and Sum-Digits in the trilogy is to place its data in the Tic-Tac-Toe[17] 3 x 3 square, which pigeonholes the amount of chapters/cantos each of the Sum-Digits used in each of the Volumes.

LA DIVINA COMMEDIA'S KAMEA OF SATURN			
Sum-Digit 7	Sum-Digit 1	Sum-Digit 4	
15	8	11	Inferno
8	18	7	Purgatorio
10	7	16	Paradiso

5. PURGATORIO'S KAMEA

To achieve the 34-chapters for Sum-Digit-1 was not easy. I tried everything imaginable and every mathematical trick I could think of within the confines of the mathematical data I had to work with to find those 34-chapters. The reason there had to be 34-Chapters for Sum-Digit 1 was because the Volumes and Sum-Digits each had 34-Cantos to their credit. Each of the Volumes is associated with a Sum-Digit number because that Sum-Digit number is mostly found in that volume: the Inferno uses the Sum-Digit-7 the most as Paradiso uses the Sum-Digit-4 the most. The diagram, La Divina Commedia's Kamea of Saturn, has Purgatorio with eighteen (18) chapters as Sum-Digit-1 uniting Purgatorio to Sum-Digit-1.

Finally, I decided to divide the amount of verses each of the nine cells uses by the amount of chapters each uses. I obtained, for the most part, ambiguous results, which I had initially rejected some months earlier as not feasible; however, in revisiting this idea I had the notion of bringing each quotient to the nearest of the 13-base numbers La Divina Commedia used to construct the system to determine if any unique pattern would come to the fore: these 13-based numbers are discussed more fully below.

This last brought forth a pattern that was obviously the symbol for the sign of Capricorn[18]. A great deal of data was revealed from this pattern, which is seen from another perspective as 34-Cantos for Sum-Digit-1.

Purgatorio's Kamea

Inferno	Purgatorio	Paradiso
2085	1163	1429
15	8	10
	145.38	142.9
139	145	142
4	1	7
1097	2601	1033
8	18	7
137.13	144.5	147.57
136	145	148
1	1	4
1538	991	2296
11	7	16
139.82	141.57	143.5
139	142	142
4	7	7

6. 34-CHAPTERS FOR SUM-DIGIT-1

DANTE'S LA DIVINA COMMEDIA'S
34-Cantos for Sum-Digit-1 (Purgatorio)

VOLUME	SD		VS	CHPS		AVER.		N-BN		N-SD		N-VS	P/M	VS
INFERNO	7	=	2085 /	15	=	139.0	=	139	=	4	=	(2085	= 0	= 2085)
INFERNO	1	=	1097 /	8	=	137.1	=	136	=	1	=	(1088	+ 9	= 1097)
INFERNO	4	=	1538 /	11	=	139.8	=	139	=	4	=	(1529	+ 9	= 1538)
PURGATORIO	7	=	1163 /	8	=	145.3	=	145	=	1	=	(1160	+ 3	= 1163)
PURGATORIO	1	=	2601 /	18	=	144.5	=	145	=	1	=	(2610	- 9	= 2601)
PURGATORIO	4	=	991 /	7	=	141.5	=	142	=	7	=	(994	- 3	= 991)
PARADISO	7	=	1429 /	10	=	142.9	=	142	=	7	=	(1420	+ 9	= 1429)
PARADISO	1	=	1033 /	7	=	147.5	=	148	=	4	=	(1036	- 3	= 1033)
PARADISO	4	=	2296 /	16	=	145.3	=	142	=	7	=	(2272	+ 24	= 2296)
			14233	100								14294	+ 39	= 14233

VOLUME = One of the three volumes of La Divina Commedia
SD = Original Sum-Digit inherent in the volume
VS = Verses in the volume the original Sum-Digit used
CHPS = Chapters in the volume the orignal Sum-Digit used
AVER. = Average number of verses the original Sum-Digit used
N-BN = New Base Number for Purgatorio's 34-Chapters/Cantos
N-SD = New Sum-Digit created by averaging original SD's verses
N-VS = The CHPS times N-BN produces total verses for N-SD
P/M = The total verses plus or minus for original SD verses
VS = The original number of verses used by the original SD

This above analysis would lead into averaging the three totals for each Sum-Digit producing yet another three totals for the **WATER** element. It was merely a matter of now placing the 12-totals into a Zodiac/Calendar circle. How do I delegate these totals to the signs/months? The Astrological Matrix I developed (3 x 4 matrix) was a great help in my serendipitously doing this. I merely put the four categories of La Divina Commedia: Volumes, Sum-Digits, Kameas and Averages in four vertical columns and then place the 12-totals obtained from these categories in synch with their Sum-Digits: these four patterns coincided with the four mystic elements: Fire, Earth, Air and Water.

7. LA DIVINA COMMEDIA'S ASTROLOGICAL MATRIX

La Divina Commedia's Astrological Matrix

VOLUME (Fire)	SUM DIGITS (Earth)	KAMEAS (Air)	AVERAGES (Water)	
4720 1	4677 6	4716 3	4704.33... 8	SUM DIGIT 7
4755 5	4731 10	4861 7	4782.33... 12	SUM DIGIT 1
4758 9	4825 2	4656 11	4746.33... 4	SUM DIGIT 4

Logically, I figured that the least amount of days in a month should have the least amount of verses. Then the four months with 30-days should receive the next four lowest numbers. It turned out that the four totals out of the Sum-Digit 7 filled that particular requirement. All I had to do was match up the four categories: Volumes (**Fire**), Sum-Digits (**Earth**), Kameas (**Air**) and Averages (**Water**) to the four mystic elements in the Zodiac.

It was in these mathematical studies on Dante's La Divina Commedia that I discovered the Star of David in the Zodiac/Calendar year. Dante had so arranged it that the 12-totals fit into the Zodiac Cycle producing three butterfly patterns, which inherently produces the Star of David in the Zodiac cycle. The three butterfly patterns are modeled after the four months with 30-days. It was at this time I conducted a great deal of research on the Calendar year, which brought be back to the dawn of Christianity and the beginning of the Julian calendar. I would discover in Dante's 14,233-verses a pattern of 38-Solar Years (365.242199 Days) and the remainder of one Moon Calendar Year (354 Days), which I believe infers the 39-books of the Old Testament. The reason I believe Dante Alighieri did this is because the New Testament is written by the esotericism codified to the Old Testament. THE NEW TESTAMENT IS A VERY TERSE AND SUCCINT COMMENTARY ON THE ESOTERICISM CODIFIED TO THE OLD TESTAMENT. This will be difficult for Christianity to understand; however, there is no doubt in my mind that the books of the Old Testament are Christian Documents. No Jew ever wrote a word of the Old Testament.

8. LA DIVINA COMMEDIA'S STAR OF DAVID

9. LA DIVINA COMMEDIA'S 13-BASE NUMBERS

Out of the one hundred chapters/cantos there are only 13-Base Numbers and these were initially analyzed ad nausea to achieve my goal of 34-Chapters/Cantos for Sum-Digit 1; however, in doing so I found the incredible sophistication that Dante imbued into his mathematical system: for No Margin of Error could be found.

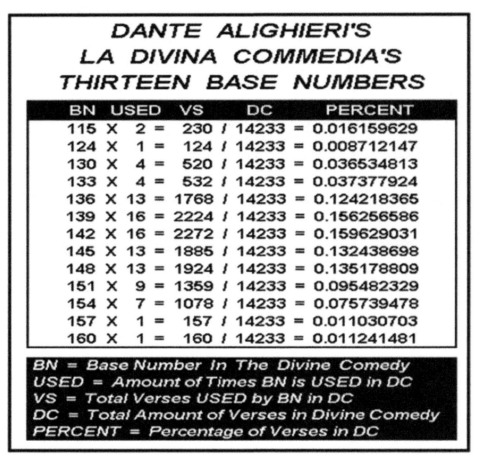

DANTE ALIGHIERI'S LA DIVINA COMMEDIA'S THIRTEEN BASE NUMBERS

BN	USED		VS		DC		PERCENT
115 X	2	=	230	/	14233	=	0.016159629
124 X	1	=	124	/	14233	=	0.008712147
130 X	4	=	520	/	14233	=	0.036534813
133 X	4	=	532	/	14233	=	0.037377924
136 X	13	=	1768	/	14233	=	0.124218365
139 X	16	=	2224	/	14233	=	0.156256586
142 X	16	=	2272	/	14233	=	0.159629031
145 X	13	=	1885	/	14233	=	0.132438698
148 X	13	=	1924	/	14233	=	0.135178809
151 X	9	=	1359	/	14233	=	0.095482329
154 X	7	=	1078	/	14233	=	0.075739478
157 X	1	=	157	/	14233	=	0.011030703
160 X	1	=	160	/	14233	=	0.011241481

BN = Base Number In The Divine Comedy
USED = Amount of Times BN is USED in DC
VS = Total Verses USED by BN in DC
DC = Total Amount of Verses in Divine Comedy
PERCENT = Percentage of Verses in DC

Notice the five central numbers: 136, 139, 142, 145 and 148 in groups of 13 and 16 chapters/cantos in relationship to the other eight numbers. This is overtly a set in the Fibonacci sequence. Notice also how each percentage of the 13-Base Numbers are within an acceptable Margin of Error when it is considered that whole numbers are being used throughout the system. This means that in all calculations the most economic amount of verses are used; thus, producing 'No Margin of Error".

Further analysis on La Divina Commedia's Kamea reveals Masonic symbolism and a Swastika. A swastika can only be created out of the Kamea of Saturn. Research on the Kamea of Saturn revealed a wealth of information concerning the swastikas pointing to the origins of the Fish symbol of Christianity, the Scarab symbol of Egypt and the symbol of Chinese clothing and architecture. Additional research on the Kamea of Saturn (a.k.a. Lo Shu in China) has revealed the origin of the I Ching and the origin of the Square, Compass and G. of Masonic symbolism[19]. This research does definitively point to the fact that Dante Alighieri did use the Kamea of Saturn as a mathematical device to construct his compositional structure for La Divina Commedia.

10. SQUARE, COMPASS AND G IN MASONIC SYMBOLISM

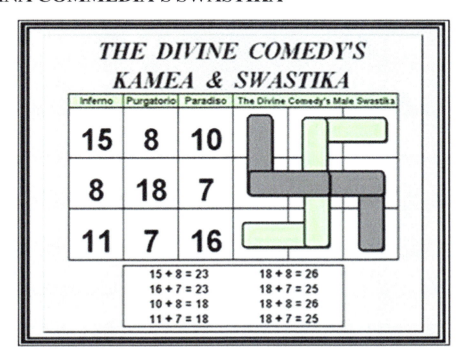

THE DIVINE COMEDY'S
Thirteen Base Numbers Distributed

	Inferno	Purgatorio	Paradiso
Sum-Digit-7	2 X 115 1 X 124 2 X 133 5 X 142 6 X 151	2 x 133 2 x 142 3 x 151 1 x 160	9 x 142 1 x 151
Sum-Digit-1	7 x 136 1 x 145	5 x 136 9 x 145 4 x 154	1 x 136 3 x 145 3 x 154
Sum-Digit-4	3 x 130 5 x 139 2 x 148 1 x 157	6 x 139 2 x 148	1 x 130 6 x 139 9 x 148

Commedia's Masonic Symbolism

Square, Compass, & G	Comedy's Base Numbers Used		
	5	4	2
	2	3	3
	4	2	3

11. LA DIVINA COMMEDIA'S SWASTIKA

THE DIVINE COMEDY'S
KAMEA & SWASTIKA

Inferno	Purgatorio	Paradiso	The Divine Comedy's Male Swastika
15	8	10	
8	18	7	
11	7	16	

15 + 8 = 23	18 + 8 = 26
16 + 7 = 23	18 + 7 = 25
10 + 8 = 18	18 + 8 = 26
11 + 7 = 18	18 + 7 = 25

12. LA DIVINA COMMEDIA'S MATHEMATICAL MATRIX

I finally did discover the mathematical model that Dante had patterned his La Divina Commedia after. It took all of twelve years to envisage it. I call it the Universal Mathematical Matrix: Prima Materia (Perennial Matrix) because it is universally used by all ancient religions around the world to structure their sacred literature, art works and monuments. This 10 x 10 matrix is a commentary on the MONAD that all the scribes of antiquity envisaged and used to write their works.

La Divina Commedia's Mathematical Matrix

136 9	115 9	139 9	145 9	136 9	139 9	142 9	142 9	139 9	154 9
142 9	139 1	151 2	139 3	139 4	145 5	148 6	139 7	148 8	139 9
136 9	151 2	148 4	157 6	145 8	145 1	154 3	142 5	154 7	142 9
151 9	142 3	151 6	139 9	139 3	151 6	145 9	148 3	142 6	148 9
142 9	124 4	151 8	136 3	142 7	136 2	145 6	148 1	136 5	139 9
115 9	136 5	142 1	133 6	136 2	154 7	160 3	142 8	148 4	145 9
130 9	136 6	136 3	145 9	154 6	133 3	145 9	148 6	148 3	148 9
160 9	136 7	142 5	139 3	151 1	154 8	142 6	139 4	142 2	142 9
133 9	133 8	139 7	136 6	145 5	139 4	148 3	145 2	154 1	151 9
136 9	130 9	148 9	151 9	145 9	148 9	130 9	142 9	139 9	145 9

I simply took the 100-Cantos of *La Divina Commedia* and sequentially placed them into the Universal Mathematical Matrix: Prima Materia (Perennial Matrix) beginning with the 34 cantos of *La Inferno* placing them into the first 34 cells of the matrix working downward then to the top of the second column and to the third and fourth column until the 34 cantos are completely accounted for. Follow the same procedures with *La Purgatorio* by placing its 33 cantos into the next 33 cells where the placement sequence left off. Placing the 33 cantos of *La Paradiso* into the last 33 cells of the Universal Mathematical Matrix: Prima Materia (Perennial Matrix) finishes off the process. Now add all the verses in the white area designated as 1-4-7 (Cardinal signs of Astrology) and the total is 2580 verses. Total the black area designated as 2-5-8 (Fixed signs of Astrology) and the sum is 2580. This is obviously not an accidental placement of data into this Universal Mathematical Matrix: Prima Materia (Perennial Matrix). This Universal Mathematical Matrix: Prima Materia (Perennial Matrix) was Dante Alighieri's guiding light in his structuring the compositional structure of La Divina Commedia.

12. LA DIVINA COMMEDIA'S SILHOUETTES OF THE TRINITY

SILHOUETTES OF THE TRINITY

Zodiac	Calendar	Sequence	La Divina Commedia	
Taurus 2	5-May	1	4825	Sum Digit
Gemini 3	6-Jun	2	4716	Kamea
Cancer 4	7-Jul	3	4746.33	Average
Leo 5	8-Aug	4	4755	Volume
Virgo 6	9-Sep	5	4677	Sum Digit
Libra 7	10-Oct	6	4861	Kamea
Scorpio 8	11-Nov	7	4704.33	Average
Sagittarius 9	12-Dec	8	4758	Volume
Capricorn 10	1-Jan	9	4731	Sum Digit
Aquarius 11	2-Feb	10	4656	Kamea
Pisces 12	3-Mar	11	4782.33	Average
Aries 1	4-Apr	12	4720	Volume
Signs	**Months**	**Numbers**	**Verses in the Elements**	

One of the most remarkable discoveries made in the analysis of La Divina Commedia's mathematics relates directly to Dante Alighieri's vision of the Trinity. Those that have read La Divina Commedia know that at the end of *La Paradiso* Dante has a vision of the Trinity. In my completion of Dante's mathematical system the very last thing I did was place the final twelve totals, which created the Zodiac/Calendar year and by extension the Star of David, into Microsoft Excel 'Area Graphic Program' and the results were absolutely stunning. I did have to tweak the sequence of the twelve totals outlined in the original image. What I did was simply place the sign of Taurus (the second sign of the Zodiac) into first place because the number two tries, as it may, to usurp the position of God, which is symbolically number one (MONAD), which Aries signifies as APRIL FIRST, which is the beginning of creation according to Jewish lore; thus, by tweaking these numbers by putting Taurus first a much more esthetically pleasing image of the Trinity was discovered. This placing the number two first is not unprecedented. The first letter of Genesis is BETH, which has the numerical value of two (2) and that is another esoteric analysis not to be discussed here in this paper.

I had, through one graphic line, the silhouettes of three heads inferring the Trinity and one was Neanderthal looking: obviously Yahweh symbolically representing ego-consciousness. The lighter area shows two silhouette faces in reverse of each other symbolizing Elohym the gods (angels) and the Most High God (Saint Paul's Unknown God or Jesus' Father). All three images appear to be laughing. These images of the Trinity are very similar to the Crown image created by the Genesis Formula extrapolated from the first word of Genesis: BERESHITH. Only a variation of the height and depth of the area graphic line produces the different images of the Crown and Trinity images: all the original authors had to do is fine tune the numbers by tweaking them.

I will add here, today[1], a codicil to this point. Dante obtained his knowledge as to how to configure this Trinitarian image through the esotericism codified to the first two written letters and one unseen letter at the beginning of the book of Genesis [PEI, BETH and RESH]. This particular nuance I just discover, yesterday, which I will not discuss here; but, I am writing another paper relating to SCHEDULING THE ITINERARY OF CHRIST'S MINISTRY where I will outline those nuances that inspired Dante into creating esoterically this image of the TRINITY in his La Divina Commedia.

It is through the demonstration of these several art forms outlined in this work that it can be seen that it was important enough for our ancestors to take this commentary on the MONAD seriously and devote their lives and resources to blanketing the globe with variations on its theme.

LA DIVINA COMMEDIA
Has No Margin of Error

Inferno	Sum-Digit-7	=	2	x	115	=	230	/	14233	=	0.01615963
Inferno	Sum-Digit-7	=	1	x	124	=	124	/	14233	=	0.00871215
Inferno	Sum-Digit-7	=	2	x	133	=	266	/	14233	=	0.01868896
Inferno	Sum-Digit-7	=	5	x	142	=	710	/	14233	=	0.04988407
Inferno	Sum-Digit-7	=	5	x	151	=	755	/	14233	=	0.0530457
Inferno	Sum-Digit-1	=	7	x	136	=	952	/	14233	=	0.06688681
Inferno	Sum-Digit-1	=	1	x	145	=	145	/	14233	=	0.01018759
Inferno	Sum-Digit-4	=	3	x	130	=	390	/	14233	=	0.02740111
Inferno	Sum-Digit-4	=	5	x	139	=	695	/	14233	=	0.04883018
Inferno	Sum-Digit-4	=	2	x	148	=	296	/	14233	=	0.02079674
Inferno	Sum-Digit-4	=	1	x	157	=	157	/	14233	=	0.01103070
Purgatorio	Sum-Digit-7	=	2	x	133	=	266	/	14233	=	0.01868896
Purgatorio	Sum-Digit-7	=	2	x	142	=	284	/	14233	=	0.01995363
Purgatorio	Sum-Digit-7	=	3	x	151	=	453	/	14233	=	0.03182744
Purgatorio	Sum-Digit-7	=	1	x	160	=	160	/	14233	=	0.01124148
Purgatorio	Sum-Digit-1	=	5	x	136	=	680	/	14233	=	0.0477629
Purgatorio	Sum-Digit-1	=	9	x	145	=	1305	/	14233	=	0.09168833
Purgatorio	Sum-Digit-1	=	4	x	154	=	616	/	14233	=	0.04327970
Purgatorio	Sum-Digit-4	=	5	x	139	=	695	/	14233	=	0.04883018
Purgatorio	Sum-Digit-4	=	2	x	148	=	296	/	14233	=	0302079674
Paradiso	Sum-Digit-7	=	9	x	142	=	1278	/	14233	=	0.08979133
Paradiso	Sum-Digit-7	=	1	x	151	=	151	/	14233	=	0.01060915
Paradiso	Sum-Digit-1	=	1	x	136	=	136	/	14233	=	0.00955526
Paradiso	Sum-Digit-1	=	3	x	145	=	435	/	14233	=	0.03056278
Paradiso	Sum-Digit-1	=	3	x	154	=	462	/	14233	=	0.03245978
Paradiso	Sum-Digit-4	=	1	x	130	=	130	/	14233	=	0.00913370
Paradiso	Sum-Digit-4	=	6	x	139	=	834	/	14233	=	0.05859622
Paradiso	Sum-Digit-4	=	9	x	148	=	1332	/	14233	=	0.09358533

The same argument that was used above in analyzing the 13-Base Numbers can be used to analyze each of the Sum Digits used in each of the volumes in the entire La Divina Commedia's trilogy.

---

[1] July 20, 2016

Basically La Divina Commedia is an esoteric commentary on the first chapter of Genesis; however, that is not at all apparent to the uninitiated (profane). There are mathematical studies that I have conducted and published on the first chapter of Genesis[20] that are far more extensive than La Divina Commedia's compositional structure; however, the trilogy's textual material have far more sophisticated esoteric data than I can envisage out of it. This is only because I do not know Italian, which is the language the storyline is best studied from in regards to an esoteric point of view; nonetheless, I will not go too much into that material for it is not appropriate for this paper; however, it is fitting that I mention that Dante structured his La Divina Commedia, for the most part, within the Kamea of the Moon: a 9 x 9 magic square.

Below there are a number of different images of the same matrix studies from a number of different perspectives.

- ❖ The first matrix represents the Multiplication Tables up to the number nine – casting-out-nines. It is the multiplication tables up to ten that Pythagoras[21] is credit with creating and in which he developed his mathematical theorems; however, Pythagoras did not create it, he independently envisaged it out of the MONAD just I did and thousands of other people did in all times and climes.
  - ➤ The first image is a 9 x 9 square: that is a given.
  - ➤ This first image is derived from the nine multiplication tables up to nine – casting-out-nines; however, realistically each multiplication table beyond the first multiplication table is a duplicate or symbolically the mirror-image and likeness of the first multiplication table. Conceptually speaking there is no difference between the first multiplication table and the others outside of their perceived quantitative values.
  - ➤ Thus each numerical digit is symbolically the MONAD symbolically expressed differently; hence, it can be envisage how the matrix is a commentary on the MONAD.
- ❖ Being that the first image is a 9 x 9 square it points to being a Magic Square: Kamea of the Moon in Talismanic Magic[22].
  - ➤ Here I have color coded the diagonal from left to right in order for the reader to easily see the number 1-81 placed into the matrix in numerical order. This order enables each of the columns, rows and diagonals to total to 369.
    - ▪ I will return to this matrix in a moment.
- ❖ The next matrix is the UNIVERSAL MATHEMATICAL MATRIX: Prima Materia (Perennial Matrix). This matrix is a product of the first matrix above.
  - ➤ A Row and a Column of nines are added to the nine multiplication tables casting-out-nines.
    - ▪ However, this is not really necessary seeing that if the commentary on the MONAD is extrapolated out infinitely the first row and column of nines will fill themselves in on a symbolic level creating the perfect 10 x 10 matrix.
    - ▪ Much can be said about this matrix symbolically and in real time but I will not go into that in this paper.
- ❖ La Divina Commedia Mathematical Matrix is an amalgamation of the three images of the matrix just described above.
  - ➤ It is a representation of the nine multiplication tables,
  - ➤ It is the Kamea of the Moon though the numbers 1-81 are not visibly enumerated,
  - ➤ And it is the Universal Mathematical Matrix: Prima Materia (Perennial Matrix)
  - ➤ Inclusive in all this is the numerical data from each of the one hundred chapters of La Divina Commedia, which I have already discussed above.
- ❖ Finally, the last image takes the data in the final image: La Divina Commedia Mathematical Matrix and analyzes it from the perspective of the Kamea of the Moon.
  - ➤ Rather than using the numerical sequence from the multiplication tables casting-out-nine the numerical data numbers 1-81 casting-out-nines is used from the Kamea of the Moon.
    - ▪ In this manner it can be easily envisaged that Dante Alighieri indeed did used the

Kamea of the Moon in structuring his compositional structure in La Divina Commedia.

- The final totals are too evenly matched for this vast quantity of numerical data to constellate on its own; thus, it *had to be* deliberate.

The next two images illustrate how Dante also pattern the symbol of Capricorn into La Divina commedia twice using the Kamea of Mars (5 x 5 Magic Square). Dante dedicated La Divina Commedia to Beatrice who was born in the month of January.

The image illustrate that Dante structured the entire La Divina Commedia with the formula of the Golden Ratio. In fact if you read the twenty-eight chapter of Purgatorio he even mythologizes the Golden Ratio in Dante's movement. In fact Dante birth, the beginning of writing and ending La Divina Commedia is based upon the Golden Ratio: June 1, 1265 to March 15, 1300 around to September 14, 1321 (Feast of the Cross)[23].

It is very interesting that the very next day September 15th is anniversary date of the Eleusinian mysteries. I believe that September 14th symbolized the date that Dante had his vision of the Trinity: i.e. Initiatic Visionary Experience. This was not a physical death it was the death of materialism and the birth of the Christ child.

If you think about the first 35-years of Dante Life and then his creating the 100-part matrix to record his journey through the three realms of spirit I think you will see that he was following the spiritual paradigm laid out in the first eleven chapters of Genesis. Dante by incorporating the Golden Ratio into his work illustrate that he was convey the concept that by having that vision he entered the Garden of Eden.

MULTIPLICATION TABLES
Up to Nine (Casting out Nines)

1	2	3	4	5	6	7	8	9
2	4	6	8	1	3	5	7	9
3	6	9	3	6	9	3	6	9
4	8	3	7	2	6	1	5	9
5	1	6	2	7	3	8	4	9
6	3	9	6	3	9	6	3	9
7	5	3	1	8	6	4	2	9
8	7	6	5	4	3	2	1	9
9	9	9	9	9	9	9	9	9

KAMEA OF THE MOON

									369
37	78	29	70	21	62	13	54	5	369
6	38	79	30	71	22	63	14	46	369
47	7	39	80	31	72	23	55	15	369
16	48	8	40	81	32	64	24	56	369
57	17	49	9	41	73	33	65	25	369
26	58	18	50	1	42	74	34	66	369
67	27	59	10	51	2	43	75	35	369
36	68	19	60	11	52	3	44	76	369
77	28	69	20	61	12	53	4	45	369
369	369	369	369	369	369	369	369	369	369

UNIVERSAL MATHEMATICAL MATRIX

9	9	9	9	9	9	9	9	9	9
9	1	2	3	4	5	6	7	8	9
9	2	4	6	8	1	3	5	7	9
9	3	6	9	3	6	9	3	6	9
9	4	8	3	7	2	6	1	5	9
9	5	1	6	2	7	3	8	4	9
9	6	3	9	6	3	9	6	3	9
9	7	5	3	1	8	6	4	2	9
9	8	7	6	5	4	3	2	1	9
9	9	9	9	9	9	9	9	9	9

LA DIVINA COMMEDIA'S MATHEMATICAL MATRIX

136/9	115/9	139/9	145/9	136/9	139/9	142/9	142/9	139/9	154/9
142/9	139/1	151/2	139/3	139/4	145/5	148/6	139/7	148/8	139/9
136/9	151/2	148/4	157/6	145/8	145/1	154/3	142/5	154/7	142/9
151/9	142/3	151/6	139/9	139/3	151/6	145/9	148/3	142/6	148/9
142/9	124/4	151/8	136/3	142/7	136/2	145/6	148/1	136/5	139/9
115/9	136/5	142/1	133/6	136/2	154/7	160/3	142/8	148/4	145/9
130/9	136/6	136/3	145/9	154/6	133/3	145/9	148/6	148/3	148/9
130/9	136/7	142/5	139/3	151/1	154/8	142/6	139/4	142/2	142/9
133/9	133/8	139/7	136/6	145/5	139/4	148/3	145/2	154/1	151/9
136/9	130/9	148/9	151/9	145/9	148/9	130/9	142/9	139/9	145/9

LA DIVINA COMMEDIA'S
KAMEA OF THE MOON by QUADRUPLICITIES

136	115	139	145	136	139	142	142	139	154

142									
136	139/1	151/6	139/2	139/7	145/3	148/8	139/4	148/9	139/5
151	151/6	148/2	157/7	145/3	145/8	154/4	142/9	154/5	142/1
142	142/2	151/7	139/3	139/8	151/4	145/9	148/5	142/1	148/6
115	124/7	151/3	136/8	142/4	136/9	145/5	148/1	136/6	139/2
130	136/3	142/8	133/4	136/9	154/5	160/1	142/6	148/2	145/7
130	136/8	136/4	145/9	154/6	133/1	145/6	148/2	148/7	148/3
133	136/4	142/9	139/5	151/1	154/6	142/2	139/7	142/3	142/8
136	133/9	139/5	136/1	145/6	139/2	148/7	145/3	154/8	151/4
	130/5	148/1	151/6	145/2	148/7	130/3	142/8	139/4	145/9

QUADRUPLICITIES
VERSES COUNTED

1	2	3	4	5	6	7	8	9
139	142	136	136	130	151	124	136	133
148	148	151	136	139	151	151	142	142
136	139	139	133	139	151	157	136	145
151	145	145	142	154	145	139	139	136
133	139	145	151	154	154	148	145	136
160	142	130	154	145	145	148	148	145
148	148	145	139	148	142	139	142	142
142	148	142	139	154	136	148	154	148
142	139	148	151	139	148	145	142	145
1299	1290	1281	1281	1302	1323	1299	1284	1272

FINAL TOTALS

1, 4, 7	2, 5, 8	3, 6, 9
1299	1290	1281
1281	1302	1323
1299	1284	1272
3879	3876	3876

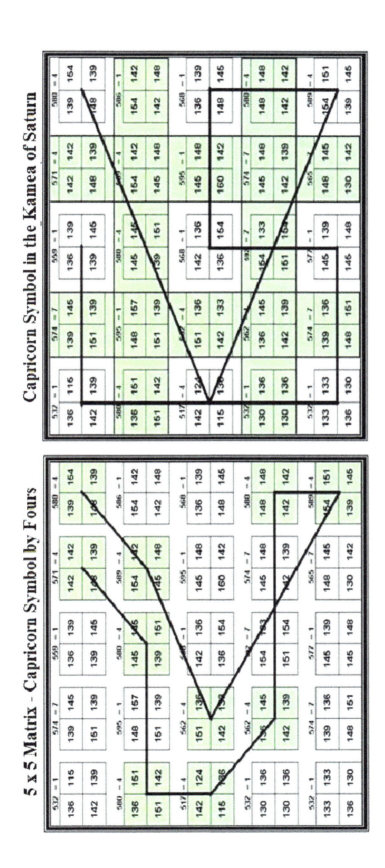

Capricorn Symbol in the Kamea of Saturn

5 x 5 Matrix - Capricorn Symbol by Fours

LA DIVINA COMMEDIA'S MATHEMATICAL SYSTEM

INFERNO			PURGATORIO			PARADISO				
136 9	115 9	139 9	145 9	136 9	139 9	142 9	142 9	139 9	154 9	1387
142 9	139 1	151 2	139 3	139 4	145 5	148 6	139 7	148 8	139 9	1429
136 9	151 2	148 4	157 6	145 8	145 1	154 3	142 5	154 7	142 9	1474
151 9	142 3	151 6	139 9	139 3	151 6	145 9	148 3	142 6	148 9	1456
142 9	124 4	151 8	136 3	142 7	136 2	145 6	148 1	136 5	139 9	1399
115 9	136 5	142 1	133 6	136 2	154 7	160 3	142 8	148 4	145 9	1411
130 9	136 6	136 3	145 9	154 6	133 3	145 9	148 6	148 3	148 9	1423
130 9	136 7	142 5	139 3	151 1	154 8	142 6	139 4	142 2	142 9	1417
133 9	133 8	139 7	136 6	145 5	139 4	148 3	145 2	154 1	151 9	1423
136 9	130 9	148 9	151 9	145 9	148 9	130 9	142 9	139 9	145 9	1414
1351	1342	1447	1420	1432	1444	1459	1435	1450	1453	14233

THE EMPYREAN[24]

"So now, appearing to me in the form
Of a white rose was Heaven's sacred host,
Those whom with His own blood Christ made His bride."[25]

"I have been in the heaven that most receives of His light,
And have seen things which whoso descends from up there
Has neither the knowledge nor the power to relate, because,
As it draws near to its desire, our intellect enters so deep
That memory cannot go back upon the track."[26]

IN CONCLUSION

This system of mathematics is obviously a highly sophisticated storage and retrieval system that is on such a level of thought that individually and collectively humanity has lost the knowledge of it.

Dante Alighieri imbued into the compositional structure of his La Divina Commedia an ancient system of thought. This system of thought was known all over the world in antiquity though it is not generally known in modernity; though, I do believe the inner hierarchies of Catholicism and Freemasonry are fully versed in esotericism. Personally, I do not see the necessity of the so-called Mystery Schools keeping this information from the general public. It is not that easy to convey to another: it is actually impossible; for the reason that, for that is God's province. Yes, I can lay out these mathematical patterns that I have envisaged in the system over a period of twelve year. I can also tell the reader that what is in this chapter is not anywhere near the tip of the iceberg that is the Esoteric Science.

The Esoteric Science is itself the secrecy that is withheld from the initiate. What that means is that no matter what I personally lay out in this paper there is a database of knowledge within this material that would make what I have outlined pale before it. Yes, the individual researcher once learning the rudiments of the system can cull out additional nuances and ideas that are not presently known. To teach esotericism in a classroom as dogma and/or tradition is not really feasible and that is why I believe the Church doesn't do it.

Yes, the mathematical system remains the same throughout all times and climes but the key is for the initiate to walk the margins of the world seeing this esoteric divine system of thought in all cultures. Every single culture around the world in antiquity has created their literature, artworks and monuments esoterically differently than all other cultures. That is the beauty of divine esotericism.

The question is, why did the ancients set up this Esoteric Science in their literature, artworks and monuments around the world? The answer is found in the individual building his or her psychic temple that he or she will live in for eternity. Yes, the literature, artworks and monuments of antiquity that we see in the outer world were created by a nation of people with a like-minded mentality knowing the art of esotericism: how to speak, write and convey the WORD OF GOD. I can't think of one nation in antiquity that did not accomplish this except of course the materialists or marauding barbarians of the world, which would often end up destroying these highly civilized and spiritual cultures, which is very similar to the mental acuity of modernity.

However, what the literature, artworks and monument convey is not gear towards the masses it is always designed for the fledgling initiate: the lone mystic.

Reading the above analysis of Dante Alighieri's La Divina Commedia's Mathematical System it is easily envisaged through the four mystic Elements: Triplicities: FIRE, EARTH, AIR and WATER that the process of building the TETRACTYS (Temple of God) in the psyche is a personal one because each psyche's idea of the Garden of Eden: the desired spiritual goal is different than every other psyche in existence. The psyche's goal is to find the soul it had lost.

If this is the case why is the Catholic Church so uniformed in its teachings? The answer to that is that the Catholic Church is the prototype of the Temple of God. It is the generic way of expressing esotericism in Christianity.

Those that read La Divina Commedia will see that Dante Alighieri is the lone pilgrim journeying through Inferno, Purgatorio and the Paradiso so there is no ambiguity as to there being anyone journeying the pilgrimage with him. Virgil is merely symbolically Dante's psychic use of reason and logic. Virgil represented what Dante Alighieri was most enamored by in the outer world: the poetry and philosophy of Virgil; therefore, nothing was more appropriate to guide Dante than Virgil. What augments this guide Virgil is the spiritual guidance, which is represented by Beatrice, Lucy and the Virgin Mary, which is symbolic of the high spiritual dynamics in the unconscious mind. Spiritual guidance made it infinitely easier for Dante Alighieri to traverse the three realms of spirit although he had a very difficult time doing it. Nobody promised him a Rose Garden. Dante had to prove himself, every step of the way.

I want to end this paper by giving the reader three examples in the past two centuries of three lone pilgrims that journey into the arms of God.

1   Mary Baker Eddy the Discover and Founder of Christian Science was on her death bed when she had her initiating vision that guided her through the second half of her life founding the Metaphysics of Christianity. What enamored her in life was the Bible; thus, it was the Bible she obtain her raison d'être.

2   Carl Gustav Jung the founder of Analytical Psychology had an insight (vision?) around the turn of the twentieth century that he tried to elucidate, in the next sixty years, through his writings. Psychiatry was his profession and that is what enamored his psyche for the rest of his life.

3   William (Bill) Wilson was an alcoholic that was condemned to be hospitalized for the rest of his life in 1935. When the door closed behind him he cried out, "if there be a God let him show himself" and instantly the room lit up and he said, "So this is the God of the preachers". He would go on to found a worldwide organization called Alcoholics Anonymous that became his raison d'être for the rest of his life: guiding alcoholics that **DESIRED** it to sobriety.

My life's work is an amalgamation of the esoteric teachings of the Bible, many of religions and Freemasonry symbolism laid out in Washington DC, the Roman Catholic Church's teachings and the metaphysical writings of Mary Baker Eddy, the Collective Works of CG Jung and the 12-Step Program instituted by Bill Wilson and many other authors.

ENDNOTES

[1] In fact in June of that year (1983) I would enter a vocational college to obtain an Associated Degree in Computer Programming and that is only because I took a GED test (1968), while serving in the Army, to obtain a High School Diploma having dropped out of school in the first two months of the ninth grade.

[2] There is one work: Dante: Numerological Studies (American University Studies, Series 2: Romance, Languages & Literature) by John J Guzzardo, published by Peter Lang Publishing (1 Nov 1987); however, this work was published one year after my initial copyright and this author does not go beyond my first illustration below.

[3] I started my personal researches in August of 1974 and it was in January 1977 that I discovered a numerical cycle in the first chapter of Genesis and completed it in October 1978; however, the crucial date of my researches that led me to analyze Dante Alighieri's La Divina Commedia was April 15, 1983. It was April 11, 1983 that I came face to face with what the cycle was that I had envisaged in the first chapter of Genesis. During that almost nine year period, from the commencement of my researches into the Holy Writ (August 1974), I learned what was not of intrinsic value esoterically; thus, learning what to accept and most importantly what to discard as trash.

[4] Assembly lines are a modern industrial gimmick, which in my mind destroys creativity.

[5] Here lies the reason for my presenting the Esoteric Science in the mathematical format rather than from the linguistic and grammatical format. The Esoteric Science is structured through the medium of the Seven Liberal Arts: Arithmetic, Music/Harmony, Geometry, Astronomy, Grammar, Rhetoric and Logic/Dialectic. Mathematics is the optimum and ideal mode in presenting the Esoteric Science seeing it is universally accepted as the universal scientific language. I hold back on discussing the Trivium's aspects of esotericism because of the problems of translation. Each language is local and not universally understood and therefore the Quadrivium (universal language) is used because it is universally understood. In addition mathematics is an abstraction of the psyche and has no concord with the world. In order to express mathematical ideas arithmetical data has to have a linguistic format to record that knowledge; therefore, numbers (digits) are in and of themselves a representation of the Trivium (Grammatical Arts). The numbers themselves is the GRAMMAR, the manner in which mathematics is used is LOGIC and the explanation of a mathematical theorem is often redundant (RHETORIC); therefore, in every sense of the word I am using all Seven Liberal Arts to outline the Esoteric Science introduced in this paper.

[6] Let me qualify this remark by saying that if the rudiments of the esoteric science are known than translation can be very helpful; however, without that prerequisite they are altogether useless.

[7] The Divine Comedy of Dante Alighieri (Inferno, Purgatorio and Paradiso), by Allen Mandelbaum, drawings by Barry Moser, published by Quality Paperback Book Club 1980

[8] This is a perfect example of how religious texts are destroyed inadvertently by taken away or adding to the texts. This is what both Moses and Saint John warned of in their writings.

[9] THE CYCLES OF DIVINE CREATION & THE UNIVERSAL MATHEMATICAL MATRIX
https://www.academia.edu/9613502/THE_CYCLES_OF_DIVINE_CREATION_and_THE_UNIVERSAL_MATHEMATICAL_MATRIX

[10] Much of the occult I would wholeheartedly agree is absolute trash; however, I, personally, believe in demonstrable evidence not hallucinations and/or mental experiences of a neurotic or psychotic individual; nonetheless, some gems unfortunately get lost between the cracks. Such a gem is Astrology as a mathematical, symbolic and linguistic tool.

[11] I do not believe or use Astrology as a fortune telling tool or predictive oracle as the profane do. I see Astrology as merely a mathematical, symbolic and linguistic tool.

[12] CG JUNG http://en.wikipedia.org/wiki/Carl_Jung

[13] Transcendent Function http://www.amazon.com/The-Transcendent-Function-Psychological-Unconscious/dp/0791459780

[14] Eucharist http://en.wikipedia.org/wiki/Eucharist

[15] Pythagoras http://en.wikipedia.org/wiki/Pythagoras

[16] Tetractys http://en.wikipedia.org/wiki/Tetractys

[17] The only reason I initially used this small mathematical tool is because I was seeking a way of understanding the patterns developed from the Volumes and Sum Digits. I had written a wordy and primitive (not scholarly) paper trying to explain these patterns I initially envisaged, verbally and submitted it as my first copyright in 1986. Just after submitting it a memory out of my teenage years came to me: my father came home one day with a brainteaser. He asked my brother, sister and myself to take the first nine numbers and place them into the tic-tac-toe box and add them up to the same total in all eight directions: vertically, horizontally and diagonally. The answer was 15 and I had it in ten minutes; however, this memory served me well in my reaching out for help in trying to obtain a handle on Dante's mathematics. Later I would discover that this 3 x 3 square was very ancient and was called the Kamea of Saturn (Lo Shu in China).

[18] The white area forms the 'V' in the Capricorn symbol if the image is turn 90° right. The gray area produces the little loop at the tip of the 'V' shape in the Capricorn symbol and the black area produces the 'U' or cup shape that goes down and under the 'V' shape in the Capricorn symbol. January/Capricorn was the month that Beatrice was born. Beatrice was the allegorical woman that Dante became enamored with and said he would write a more worthy work dedicated to her. This Capricorn symbols would be found throughout La Divina Commedia in more spectacular ways, which will not be discussed further in this paper. See my other writings on Dante. Personally, I believe that Beatrice represents the soul/psyche.

[19] This material can be found in my work: THE SECRETS & THE MYSTERIES OF GENESIS: Antiquity's Hall of Records, by William John Meegan, published by Trafford Publishers 2003 and THE SISTINE CHAPEL: A Study in Celestial Cartography,

The Mysteries and Esoteric Teachings of the Catholic Church, by William John Meegan, published by Xlibris Publishers November 30, 2012

[20] ibid

[21] Theoretic Arithmetic of the Pythagoreans (1816), by Thomas Taylor, Kessinger Publishers

[22] I do not believe in such nonsense as amulets; however, I do believe in the mathematics that is preserved in these so-called Magic Squares.

[23] Dante Alighieri was born on June 1, 1265; though, that exact date may be disputed. He began writing La Divina Commedia on March 15, 1300, which from his birth is the first swing of the Golden Ratio, which is the anniversary date of the assignation of Julius Caesar and Julius Caesar is referenced in the first chapter of La Divina Commedia. Julius Caesar symbolizes the death of Dante's ego. The second swing of the Golden Ratio begin from March 15, 1300 to September 14, 1321 (Feast of the Cross) and the day before the anniversary date of the Eleusinian mysteries. Take the whole of Dante Alighieri life: 56.29 years and do the math.

[24] THE DORE ILLUSTRATIONS FOR DANTE'S DIVINE COMMEDIA (p. 134), 1976 (136 plates by Gustave Dore), published by Dover Publications Inc., New York

[25] DANTE: The Divine Comedy; Vol. III: Paradise, translated by Mark Musa, Penguin Classics, published by Penguin Books, Viking Penguin, Inc. New York, USA, Copyright by Mark Musa 1984, 1986

[26] The Divine Comedy, by Dante Alighieri, translated by Charles S. Singleton (Paradiso. 1: 4-9). Visions like this point to the origins of Mystery Schools' secrecy traditions when no initiate could talk about the experience even if he or she wanted to.

I personally experience such a spiritual vision in June 1978 {*I mentally envisaged the sum-total of all knowledge - I had a glimpse of Eternity, which explained to me unambiguously and in an infinite amount of ways that there was no such thing as death: my mind was peppered with billions, if not trillions, of pieces of information. At the same time that mental vision was taken place I had an inward visual experience (**through the third eye? This was not a corporeal vision**) of going down a tunnel directly into the light (I was wide-awake: not asleep).* I understood instantaneously that this vision was of Omniscience: God. The vision did not last but a nanosecond because instantaneously the vision ended because of my own thought processes (it was similar to a kneejerk or flinching reaction when suddenly my mind was infringed upon by such an alien light). Trying 'corporeally' to understand the vision I believe caused the vision to end or was it because that was the entire vision? I am uncertain as to the truth of the matter. There is of course no way of retaining the detail knowledge of such a vision; however, from that point onward I lost my fear of death and I was given the ability for pattern recognition and my memory improved greatly. Do not get me wrong. Just because someone has such a vision does not mean he or she does not have to struggle to obtain the answers he or she is searching for in life. It is in the quest to know God that the initiate unwittingly demonstrates (to the spiritual forces in creation?) that he or she is worthy to move on spirituality. Without this struggle and freely relinquishing the material world there is no other way to demonstrably demonstrate to the Empyrean that one is worthy of spiritual grace. I believe that such visions points to the beginnings of the true spiritual life no matter what progress one 'think' he or she had previously made. In fact all previous research into religion and/or spirituality is as if it was for naught. The long sought after vision of God does not come by trying to experience it or through a lifetime of research. It comes through 'DESIRING', above anything else, to know about God and life with no expectation of reward for oneself.

CONCLUSION

This volume from an iconoclastic perspective was extremely fast and loose and I totally agree with that assessment concerning the content of this work.

From an iconographic perspective it should take years for the reader to finish this book. Actually, the initiate will never finish it or validate its claims completely simply; for the reason that, by continuously reading it iconographically more nuances (knowledge) will flow out of it, which I neither envisaged nor did I include in this volume. Much of my research, not found in this volume, will be found in my other writings. Also from an iconographic perspective I did not go into too many details relating to all the aspects of this work for every thought, word or deed in envisaging this Esoteric Science would be too tedious, boring and laborious: i.e. excruciating for even the spiritually inclined and motivated to get through it all. In addition too much detail would inflame my own ego, which should remain deflated.

From my own experiences I have found that by rereading and contemplatively meditating on the actual indigenous lettering and wording of the sacred scriptures and their numerical (iconoclastic) Gematria (iconographic) values and continuously conducting a comparative analysis of my research, against that biblical analysis, by going over the length and breadth of it, which spans forty-two years, additional spiritual nuances flows from it like a clear river of water.

There is an ancient Jewish legend that explicitly states that all interpretations of the Torah are the Torah. This is a very beautiful concept that should aid the initiate in keeping his or her ego deflated; for the reason that, no lone individual's or collective's remarks or interpretations about the sacred scriptures or the MATRIX OF WISDOM is the end all or be all. For example the canonized Judaeo Christian Scriptures are hermetically sealed because they have been fully vetted esoterically via the Seven Liberal Arts. To add or take away from those hermetically sealed mathematical patterns would skew the entire systemic system that is the WORD OF GOD in the flesh (those archives); whereas, Kabbalists, Gnostics and Mystics, etc., can interpret and write commentary, like me, on the texts of the sacred scriptures; however, the ancient spiritual sages used the same symbolic and alphanumeric structuring that the canonized Old and New Testaments were structured by. This would mean that the indigenous language that the Kabbalists and Gnostics texts were written in would not necessarily be heretical texts. I say this; for the reason that I provided in the Appendix of this work an esoteric analysis of Dante Alighieri's La Divina Commedia's Mathematical System. Dante's work is of course not part of the canonized scriptures. His work is of the Kabbalists, Gnostics and Mystics, etc., genre of thought. I don't know anything about the Italian language so I cannot comment much about the esotericism of the storyline's mythoi; however, because of some nuances in the surface iconoclastic storyline I do take for granted that the texts are also esoterically structured; because, the translated storyline agree wholeheartedly with the mathematics.

In addition Catholicism is also an autonomous sect of Kabbalists, Gnostics and Mystics, etc., and the Roman Catholic Church truly cannot escape that religious classification; for the reason that, a study of all it religious buildings (Churches, Cathedrals, Basilicas) can be envisaged as esoteric or the works of Kabbalists, Gnostics and Mystics, etc., commentaries on the canonized Judaeo Christian Scriptures.

Heretics are complete idiots and I will not discuss them whatsoever.

All I can possibly do, in presenting this work, is give a personal thumbnail version of an infinite subject matter that is viewed disparately by every autonomous psyche in the world and that per se is essentially what makes the phantasmagoria of the psyche a Garden of Eden. If everybody lived with automaton psyches humanity individually and collectively would live in a modernistic, instant gratification, world that they are presently inundated and surrounded by.

AFTERTHOUGHTS

I truly believe that the world I live in is a very spiritual realm; for the reason that, the material world does not exist outside of the phantasmagoria of the psyche and one of the purposes of my writing this volume was to illustrate that psychic phenomenon. Now I know that when I write a book such as this I am educating myself with God as my only confidant; for the reason that, in the midst of my meditational contemplative thoughts I am actually ethereally walking amidst the environs that is the Ambiance of God in the Garden of Eden.

Having been born and raised amidst the mythoi of the my life, after all the years of my research, I have to stand back, and try if that is at all possible, to contemplatively conceptualize what the actual governing principle is that is in my psyche's environs that enables my soul to visualize the Ambiance of God and His spiritual teachings.

I know that every single soul lives in its own universe and it is as if there is no other living entity in a soul's autonomous universe. Iconoclastically that sounds absolutely inane; yet, when I look back over the serenity and peacefulness of the silence I have lived in over the span of most of my life I cannot help but believe that the universe was created solely for my soul's benefit to edify my soul as to its true nature: i.e. being a spiritual being.

Knowing that life is lived spiritually and symbolically between the ears I have no doubts whatsoever that my soul creates its own world (manifested creation) solely based upon its daily psychic activities. The MATRIX OF WISDOM convinces me that it is the environs that provide all my souls needs before I know I need them. The MATRIX OF WISDOM does not provide things that a soul wants.

I know that in my next lifetime the spiritual forces in creation: God will take the better part of me and provide my soul with a whole new raison d'etre (reason for existence): a whole new universe and this I believe goes on infinitely. The better parts of each previous life time is extrapolated psychically onto the next experience. Because, I have developed this research over the span of my life my next experience will begin from those accomplishment. I do believe that I will end up in a world as perfectly as I have envisioned it here in this life; however, my new environs will be a more perfect religious atmosphere where I will be set to pick-up psychically where I left off here.

CPSIA information can be obtained
at www.ICGtesting.com
Printed in the USA
BVOW07s0054041016
464048BV00003B/3/P

9 781478 780472